Born of the
Same Roots

CHINESE LITERATURE IN TRANSLATION

Editors
Irving Yucheng Lo
Joseph S. M. Lau
Leo Ou-fan Lee
Eugene Chen Eoyang

Born of the Same Roots

Stories of Modern Chinese Women

Edited by Vivian Ling Hsu

Indiana University Press • Bloomington

To the women of China
past and present
who have inspired these stories

Library of Congress Cataloging in Publication Data
Main entry under title:

Born of the same roots.

(Chinese literature in translation)
Bibliography: p.
Contents: Caterpillar / Lao She—Two women / Wu
Tsu-hsiang—On the Oxcart / Hsiao Hung—[etc.]
    1. Chinese fiction—20th century—Translations into
English. 2. English fiction—Translations from Chinese.
3. Women—China—Fiction.   I. Hsu, Vivian Ling.   II Se-
ries.
PL2658.E8B6   895.1'301'08352042   81–47009
ISBN 0–253–19526–8   AACR2
ISBN 0–253–20270–1 pbk
                    1 2 3 4 5 85 84 83 82 81

Contents

PREFACE

CHINESE LITERATURE written after the May-Fourth era, particularly fiction, has been recognized in recent years as a potentially powerful vehicle for enhancing Western understanding of China. The rapid growth in the translation of this literature into English, both in terms of quantity and quality, is beginning to transform this potential into reality. Within a period of just fifty years, Chinese fiction spanned myriad stages: from the romantic, self-centered, often semi-autobiographical literature of the early twenties to the more socially and politically oriented literature of the thirties, the literature engagé during the War of Resistance against Japan, the literature that served the socialist society in communist-ruled China, the multifarious flowering in Taiwan literature following a vacuous and "lost" decade in the fifties, and the literature by a generation of intellectual émigrés.

The language, the style, and central concerns of this literature are as diverse as the backgrounds of the writers themselves. However, almost all modern Chinese writers are linked by one common thread—their writings invariably, though to different degrees, reflect the sociopolitical conditions of their times. Through their stories, the reader is brought into touch with the events of twentieth-century China that have shaped, governed, and tortured the lives of the authors. In this literature, the history, the political documents, and the public pronouncements take on real life. Through it, the reader gains personal appreciation for their effect on individual human beings. In short, this literature is the flesh and breath to the bare bones of history. Whereas history records the external events, fiction reflects the mind and soul of society.

Chinese literature of the twentieth century has often been unfairly criticized for its immaturity, crudity, and lack of sophistication. The fact is, the best fiction by Chinese writers of the past fifty years rivals the best in the West. However, alongside the gems of twentieth-century Chinese literature, there exists a huge bulk of second- and third-rate products, some of which have for one reason or another gained sizeable readerships, misleading the nondiscriminating Western critic to form an erroneous low opinion of modern Chinese fiction. The quality of this literature is in fact remarkably high when one considers its relative newness, and especially when one takes cognizance of the fact that for a whole generation, writers struggled for individual expression under the dual pressures of Kuomintang censorship and the erratically shifting "guidelines" of the communists, sometimes risking and losing their very lives in this struggle. Writing under the communist regime has the handicap of having to conform to the didactic needs of a socialist society, and these needs are periodically redefined. The best writers in China have not lost sight of aesthetic values however; they continue to struggle to reconcile didactic needs with aesthetic values, some succeeding admirably on their own terms.

The most emotion-charged and effectual sociopolitical issues of twentieth-century China are perhaps the ones that concern half of China's people, the women. In less than two generations, China has moved from a society where it was felt that "it is better to raise geese than daughters" to the People's Republic, in which women's ability "to hold up half the sky" is publicly recognized, even if not fully realized. The issues relevant to women's lives in twentieth-century China have been amply and dramatically brought to life in literature by women writers who have a natural propensity to portray themselves and also by male writers who recognized that their own lives are inseparable from those of the women around them, and whose insights into women's problems and psyche are in many cases acutely penetrating.

This volume brings within reach of the English reader the fiction that concerns itself with women. The selection is based not primarily on the sex of the authors, but on the quality and representative nature of the works. In order to be of maximum service to the field, it does not include works that are readily available in English translations, such as the several powerful portrayals of women by Lu Hsün and such moving pieces as Jou Shih's "Slave Mother." This volume includes well-known writers like Lao She and Chen Jo-hsi as well as hitherto little-known writers like T'ien T'ao. Represented here are stories from the May-Fourth period; the War of Resistance; the period following Mao's Yenan Forum of 1942; post-1949 China, where the regime's control over literature became absolute; and the new generation that grew up on Taiwan as well as a few writers who emigrated to the United States.

Although the backgrounds of the writers are widely divergent, some themes recur surprisingly in different social contexts. The age-old prejudice against daughters is depicted in T'ien T'ao's "Parting." Women of the downtrodden class mourning the fate of their lost husbands are portrayed in Hsiao Hung's "On the Oxcart," set in a war-torn and disrupted China, and again in Wang T'o's "May He Return Soon," set in relatively prosperous and stable Taiwan. Though women characters are often oppressed and downtrodden in Chinese fiction, they are rarely portrayed as hopeless whimpering weaklings. More often than not, they are resilient individuals who have great strength to survive, and at times to triumph, like Ch'un-t'ao in Lo Hua-sheng's "Garbage Gleaner" and the protagonist in Ping Hsin's "Chang Sao." The struggle between career and domestic life is the theme of Ping Hsin's May-Fourth era "West Wind." The perennial theme of ennui and boredom in marriage and domestic life occurs in Wu Tsu-hsiang's "Two Women" and Pai Hsien-yung's "A Day in Pleasantville," set in an American suburb. Prostitution will probably be a subject in literature for as long as it exists in society. In this anthology, it is explored in Ch'en Ying-chen's "A Rose in June." Some topics are unique to certain historical periods in that they reflect a particular societal condition or consciously promote a certain ideal attitude advocated by the regime at the time. The stories "Born of the Same Roots" by Yang Ch'ing-ch'u and "My Friend Ai Fen" by Chen Jo-hsi fall into the former category, whereas Ts'ao Ming's "Spring is Just around the Corner" and Sung Shun-k'ang's "Old Team Captain Welcomes a Bride," both written in post-1949 China, belong in the latter category. The intersexual relationships of men and women have engaged the attention of writers throughout the past fifty years. We find this theme in Lao She's "Caterpillar," Ai Wu's "Rain," Teng Yu-mei's "At the Precipice," and Yü Li-hua's "Nightfall." This theme, which reminds one of the song refrain "What is this thing called love," will probably receive writers' attentionfor as long as there remains a bisexual society.

Through the nineteen stories represented in this volume, the English reader is invited to share the experiences of women in twentieth-century China, their joys, sorrows, and struggles, as portrayed by China's best modern men and women writers.

I would like to express gratitude to all the friends and students who have collaborated in these translations, to James Shu for his critical reading of the manuscript, and to Joseph S. M. Lau and Leo Ou-fan Lee for their good advice. Special thanks are also due Joanne Thodt, who typed the manuscript and who, as the first to read these translations with the fresh eye of an English reader, provided feedback and suggestions.

*Born of the
Same Roots*

LAO SHE

(1897–1966)

Lao She (real name Shu Ch'ing-ch'un) was the son of a Manchu palace guard. He was unique among modern writers in that his native home was Peking and he excelled in writing in the colloquial Peking dialect. Not much is known about his childhood, but most likely it was a difficult one, given his father's relatively lowly status and early death. He did, however, attend a normal school and later Yenching University. He taught high school for several years after graduating from college, then he went to study and teach Chinese in England. Lao She wrote his first novels The Philosophy of Old Chang (Lao Chang te che-hsüeh, 1928), Chao Tzu-yüeh (1928), and The Two Ma's (Erh Ma, postwar edition 1948) while he was in England. They were published in serial form in the Short Story Monthly (Hsiao-shuo yüeh-pao) in the period 1926–1929. On his way home from England in 1929 Lao She was waylaid for a year in Singapore, where he taught at a high school and wrote the children's novel Hsiao P'o's Birthday (Hsiao P'o te sheng-jih, 1934). He arrived home in 1930, married, and taught college briefly in Peking and Tsingtao before being appointed dean of the School of Humanities at Cheloo University in Shangtung. With the outbreak of the war of 1937, Lao She resigned his teaching post to become a professional writer in support of the war effort. He helped to found the All China Writers' Anti-Aggression Association (Chung-hua ch'üan-kuo wen-i-chieh k'ang-ti hsieh-hui) and headed it throughout the war years, himself producing many ballads and several wartime plays. These works were intended to be disseminated widely to arouse patriotic and anti-enemy sentiments among the populace. As such, they lack the subtlety and humor of his earlier novels and short stories. In the period 1943–1946, Lao She took to writing novels again, but the products all fell short of the potential he demonstrated earlier. After the war, he came to the United States on a cultural exchange program, along with the playwright Ts'ao Yü. It was during this sojourn that his novel Rickshaw Boy (Lo-t'o Hsiang-tzu, Chinese edition 1938) was translated into English by Evan King (with an ending revised by the translator) and became a bestseller in the United States. A new translation by Jeanne James has rendered the ending faithful to the original (Rickshaw, Honolulu, 1979). With the founding of the People's Republic of China in 1949, Lao She returned to China. After making some concessions to the criticisms typically leveled at writers at that time, he regained his former status and served as a vice chairman of China's Federation of Writers.

His post-1949 works, however, are all in the service of the regime. His former style, biting humor, and wit are all but lost in his work of this period, which consists of several plays, including the vastly popular **Dragon Beard Ditch** *(Lung-hsü kou, 1953). Lao She survived the Anti-Rightist campaign of 1957–1958, but with the start of the Cultural Revolution, he was singled out for "struggle" by Red Guards and young members of his own writers' organization. There are conflicting accounts of his death, but it is almost certain that it was either a suicide under pressure or a murder. He was vindicated after the downfall of the Gang of Four. A volume of his plays has been reissued, and his honor as a "people's writer" has been publicly restored.*

Lao She was one of the most prolific writers of twentieth-century China. His works have been widely translated. "Caterpillar" (Mao-mao-ch'ung), probably written in the 1930s, is drawn from the collection **Wei-shen Chi** *(1947).*

Caterpillar

Translated by Michael S. Duke

ON THIS STREET we all call him the Caterpillar. He's a pretty snappy dresser in his imported suit, overcoat, leather shoes, all bright and spiffy; but he's unpleasant to look at, with a pair of large sheep's eyes in his round gourd-shaped face, always looking down on others it seems. His way of walking is especially peculiar. He doesn't walk really; he twists and turns to propel his bent body forward. On cold days, he scrunches up his neck, sticks his hands in his coat pockets, and bends his way along the side of the wall, looking all the more like a caterpillar. The neighbors didn't pay much attention to him because he didn't pay any attention to anyone; after a while everyone got used to it and thought it quite natural—the Caterpillar really does not talk very much. We don't bother much about him, but almost all of us know what his home is like, how many chairs there are, where the spittoon is located . . . ; and we know that the Caterpillar doesn't really eat leaves; his home has a small kitchen with plates and dishes and so forth.

Almost all of us have been to his house. Our opportunity comes at the end of every month, when he receives his salary. As soon as he comes home with his salary, Mrs. Caterpillar faints dead away for at least half an hour or more. We don't bother with him, but we all go over to rescue Mrs. Caterpillar. She is very easy to revive. As soon as we arrive, we give her a drink of sugar water; she then revives and puts on a crying fit for us. He doesn't say a word; only rolls his eyes angrily at the wall. Once we see that she is crying vigorously, we all go home together, leaving everything else for the Caterpillar to handle. After a couple of days, Mrs. Caterpillar once again dresses herself up attractively and comes out to show off, walking down the street carrying her little red handbag; knowing that the Caterpillar has taken care of everything, we all feel quite relieved and yet somewhat annoyed that time always passes too slowly, and the end of the month does not arrive quickly enough for us.

It might be said that we should not be so heartless as to look forward to her fainting, but we have our reasons. After we revive her, she doesn't even thank us; when she runs into us, she doesn't pay us any notice. She is away from home all day; according to her maid, she is out playing mahjong. The place where she plays is not on our street. On that account we are not too kindly disposed toward her, but then we could hardly not rescue someone threatening death. Furthermore, at the end of every month it's always she who faints dead and Caterpillar who only looks on angrily; we cannot help favoring her even though she doesn't play mahjong with us. If she would play mahjong with us, perhaps she wouldn't need to faint dead away at the end of every month, for we are confident that a way can be found to fix up the Caterpillar.

Then again we are annoyed with her not only because she doesn't play mahjong with us; she has other unbecoming traits as well. She does not take care of her two children—a boy and a girl, very nice children. Heng! They tag behind the maid all day long like a couple of orphans; as soon as they wake up in the morning, they stand on the street outside their gate eating peanuts with their hair uncombed and their faces never ever washed, like little urchins. That doesn't go over well with us. Even though we play mahjong too and sometimes also yell at our children because of our mahjong game, still we would not give our children peanuts to eat first thing in the morning. We all know how to feed our children powdered milk. We believe that this street of ours is very civilized. If it wasn't for the Caterpillar family, we could very well change the street name to "Model Street." We cannot force them to leave, though, and we're not their landlord, so we cannot meddle in things that are none of our business. And besides, he's a college graduate and works in a government office, and she dresses very smartly and has her hair curled in a permanent wave. Having them around certainly beats having some low-class trash move in; our street will not accept low-class trash.

They have lived here now for more than a year, and after some visiting back and forth we have come to understand Caterpillar's history. We did not really investigate, but when the Caterpillars' maid blurted everything out we couldn't very well stop our ears. After we learned their real background, our opinions were not as unanimous as before. At first we were all rather unconcerned about them. He didn't socialize with us—so what? We were not about to cozy up to him, even if he did wear a fancy imported suit. On the other hand, even though she was unappreciative, whenever she fainted away we couldn't turn our backs and not perform a charitable act. After all, everyone knows that our street donated the most millet to the Philanthropic Society. When everyone became privy to their story, however, some sympathized with the Caterpillar and some with Mrs. Caterpillar. We even argued about our different opinions. As the saying goes, "Some lean toward the lamp, and some lean toward the flame." There's truth in that.

Here is the story as we heard it. The Caterpillar was a college graduate, but he had a country wife with bound feet who still wore her hair up high in a bun; so he wanted nothing more than to take another wife. Our critical comments diverged at this point. Those of us who had graduated from college said the Caterpillar could be forgiven, but the older generation merely snorted. We simply didn't dare to bring the subject up again while playing mahjong; if this leads to a fight it really wouldn't be worth it. Anyway, eventually the Caterpillar took this new wife. Having heard this much, most of us called him a dirty cheat. There was still more to the story, however; there was a condition: besides providing her with food and clothing, every month he had to give his new wife forty dollars spending money. This made us go a little easier on the Caterpillar, but in our eyes Mrs. Caterpillar's status immediately plummeted. After they were married—that maid knew everything—the two of them got along quite well; he was very satisfied and she had forty dollars a month to spend. They both thought it was a good bargain.

After a short, while, however, that bound-footed wife came looking for them. Needless to say, they had a blowup that turned everything topsy-turvy. The Caterpillar had to accept yet another condition: he would give that bound-footed wife fifteen dollars spending money every month, and two month's money to start off. She took the thirty dollars and returned to the country; as she was leaving she promised to be back some time or other! We were just about to pronounce the Caterpillar most unfortunate indeed, when the story took another twist. He intended to take the fifteen dollars for his bound-footed wife out of his new wife's forty dollars; he said he could not afford to give them fifty-five dollars in total. "If you can't pay the price, then don't embrace two brides," we all said on his new wife's behalf.

At the end of every month the two of them would have a knock-down, drag-out fight over this. At that time she had not yet invented the idea of fainting away for half an hour. She didn't often go out to play mahjong then either. Not until the Caterpillar asked her, "Isn't twenty-five dollars enough? Why do you have to have forty dollars?" did she conceive of the notion of going out to play mahjong. She put it very bluntly: "Give me the full amount and you need not be concerned; otherwise, if I lose you'll have to pay my debts!" The Caterpillar didn't say anything then, but at the end of the month he *still* did not give her the full amount. She wasn't one to be bested. Sometimes she would stay in bed for two or three days, refusing to get up until she received her money; when she got her money, she would again make herself up, put on an attractive dress, and go out as if she didn't have a care in the world. "You're the buyer and I'm the seller; the money and goods are both square," she seemed to be saying.

A few months later, she was about to have a baby. The Caterpillar hated children; his bound-footed wife already had three with her, and they were a burden as far as he was concerned. He never imagined that his new wife might also have children. He decided on an attitude of laissez faire. If she wanted to have it, then have it; what he didn't see wouldn't bother him he figured, so he pretended not to notice her swelling stomach. He didn't pay much attention to the whole thing, and his bound-footed wife didn't give it much thought either. When it was just about time for the child to be born, she came hobbling along to take care of the new wife. The Caterpillar thought that was very fine; his new wife was having a baby and his old wife was looking after her, not bad at all. It was only after the child was born that the old wife showed her true intentions. She knew that by striking then she could get back at the new wife who was extremely weak after the delivery. She could practically harass her to death; her opportunity for revenge was at hand. She sat herself down squarely in front of the new wife, pointed a finger right in her face, and cursed her; she cursed her up and down until she fainted dead away several times and she didn't even give her a little sugar water to drink. After cursing her for three days, she hobbled away, handing her over to God; she could live or die as she pleased, but the old wife would not have to accept the blame for driving her to her death. The new wife didn't feel like living either; although she was not driven to death by the bound-footed one, she tried to kill herself by wildly overeating within the first month after giving birth.

By that time the Caterpillar felt things were getting out of hand. If his new wife died, getting another one would surely cost a fortune; so he sent for a doctor. By and by, she recovered. And after she recovered she negotiated with the Caterpillar, making it clear that she was not about to look after the child. The Caterpillar didn't say anything, and thus neither one of them looked after the child. Mrs. Caterpillar went out to play mahjong just as before; at the end of every month she demanded her forty dollars just as before, and, if the Caterpillar didn't give it to her, she had by now invented a new weapon—she would faint away for half an hour. That's how it was with the first child, and the second child was the same. That's the way their story went.

Once we had heard it all, none of us could draw any conclusions anymore; no matter how we judged the matter, it didn't seem right. Suppose we say the bound-footed one was wrong; she should not have acted so cruelly, but she herself has to live like a widow. Suppose we say the new wife was wrong; that doesn't make sense either, because she too has suffered indignities. At most we could only blame her for taking her frustration out on her children; but, when we think about that again, her position seems reasonable too. Why should the Caterpillar be able to hand all the grief and trouble over to her and not have to bear any hardship himself? Since she was really purchased—forty dollars a month spending money is only a euphemistic way of putting it—why should she have to take care of the children, especially since the Caterpillar wasn't giving her any additional money for it? With all that said, it would seem that the Caterpillar was the one in the wrong; but, as soon as we give more careful thought to his plight, we see that he also has more grief than happiness. His first wife takes his money and hates him, his new wife also takes his money and hates him, and in the end he has to break his neck trying to make money.

After giving their story so much thought, none of us dared bring it up again; for as soon as we did, we'd feel perturbed. Our attitude toward those two children changed somewhat, however; we felt that the two of them were quite pitiful—there were really quite a few kind-hearted people on our street—every time we see those two children playing on the street now, we go over and pat them on the head and sometimes even give them something to eat. Sometimes we feel those two adults are pitiful and sometimes we find them exasperating. No matter how we feel, however, in their lives we have caught a glimpse of something that we had never seen before, something like the meaning contained in a solemn tragedy. It's as though their problems are not completely of their own making, but rather like the curse of the age being played out in their lives. Thus at the end of every month now, according to established pattern, she faints dead away for half an hour. More people go over to rescue her than before. Who knows what's going to become of them?

WU TSU-HSIANG

(1908-)

Wu Tsu-hsiang was born in 1908 into a landlord family of south central Anhwei. He began to write while he was a student of Chinese popular fiction at Tsinghua University. In 1934 the prestigious Shanghai journal Literature Quarterly *(Wen-hsüeh chi-k'an) published his short story "Eighteen Hundred Piculs" (I-ch'ien-pa-pai tan, 1934), and overnight Wu was touted as a highly promising writer of rural fiction. With the publication of two collections of stories in 1934 and 1935, Wu's literary star continued to rise only to burn out in the cataclysmic fifteen years that followed. Instinctively aware of the dangers of the didactic heresy, Wu kept the ideological freight of his stories light and artistically integrated, so that his moral perceptions are transmitted keenly and soundly. Wu Tsu-hsiang has clearly demonstrated brilliance in his writings, but his output is rather meager. He stopped writing altogether after the War of Resistance. He taught Chinese at Peking University from 1949.*

The following miniature piece was written in 1935. Though not the best example of Wu's craftsmanship, it nonetheless demonstrates well his skill at conjuring up instant human drama couched in lively dialogue.

Two Women

Translated by Paul Crescenzo and Vivian Hsu

THE MAID WAS about twenty, with a flat nose and flat lips, coarse eyes, coarse hands, and a bulky waist. She lightly pushed open the door and tiptoed inside.

"Mistress, I th-th-think . . . I'd l-like . . ." She was wringing her thick hands and staring at her bare fidgeting toes as she spoke. Affecting feminine modesty seemed to require an effort on her part, and her attempt at polite address clashed with her big rustic appearance.

T'ai-t'ai, the mistress, was about the same age, but looked much younger. Standing before her, the maid was only a plain, rough clay figurine. Together these two women made an interesting contrast: one unpolished and crude, like a shard of ancient pottery just unearthed; the other very delicate and sophisticated, an exquisite porcelain toy.

T'ai-t'ai was just regaining her composure after a quarrel with her husband. He had gone to see a movie without inviting her. And the night before she had prepared a big dinner, but he didn't come home until eight and then informed her that he had eaten out. "Eaten already! Why didn't you tell me earlier?" She had gotten so angry that her stomach was upset all night long.

She could no longer hold back her anger and it broke out in a quarrel. Her husband had his own reasons, he refused to apologize, and he didn't even pretend to humor her. That only made her more furious. "I know you don't care for me any more!" she yelled at him, and collapsed onto the bed to sob. Her husband picked up a book and stared at it for a moment, then reached for his hat and stomped out of the house.

T'ai-t'ai was alone in the bedroom, lying down and feeling very listless. Her pillow was damp and cold and stuck to her face. She pushed it away and sat up. To occupy herself, she opened her bureau and began to put a messy pile of assorted stockings in order.

The door opened and her maid stepped in, fidgeting in a ridiculous manner. T'ai-t'ai had to laugh to herself. She thought, "How amusing." A week ago when the employment agency had sent over this woman, her husband asked whether or not she was satisfactory. T'ai-t'ai had said, "It will be amusing to watch such a simpleton," and decided to keep her. How even though T'ai-t'ai had stopped crying, she still had a bellyful of anger, and she was weary and bored. She needed someone to talk to. So she turned her head and asked tolerantly, "Well, what do you want? Speak up, you can tell me."

"I thought T'ai-t'ai might read a letter for me."

"Of course," said T'ai-t'ai haughtily, with a condescending nod.

The maid fumbled with her jacket and drew out an unsealed, crumpled letter. With much embarrassment, she handed it to her mistress.*

T'ai-t'ai looked over the contents twice very carefully, and then with an amused smile she said, "Ah, this letter is from your husband!"

The other woman was about to say something and raised her

---

*The letter that follows is omitted in this translation. It is incoherent and full of incorrect expressions—obviously the work of a semi-literature person.

head, but she dropped it again and stared at her wiggling toes. She said nothing after all.

T'ai-t'ai went on, "Your husband says he's very sorry about the argument you had, and he begs you to come home in the spring to help with the planting. He won't curse you anymore, and your father and mother-in-law won't beat and curse you anymore either. He says Little T'an has no milk, so he wants you to hurry and send money home . . ."

T'ai-t'ai explained the letter once, then again, watching her maid's reaction. Her neck reddened first, then the blush rose into her cheeks and finally crimsoned her ears.

"Curse them!" she snapped suddenly, and then with hatred she spit out, "Those devils!" In just an instant, her bashful manner vanished.

T'ai-t'ai found this rather interesting. As if she were speaking to a child, trying to draw her out, she said, "So you had a fight and ran away from home! You certainly have guts! How did you manage to get away? Where did you live? Tell me the whole story."

The other woman wrung her hands once or twice and grew bashful once again. Hemming and hawing, she finally said, "I am cursed, cursed! At home I worked in the fields, planting the rice seedlings. Those two old scoundrels would beat and curse me every day. The year there was a flood, they said I brought it on! This year there was a drought, and they blamed me again. I brought it! I brought it! Maybe so, but I didn't mean to. Then that wife-beating devil of a husband, he started in on me too! When I planted seedlings or weeded the fields, that little devil, that Little T'an, he'd be bawling on my back! He would cry and cry, even in June when I had to tread the water mill, I had to carry him too. I'd work into the evening, and be sweaty and smelly. The dew would fall, and Little T'an would cry to high heavens. And then he caught a fever. I got heat rash all over my back from him. But they said I gave the heat rash to . . . they said I made Little T'an sick! My husband . . . he took the hoe and started to beat my legs with it. He beat me and beat me and beat me!" Noisily she sucked in her own saliva.

T'ai-t'ai watched her become frenzied as she spoke: she was swallowing hard, nodding her head violently, and shaking all over. Her mistress repressed a smile and put on a very shocked face. "Ugh! He beat you!? How could anyone do such a thing? Calm down, speak slower!"

"Damn them! I was getting only three bowls of rice a day under his roof, scraped rice at that! Damn them! I thought to myself, 'I can't stand this, I . . . I just . . . I just couldn't take any more! So I sold the silver hair clasp my mother had given me to Red Feather.

Red Feather, what an old chap! I left with him. He didn't want to take me but I knew he was going to Shanghai. I nagged and begged him, so he finally let me come. I used three hundred in cash to get to Nanking. Then I met San Ting-tzu and Hsin Sao-tzu and Erh Sao-tzu and even Fu-t'ou's mother! They were all at the agency. They all refused to slave in the fields and they ran away too!"

"These women, they are all your chums from the village?"

The maid nodded.

"How gutsy you all are!" exclaimed T'ai-t'ai, settling back in her chair.

"That old coot Red Feather, he tried to scare me with all sorts of lies. He made my heart pound sometimes! He said the foreign devils in Nanking and Shanghai plucked out people's eyes! He said there were airplanes that dropped bombs. I would become a beggar if I left the village. He went on and on and on! But I wasn't really afraid. I wasn't going to put up with all that abuse back home just to get my keep. I knew I'd find a way for myself. I wouldn't starve. I wasn't really afraid!"

"But your child, Little T'an . . . don't you care about him?" asked T'ai-t'ai with genuine concern. She had suddenly and unconsciously become involved in her maid's story and no longer found it trivial.

The other woman stared at her wiggling toes again and said nothing. After a while, she blurted out, "Could T'ai-t'ai loan me two dollars? Could she write a letter for me?"

"The money is no problem, I'll give you an advance on your wages. But a letter . . . do you have any way of sending it? Your husband says to send letters to Hung-sheng-hsien. What is that? A man, a shop, or an address?"

The maid stared blankly out the window. "Probably it's a shop in the city, a tea shop, run by someone named Hung."

"Who do you know that's named Hung? There is no such surname!"

"Damn it! He can't even write clearly!"

"Did your husband write this letter himself?"

"Him? Write? He couldn't recognize the simplest character even if it were as big as a shoulder pole! . . . I'll have to go ask Erh Sao-tzu." She excused herself and lumbered out.

T'ai-t'ai sighed deeply. Her eyes fell upon her pillow, with its large wet stain. Her face flushed. She no longer found her maid "amusing." She admired her, almost envied her. But her own problem? What was she to do? She wondered . . .

HSIAO HUNG

(1911–1942)

Hsiao Hung's popularity as a writer has grown considerably in recent years. Her highly evocative style, masterful recreations of life in Northeast China (Manchuria), and accent on the feminine experience are drawing readers and critics to her work in increasing numbers.

She was born Chang Nai-ying in 1911, to a landlord family near Harbin in Northeast China. Hsiao Hung's world view was largely formed by a generally unhappy and lonely childhood. Her rise to prominence on the Chinese literary scene dates from her first and, in the eyes of some critics, finest novel, The Field of Life and Death (Sheng-szu ch'ang), published in December 1935. It was acclaimed as a major literary and political event, for it deals with the issues of Japanese aggression in Northeast China and the burgeoning attempts by Chinese peasants to resist.

From 1936 to 1940, the early years of the Sino-Japanese War, Hsiao Hung continued the vagabond, somewhat Bohemian existence that characterized most of her adult life. Her literary output over these years was limited to several small volumes of short stories and essays of uneven quality.

In 1940 Hsiao Hung fled from the wartime capital of Chungking to Hong Kong. At the age of thirty, she died in a hospital there on January 22, 1942, barely a month after the city fell to the Japanese. During her refuge in Hong Kong, she produced three novels. One of them, Tales of Hulan River (Hu-lan-ho chuan, 1942), which she had begun in her final years in Chungking, is generally regarded as her masterpiece. It is a moving and highly artistic reminiscence of the author's home, and it was only after the national wartime emotions had cooled that this novel began to enjoy the acclaim and popularity it rightly deserves.

The most comprehensive study of Hsiao Hung's life and works in any language was written by Howard Goldblatt (Hsiao Hung, Boston, 1976). He has also translated into English Tales of Hulan River and, with Ellen Yeung, The Field of Life and Death, both of which have been published in one volume (Indiana University Press, 1979).

"On the Oxcart" (Niu-che shang) was written while Hsiao Hung was in Japan and was first published in Literature Monthly (Wen-hsueh yüeh-k'an) in 1936. In the following year it was reprinted in a collection with the same title by Cultural Life Publishing Company (Wen-hua sheng-huo ch'u-pan-she).

On The Oxcart

Translated by Howard Goldblatt

LATE MARCH. Clover covers the banks of the streams. In the early
light of the morning our cart crushes the red and green grasses at
the foot of the hill as it rumbles through the outskirts of Alter-
grandfather's* village. The carter is a distant uncle on Mother's side.
He flicks his whip, but not to strike the rump of the ox; the tip
merely dances back and forth in the air.

"Are you sleepy already? We've only just left the village! Drink
some plum cider now, and after we've crossed the stream you can
sleep." Alter-grandfather's maid is on her way to town to visit her
son.

"What stream? Didn't we just cross one?" The yellow cat we're
bringing back from Grandfather's house has fallen asleep in my lap.

"The Hou-t'ang Stream."

"What Hou-t'ang Stream?" My mind is wandering. The only
things from Alter-grandfather's village still visible in the distance
are the two gold balls topping the red flagpole in front of the ancestral temple.

"Drink a cup of plum cider, it'll perk you up." She is holding a
cup of the dark yellow liquid in one hand as she puts the lid back
on the bottle.

"I don't need anything . . . perk me up? You perk yourself up!"

They both laugh as the carter suddenly cracks his whip.

"You young lady, you . . . you sharp-tongued little scamp . . . I, I
. . . " He walks over from alongside the axle and reaches out to grab
hold of my hair. Drawing my shoulders back, I clamber to the rear
of the cart. Every kid in the village is scared of him. They say he
used to be a soldier, and when he pinches your ear it hurts like the
dickens. Wu-yün Sao† has gotten down off the cart to gather a lot of
different kinds of flowers for me. Now the wind blowing in from
the woods has picked up a bit, and her scarf is flapping around her
head. It reminds me of a raven or a magpie, like the ones I saw in
the village. Look at her jumpin' up and down, just like a kid! She's

---

*The distinction between maternal and paternal relations is marked in Chinese
kinship terms. In this translation, the prefix "alter-" is used to distinguish maternal
grandfather from paternal grandfather.

†The term sao designates the wife of one's older brother, but it is also used loosely
in informal familiar address to any middle-aged woman.

back in the cart now, singing out the names of all kinds of flowers. I've never seen her so happy and carefree.

I can't tell what those low, coarse, grunting noises from the carter mean. Puffs of smoke from his short pipe float back on the wind. As we start off on our journey, our hopes and expectations are far off in the distance.

I must have fallen asleep. I remember waking up once, some-where after we crossed Hou-t'ang Stream—I don't know exactly where—and through the cobwebs of my mind I thought I saw the boy who watches over the ducks beckon to me. There was also the parting scene between me and Hsiao-ken as he straddled the ox. And I could see Alter-grandfather again taking me by the hand and saying, "When you get home tell your grandpa to come on over during the cool autumn season and visit the countryside. You tell him that his old in-law's quail and his best sorghum wine are wait-ing here for us to enjoy together. You tell him that I can't get around so well anymore; otherwise the past couple of years I would have gone."

The hollow sound of the wheels wakes me up. The first thing I see is the yellow ox plodding along the road. The carter isn't sitting there by the axle where he should be— there he is, on the back of the cart. Instead of the whip, he's holding a pipe in his hand. He keeps stroking his jaw with his other hand; he is staring off into the horizon. Wu-yün Sao is holding the yellow cat in her lap and strok-ing it's tail. The blue cotton scarf around her head has dipped below her eyebrows, and the creases on her nose are more distinct than usual because of the dust that has gathered around them.

They don't know I'm awake.

"By the third year there were no more letters from him. You soldiers . . ."

"Was your husband a soldier too?" I couldn't hold back. My carter-uncle pulls me backwards by my pigtail.

"And no more letters at all after that?" he asks.

"Since you asked me, I'll tell you. It was just after the Mid-Autumn Festival—I forget which year it was. I had just finished eating breakfast and was slopping the pigs in front of the house. 'Soo-ee, soo-ee!' I didn't even hear Second Mistress from the Wang family of South Village as she came running up, shouting, 'Wu-yün Sao, Wu-yün Sao! My mother says it's probably a letter from Brother Wu-yün.' She held a letter right under my nose. 'Here, let me have it. I want to see . . . ' I don't know why, but I felt sick at heart. Was he still alive? He . . . A tear dropped on the red-lined stationery, but when I tried to wipe it off, all I did was make a red smudge on the white paper. I threw the slop down in the middle of the yard and went into my room to change into some clean clothes. Then I ran as fast as I could to the school in South Village to see the schoolmaster. I was laughing through my tears. 'I've got a letter here from someone far away; would you please read it to me? I haven't had a single word from him for a year.' But after he read the letter he said it was for someone else. I left the letter in the school and ran home. I didn't go back to feed the pigs or put the chickens to roost; I just went inside and lay down on the brick bed. For days I was like someone whose soul had left her."

"And no more letters from him since then?"

"None." She unscrews the lid from the bottle of plum cider and drinks a cupful, then another.

"You soldiers, you go away for two or three years, you say, but do you return home? How many of you ever do? You ought to at least send your ghosts home for us to see."

"You mean . . . ?" the carter bursts out. "Then he was killed in battle somewhere?"

"That's what it amounted to; not a word for more than a year."

"Well, was he killed in battle or wasn't he?" Jumping down from the cart, he grabs his whip and snaps it in the air a couple of times, making sounds like little explosions.

"What difference does it make? The bitter life of a soldier doesn't allow for much good fortune." Her wrinkled lips look like pieces of torn silk, a sure sign of an unrooted nature and a life of misfortune.

As we pass Huang Village the sun begins to set and magpies are flying over the green wheat fields.

"Did you cry when you learned that Brother Wu-yün had died in battle?" As I look at her, I continue stroking the yellow cat's tail. But she ignores me and busies herself with straightening her scarf.

The carter scrambles up into the cart by holding on to the handrail and jumping in, landing right above the axle. He is about to smoke; his thick lips are sealed as tightly as the mouth of the bottle.

The flow of words from Wu-yün Sao's mouth is like the gentle patter of rain; I stretch out alongside the handrail and before long I've dozed off again.

I awake to discover that the cart is stopped alongside a small village well—the ox is drinking by the well. Wu-yün Sao must have been crying, because her sunken eyes are all puffed up and the crow's-feet at the sides of her eyes are spread open. The carter scoops up a bucketful of water from the well and carries it over to the cart.

"Have some—it's nice and cool."

"No thanks," she replies.

"Go ahead and drink some. If you're not thirsty, at least use some of it to wash your face." He takes a hand towel from his waistband and soaks it in the water. "Here, wipe your face. Your eyes are all dusty."

I can't believe it, a soldier actually offering his towel to someone! That strikes me as peculiar, since the soldiers I've known only know how to fight battles, beat women, and pinch children's ears.

"That winter I traveled to the year-end market to sell hog bristles. I stood there shouting, 'Good stiff hog bristles . . . fine long hog bristles . . .' By the next year I had just about forgotten my husband . . . didn't let him tear at my heart anymore. What good was there in thinking of him, I told myself. After all these years, he's got to be long gone! The following autumn I went into the fields with the others to harvest kaoliang . . . here, look at my hands—they've done their share of work.

"The next spring I hired myself out for a season's work, so I took the baby with me, and the household was broken up for two or three months. But I pulled it back together the next winter. All kinds of ox hairs . . . hog bristles . . . even some bird feathers, I gathered them up. During the winter I sorted them, cleaned them, and took them into town to sell whenever there was a thaw. If I could catch a ride on a cart, I took Little Baldy into town with me.

"But this one time I went in alone. The weather that day was awful—it had been snowing almost every day—and the year-end market lacked its usual bustle. I'd only brought a few bundles of hog bristles but I couldn't sell them off. I squatted there in the marketplace from early morning till the sun was setting in the west. Someone had put a poster up on the wall of a large store at the intersection, which everyone stopped to read. I heard that the 'proclamation' had been put up early in the morning, or maybe it had only been there since around noontime. Some of the people read part of it aloud. I didn't know what it was all about. They were saying, 'proclamation this' and 'proclamation that,' but I couldn't figure out just what was being 'proclaimed.' I only knew that a proclamation was the business of officials and had nothing to do with us common folk, so I couldn't figure out why there were so many people interested in it. Someone said it was a proclamation about the capture of some army deserters. I overheard a few other tidbits here and there . . . in a few days the deserters were going to be delivered to the county seat to be shot."

"What year was that? Was that the execution of the twenty-odd deserters in 1921?" The carter absent-mindedly lets down his rolled-up sleeves, and strokes his jaw.

"How should I know what year it was? Besides, execution or not, what business was it of mine? Anyway, my hog bristles weren't selling so well and things were looking bleak." She rubs her hands together briefly and suddenly stretches out her hand as though she were catching a mosquito.

"Someone was reading out the names of the deserters. I saw a man in a black gown and said to him, 'Read those names again for me!' I was holding the hog bristles when I heard him say Chiang Wu-yün . . . Chiang Wu-yün . . . the name seemed to be echoing in my ears. After a moment or two, I felt like throwing up, like some foul-smelling thing was stuck in my throat; I wanted to swallow it, but couldn't. My eyes were burning. The people looking at the 'proclamation' crowded up in front of it, so I backed off to the side. I tried to move up again and take a look, but my leg wouldn't hold me. More and more people came to look at the 'proclamation,' and I kept backing up . . . farther . . . farther . . ."

I can see that her forehead and the tip of her nose are beaded with perspiration.

"When I returned to the village it was already late at night. Only when I was getting down from the cart did I remember the hog bristles . . . they'd been the farthest thing from my mind at the time. My ears had turned as stiff as two chips of wood . . . my scarf had fallen off, maybe on the road, maybe in the city . . ."

She lifts up her scarf to show us and, sure enough, her earlobes are missing.

"Just look at these; that's what it means to be a soldier's wife . . ."

The ends of her scarf, which she has fixed tightly over her head again, flutter slightly when she speaks.

"So Wu-yün was still alive, and I wanted to see him; after all we had been husband and wife for a time.

"In February I strapped Little Baldy on my back and went into town every day. I heard that the 'proclamation' had been put up several more times, though I never went to see that God-awful thing again. I went to the yamen to ask around, but they only said, 'That's none of our business!' They sent me to the military garrison . . . ever since I was a kid I've had a fear of officials . . . a country girl like me, I'd never seen a single one. Those sentries with their bayonets sent shivers up and down my spine. *Oh, go ahead! After all, they don't just kill people on sight.* Later on, after I'd gone to see them lots of times, I wasn't afraid any longer. What more was there to lose? After all, out of the three people in our family, they already had one in their clutches. They told me that the deserters hadn't been sent over yet. When I asked them when they would be, they told me, 'Wait another month or so!' But when I got back to the village I heard that the deserters had already come from some county seat or other—even today I can't remember which county seat it was, since the only thing that mattered to me was that they had been sent over—and they said if I didn't hurry and go see him, it'd be too late. So I strapped Little Baldy on my back and went back to town, where I asked around again at the military garrison. 'Why all the impatience?' they asked me. 'How many dozens of times are you going to ask? Who knows, maybe they won't be sent over at all.' One day I spotted some big official riding in a horsedrawn carriage with its bells jingling as it came out from the garrison buildings. I put Little Baldy down on the ground and ran over; the carriage was heading straight toward me, so I knelt down in front of it . . . I didn't even care if the horse trampled me.

"'Venerable sir, my husband . . . Chiang Wu- . . . ' Before I even got his name out I felt a heavy blow on my shoulders . . . the carriage driver had pushed me over backwards. I must've been knocked over . . . I crawled over to the side of the road. All I could see was that the driver too was wearing a military cap.

"I picked myself up and strapped Little Baldy on my back again. There was a river in front of the garrison, and for the rest of the afternoon I just sat there on the bank looking at the water. Some people were fishing and some women were washing clothes. Farther off, at the bend in the river, the water was much deeper, and the crests of waves passed in front of me, one after the other. I don't know how many hundreds of waves I saw passing by as I sat there. I felt like putting Little Baldy down on the bank and jumping straight to the bottom. Just leave that little life behind; as soon as he started crying, someone would surely come and pick him up.

"I rubbed his little chest and said something like, 'Little Baldy, you go to sleep.' Then I stroked his little round ears . . . those ears of his, honestly, they're so long and full, just like his daddy's. Looking at his ears, I was seeing his daddy."

A smile of maternal pride spreads across her face.

"I kept on patting his chest and said again, 'You go to sleep, Little Baldy.' Then I remembered that I still had a few strings of cash on me, so I decided to put them on his chest. As I reached over . . . reached over to put . . . when I was putting them on his . . . he opened his eyes . . . just then a sailboat came around the bend, and when I heard a child on the boat shouting 'Mama,' I quickly picked up Little Baldy and held him against my bosom."

Her tears fall as she tightens the scarf under her chin.

"But then . . . then, I knew I had to carry him back home. Even if I had to go begging, at least he would have his mother . . . he deserved a mother."

The corners of her blue scarf quiver with the movements of her jaw.

A flock of sheep cross our path; the shepherd boy is playing a willow whistle. The grass and the flowers in the woods all blend together in the slanting rays of the sun, so that all we can see is a vast jumbled patch of yellow.

The carter is now walking alongside the cart, raising trails of dust on the road with the tip of his whip.

"It wasn't until May that the people at the garrison finally told me, 'They'll be coming soon.'

"Toward the end of the month a big steamship pulled up to the wharf in front of the garrison. God, there were a lot of people! Even on the July Fifteenth Festival you don't have that many people coming out to watch the river-lanterns."

Her sleeves were waving in the air.

"The families of the deserters were standing over to the right, so I moved over there with them. A man in a military cap came over and pinned a kind of badge on each of us. I had no idea what the badge said, since I can't read.

"When they were about to lower the gangplank, a troop of soldiers came up to those of us who were wearing the badges and herded us into a circle. 'Move a little farther back from the river, move a little farther . . .' They pushed us back some thirty or forty feet from the steamship with their rifle butts. An old man with a white beard stood next to me, holding a bundle in each hand. 'Uncle, why did you bring those things along?' I asked him. 'Huh? Oh, I have a son and a nephew . . . one bundle for each . . . when they get to the next world it wouldn't be right for them not to have clean clothes to wear.'

"They lowered the gangplank. Some of the people began to cry as soon as they saw the gangplank being lowered. Me, I wasn't crying. I planted my feet squarely on the ground and kept my eyes on the ship, but no one came out. After a while, an officer wearing a foreign sword leaned over the railing and said, 'Have the families move farther back; they're going to be leaving the ship now.' As soon as they heard him bark out the order, the soldiers herded us even farther back with their rifle butts, all the way back to the bean field by the edge of the road, until we were standing there on top of the bean shoots. A rumble sounded on the gangplank, and out they came, led by an officer, their leg-irons clanking along. I can still see it: the first one out was a little short man . . . then five or six more . . . not one of them with broad shoulders like Little Baldy's daddy . . . really, they looked wretched, their arms hanging stiffly in front of them. I watched for a long time before I realized that they were all wearing manacles. The harder the people around me cried, the calmer I became. I just kept my eyes on the gangplank . . . I wanted to ask Little Baldy's daddy, 'Why couldn't you just be a good soldier? Why did you have to desert? Look here at your son; how can you face him?'

"About twenty of them came down, but I couldn't spot the man I was looking for; from where I stood they all looked the same. A young woman in a green dress lost control and burst through the rifles holding us back. Naturally the guards didn't allow her to pass; no, they went out and grabbed her, and she started rolling in the dirt and crying, 'He hadn't even been a soldier for three months . . . not even . . .' Two of them carried her back. Her hair was all mussed up and hanging over her face. After God knows how long they finally led those of us wearing badges over. The more we walked, the closer we got, and the closer we got, the harder it was for me to spot Little Baldy's daddy. My eyes started to blur . . . the weeping all around made me panicky . . .

"Some of them had cigarettes dangling from their mouths, some were cursing, some were even laughing. So this was the stuff soldiers are made of. I guess you could say that soldiers don't give a damn what happens to them.

"I looked them over; Little Baldy's daddy wasn't there for sure. *That's strange!* I grabbed hold of an officer's belt: 'What about Chiang Wu-yün?' 'What's he to you?' 'He's my husband.' I put Little Baldy down on the ground and the little pest started to cry. Pah! I slapped him across the mouth, then I began hitting the officer: 'You've destroyed him! What have you done with him?'

"'Good for you, lady, we're with you.' The prisoners shouted as one, stamping their feet. When the officer saw what was happening, he quickly called some soldiers over to drag me away. 'It's not only Chiang Wu-yün,' they said. 'There are a couple of others who haven't been sent over yet; they'll be over in a day or two on the next ship. Those three were the ringleaders of the deserters.'

"I put the child on my back and left the riverbank, with the badge still pinned on, and walked off. My legs were all rubbery. The streets were filled with people who had come over to watch the excitement. I was walking behind the garrison buildings, and there at the base of the garrison wall sat the old man with the bundle, but now he had only one left. 'Uncle, didn't your son come either?' I asked him. He just arched his back, chewed on the ends of his beard, and wept.

"He told me, 'Since he was one of the ringleaders, they carried out their capital punishment on the spot.' At the time I didn't know what 'capital punishment' meant."

At this point she begins to ramble.

"Three years later, when Little Baldy was eight, I sent him to the beancurd shop . . . that's what I did. I go to see him twice a year and he comes home once every two years, but then only for ten days or a couple of weeks."

The carter has left the side of the cart and is walking along the berm, his hands clasped behind his back. With the sun off to the side, he casts a long shadow which makes a huge fork with every step he takes.

"I have a family too . . ." The words seem to fall from his lips, as though he is speaking to the woods.

"Huh?" As Wu-yün Sao loosens her scarf a little, the wrinkles above her nose quiver momentarily. "Really? You're out of the army, and still you don't go home?"

"What's that? Go home, you say! You mean go home with nothing but the clothes on my back?" The carter sneers as he rubs his nose hard with his coarse hand.

"Haven't you put a little something away these past few years?"

"That's exactly why I deserted, to make a little money if I could." He cinches his belt tighter.

I put on another cotton jacket and Wu-yün Sao throws a blanket over her shoulders.

"Um! Still another mile to go. Now if we had a cart horse . . . um! We could be there in no time flat! An ox is something else. This beast just plods along with no spirit, and it's no good at all on a battlefield."

The carter opens his straw bag and takes out a padded jacket. Pieces of straw fall off and swirl in the wind. He puts it on.

The winds at dusk are just like February winds. In the rear of the cart the carter opens the jug of wine that my mother's father had brought for Grandfather.

"Here, drink! As they say, 'In the midst of a journey open a jug of wine, for the poor love to gamble.' Now have some." After drinking several cups, he opens his shirt and exposes his chest. He is chewing on some pieces of jerky, causing froth to gather at the corners of his mouth. Whenever a gust of wind blows across his face, the bubbles on his lips expand a little.

As we near the town, through the gray overcast we can tell only that it is not a patch of open country, or a mountain range, or the seashore, or a forest. The closer our cart comes, the more the town seems to recede. Our hands and faces feel sticky. Another look ahead, and this time even the end of the road is lost from view.

The carter puts the wine jug away and picks up his whip. By now even the ox's horns have become indistinct.

"Haven't you returned home even once since you left? And you don't hear from them either?" Apparently the carter doesn't hear her. He whistles to urge the ox on. Then he jumps down from the cart and walks along up front with the animal. An empty cart with a red lantern hanging from its axle comes rolling up to us.

"A heavy fog!"

"You said it!"

The carters thus hail each other in passing.

"A heavy fog in March . . . that means either a war or a year of famine . . ." The two carts pass on the road.

LO HUA-SHENG

(1893–1942)

Lo Hua-sheng, born Hsu Ti-shan, was the son of a Chinese official in Taiwan. When Taiwan was ceded to Japan as a result of the Sino-Japanese war in 1895, his whole family moved back to their native province of Fukien. Although his family was of the gentry, it was economically on the decline. As a child, he was exposed to both Buddhist and Christian beliefs, and that may account for his preoccupation with religion when he reached adulthood. He received enough education in his teens to become a teacher at a provincial school at age nineteen. Later, he received missionary support to attend Yenching University, where he was graduated in 1920. Even as a student he was an active writer, and he was one of the twelve founding members of the Literary Association. Between 1923 and 1926, he studied comparative religion at Columbia University and Oxford University, earning his M.A. from Columbia in 1925. Upon his return to China, he taught at the top universities in Peking—Yenching, Peking, and Tsinghua. Lo Hua-sheng's interests ranged far beyond literature. In this period, he wrote several books on religion, Indian literature, and even Sino-British diplomatic history. In the early 1930s he went to Southeast Asia and taught there briefly. The last several years of his life were spent in Hong Kong, where he taught Chinese literature at Hong Kong University until his death from a heart attack at age forty-nine.

Lo Hua-sheng's writings are unique in that they reflect his belief in religious ideals and in the human spirit. The Buddhist concept that all human beings, all living creatures in fact, possess equal worth is present in his stories. His adopting the pen-name Lo Hua-sheng, "Peanuts," reflects his humble attitude toward himself. The characters in his stories may be downtrodden and may be trapped in seemingly hopeless circumstances, but with faith, patience, resilience, and good will, their human spirit and dignity triumph in the end. It is significant that Lo Hua-sheng tended to choose women for his protagonists. It is extremely difficult to portray characters with the above-mentioned qualities who could at the same time be realistic and convincing. Lo Hua-sheng does not totally succeed at this, but comes powerfully close to it in his final story, "Yü Kuan," published posthumously. His literary output consists of a dozen or so short stories. The mainland Chinese literature journal Chinese Literature has published several of Lo Hua-sheng's stories in translation, including "Big Sister Liu" (originally "Ch'un-t'ao," Chinese Literature, 1957, no. 1). "Merchant's Wife" (Shang-jen fu, 1921) and "Yü-kuan"

23

(1939) are available in English translation in Modern Chinese Stories and Novellas, *edited by Joseph Lau, C. T. Hsia, and Leo Ou-fan Lee. "Garbage Gleaner" is a second and improved translation of "Ch'un-t'ao."*

Garbage Gleaner

Translated by Vivian Hsu and Juliani Sidharta

THE SUMMER WAS especially hot in Peking that year. Although the street lamps were already lit, the man who sold sour plum cider at the corner of the lane was still clanging his brass bowls, like the accompaniment of the women ballad singers. A woman carrying a basket full of scrap paper on her back passed by the vendor. Her face was hidden beneath the battered straw hat, but as she hailed him, her even white teeth flashed momentarily. The burden weighed heavily on her back, keeping her from straightening up at the waist; just like a camel, she walked sternly step by step to her gate.

The gate opened into a small compound. The woman lived in two dilapidated rooms. Most of the compound was scattered with rubble. By her door was an arbor of cucumbers and some corn. Beneath her window there was still a row of tuberoses. Some rotted beams under the arbor were probably the most prized seats of her home. As she reached the gate, a man came out and helped her lay aside her heavy load.

"Wife, you are late today."

The woman looked at him, as if surprised at his words. "What do you mean? You've gone mad thinking of a wife. Don't call *me* wife, I tell you." As she entered the room, she took off her battered straw hat and hung it behind the door. Then, with a bamboo ladle she scooped some water from a vat, several ladlefuls in succession, and drank until she ran out of breath. She stood for a moment, gasping, then pulled the basket aside and sat down on a rotted beam in the arbor.

The man's name was Liu Hsiang-kao. He was about the same age as the woman—thirtyish. The woman's surname was also Liu. Except for Hsiang-kao, no one else knew that her given name was

Ch'un-t'ao. The neighbors called her Big Sister Liu, the scrap collector, because she made her living by rummaging through rubbish heaps in the streets and lanes, sometimes calling out as she went along, "Matches for your scrap paper!" Though she swallowed dust from morning until night, under the blazing sun or out in the cold wind, she always loved cleanliness. Be it winter or summer, each day when she came home she always bathed and washed her face. It was always Hsiang-kao who prepared the water for her.

Hsiang-kao was a graduate of a rural elementary school. Four years earlier soldiers had marauded his village and his whole family had scattered and fled. On the road he met Ch'un-t'ao, who was also a refugee. They traveled together several hundred *li* and then went their separate ways.

She had somehow followed some people to Peking. A Western woman wanted to hire a fresh, innocent country girl as an Amah, and she was recommended for the job. The mistress was impressed with Ch'un-t'ao's cleanliness and robust grace and became very fond of her. Ch'un-t'ao on her part could not get used to seeing her masters eat beef, smear butter on their steamed buns, and even add milk to their tea. They exuded an odor that she couldn't get accustomed to. One day, her master asked her to take their child to the zoo. It dawned on her then that they all smelled like the tiger and wolf cages. She became more and more troubled in her heart. In less than two months, she quit her job. Then she went to an ordinary household, but country folks are not used to being bossed around and cannot stand to be scolded, so she did not stay there very long either. When her money was about to run out, she decided to try her hand at collecting scrap paper. With this occupation she managed to eke out a living from day to day.

The story of Hsiang-kao after he and Ch'un-t'ao parted ways was quite simple. He went to Chochou, but could not find any of his relatives. Erstwhile friends, hearing that he had come as a penniless refugee, were reluctant to have him stay with them. Somehow, he too drifted to Peking. He became acquainted with Old Wu, the sour plum cider vendor at the street corner. Old Wu loaned him the run-down living quarters in the compound, with the understanding that when someone came to rent the rooms, he would have to find himself another place. He had no job, so he helped Old Wu keep his accounts and sell the cider. He received no cash for this service, but he was provided with the two rooms plus two meals a day.

Ch'un-t'ao's scrap paper collecting business gradually picked up, but the people with whom she was staying would not allow her to store her merchandise there. So she looked for another place along the north city wall. When she knocked at a gate, it was answered by none other than her old acquaintance, Hsiang-kao. Without much ado, she rented the rooms from Old Wu and let Hsiang-kao stay to help her. That was three years ago. With his knowledge of a few characters, Hsiang-kao could help Ch'un-t'ao sort out the scrap papers she collected. He was able to pick out those that were valuable, such as inscribed paintings, or scrolls and letters written by prominent generals and ministers. With the two of them working together, the business improved. Sometimes Hsiang-kao also tried to teach Ch'un-t'ao to read, but without much success. As his own knowledge was limited, he found it very hard to explain the characters.

For the several years that they lived together, they got along quite well. Even though they did not enjoy the connubial bliss of a pair of mandarin ducks, it could be said that they led the cheerful life of a pair of common sparrows.

As Ch'un-t'ao now entered the room, Hsiang-kao followed her with a bucket of water. "Hurry and wash up, wife," he chirped, "I've been starving waiting for you. Tonight let's have something good—onion griddle cake, how about that? If that sounds good to you, I'll buy the fixings."

"Wife, wife! Stop calling me that, OK?" Ch'un-t'ao became impatient.

"If you promise to answer just once, tomorrow I'll go to a second-hand shop at T'iench'iao and buy you a nice straw hat. Didn't you say that you need a new one?" Hsiang-kao pleaded.

"I don't like to hear it."

He knew that she was getting annoyed, so he changed the subject and asked, "What would you like to eat then?"

"Whatever you'd like to eat, I'll make it for you. Go!"

Hsiang-kao bought a few stalks of onions and a bowl of sesame sauce. As he placed them on the table, Ch'un-t'ao, already bathed, came out holding a red card.

"This must be some big shot's marriage certificate. This time, don't give it to Old Li from the Little Market. Have someone take it to the Peking Hotel; we can sell it there for a better price."

"It's ours! Otherwise I wouldn't have the right to call you wife, would I? I've tried to teach you the characters for a couple of years now, and you can't even recognize your own name!"

"Who can recognize so many characters? Cut out this wife! wife! nonsense. I don't like to hear it. Now who wrote this?"

"I did. This morning a policeman came to check up on the tenants. He said that they are tightening up the martial law these days. Every house has to report exactly how many there are in the household. Old Wu said that we could save ourselves a lot of trouble if we were reported as husband and wife. The policeman also said that it wouldn't do to register a man and a woman living together. So I filled in the blank marriage certificate that we didn't sell last time. I put down that we were married in 1931."

"What! 1931? I didn't even know you then! Aren't you making a big mess here! We haven't kowtowed to Heaven and Earth together, nor have we exchanged wedding toasts. How can you say that we're husband and wife?"

Even though Ch'un-t'ao resisted the idea, she spoke calmly. She had changed into a pair of blue trousers topped with a white tunic. Although she wore no make-up, her face exuded a natural grace. If she was interested in finding a husband, the matchmaker could easily pass her off as a twenty-three or twenty-four-year-old widow. She could have commanded a bride price of at least one hundred and eighty dollars.

Smiling, she folded up the card and said, "Don't be crazy. What a marriage certificate! Let's make our griddle cakes and eat." She lifted the stove lid and thrust the card into the flames, then she walked to the table and started to knead the dough.

"You can burn it if you like," Hsiang-kao said with a grin, "but the policeman has registered us as husband and wife. If an inspector comes, couldn't I just say the certificate was lost on the road while we were fleeing? From now on I am going to call you wife. Old Wu recognizes our marriage, and so does the policeman, so I'm still going to call you wife whether you like it or not. Wife! Wife! Tomorrow I'll buy you a new straw hat. Ayee! I can't afford a ring."

"If you don't stop calling me that, I'll get mad."

Hsiang-kao was not as high-spirited as he had been moments before. "It looks like you're still thinking of that Li Mao," he muttered to himself, not intending for Ch'un-t'ao to hear him, but she did.

"Me? Think of him? Husband and wife for just one night, then not a single word for four or five years. Isn't that nonsense?" She had once told Hsiang-kao what had happened on her wedding day. As the wedding sedan chair entered her husband's gate, even before the guests had a chance to sit down for the reception, people came in from two neighboring villages warning that a big troop of soldiers had arrived and were nabbing men from everywhere to dig trenches. At this news, everyone took flight. The new couple hurriedly bundled up a few belongings and fled with all the others toward the west. They walked all day and all night. The second night on the road, they suddenly heard people ahead shouting, "The bandits are coming, hide quickly!" In the mad scramble, everyone rushed to get out of sight, and no one could attend to anyone else. When day broke, about a dozen people were missing, Ch'un-t'ao's husband, Li Mao, among them.

"I think he must have been taken by the bandits, and maybe they killed him long ago. Well, forget it! Let's not bring him up any more.!"

Ch'un-t'ao finished making the griddle cakes and set them on the table. Hsiang-kao scooped a little bowl of cucumber soup from the pot. Having nothing to say, they ate their meal in silence. After the meal, they sat as usual in the arbor and chatted. There were flickers of light between the cucumber leaves. The cool breeze had brought the fireflies down to the arbor, like a myriad of shooting stars. The night-blooming tuberoses gradually opened and filled the courtyard with their perfume.

"How lovely they smell." Hsiang-kao plucked a flower and placed it in Ch'un-t'ao's hair.

"Don't spoil my tuberoses. Wearing a flower at night—I'm not a prostitute!" She took the flower out, sniffed its fragrance, and placed it on the wooden seat.

"Why were you late coming home tonight?" asked Hsiang-kao.

"Huh! Today I did a good piece of business! As I was about to come home this afternoon, I passed the Houmen Arch and saw a street cleaner pushing a big cart of papers, so I asked him where he had gotten them. He said that they had been thrown out at the Shenwu Palace Gate. I saw that there were a lot of red and yellow document papers and asked him if he would sell them to me. He said that if I really wanted them, he'd give me a bargain. Look here!" She pointed to the big basket under the window. "I paid only a dollar for that basketful. But I'm not sure if we'll get our money's worth. We can look them over tomorrow."

"You can't go wrong on stuff from the Palace. It's things from the schools and the foreign business offices that I dread. Not only are their papers heavy, but they also smell bad. We can never be sure of what we're getting."

"In these past few years, all the shops have been using foreign newspapers for wrapping. I can't imagine who all these people are that read the foreign newspapers. They are heavy to handle and not worth that much money," said Ch'un-t'ao.

"More and more people are reading foreign books, and everyone wants to read foreign newspapers, so they can do business with foreigners."

"Let them do business with foreigners, we'll stick to collecting foreign wastepaper."

"Looks like everything will have foreign labels from now on. Ricksha pullers are pulling 'foreign' rickshas, donkey drivers will want 'foreign' donkeys, the next thing you know there will also be 'foreign' camels!'' Hsiang-kao coaxed a laugh out of Ch'un-t'ao.

"You shouldn't mock other people. If you had the money, you'd also want to learn to read foreign books, and get yourself a foreign wife."

"Heaven knows! I'll never be rich. Even if I get rich I wouldn't want a foreign wife. If I were rich, I'd go back to the country and buy myself a few acres of land. We could till it together."

Ever since Ch'un-t'ao fled from her home and lost her husband, the word "country" always had bad associations for her. "You're still thinking of going back?" she countered. "I'm afraid that even before you buy the land, you and your money would have been gobbled up! Even if I were starving I wouldn't go back."

"I'm talking about going back to my village, Chinhsien."

"These days, the country is the same wherever you go. If it's not marauded by the soldiers, then it's raided. If it's not raided by the bandits, then it's the Japanese. Who dares to go back? We're far better off staying here and collecting scrap paper. What we need is one more helper. If we had one more person at home to replace you in sorting out the papers, you could set up a stall by day and sell directly to customers. We'd do away with the middleman, and we'd be less likely to pass over choice items."

"Three more years as apprentice at this trade and I'll be set. If we let any choice items pass, we can't blame anyone but ourselves. I've learned plenty these past few months. Now I know pretty well which stamps are valuable and which are not. I'm also getting the hang of spotting the writings of famous men. Remember that piece by K'ang Yu-wei I picked out of the pile the other day? Guess how much I sold it for today!" He gestured proudly with his thumb and index finger. "Eighty cents!"

"What did I tell you! If we can pick eighty cents out of the scraps every day, we've got it made. What's the point of going back to the country? Isn't that just looking for trouble?" Ch'un-t'ao's happy voice sounded like the oriole's warble in late spring. "I bet we'll find all kinds of goodies in the pile I brought home today. I hear that there will be more tomorrow. This man told me to wait for him at the Houmen Arch first thing in the morning. Things are being cleaned out at the Palace these days. They are packing up and moving south, and discarding a lot of papers from the offices. I noticed that sacks of them have been thrown out at the Tunghua Palace Gate as well. Tomorrow you should go down there and find out about it too."

They chatted in this high-spirited vein. Before they knew it, it was past ten o'clock. Ch'un-t'ao stood up and stretched. "I'm tired, let's get some rest."

Hsiang-kao followed her inside. Against the window there was a brick oven-bed wide enough for three to sleep on. In the dim light of the oil lamp, two pictures were faintly visible on the wall. One was of the Eight Fairies playing mahjong, and the other was a cigarette advertisement poster. If Ch'un-t'ao took off her battered straw hat and put on a decent dress—not necessarily one from a fancy shop in Shanghai, even a second-hand Chinese gown from the T'iench'iao market would do—and sat on a grassy knoll, she wouldn't look much different from the fashionable girl in the advertisement. Hsiang-kao often teased Ch'un-t'ao, saying that it was her photograph.

She got up on the bed and undressed. Then she pulled up a thin coverlet and lay face down on one side of the bed. Hsiang-kao, as usual, gave her legs and back a massage. And as usual, she gradually relaxed and smiled faintly under the flickering light of the oil lamp. Half asleep, she murmured, "Hsiang-kao, go to bed too. Don't work tonight, we'll have to get up early in the morning."

Soon she made a steady, faint snoring sound, and Hsiang-kao put out the lamp.

At daybreak the man and the woman both got up promptly, and like a pair of ravens searching for food, went flying hastily to their own work.

As the midday cannon sounded and the gongs and drums of the Ten Monasteries Lake reached their peak, Ch'un-t'ao came through the Houmen Arch carrying a basket of scrap paper on her back, and headed west toward Puya Bridge. As she neared the marketplace, she heard someone calling her from the side of the road, "Ch'un-t'ao, Ch'un-t'ao."

Even Hsiang-kao called her by this pet name only once in a blue moon. Since she had left her village four or five years before, no one had ever called her that in public.

"Ch'un-t'ao, Ch'un-t'ao, don't you recognize me?"

As if by reflex she turned her head and saw a beggar sitting on the roadside. The piteous call had come from a mouth buried under a heavy beard. He could not get up, because he had no legs. Draped on him was a tattered grey army uniform, with all the metal buttons rusted. His skin showed through the split shoulder seams, and a nondescript army cap sat askew on his head, its insignia long gone.

Ch'un-t'ao stared at him, speechless.

"Ch'un-t'ao, I'm Li Mao."

She took two steps forward. Grimy tears ran from the man's eyes down his unkempt beard. Her heart beat wildly. For a long time she could not utter a word. At last she said, "Mao, are you really a beggar? How did you lose your legs?"

"Ai, it's a long story. How long have you been in Peking? What are you selling?"

"Selling? Why, I collect scrap paper. Let's go home, and then we can talk."

She hired a ricksha, raised Li Mao onto it, and also placed her basket in it. She herself went to the back and pushed along. At Tesheng Gate the ricksha puller helped her put Li Mao down. As they entered the lane, Old Wu was there clanging his small brass bowl.

"Big Sister Liu, you're early today, good business, eh?"

"A relative has come from the country," she replied.

Li Mao crawled like a circus bear, using his hands and dragging his mutilated legs. Ch'un-t'ao unlocked the door and guided Li Mao in. She took out a suit of Hsiang-kao's clothing, and as Hsiang-kao did for her every day, she went to the well and drew two buckets of water. She filled a small wash basin and told Li Mao to bathe; then she gave him another basin so he could wash his face. She helped him to a seat on the brick bed and went into the next room to bathe herself.

"Ch'un-t'ao, this place of yours is nice and clean. Do you live here by yourself?"

"My partner lives here, too," she answered with no hesitation.

"Are you in business?"

"Didn't I tell you I collect scrap paper?"

"Collect scrap paper? How much can you earn in a day?"

"Stop asking questions about me. Tell me about yourself first."

Ch'un-t'ao dumped out the bath water. She came back inside, combed her hair, and sat down opposite Li Mao.

"Ch'un-t'ao, ah, it's too long. I'll just tell you the bare outline. Since that night when the bandits captured me, I hated their guts because they made me lose you. I waited for my chance, then I grabbed one of their rifles and killed two of them. Then I ran for my life. I managed to flee to Shenyang, just as they were recruiting for the border guards, so I joined up. All through the next three years I kept trying to get some news from home, but everyone said that our village had been razed. I don't even know who has the title deed for our bit of land. I had forgotten to take it when we fled. So, in those few years, I never asked for leave to go home to have a look around. I was afraid that if I did, I'd lose even the few dollars that I was earning each month.

"I settled down to being a soldier, living from month to month just for my pay. As for becoming an officer, I didn't dare hope for that. I must have been born unlucky. At the end of last year, the colonel of our regiment issued an order that any man who could hit

the target nine times in a row would get double pay and be promoted. No one in our regiment could hit the target more than four
times in a row, and even those did not hit the bull's eye. But shot
after shot I hit the bull's eye, nine times in a row. Not only that,
with the remaining bullet, I thought I'd really show my stuff. To
show how good I was, I turned around, bent over and fired from
between my legs, and sure enough I hit it dead in the center. I was
so pleased with myself at the time.

"When the colonel sent for me, I prepared to receive at least some
praise. Instead, the last thing I expected happened. The ass became
very angry at me. He swore that I must be a bandit to be able to
shoot so well, and wanted to have me shot. Nobody but a bandit
could shoot so well, he said. My sergeant and my lieutenant both
pleaded for me; they guaranteed that I was not a bad lot. Well, that
saved me from being shot, but they took away my rank as a private,
and wouldn't even let me be a second-class private. The colonel said
an officer is bound to hurt the feelings of his men sometimes, and
with a sharpshooter like me in the ranks, he could be shot in the
back during a battle. Although he'd be considered killed in action,
it still wouldn't be worth it to be killed for someone's revenge. No
one could say anything to that. They could only advise me to leave
the army and look for another livelihood.

"Not long after I was discharged, Shenyang fell to the Japanese.
That dog of a colonel led his troops to surrender without a fight.
When I heard that, I really got furious. I swore I'd get the bastard,
so I joined the Volunteers. We fought around Haich'eng for a couple
of months, but then we had to give ground gradually and retreat to
south of the pass. Two months ago we were fighting northeast of
P'ingku. I was on patrol duty when I ran into the enemy. I was
wounded in both legs. I could still walk, so I took cover behind a
boulder and killed a couple of them. When I couldn't hold out any
longer, I threw my rifle away and crawled toward the fields. I
waited one day, two days, but still no sign of the Red Cross or the
Red Salvation. The wounds were swelling badly and I couldn't
move. I had nothing to eat or drink. I just lay there and waited for
death. Luckily a big cart passed by, and the driver helped me up
and rushed me to an army first-aid tent. They took one look at me,
put me in a car, and sent me to a hospital in Peking. It was already
the third day. The doctor opened up the bandage and said that my
legs were too far gone. There was no way but to amputate.

"I stayed in the hospital for more than a month. I recovered but
my legs were gone. I had no relatives here that I knew of, and I
couldn't go back to the village either. Even if I could, with no legs,
what could I do on the land? I pleaded with the hospital to take me

on and give me some odd jobs to do. But the doctor said that the hospital treats people but cannot support them or find jobs for them. There is no home for disabled veterans in this city, so what could I do but beg on the streets? Today is only the third day. In the past two days, I'd been thinking that if this is what life is going to be I might as well hang myself."

Ch'un-t'ao listened intently, tears welling up in her eyes. She was speechless. Li Mao wiped the sweat from his brow, and paused for a while.

"Ch'un-t'ao, what about you? This place of yours, although it is cramped and nothing like our broad open country, it looks like you're not suffering too much hardship."

"Who's not suffering? Even if things are bad, a person still has to find a way to live. Aren't there people who put on smiles even at the gate of hell? These past few years I have been collecting scrap paper for a living. A man by the name of Liu is my partner. The two of us share everything and we can get by OK."

"You and this person Liu live here together?"

"Yes, we both sleep on this brick bed." Ch'un-t'ao did not hesitate a bit, as if she had made up her mind on the matter a long time ago.

"Are you married to him then?"

"No, we just live together."

"Hm, in that case, you mean you are still my wife?"

"No, I'm not anybody's wife."

Li Mao's pride as a husband was wounded. But what was there to say? His eyes were fixed on the ground, not that he was looking at anything of course, but just that he was somewhat afraid to look at his wife. At last he spoke in a low voice, "People would laugh at me and call me a living cuckold."

"Cuckold?" As the woman heard his words, her expression stiffened, but her attitude remained calm. "Only people with money and status are afraid of being called cuckolds. A man like you, who gives a damn? No one even knows you're alive. Cuckold or not, what's the difference? I'm on my own now. Whatever I do can't have any effect on you."

"But we're still husband and wife after all. As the saying goes, 'One night of marriage, a hundred days of affection.'"

"I don't know anything about any 'hundred days of affection,'" Ch'un-t'ao cut in. "If you count the days of affection, more than ten 'hundred days of affection' have passed. No word of each other for four or five years . . . I'm sure you never dreamt that we'd meet up like this. I was here all alone, I had to live and I needed a helper. After living with him like this for all these years, if we are to speak of affection, naturally I don't feel the same for you. Today I brought you home because our fathers were friends, and we're still from the same village. You may claim that I am your wife, but I shall deny you. Even if you take me to court, I'm not so sure you'll win."

Li Mao fumbled at the pouch by his belt, as if looking for something. He stopped and stared at Ch'un-t'ao, and his hand dropped back and rested on the mat.

Li Mao was silent. Ch'un-t'ao wept. Neither uttered a word. The shadows quietly lengthened.

Li Mao finally gathered his thoughts.

"All right, Ch'un-t'ao, have it your way. We both know I'm crippled, so even if you are willing to come back to me, I couldn't support you."

"I'm not throwing you over just because you're crippled. But I've grown too attached to him and can't give him up either. Why don't we all just live here, no one needs to think about who is supporting whom, how about it?" Ch'un-t'ao, too, spoke what was in her heart.

Li Mao's stomach rumbled faintly.

"Oh, we've been talking here all this time and I haven't even asked you what you would like to eat. You must be very hungry."

"Anything would be fine, whatever you have. I haven't had a bite to eat since last night. I've only had water."

"I'll go buy something." As Ch'un-t'ao was hurrying out the door, Hsiang-kao strode gaily into the courtyard, and the two collided squarely in the arbor.

"What are you so happy about?" she asked. "And how come you're home so early today?"

"I did some terrific business today! This morning I went through that basket you brought home last night, and right in there was a bundle of petitions sent by the Korean Emperor in the Ming Dynasty—worth at least fifty dollars apiece, and we've got ten of them! I brought just a few sheets down to the shops to see what price they can fetch from customers, then I'll bring out the rest later. And then there were two documents bearing the Tuan-ming Palace seal. Some expert said that they are from the Sung Dynasty and offered sixty dollars for them right off, but I was afraid to sell it, afraid that I'd be taken for too low a price. I brought them back for you to take a look. See here." He opened the bundle and took out the petitions and old documents.

"This is the imperial seal from the Tuan-ming Palace." He pointed to the stamped imprint. "If it weren't for this seal, I sure wouldn't have seen anything special in this piece of paper; even fine foreign paper is whiter than this. Those Palace officials must be as blind as I am." Although Ch'un-t'ao looked at the paper, she still could not see the value in it.

"We're lucky they're not more sharp-eyed; otherwise, how could people like us make a couple of bucks now and then?" Hsiang-kao put the documents back into the bundle along with the petitions. Grinning, he said to Ch'un-t'ao, "I say, wife . . ."

Ch'un-t'ao gave him a sharp look and said, "I told you not to call me wife."

Hsiang-kao didn't pay any attention to her and went straight on. "Well, you're home early too. Business must have been good."

"This morning I bought another basketful, just like yesterday's."

"Didn't you say that there was a lot more?"

"They had all been sent to the Morning Market to be sold in the country for wrapping peanuts!"

"Never mind, after all, we've done well today. It's the first time we've done over thirty dollars' worth of business in a day. Say, it's not often that we're home together in the afternoon. Let's go to the Ten Monasteries Lake for some fun. It's a nice cool spot to spend a hot day. How about it?"

Without waiting for an answer, he entered the house and put the bundle on the table. Ch'un-t'ao followed him in. "We can't, we have a visitor today." As she spoke she raised the door curtain to the inner room and nodded to Hsiang-kao. "Go on in."

He went in, and she followed. "This is my husband," she said to Hsiang-kao; then to Li Mao whe said, "This is my present partner."

The two men stared at each other, eyeball to eyeball. Both remained speechless; even the two flies on the window sill were still. In that silent spell, the shadows inched on.

"Your name, sir?" Hsiang-kao knew it very well, but he followed the usual courtesy just the same.

At last they began to chat.

"I'll go buy something to eat." Ch'un-t'ao then turned to Hsiang-kao. "You haven't eaten yet either, have you? How about griddle cakes?"

"I've eaten already. Stay home, I'll go and buy them."

The woman pulled Hsiang-kao to a seat on the brick bed. "You stay home and chat with our guest," she insisted with a smile, then went out herself.

The two men remained in the room. In such a situation, either they had to love each other like old friends from the start, or they would have to fight to the death. Fortunately, the former turned out to be the case—and it wasn't because Li Mao could not fight. Just because he had lost both legs didn't mean he was helpless. It must be remembered that Hsiang-kao's only exercise in the past four or five years had been wielding a pen; if Li Mao used all his strength he could easily have crushed Hsiang-kao to death. If he had a gun, it would have been an even simpler matter; one crook of the trigger finger and Hsiang-kao would have crossed the bridge to the nether world.

Li Mao told Hsiang-kao that Ch'un-t'ao's father was a well-to-do landowner in their village. His own father managed the donkeys and did other odd jobs for that household. Because he could shoot so well, Ch'un-t'ao's father was afraid that he would go off and join the army. To make sure that Li Mao would stay and protect the local villagers, the old man gave his daughter to him in marriage. This was something Ch'un-t'ao had never before told Hsiang-kao. Li Mao went on to tell Hsiang-kao about the conversation he had with Ch'un-t'ao that day. By and by, their talk pressed in on the issue that weighed on both their minds.

"Now that you are united again, of course I must step aside," said Hsiang-kao reluctantly.

"No, we have been separated for such a long time; and what's more I'm a cripple now, I can't support her. It wouldn't be of any use. You two have lived together these past few years, why break it up? I can go to a home for the disabled. I heard that there is one around here; and with the right connections, I may be able to get in."

Hsiang-kao was surprised to hear these words. He never expected a rough soldier like Li Mao to harbor such a noble spirit. Although his heart wanted to accept Li Mao's magnanimity, his mouth continued to refuse the idea. Such is the trickery of "propriety" understood by all who have studied the Books.

"That wouldn't be right, I couldn't live with myself if I came to be known as wife-snatcher. And looking at it from your angle, how can you willingly let your wife live with someone else?"

"I can write out a divorce paper for her, or a bill of sale for you. Either one will do," Li Mao said with an earnest smile.

"Divorce? She hasn't done anything wrong; you can't divorce her! I won't have her losing face either. Sale? Where do I have the money to buy her? All my money is hers."

"I don't want any money."

"What do you want then?"

"Nothing, I don't want anything."

"Then why bother to write a bill of sale?"

"Because a verbal agreement has no validity. If anyone has regrets later, we'd have a terrible mess. It's better that we be a little petty now, to be sure that we'll be honorable later."

At this point, Ch'un-t'ao returned with the griddle cakes. Seeing that the two men had hit it off, she felt very happy.

"Lately I've been thinking a lot about getting a third person to help out. Now by a lucky coincidence Brother Mao has come on the scene. Since he cannot move about, he'd be perfect for managing things at home, sorting paper, and whatnot. You can make the rounds outside selling the goods. I'll stick to collecting the paper. The three of us can set up a business!" Ch'un-t'ao came out with this idea of her own.

Ignoring the usual courtesies, Li Mao reached for a griddle cake and stuffed it into his mouth. He was so starved, he had no time to speak now.

"Two men and one woman start up a business? And you put up the capital?" Hsiang-kao asked the unnecessary.

"Why? Don't you want to?" It was the woman's turn to ask.

"No, no, I don't have any objections." Hsiang-kao could not bring himself to say what was weighing on his heart.

"What can I do? What use would I be, sitting in the house all day?" Li Mao was rather hesitant too. He could guess what was on Hsiang-kao's mind.

"Don't you two worry about it, I've got it all figured out."

These words didn't set Hsiang-kao's mind at ease; he moistened his lips, then swallowed hard. Li Mao continued eating, but his eyes were fixed on Ch'un-t'ao, waiting to hear her plan.

Collecting scrap paper was probably an occupation in which women played the leading role. She had already decided that Li Mao would stay home and pick out the used postage stamps and the picture cards from the empty cigarette packs. That job required only hands and eyes; he could easily do it. She figured, if Li Mao could pick out a hundred-odd picture cards from cigarette packs every day, the income from it would cover his food. And if he could in addition find two or three rare stamps every day, he would be doing pretty well. The sale of foreign cigarettes in the city came to about ten thousand packs a day; for her to collect one percent of those wrappers should not be too difficult. As for Hsiang-kao, she would still have him sort out famous peoples' letters and other relatively valuable things. He was, needless to say, already an expert of some sort and could carry on without any guidance. Ch'un-t'ao herself would continue the most strenuous job. Unless there was a really heavy rainstorm, she would go out collecting. The hot sun and cold wind would not keep her home; she would work all the harder in bad weather, because some of the other scrap collectors would not be out giving her competition on such days.

Ch'un-t'ao glanced at the sun through the window. She knew that it was not yet two o'clock. She went out into the courtyard, put on her battered straw hat, then peered into the room and instructed Hsiang-kao, "I'm going to find out whether anything more is being thrown out at the Palace. Stay home and look after him. I'll be back tonight; we can discuss this some more then."

Hsiang-kao knew he could not hold her back, so he let her go.

Several days went by quietly. But two men and one woman sleeping on the same brick bed would inevitably be awkward. Societies based on the polyandrous system could never become very widespread. One reason is the fact that the average man cannot rid himself of the primitive concepts regarding his rights as husband and father. It is on the basis of these concepts that our customs, habits, and moral precepts were formed. But the fact is, only the parasites and exploiters in our society observe these so-called customs and traditions. As for those who make their living with their own sinews, they have very little regard for these things.

Take Ch'un-t'ao, for instance. She was neither a madam nor a lady. She would never attend a diplomat's ball, nor would she ever have the chance to play a leading role at some important social function. Her conduct was not subject to anyone's criticism or question. Even if it was, it would not bother her one whit. The only ones who paid any attention to her were the local policemen, and they were not difficult to handle.

And the two men? Hsiang-kao admittedly had some schooling, and he had some ideas about the philosophies of the ancients. But aside from a mild interest in keeping up appearances, he felt more or less the same as Ch'un-t'ao. But ever since he and Ch'un-t'ao started living together, he had depended on her completely for his livelihood. Ch'un-t'ao's words were like vitamins absorbed through his ears; he listened to her because that was good for him. Ch'un-t'ao told him not to be jealous, so he cast aside even the seeds of jealousy.

As for Li Mao, he was thankful for each day that Ch'un-t'ao and Hsiang-kao let him stay with them; if they regarded him as one of the family, he was more than satisfied. After all, a roving soldier is bound to lose a wife or two. His problem was also just one of appearances.

Nevertheless, although Hsiang-kao didn't feel jealous, various kinds of uneasy feelings floated between the two men.

The heat of the summer had not let up. Ch'un-t'ao and Hsiang-kao were not the kind that went to resorts like T'angshan or Peitaihe. Regardless of the weather they had to carry on to make a living. At home, Li Mao was beginning to catch on to this trade; he could already distinguish those papers that could be sent to the toilet paper manufacturers from those that should be kept for Hsiang-kao's appraisal.

One night when Ch'un-t'ao came home, she found Hsiang-kao

waiting for her as usual. It was already late, and she could smell mosquito-repelling incense burning as she entered the courtyard.

"Since when did we start burning incense?" She directed that at Hsiang-kao who was sitting in the arbor. "You're liable to burn the house down too if you're not careful."

Before Hsiang-kao could reply, Li Mao piped up, "It's not for driving away the mosquitos, but for getting rid of the musty smell. I asked Big Brother Liu to light it. I'm thinking of sleeping outside tonight. It's too hot in the room. With three people sleeping on the brick bed, it really gets uncomfortable."

"And whose red card is this on the table?" Ch'un-t'ao picked it up to examine it.

"We talked it over today." His voice came from the brick bed. "We agreed that you should belong to Big Brother Liu. That's the contract of sale I gave him."

"So, you two have settled this between yourselves! What makes you think you can dispose of me just like that?" She walked over to Li Mao with the red card. "Was this your idea, or his?"

"It's both of ours. The way we've been living, I was miserable, and so was he."

We've talked about this over and over, and you two are still hung up on it. Can't you just forget about this husband and wife business?"

She tore the red card to shreds, and her voice became angry. "How much did you sell me for?"

"We put down some figure just to make it look decent. Only a good-for-nothing man would give away his wife for nothing."

"So you think selling your wife would make you into a good-for-something?"

She walked out to Hsiang-kao. "Now that you have money, you think you can buy yourself a wife. If you spend just a little more . . ."

"Don't talk like that, don't talk like that," Hsiang-kao pleaded. "Ch'un-t'ao, you don't understand. For the past few days, the people in the trade have all been laughing at me."

"What's there to laugh about?"

"They laugh at . . ." Hsiang-kao couldn't say it out loud. In reality he did not have strong feelings about the matter. Whatever Ch'un-t'ao wanted, nine cases out of ten, he would obey. He himself did not understand why she had such power over him. When she was not with him, he knew which things should be done and had definite ideas about how things were to be done; but as soon as he came face to face with her, it was as if he were before the Dowager, and he would obey her every wish.

"So you can't forget your genteel ideas—just because you've

studied a few books, scared to death that people will make fun of you."

Since the earliest times, real control over the people has come not from the teachings of the sages, but from cursing tongues and blows of the whip. It is these curses and blows that have maintained the customs and habits. But through her experience, a certain attitude had taken hold in Ch'un-t'ao's heart; she was ready to return "a curse for a curse, a blow for a blow." She was not a weakling; she did not pick on others, but she wouldn't take abuse from others either. All this was clearly demonstrated in the way she instructed Hsiang-kao.

"If anyone laughs at you, why don't you let him have it? What's there to be afraid of? Our affairs are nobody else's business."

Hsiang-kao had nothing to say.

"Let's not talk about this any more. The three of us will just go on living like this, okay?"

The whole room was silent. After dinner, Hsiang-kao and Ch'un-t'ao sat in the arbor as usual, but both were exceptionally taciturn that night. They didn't even talk about the day's business.

Li Mao called Ch'un-t'ao into the room and urged her to become Hsiang-kao's wife officially. He said that she did not understand a man's heart. No man would willingly be a cuckold, nor would a man like to be known as a wife-snatcher. He took a faded red card from his waistband and handed it to Ch'un-t'ao.

"This is our marriage certificate. That night when we fled, I took it from the shrine and stuffed it inside my shirt. Take it now, and let's just say we are no longer a couple."

Ch'un-t'ao took the card without a word; she just stared at the torn mat on the brick bed. Involuntarily she sank down next to the crippled man,

"Mao, I can't take this; take it back. I'm still your wife. As the saying goes, 'One night of marriage, a hundred days of affection.' I can't wrong you like this. What kind of a person would I be if I threw you over just because you can't walk and can't do heavy work anymore?"

She put the red card down on the brick bed.

Li Mao was deeply moved by her words. "I can see that you like him a lot," he said softly to Ch'un-t'ao. "It's best that you live with him after all. When we have a little more money scraped together, you can send me back to the village, or to a home for the crippled."

"Truth to tell," Ch'un-t'ao's voice became very soft, "he and I have lived like a couple these past few years. We get along very well and we've grown fond of each other. I'd be loath to let him go now. Let's ask him in. We'll talk it over and see what he thinks."

She called through the window, "Hsiang, Hsiang." But there was no reply. She went out to look, but Hsiang-kao was already gone. This was the first time he had ever gone out at night. Ch'un-t'ao was stunned. She turned toward the room. "I'll go look for him."

She was sure that Hsiang-kao would not have gone very far. But when she went up to the corner of the lane and asked Old Wu, the old man said he was headed toward the main street. She went to all his usual hangouts, but Hsiang-kao was nowhere to be found. It's easy to lose someone; once he gets out of sight, he can disappear for good, just like that. It was almost one in the morning before Ch'un-t'ao returned home dejected.

The oil lamp in the room had already gone out.

"Are you asleep? Has Hsiang-kao come back?" She struck a match, lit the lamp, and glanced over at the brick bed. Cold terror gripped her. Li Mao was hanging by his own belt from the lattice of the window. But she managed to stay coolheaded enough to climb up and untie him. Luckily he had not been there long, and there was no need to alarm the neighbors. Slowly she massaged him, and he gradually came around again.

Taking one's own life for the sake of another is a noble deed befitting a knight-errant. If Li Mao hadn't lost his legs, he would not have had to resort to this. But in the past few days, Li Mao had felt that there was no future for him. He had come to the conclusion that it would be best to kill himself, so that at least Ch'un-t'ao could have a better life.

Although Ch'un-t'ao did not feel love for him, she had a strong sense of duty toward him. She comforted and reassured him, talking to him until it was almost daybreak. At last he fell asleep. When Ch'un-t'ao got down from the brick bed, she found on the floor the charred remains of that red card—the marriage certificate that Li Mao had tried to give her. She stared at it transfixed.

She did not go out at all that day. In the evening she sat beside Li Mao on the brick bed.

"What are you crying about?" Ch'un-t'ao saw the hot tears rolling down Li Mao's cheeks.

"I've wronged you. Why did I have to come here?"

"No one is blaming you."

"Now he has left, and I don't have any legs . . ."

"You mustn't think like that; he'll come back."

"I hope he'll come back too."

Another day went by. When Ch'un-t'ao got up the next morning, she went out to the arbor and picked two cucumbers. She fixed a dish with them, and slapped together one large grilled wheat cake. She and Li Mao shared the simple meal together.

Then, as before, she put on her old battered straw hat, and carried her basket on her back.

"Since you're depressed today, why don't you just stay home?" Li Mao said to her through the window.

"I'd feel worse sitting around the house."

Slowly she walked through the gate. It was her nature to work; even when she was depressed and unhappy, she still wanted to work. Chinese women seem to be concerned only with life and not with love. Advancement in life is what occupies their consciousness, whereas love is only something that stirs in the dark, stifled recesses of their hearts.

Of course, love is only an emotion, while life is tangible and real. The art of chattering about love all day long while lounging behind a silk curtain or sitting in a secluded forest glen was imported by ocean-going steamers—the Empress this or the President that. Ch'un-t'ao was not a woman of the world and she never studied with blue-eyed foreigners. She did not understand this fashionable "love." All she knew was a dull weariness.

She wandered from one lane to another. Endless dust and endless streets engulfed this heavy-hearted woman. Now and then she shouted "Matches for scrap paper," but at other times she would even pass up a pile of paper for which she did not have to exchange anything. Sometimes she would give someone five boxes of matches when she was supposed to give only two. After muddling through the whole day, she followed the black ravens—who only knew how to caw raucously and to snatch food—and reached home. She lifted her head and saw posted on the gate a new resident's identification card, stating that Liu Hsiang-kao and his wife Liu were the occupants. The sight made her heart sink even deeper.

Just as she stepped into the courtyard, Hsiang-kao came running out of the house.

Her eyes opened wide in disbelief. "You've come back . . . " Her eloquent tears said the rest.

"I cannot leave you; everything I have I owe to you. I know you need my help. I can't be so heartless."

Actually, for the past couple of days Hsiang-kao had been wandering aimlessly. As he walked the streets, his feet felt as if they were dragging heavy fetters, with the other end of the chain fastened to Ch'un-t'ao's wrist. What's more, wherever he went, he ran into the cigarette ad with the girl who looked just like Ch'un-t'ao, which struck him repeatedly at the heart. He was so miserable that he didn't even notice when he was hungry.

"I've talked it over with Brother Hsiang already." It was Li Mao's turn to speak. "He's the head of the household here, and I'm the co-occupant."

Hsiang-kao helped her unload her basket as always, and at the same time wiped the tears from her face. "If and when we all go back to the country, he'll be the head of household and I'll be the co-occupant. You are our wife."

She did not utter a word, but went straight into the house, took off her hat and clothes, and took her daily ritual bath.

The chatter about business was resumed once again in the arbor. They talked about selling those documents from the Palace, then Hsiang-kao could set up a stall in the market, or perhaps they could move to a slightly bigger place to live.

In the room, the tiny flame of the oil lamp was suddenly snuffed out by a moth diving into it. Li Mao had long been fast asleep, for the Milky Way was already low in the sky.

"Let's go to bed too," said the woman.

"Get into bed first. I'll come give you a massage in a minute."

"There's no need, I didn't walk very much today. We'll get up early in the morning; don't forget to take care of that piece of business. We haven't done any trading for a couple of days now."

"Say, I forgot to give this to you. When I came back today, you hadn't come home yet, so I made a special trip to the T'iench'iao market to buy you a hat. It's practically brand new. Look!" He groped in the dark for the hat, and handed it to her.

"How can I see anything in this dark! In any case, I'll put it on tomorrow."

All was quiet in the courtyard; only the fragrance of the tuberoses wafted in the night air. In the room faint voices could be heard.

"Wife . . ."

"I don't like to hear that, I'm not your wife."

PING HSIN

(1900–)

Ping Hsin (born Hsieh Ping-hsin, also named Hsieh Wan-ying), a native of Fukien province, was born in 1900. She is remarkable in that her fame as a woman writer of fiction, essays, and poetry has spanned the past sixty years.

Ping Hsin, the daughter of a prominent naval officer, came from a well-to-do, comfortable home. She received her high school education at a missionary school in Peking, her college education at the American-associated Yenching University, and her M.A. from Wellesley College in 1926. After returning to China, she taught literature at Yenching University and married one of her colleagues, Professor Wu Wen-tsao, a sociologist. During the war, she taught in the United Southwest University in the interior. For a time she and her husband were active in the service of the Kuomintang government. In 1943, Ping Hsin became the editor-in-chief of the bi-monthly magazine Women's Culture (Fu-nü wen-hua) founded by Mme. Chiang Kai-shek. In 1946, when her husband was appointed the Cultural Attache to the Chinese Embassy in Japan, her whole family went to live in Tokyo, returning in 1952. Nothing was heard of Ping Hsin for the next two decades. But given her class background, foreign associations, and "capitalist bourgeois mentality," it is not hard to surmise that she suffered criticism and "rectification" in this period. We do know that she received "re-education" in the countryside in Hupei for fourteen months in 1970–71.

Having been "re-educated," Ping Hsin resurfaced in 1973 as a representative on the Japan-China Friendship Association delegation to Japan. Since that time, she has been a visible personage in Peking, often meeting foreign cultural visitors and working as an editor for juvenile literature.

Ping Hsin was a productive writer of fiction only in college and for a brief period afterwards. During the past forty years she has been active more as an essayist. Her fiction has a fairly narrow range, but within its limits Ping Hsin demonstrates a keen sensitivity for the psyche of women and children. Her fiction is often pessimistic in tone, but it also reflects her faith in nature, children's innocence, and motherly love. Her writings sometimes contain an overdose of feminine sentimentalism, although it seems relatively restrained when compared with its occurrence in works by other women writers of the 1920s and 30s.

Ping Hsin has to her credit several volumes of essays and travelogues, one volume each of short stories and poems, and translations of two of

44

Tagore's works and Gibran's The Prophet. *"West Wind" (Hsi-feng) was published in 1936 and "Chang Sao" appeared during the War of Resistance.*

West Wind

Translated by Samuel Ling

CH'IU-HSIN RECLINED by the window of the train, staring abstractedly at the forlorn landscape rushing past her eyes. "Late autumn is upon us," her heart murmured as she took in the passing scene.

In the fields the crops had just been harvested. The short stubby stems of sorghum left standing cast long slim shadows in the setting sun. The weeds had turned sere, and cracks appeared in the parched fields. The brown willow trees along the railway swayed in the dust whipped up by the autumn wind, adding to the somber mood. "Late autumn is here," Ch'iu-hsin muttered under her breath.

The mood that had lately come upon Ch'iu-hsin had become almost overwhelming the last day or two. She was in the grip of deep melancholia as she surveyed the endless vista of swirling leaves outside the train window.

Distractedly, Ch'iu-hsin smoothed her dress and sat up straight. Her fellow passengers all looked tired from the prolonged monotony of the jolting train. Those who had been engaged in conversation stopped talking, yawned, and asked for tea. Mothers stared out the windows as their children slept in their laps. Everything evoked a feeling of weariness, unrest, and ennui.

"And these are my traveling companions in life's journey!" Ch'iu-hsin knitted her brows and looked out the window.

"Ch'iu-hsin, I now bid you a fond goodbye! Yours is a sacred calling. Who am I, an ordinary mortal, to becloud your bright future? Much as it hurts, I now bid you farewell. I shall retreat to a corner of the wall and, like a solitary flower, gaze at you as you, like a full moon, make your way up to the sky.

"Farewell, my friend. Allow me to offer my last good wishes and to pledge my unwavering loyalty. The day will come when middle age will catch up with us, the wind will sweep the earth and the waning moon will peep through the curtain. If and when your heart should be touched by loneliness and sorrow, don't forget there is one person who will still be with you in spirit, ever ready to proffer his humble solace."

These were the last paragraphs of the last letter that Yuan wrote her after receiving her letter of rejection. Now that the day envisaged by Yuan had indeed arrived, Ch'iu-hsin could not help but recall what Yuan had said in the letter.

Ten years had gone by. She knew Yuan had married shortly after writing that letter. "That's men for you!" Ch'iu-hsin thought derisively at the time. "All they want is a wife to cater to their creature comforts. Love and loyalty are merely words to be bandied about in courtship. Didn't Yuan say that without me the future would have no meaning? and hasn't he managed very well without the things he claimed were dearest to his heart?"

Ch'iu-hsin was young then. Despite her deep feelings for Yuan, she was not quite ready to give up her own promising future, for which her education and training had so well prepared her. She was not ready to play a secondary role as wife and mother. In a way, she was happy to know that Yuan had settled down. Although somewhat miffed, she had written Yuan a warm congratulatory letter at the time of his marriage.

She had lost contact with Yuan. She did learn, indirectly, that he was doing well and that he often visited Peiping.* Who knows? Perhaps Yuan had made a deliberate effort to avoid her. Or perhaps circumstances had conspired against such a meeting. Be that as it may, Ch'iu-hsin could not completely banish him from her mind.

"If and when your heart should be touched by loneliness and sorrow . . ." Ch'iu-hsin heaved a soft sigh. She stood up, dusted herself off, took up her briefcase, and made for the dining car.

There were only three or four people there, and they were either reading or smoking. Although they had all eaten, they remained in their seats. Perhaps the dining car offered more elbow room than their cramped quarters. Chi'iu-hsin seated herself at a table near the door and ordered a cup of coffee.

Steadying the saucer with her left hand and holding a spoon with her right, Ch'iu-hsin stared at the steam rising from her cup. The words "Don't forget there is one person who will still be with you in spirit . . ." floated into her mind.

The door of the dining car snapped shut with a bang, breaking her train of thought. She raised her head and could hardly believe what she saw. Her heart beat violently; her face suffused with a

---

*Peiping, "Northern Peace," was renamed Peking, "Northern Capital," in 1949.

warm glow. The person who came through the door was none other than Yuan! In the confusion of the moment, they greeted each other as if by reflex action. With a tremulous smile, Yuan seated himself across from Ch'iu-hsin.

Regaining a measure of composure, Ch'iu-hsin observed that the ten-year span had hardly left its mark on Yuan. His face was fuller, but he appeared as youthful as ever. He was impeccably dressed and wore a ring on the third finger of his right hand.

Yuan, of course, was looking at her too. From the startled look on his face, Ch'iu-hsin could see the ravages that time had wrought on her own person. She was momentarily disheartened. As soon as he had regained his composure, Yuan sat back with a smile.

"This is indeed a surprise. How have you been all these years? I hear you are making great strides in your career."

"Things have been going pretty well," Ch'iu-hsin replied. "How about you?" Somehow, the words came out like a sigh.

"We live in Shanghai. That's also where I work," Yuan replied. He ordered a cup of coffee and something to eat. "Life is one long grind, but I have no complaints. The family is fine. I'm the father of two children now."

He asked Ch'iu-hsin to help herself to the food. He then inquired where she was going.

"I'm boarding a steamer at T'angku to attend a meeting in Shanghai," Ch'iu-hsin replied. "It's been a long time since I traveled by boat. The voyage should give me a little time to relax."

"What a coincidence!" Yuan exclaimed excitedly. "Are you sailing on the Shun-t'ien? That's my boat too. I just love to watch the moon on the sea. We who live in Shanghai hardly ever get a good look at the moon."

They were both looking out the window. Before them was an endless expanse of reeds growing in shallow water. T'angku itself loomed in the distance.

Ch'iu-hsin stood up and said happily, "We'll be there in a moment. I think I'll go get my things together."

Yuan also stood up and said, "I'll be coming shortly. I'll take care of the bill and see you later."

As he spoke, he opened the door for Ch'iu-hsin. From the smile on his face, his words, and everything about him, Ch'iu-hsin could hardly believe that a long ten years had elapsed since they had last met.

A mini-train took them to the boat. They were welcomed aboard by the smiling, white-clad captain and his crew lined up along the railing. After being led to her cabin, Ch'iu-hsin put down her suitcase and looked out the porthole. The gangplank had been taken down and the boat was slowly moving away from the shore. She could hear the muddy water sloshing against the side of the boat. It was getting dark, so she switched on the light.

She looked into the mirror. Her hair was flecked with dust. Her eyes had dark rings around them. Her face had a weary and emaciated look.

"That's not the face that was!" she could not help noticing.

The dinner bell had sounded, rudely awakening her from her reverie. She hastily changed into fresh clothes, washed her face and applied, for the first time in a long while, a touch of rouge on her face.

In the dining room, Ch'iu-hsin found that everybody had been seated. Most of the passengers were foreigners. A waiter took her to a small table where Yuan was seated by himself.

Yuan, too, had changed clothes. Under the light, his collar appeared snow-white. He was wearing a blue necktie with white dots and a blue woolen suit. His freshly washed face had a robust glow. As Ch'iu-hsin approached, he rose and pulled out a chair for her. The tableware, the cuisine, and the foreign languages spoken in the dining room all brought back memories they had once shared in a foreign country.

Somewhat at a loss for words, they chatted politely about the relative merits of Chinese and Western food. As they talked, Ch'iu-hsin appeared to Yuan younger than she looked when they had met unexpectedly that afternoon. The pale blue dress with white flowers was a perfect fit for her slender frame. Her eyes were as captivating as ever. Her make-up, however, could not conceal the faint wrinkles around her eyes. Absent, too, was the lively glint that used to animate her large dark eyes.

They finally got the conversation going at a lively clip. As they exchanged the latest information about their mutual friends, they could not help but lament the passing of the years. Ch'iu-hsin even broke into spontaneous laughter as they reminisced about hilarious situations involving their friends.

Dinner over, Ch'iu-hsin stood up and slowly walked to the door with Yuan following her. The boat had already left Taku* behind. The moon was rising out of the sea, and a brisk sea breeze was blowing. As if propelled by an invisible force, they slowly made for the highest deck.

The moon was in all its glory. The long shadows of the masts looked like dark lines etched on the deck. On the bridge outside the control room, the white-clad officers could be seen pacing back and

---

*Taku is further down the coast from T'angku.

forth under the moon. They were smoking and occasionally laughing at some joke. After looking around, Ch'iu-hsin seated herself on a deck chair facing the moon. Yuan seated himself beside her.

In that setting, the world seemed to have ceased to exist. The only realities were the shining moon, the expanse of water, and a boat making its way toward the distant horizon. She was all alone with Yuan, the person she had cherished for the past ten years. It was like a miracle. As the words "And gaze at you as you, like a full moon, make your way up to the sky . . . Don't forget there is one person who will forever be with you in spirit . . ." came back to her, she turned to look at Yuan, her heart filled with a sense of regret not untinged with bitterness.

Yuan did not look at her or at the moon. He was staring at the sparkling, restless waves until he sensed that Ch'iu-hsin was looking at him. He smiled and was about to speak when, in the moonlight, he saw tear-drops welling up in Ch'iu-hsin's eyes. Caught off guard, he gave a slight cough, but remained silent.

With a forced smile, Ch'iu-hsin lifted her head toward the moon so that her tears rolled back into her eyes.

"The moon at sea seems to have a coolness all its own," she said. "I'm a little chilly."

"Let me go to your cabin and get your coat," said Yuan, standing up.

Ch'iu-hsin also got up. "No, that isn't necessary," she said. "I'm a little tired. It's time to retire anyway."

Yuan walked her to the door, wished her good night, and left. Ch'iu-hsin closed the door and made ready for bed. The events of the day had come upon her so suddenly and unexpectedly that they seemed to have come out of a dream. How could she explain it? She had been totally immersed in her career for the past ten years and yet, when she met the person she had earlier rejected, she could not restrain her tears.

"That's a woman's fate!" she muttered to herself. "I had known all that before I made my choice between marriage and a career . . . Yuan has nothing to do with it. This is but a foolish, fleeting feeling. It is the sea voyage, the moon, the romantic aura of it all! It is my vulnerable emotions . . ."

She looked into the mirror and broke into a smile as if to shore up her own morale. She then hung up her clothes, turned out the light, and crept into bed.

Even with her eyes closed, she could not shut out the moonlight. She opened her eyes and found her cabin flooded with light from the moon. It was a little warm, so she got up and opened the porthole a little wider. She returned to bed, pulled up the blanket, and laid her head on her arm. She could hear the sea breeze outside the window and rhythmic footsteps pacing the deck. She also heard the faint sounds of singing and laughter.

"I wonder if Yuan has retired." She let her thoughts wander just a bit, "On this moonlit night . . . just the two of us . . . If, ten years ago, I had made a different decision . . ." She shook her head, pulled the blanket over her shoulders, and closed her eyes.

Before breakfast Ch'iu-hsin had already made up her mind. "Don't betray your feelings to Yuan. Actually, what feelings are there to betray? Just avoid meeting him and talking with him. There is so much I have to do, not to mention the speech I have to write for the conference . . ."

She took out her fountain pen and her notebook so she could work in the study after breakfast. She walked out the door, but immediately turned back and put on a simple but attractive dress.

As he did the previous evening, Yuan stood up and pulled out a chair for her. He looked, as usual, calm and collected. His face was full and had a healthy glow. She tried to carry on a conversation in a natural manner, but her eyes smarted and her head ached. "Insomnia isn't much fun," she thought to herself.

Yuan told her that the boat was due to arrive at Chefoo at nine and asked her, since it would remain in dock for the larger part of the day, whether she would like to go ashore. After a moment's thought, Ch'iu-hsin replied with a smile, "I hope you'll excuse me, but I still have a speech to write and it's easier to write when the boat is not in motion. I think I'll make use of the time to do some work." Yuan did not insist. He excused himself when breakfast was over.

Winding through green-clad hills along the inlet, the boat slowly made its way into the harbor. In the morning light, the sea and the hills appeared to be shrouded in a luminous mist. Like fish scales, the grey tiles of the houses peeped through the foliage. The white lighthouse in the foreground was partly hidden by trees and rocks. Like little fishes, a flotilla of sampans converged on the boat. Yuan boarded one of the sampans. He was wearing a hat and holding an overcoat. He looked up and waved to her.

Ch'iu-hsin turned and headed for the study. She opened her notebook and proceeded to jot down the topic of her speech: "The Two Problems Facing Women—Career and Marriage." Somehow, she could not continue. She distractedly doodled circles around the characters she had committed to paper.

She had a leisurely lunch by herself. After lunch, she took a nap. She was awakened at three o'clock by noises outside her window. "The boat is about to set sail. Yuan should be back any moment now," she thought. She got up, washed her face, and went up to the deck.

Yuan was walking up the gangplank. He had a paper bag under his left arm and a basket in his right. He said with a smile, "Chefoo is famous for its fruit, you know. Take a look at these grapes. My children just love them."

Ch'iu-hsin looked into the basket and said, "They are really huge and they smell so sweet! What's in the paper bag?"

"That's Chefoo embroidery," Yuan replied. "My wife told me it's known to be fine and reasonable and that I should stock up on some for gifts. I am not a knowledgeable buyer, so I just bought some at random. You should have come with me."

Ch'iu-hsin smiled but said nothing.

The boat moved slowly away from the wharf. A number of foreigners had come aboard. Most of them were returning from their summer vacation with their children. The deck was alive with noise and gaiety. Ch'iu-hsin and Yuan leaned on the railing watching the children skipping rope.

"How old are your children?" Ch'iu-hsin asked. "Whom do they look like?"

"The boy is eight," Yuan replied, "and the girl is just five. It's difficult to say whom they take after. The funny thing is, when you hold them up and look into the mirror, you seem to see them as yourself, and yet they are so different."

Ch'iu-hsin was looking into the distance, so Yuan held his silence. Ch'iu-hsin then turned to Yuan and said with a smile, "I heard what you said. Your wife must be very young and beautiful and yours must be a very happy family."

"Yes, indeed," Yuan said after a pause. "My wife is about ten years younger than I. When you come to Shanghai, you must spend a few days with us."

"Thank you," Ch'iu-hsin replied. "I certainly will."

At the sound of the dinner bell, they went to the dining room.

Seated at their table were a young foreign couple and a little boy. Yuan was acquainted with the man and went over to say hello. Upon being introduced, the adults all shook hands and took their seats. The boy was about four or five. He had big eyes and rosy cheeks. His mother gave him a nudge and said, "Aren't you going to say hello to Mr. Chang?"

With a smile, the boy said, "Hello, Mr. Chang." He then turned to Ch'iu-hsin and said, "How are you, Mrs. Chang?" Ch'iu-hsin blushed and was about to say something when Yuan explained, "This is Miss Ho."

The boy's mother smiled and said to the boy, "Say you are sorry.

I failed to make the proper introductions." The boy looked at Ch'iu-hsin and laughed.

Ch'iu-hsin was not in the mood for conversation and confined herself to a few words with the foreign woman. Yuan, on the other hand, carried on a lively conversation with the man.

After dinner, the woman, with the boy in tow, retired while Yuan went with the man to the smoking room. Ch'iu-hsin went to her cabin to get a coat and went on deck.

The moon appeared clearer and cooler than the night before. The wind, too, was blowing hard. It was too cold to stand by the railing. She pulled up a deck chair and sat under the shadow of the lifeboat away from the wind, watching the moon.

There was not a single soul on deck. All was silence except for the sound made by the boat and the waves and the wind. Under the moonlight, the sea was a sheet of white. A myriad of twinkling stars formed a path from where she sat to the moonlit horizon.

"If it were only possible to ride the ocean breeze and travel the high road to the end of the horizon . . ." she mused, waxing poetic. So immersed had she been in the mundane affairs of living the past ten years that she had seldom had the chance to give free rein to her fantasies.

"What high road? It is no more possible to travel the high road than to walk on the waves. What appeared yesterday to be a high road leading to happiness may turn out to be a low road leading to darkness and destruction. The high road that promised to lead to happiness ten years ago is now . . ." Ch'iu-hsin mused, her hands cradling her cheeks.

As Ch'iu-hsin roused from her mind's wanderings, she was surprised to see Yuan leaning on the railing, looking at her with a smile.

Blushing, Ch'iu-hsin said, "When did you get here? And why the silence? You really scared me."

Yuan sat down next to her and said, "I've been here quite a while. Your face was buried in your hands, so I didn't want to disturb you."

Ch'iu-hsin looked at Yuan but said nothing. She clasped her knees, looking at the moon.

After a while, Yuan volunteered, "You seem somewhat upset. What does a child know and why let it bother you? You haven't changed . . ."

Ch'iu-hsin stood up and asked, "What have I got to be upset about? I paid no attention to what the child said. And tell me, what was I like before?"

Obviously displeased, she look at Yuan as she held on tightly to her coat.

There was a tenderness in Yuan's eyes as he said in a low voice, "It's not as if we just got acquainted. Do you really believe I'm insensitive to your moods? You hardly spoke a word all evening. That was why I did not impose myself on you after dinner. I can tell you have been upset the last couple of days and not just tonight."

Although Ch'iu-hsin tried not to betray her emotions, she felt a tug at her heart. She lowered her eyes and sat down again.

"I'm sorry," she said, "if I appear to be upset. All these years I have been totally wrapped up in my work. When I have a moment to myself, I tend to be beset with a feeling of weariness. The reason I took this boat trip was to avoid familiar faces and familiar situations. I hardly imagined . . ."

Yuan, too, sat down and said in a serious tone, "Really, I'm very anxious to know how you have been. How well do you cope with the pressure of work? What do you do for relaxation? You know as well as I do that all work and no relaxation often brings on a feeling of ennui and frustration."

With a sign, Ch'iu-hsin replied, "All in all, I'm quite happy with my career. That is not to say, of course, that it's been a bed of roses. I used to visit my family whenever I had the time. Since my mother passed away, however, my brothers have gone their separate ways. In the last ten years, my friends, too, have moved, making it difficult to find somebody congenial to talk to. Sometimes, this feeling of loneliness . . ." She smiled wanly and continued, "Actually, it's not all that serious except that, after a hectic day, one gets a vacuous feeling . . ."

Yuan looked at the sky but kept his silence.

The moon was high in the sky and the wind was blowing harder. Ch'iu-hsin stood up and said, "Let's go now. It's getting late."

Yuan put out his hand and stopped her. "You still have a friend, a friend who will forever remain true. My home is your home. We would love to have you visit us."

Smiling a cheerless smile, Ch'iu-hsin said, "Thank you, but you have a happy family and the presence of an intruder . . ."

Holding her hand, Yuan said, "I made my proposal a long time ago. If you had . . ."

At that, Ch'iu-hsin could no longer hold back her tears.

"Loneliness! I, too, know its meaning," Yuan continued. "I love my children and I know my duties as a husband. And yet, there are times when I cannot help thinking if at the time . . . things would have been vastly . . ."

Several people were coming up the stairs, talking and laughing. Yuan and Ch'iu-hsin let go their hands and parted company.

In her cabin, Ch'iu-hsin sat on the edge of the bed. She hated herself for having said what she had not intended to say. Why ex-

pose your own weaknesses to Yuan after all these years and why
sow discord in Yuan's family? The more she thought about it, the
worse she felt. "Until we dock," she vowed, "I will not see Yuan
again."

The next morning, Ch'iu-hsin was at first going to ring for room
service so she could have breakfast without leaving her cabin. But
she decided that that might give Yuan the satisfaction of thinking
she was probably suffering from a bout of depression, and so she
went to the dining room.

Yuan appeared calm and self-possessed, as usual. During breakfast they engaged in polite talk about nothing in particular. Ch'iu-
hsin then spent the whole day at her desk and drafted two
speeches. She felt almost elated.

It was almost time for dinner. After resting a while, she tidied up
her hair, went on deck, and stood by the railing. The moon was full
and there was a haze over the shimmering sea. After an entire day
by herself, she was again assailed by a feeling of melancholy. "This
is the last day of the journey," she said to herself with a sigh, "the
last day to look at the moon . . . With the dawn of another day, it's
back to the rat race!"

She could sense Yuan making his way in her direction, but she
pretended not to have noticed. At the sound of the dinner bell, she
followed the other passengers into the dining room.

After dinner, the young foreign couple, having put their child to
bed, suggested going on deck to watch the moon. With no great
enthusiasm, Ch'iu-hsin nodded consent. In the absence of any objection on the part of Ch'iu-hsin, Yuan followed them up to the
deck.

They carried on an animated conversation under the moon. The
foreign couple, in particular, appeared light-hearted and gay. They
poked fun at each other as they talked about their falling in love.

"He claimed that unless I married him," the young woman ban-
tered, "he would never know the meaning of happiness. He vowed
that unless I married him, he would never again look at the autumn
moon or sit by the fireside on a winter night. So you see, the only
reason I married him was to save him from the fate of never again
looking at the moon or sitting by the fire."

"Do you really believe all that?" the man countered. "The only
reason I married her was so she would not end up being an old
maid."

While Yuan and the others roared with merriment, Ch'iu-hsin
gave only a perfunctory short laugh.

After a while, Yuan stood up and said, "If you will excuse me, I
think I'll go now. The boat will dock early tomorrow and I have to
get my things together."

"What's the rush? It's not often you get to see such a lovely moon," the man said. "Let's stay a while longer."

Looking at Yuan, Ch'iu-hsin added, "Yes, why don't we?"

Smiling, Yuan replied, "The thing is, my children will be there to meet me tomorrow morning. The things I bought them in Peiping are at the bottom of the trunk, and if I don't take them out now, there'll be a lot of rummaging when they ask for them tomorrow."

Ch'iu-hsin made no reply.

The foreign couple got up and said with a smile, "You're truly a model father! We have to go too. If the boy should wake up and not find us, there'll be no end of trouble."

Ch'iu-hsin lifted her head and said, "Go ahead. I'd like to sit here a little while longer."

At the head of the stairs, Yuan turned his head and said tenderly, "The night air is getting chilly. Don't stay too long now."

It was hazy when the Shun-t'ien steamed into Wusung harbor. Ch'iu-hsin, who had hardly slept, was standing alone by the railing. The only people around were the deck-hands swabbing the deck. Through the morning mist could be seen tiers of buildings and billboards on both banks of the river.

With knitted brows, Ch'iu-hsin muttered to herself, "Another cloudy day . . . It's enough to make anybody miserable! Wonder if there'll be anybody from the association to meet me . . . Yuan's children, his family . . . perhaps he would . . ." At that, Ch'iu-hsin shook her head and went into her cabin.

By then, all the passengers were up and had had their breakfast. They were busy getting their boxes and other pieces of luggage together and instructing the stewards to move them to the railing by the gangplank. Amid all this confusion, Ch'iu-hsin put on her coat and emerged from her cabin with a briefcase and a suitcase.

The buildings on both banks of the river loomed larger and larger and the babble on the wharf grew louder and louder as the boat eased itself into the dock. Suddenly she heard Yuan, who was standing behind her, calling to somebody. Ch'iu-hsin turned and saw him beaming and waving to somebody on the wharf. She followed Yuan's eyes and saw a young woman with her hands on the shoulders of two children. The moment the gangplank was lowered, they scrambled up to the boat. Yuan led them by the hand to the door of the parlor.

So engrossed was Ch'iu-hsin with the sight and sound of the happy throng, that she stood where she was, instead of disembarking with the other passengers. Yuan's wife was young and slim. Her hair had a smooth permanent wave, and she wore pearl earrings. Her full face was attractive and tastefully made up. She was wearing a white silk dress with big red flowers. On another woman, all this might have appeared vulgar, but on her person it only accentuated her youth.

The boy wore a white shirt and green corduroy pants, and a hat dangling from his neck. The little girl had neatly bobbed hair with bangs. She wore a pale yellow, round-necked short-sleeved coat over a pale yellow dress. Both children showed off a pair of chubby legs.

They were laughing and asking many questions. With head raised, the girl held on to her father's legs. She had clearly defined eyebrows and she bore an uncanny resemblance to her father. The boy was smiling and holding his mother's hand. His dainty lips looked so much like his mother's!

When Yuan turned his head and saw Ch'iu-hsin standing at the gangplank, he led his wife and children to her. As soon as the introductions were over, the children tugged at Yuan's hands and said, "Daddy, the car is at the wharf. Let's go."

While trying to restrain his children and get his luggage together, Yuan asked Ch'iu-hsin, "Is someone meeting you? If not, why don't you come with us and stay a while?"

"Thank you very much," "Ch'iu-hsin replied. "I'm being met. In fact, I see them on the wharf now. Why don't you go ahead?"

Yuan and his family walked down the gangplank. After getting in the car, they waved to her. The car moved and disappeared around the corner.

Most of the passengers had disembarked and left. The wharf was almost deserted. Ch'iu-hsin walked slowly down the gangplank with her luggage. She stood on the wharf for a while, looking at the desolate scene around her. A gust of westerly wind blew across her impassive face, sweeping up swirling pieces of straw and scraps of paper on the wharf.

Chang Sao

Translated by Samuel Ling

I DON'T FEEL at liberty to call Chang Sao* "my Chang Sao" and that's a pity, but the fact is I cannot claim her to be mine in any

---

*The term *sao* designates the wife of one's older brother, but is also loosely applied to any middle-aged woman in informal, familiar address.

capacity. She was neither my neighbor nor my maid, and she would be the last to consider herself a friend of mine. She was only the wife of Old Man Chang, the custodian of the temple.

I lived on the floor above the temple. The ground floor was occupied by the elderly Mr. and Mrs. Li, proprietors of the temple. Old Man Chang and his wife were given the use of a small room adjacent to the front door.

The Lis' daughter was a student of mine. After showing me around the temple, she said, "This is a secluded spot, an ideal place to do your writing. It's true, up here on the hill, there are certain inconveniences, but you can always get Chang and his family to run errands for you."

At the mention of his name, Chang, who was at the door sill, stood up and smiled, baring a mouthful of yellowed teeth. He was about forty years of age, short, and with honesty written all over his face.

"Where's your Chang Sao?" my student asked.

"She's gone to fetch water," he replied.

As my student took me upstairs, she said to me, "His wife is very capable, a lot smarter than her husband and strong to boot. If there's anything you want done, it's better to get her to do it."

For the sake of convenience, I boarded with the Lis. That way, I wouldn't have to go down the hill in inclement weather. Besides, the eating places in the village were infested with flies, especially in the summer.

The elderly Lis were natives of Shansi Province. They were a kind and friendly pair. Mrs. Li, who was a good cook, prepared all the meals.

In the morning, I would go down to the kitchen to fetch water to wash my face. I would then tidy up my room. Except for mealtimes, I hardly saw the Lis.

The Lis kept early hours. Even during the day, they hardly made a sound. There was nothing to disturb the quiet pervading the premises. What a contrast to the lodgings I took in the city! I felt completely at ease.

On the third day, I went to see Chang Sao to ask her to do my laundry. As she emerged from her dingy little room into the sunlight, I was able to take a good look at her. She had stringy hair, the color of burnt toast. She wore a bun high on the back of her head. Her face was swarthy and lined with wrinkles etched by wind and sun. She had a large mouth framed by thin lips. There was a glint in her eyes. Her figure was not tall but wiry and charged with energy.

"What can I do for you?" she asked with a big smile.

"I have some clothes that need to be washed," I replied. "They are white, so be careful."

"I understand," she said. "Your clothes require particular care. I need a piece of soap."

Mrs. Li, who was leaning on the door and who overheard the conversation, beckoned to me. When we had gone into the room, she said to me in a whisper, "I suggest you get somebody down the hill to do your laundry. This woman is just too much. Every time she is asked to do the laundry, she asks for a piece of soap. She keeps what's left over and sells it. That's why we always do our own laundry."

After a moment's thought, I said with a smile, "I'll think about it, but let it go this time."

Early next morning, Chang Sao brought back the clothes and the bedsheets, which she had washed to a dazzling white. She laid them on my bed, all neatly folded, and said, "Sir, here are your clothes and here's what's left of the soap."

I thanked her, well pleased with my "good fortune." I must say she gave me a good impression.

As I came to know her better, she often came upstairs to sweep the floor, deliver my mail, take my washing, and empty my waste-basket. My worldly belongings had always been few and simple, and she knew where everything was. Although I never locked the door, I never lost anything, be it money, clothes, or books. As for such things as matches, snacks, towels, and soap, I never kept track of them anyway. Mrs. Li had warned me a number of times to be careful with my things, but why should I bother? They were not worth anything. Chang Sao did a fine job of keeping my room neat and clean and that was good enough for me.

Although Chang Sao seemed to cotton to me, she was not so ac-commodating as far as Mr. and Mrs. Li were concerned. She would, for instance, raise the price for fetching water every two or three days. No, she would not come right out and ask for more, but, by using slow-down tactics, she left no doubt what she was trying to get across.

On one occasion, Chang Sao did not appear for a couple of days. The water in the vat ran out. Somewhat put off, Mrs. Li asked Chang Sao's husband, "Where's your wife?"

"She's working for somebody in the field," Chang replied with a smile.

Of course, you could ask Chang to fetch water. The trouble was he would say yes and then never get around to it. It was not until I had come downstairs several times to remind him that he finally saw fit to go out with buckets slung over his shoulders.

From where I stood at the bannister, I saw Chang Sao coming in from the field. She stopped at the foot of the hill and stood talking to her husband.

After fetching two buckets of water, Chang lay down and complained about a stomachache. He did not appear the next day.

Obviously annoyed, Mr. Li said, "This is nothing short of extortion. Do they think there's nobody else to do the job? I'll go down the hill and look for somebody myself!"

Mr. Li sat for hours at the teahouse, trying to find somebody in the village to do the job. The people he talked to all shook their heads and said with a smile, "It's a steep climb up the hill. You'll have to pay more." When they indicated the amount they wanted, Mr. Li went back up the hill in a huff. What they asked for was even more than Chang Sao was getting.

I quietly went down the hill and found Chang Sao in the field. I said to her, "Go get the buckets. There's no water to drink."

"I haven't got the time," she replied with a smile.

I smiled and said, "Now, you know that's not true. I know what's on your mind. From now on, I'll pay for the labor. After all, I have to use it too."

She smiled and followed me up the hill, carrying a basket on her back.

Since then, she has never failed to keep us supplied with water no matter how busy she might be on the farm, except for the few days she took off to have her baby. Then it was her husband who took over the chore.

Chang Sao wore loose-fitting clothes, so I never noticed anything unusual about her appearance. Then one day, Mrs. Li said to me, "Chang Sao is getting heavy. I suggest you speak to her husband about the water situation just in case he takes it into his head not to do it at the last minute."

I wasn't sure how I should approach the subject. Only a short while ago, I had seen Chang Sao carrying a large basket of beans up the hill. I didn't think anything was about to happen any time soon, so I did not mention the subject.

The next morning, Chang Sao did not come upstairs to clean my room. While we were having breakfast, her husband came in with a small basket of eggs. I asked him where his wife was. With a broad grin, he said, "She had a baby last night." Offering our congratulations, we inquired whether it was a boy or a girl.

Mrs. Li said, "Its amazing how these people can deliver a baby all by themselves. This is their first baby too. It seems giving birth to a baby is no more complicated than laying an egg!"

I went upstairs, wrapped a fifty-dollar bill in a piece of red paper and gave it to Chang. "This is for buying brown sugar for Chang Sao."

Mrs. Li also brought Chang a red paper envelope.

Accepting the gifts with a smile, Chang said, "Thank you very much. Would you, Mrs. Li, like to see your nephew?*" Mrs. Li appeared pleased as she went into the murky room.

Mr. Li and I were chatting in the hall when Mrs. Li returned. She was shaking her head and laughing when she said, "Such a big baby boy, so dark and sturdy! You know what Chang Sao was doing? She was sitting on the bed-board making a fishing net! She just had the baby in the middle of the night and now she is already hard at work, and she doesn't even look the least bit exhausted. She's got to be made of steel!"

She then told me that Chang Sao had been adopted by the Changs at the age of twelve as an intended daughter-in-law and was married to their son at the age of fifteen. While she was alive, Mrs. Chang often beat her, and Chang Sao would hide in a cave to cry her heart out. It was not until Mrs. Chang died the year before that she was able to live in peace with her weakling of a husband. She was no more than twenty-five.

That came as a complete surprise. I had always thought of her as being somewhere between thirty and forty. Hard work had robbed her of any vestige of youth! She was the type of person who never asked why, never had any doubts, never harbored any grudge or resentment. She rose with the sun and worked till dusk, carrying water, chopping firewood, doing the laundry, working on the farm. She worked nonstop like a windmill, climbing up the hill and going down to the valley. So long as there was a ray of light, she could be counted on to be doing something. Even on moonlit nights, she would take advantage of the light to pick beans the whole night through.

It continued to rain for five or six days. When the sun came up on the seventh day, Chang Sao was seen going out with a basket on her back and a scythe in her hand. While she was away, the baby was left in the care of her husband, who could be heard humming and grunting in the room. When Chang Sao was late coming home and the hungry baby started to cry, Chang would pace back and forth at the door, not knowing what to do.

We said to him laughingly, "It's a lot less trouble for you to go down the hill and let your wife tend the baby. As it is, when your wife comes home, she has to make dinner and feed the baby too. It's enough to kill anybody."

Chang shook his head and answered with a smile, "People want her. She does her job well. I'm useless!"

Chang was at least being honest. I often felt ashamed. When I sat with a book in my hand, I would see Chang Sao hurrying in and

---

*"Nephew," designating the baby, is applied loosely to the son of a close friend.

out, always carrying something on her back, her shoulders, her hands and her waist. She had no idea she was doing the most basic, backbreaking, and productive work in the rear during the war. As for me, whenever I wrote to my friends, I felt obliged to complain of my weariness, poverty, and ennui. While in reality, here I was, comfortably ensconced in the hills amid the pines, moaning and groaning without a cause! Seeing Chang Sao going about her endless chores with such enthusiasm is enough to make me throw down my book and get on my feet.

One day, my student and her schoolmates in the propaganda squad came to plaster war slogans on the temple door. One of the slogans carried the message "Redouble your efforts in decimating the enemy at the front and increasing production in the rear." Chang Sao was standing behind the crowd, not quite knowing what was going on. When she saw me, she asked with a giggle, "What does that say?" "The first line," I replied, "is about your country folk doing battle at the front. The second line is about people like you."

Uncomprehending, she asked, "What about you, sir?"

Bowing my head in shame, I replied, "Me? There's no place for me up there."

LING SHU-HUA

(1900–)

Ling Shu-hua, a native of Kwangtung province, comes from a comfortable family background. She was a student of literature along with
Ping Hsin at Yenching University, graduating in 1923. While a student,
she impressed Ch'en Yuan, a writer and professor of English, with her
literary talents, and became his protégé and later his wife. Ling Shu-hua
left China after the War of Resistance and, with the exception of brief
visits, has remained abroad ever since. For most of this period, she has
lived in London, where her husband served as China's chief delegate to
UNESCO. Between 1954 and 1960 Ling Shu-hua was a professor of literature at the Chinese Nanyang University in Singapore. As of this writing,
she is still living in England.

Ling Shu-hua's literary reputation rests on her several collections of
short stories published in the late 1920s and early 30s. These stories are
distinguished by her sensitive, sympathetic, yet convincing, portrayals
of women, especially women of the upper class in a changing Chinese
society. "Little Liu" (Hsiao Liu) first appeared in the collection Women
(Nü-jen) in 1930. It portrays in two well-sketched scenes the humbling
of the youthful spirit of a teenage girl as she matures into womanhood.

Little Liu

Translated by Vivian Hsu with Julia Fitzgerald

I WAS THEN IN the second year of middle school. All my classmates
were girls of fourteen or fifteen. The weather had turned warm.
After lunch, we would all hang out in the schoolyard by threes or
fives, walking around arm in arm and kidding with each other; or
we would sit on the steps, chit-chatting over our needlework. Since
our afternoon classes didn't require any preparation, nobody was
dumb enough to pass up a chance for some fun. After all, who
would want to get the reputation of being a grind?

"Hey, Phoenix, come over here!" I heard Little Liu calling out to
me as I walked across the schoolyard.

"What's . . . up?" I mimicked her offbeat Hupei accent. She and five other girls were all squeezed together on a bench.

"I've got a great story!" Flashing from her smooth, round, water-chestnut of a face, her big black eyes slid over me an instant, her rosy cheeks full of mischievous laughter.

"Hah! Great story, I'm sure. Probably just your naughty gossip again!" Though I scoffed with my tongue, my legs were already carrying me toward the bench.

"Well, Smarty, so what brings you here after all?" Little Liu knew she had scored a small triumph, but just the same, in feigned annoyance, she puckered up her little mouth into a wrinkled knot. Sparks flew from her big round eyes, but all I could see were the long lashes, framing those bright adorable eyes.

I suddenly grabbed her lips. "A dumpling!" I cried, "Who wants to eat a nice tender dumpling?" All the schoolgirls shrieked with laughter. Then Liu stuck out her foot and tripped me. I lost my balance and, my arms flailing, fell square on top of her.

To get even, I quickly took advantage of my position and nestled down with my cheek in the soft crook of her arm. I turned my face toward her chest, flung my arms around her, and began to whimper "Ma, ma-mee . . ." like a suckling baby.

Little Chou, famous for her naughty antics, didn't miss this perfect chance to pull a pun on Little Liu. "Ha-ha, Little Cow,*" she chanted loudly, "shameless cow, suckling a baby, ha-ha." That immediately drew another round of shrieking laughter.

"Get off me, you scab, get off!" Little Liu's face was flaming as she shoved me with all her might.

Not one to be shoved off, I stood up. "OK, OK, I'm off." I put on a smile. "So now tell me what this great story was that got you all so excited just now." To keep her from running off, I sat right down by her and draped my arm over her shoulder.

"I forgot!" she said spitefully.

"Now now, my good little cow, you really do have to tell me . . ." I shook her shoulder. Whenever we Southerners got into a silly mood, we would let our tongues slip, changing *Liu* to *niu* — "cow."

"Come on, finish what you were telling us, or we'll die of suspense. So what happened to that pitiful 'duck'?" Little Chou squinted her eyes, nudging Little Liu with a smile.

"What duck, what duck?" I demanded, giving Little Liu a pinch. "Hurry up, you've got to tell us."

"You mean to tell me you don't know about ducks?" Little Liu

---

*The surname Liu and the word *niu*, "cow," already close enough in Mandarin Chinese for a pun, become identical in the Hupei dialect, in which the initial *l* is merged into the initial *n*.

feigned a sober air. "When we get to biology class, why, Master
Kowtow is going to quiz you about it." Master "Kowtow" had gotten this nickname bestowed on him from the inept way he pronounced the word "tadpole"—*ketou*. He slurred it, from "ketou" to
"k'out'ou"—"Kowtow."

"Come on, don't keep us hanging like this." I gave her a fiercer
pinch.

"Oh, what a blockhead you are. Such a big fat duck right in front
of your eyes and you don't even see it." Little Liu giggled with a
hand over her mouth. Then in a flat voice as if she were reciting a
lesson, she began. "Consider the shape of a duck: a duck is puffed
out in front and protrudes in back. A duck walks with clumsy flapping feet and points its toes inward, waddling from side to
side . . ."

Before Little Liu could finish, the laughter of the schoolgirls
drowned out her mock lecture. Everyone was shaking and gasping,
wild-eyed with mirth.

"OK, you guys, don't be so mean. She's pathetic enough without
you all making such fun of her." Li Hui-sheng, who had had her
share of merriment, admonished us in a serious tone when the
swirl of laughter finally subsided.

"Now seriously, who is this 'duck' that you're all gabbing
about?" I demanded in a low voice.

"That new one," Little Liu murmured back. "Look over there.
Look good and hard and see if you don't think 'Duck' or 'Waddles'
isn't the perfect nickname for her."

My eyes followed to where Liu had gestured, and there, waddling
along under the walkway, was the new student, the one who was
auditing classes, named Chu. She waddled along with her chest
puffed out and her fat rear end protruding, her obviously just-
unbound feet stuffed into a dumpy pair of shoes that looked like
boats—and pointing in like pigeon toes. Her body was so lumpy
and squat . . . Sure enough, I had never in my life seen anyone that
fit the nickname "Waddles" more perfectly.

"She is a sad sight, and nobody wants to talk with her." I began
to feel sorry for her.

"You think that's sad?" Little Liu replied, "Then get this—she
has only just now gotten down off the bridal sedan chair . . . Get
that! Here she is, coming to classes with her ears still ringing from
the sound of wedding gongs and cymbals . . . Do you think any
lessons could sink into such a sad befuddled head as that?"

"You mean she's really just married?" I asked in amazement.

"Sure she's married. You've seen the padded jackets she wears,
bright red one day, bright green the next—all the colors of a sweet

young newlywed," Little Liu was snickering. "And not only is she just married, she's even half a . . ." She stopped short.

"Half a what? Half a what? You're awful, Liu! You're teasing us . . ."

"What's this business with 'half' and 'whole.' Go on, tell us." Even Big Wu who is taciturn by nature, was getting impatient.

"Now don't tell me you're a bunch of three-year-old babies. You mean you don't know about the birds and the bees?" Little Liu was still wearing her sober face.

"Ah ha!" cried Little Chou, who was always the sharpest. "This 'half' . . . oh, clever, Little Liu, *clever*! You don't mean . . ." Then she leaned over and buzz-buzzed into Little Liu's ear, while Liu just kept nodding slightly.

"Ha, ha!" Now Hui-sheng cried out that she understood too. But she pinned Little Liu down with a sharp look. "But how do you know?" Hui-sheng demanded. "You better not be making it all up!"

"Do I ever lie to you?" Little Liu retorted. "I might as well tell you the whole thing. This morning as I was getting off my ricksha, I heard this ricksha puller cursing like the devil: 'Damn ricksha seat's got this filthy puke all over it. A woman having her morning sickness out in public, that's got to be news!' I took one quick look, that cursing ricksha puller turned out to belong to Waddles!"

"Disgusting!" Little Chou spat on the pavement in contempt. The rest of us all stared at Little Liu in silence.

Finally, Hui-sheng said, "If you ask me, things are getting out of hand at this school—letting married women come to a girls' school! You'd think they'd have more discrimination."

"Isn't that the truth! They are getting more and more slipshod. Granted, they are quite generous: full tuition for adults, free for accompanying 'children.'" Little Liu snickered.

"You are really mean!" Hui-sheng said, but she continued, "My cousin was telling me that other people have started making fun of our school, calling it the 'Institute for Cultivating Good Wives and Wise Mothers.'"

"Last year there were that Ms. Pai and that Ms. Ch'ü—if that wasn't enough to set mouths yapping . . . In one case, the old master of the house personally escorting his wife right into the schoolyard! And in the other, a young master coming every day to fetch his *mother* from the classroom! And do they think we're blind? It's only the principal who's pretending to be deaf to these scandalous goings-on. Why, he's ignoring the whole thing as if it didn't exist!" Little Liu ranted on.

"I think we'd better go have a good talk with the principal." Little Chou too was getting indignant.

"But do you think he'll listen? No! You heard him the last graduation. He's no 'modern man'—you heard him. Giving us that stuff about being good wives and wise mothers." Little Liu was quick to remember.

"We've been acting like a bunch of simpletons; in all the other schools the students are . . ." Hui-sheng was a couple of years older than the rest of us, she knew a thing or two about goings-on in the outside world.

"You're right, we really have been simpletons!" two or three voices echoed.

"Yeah, aren't we good girls?" Little Liu snickered sardonically, "walking the straight and narrow. We just swallow up the 'three obediences and four virtues.' That will sure turn us out to be 'virtuous wives and wise mothers!'"

Everyone fell silent, feeling both ashamed and indignant. Then, suddenly, Little Chou leapt up. "Sure we can talk to him," she said bitterly. "We can talk and talk until we're blue in the face, but will it change anything? No. That old man is so slick; he'll never listen to us."

"But are we just going to sit back and let him go on doing whatever he wants?" Little Chou's eyes were blazing now.

"You guys are a bunch of real blockheads, that's all I can say. So you don't want wives and mothers coming to our school? You think that's a problem? That's no problem at all." All eyes were riveted on Little Liu now. "But going to the principal won't do it. No, what we've got to do is pull a 'Build the walls and clear the fields.' Yes, that'll be a million times more effective than going to the principal."

Now this was an expression everybody understood. It had been on the history exam just last term. Question One: "What were Russia's tactics when under the severe threat of Naploleon's invading forces?" Answer: "Build the walls—that is, fortify defenses; and clear the fields—or, leave nothing for the invading army to eat or sleep in. Ravage the countryside." It was a dull enough principle to have to memorize, but when Little Liu turned it to the matter at hand, whew! We were all bedazzled by her cleverness.

"Right!" cried Little Chou exuberantly. "We'll fortify the walls! We'll clear the fields! Little Cow, you will be the vanguard."

"Now cool down! I didn't say we had to go to war!" Little Liu had already assumed her leader's role. "But actually, we will need a general, somebody to give the orders and get things organized. You all listen and do what I say."

Of course everyone right away yelled out jubilantly, "Liu, Liu! Let Little Liu be the General."

"Well, sisters," Little Liu smiled with a slight wrinkle of pride on her brow, "let's not stir up a hurricane about it. After all, we've got to stick together to make this thing work, don't we?"

Well, we were all teenage kids and loved to stir things up. Even when nothing was going on we loved to make big hullaballoos out of everything—so you can imagine the uproar and excitement when we really had something to shout about. Then the whole bunch of us huddled around hashing out the various tactics, and, following the General's command, went forth to mobilize other students. The sooner we got to it the better, so it was decided that the strategy of "fortify the walls and clear the fields" be carried out during sewing class that very afternoon.

Our timing couldn't have been better even if we had planned it in advance. Just as the whole thing was more or less organized, the bell rang for afternoon classes to begin. Of course science class, which came first, was interminable—nobody was in any mood to listen to the teacher. We were all passing notes, giving each other sly winks, making faces. As if this weren't enough, those on the outskirts of the action were throwing spit balls into the center. It was lucky for us the teacher was a "good guy"—he was the kind that if you didn't know the answer, he wouldn't make you stand there turning red and wishing you could melt into the floor; no, he'd answer for you, quick. He was nice. No matter how bad we were, he'd just turn his head and pretend not to see.

The fifty minutes were endless and we were prancing with impatience. The bell rang; we all grinned like monkeys. As soon as the teacher stepped off the platform, we lunged ahead in a mad stampede to the sewing class upstairs.

The sewing teacher was a great lady too. She had been a widow since she was fairly young, and was very straight-backed and proper, so we called her "Li Kungts'ai"*—the Imperial Tailor Li. Since it wasn't really a derogatory name, calling her by it soon became a most natural habit with us. In fact, sometimes we'd even use it in sewing class, and I know she must have heard it, but she never got mad.

It had always been customary for us to cut up in sewing class. But today—wow, the floorboards were louder than ever; even the window panes shook. The noise must have gotten to the third-year kids downstairs, the more take-charge ones ran out into the yard and yelled up at us, "Hey! You got wild horses up there or something?"

---

*Li Kungts'ai is a character in *The Dream of the Red Chamber*, who, widowed at a young age, dedicated herself to the upbring of her fatherless son. The name sheds light on her upbringing, for while still a young girl, she was deliberately encouraged to develop her interest in the "feminine" occupations of needlework and tailoring rather than in intellectual activities.

We didn't give them a second glance; not even the promise of a juicy argument could pull us away from the schemes we were hatching that day. But Little Liu was not about to miss a chance to match her wit. She dashed to the window and flung out a clever retort. "Horses? Yes, heavenly horses. We've got the horses of Heaven on the run up here and look how all the gods are paying court!"

The Imperial Tailor Li was usually late for class, and so we usually got to have at least five or ten minutes of uproar and chaos. But today, we had our plan all set, and way before the usual time to pipe down, we were in our places ready for the action to begin. And of course, "Waddles" was sitting there, waiting with the rest of us.

We were all still chattering like a flock of birds, when up jumped Little Liu. "I've got some news for you guys," she said in this loud voice. "Got some news! Shut up and listen . . . Just now I was going to the storeroom to get some paste. I ran into this old lady hugging this bag of clothes to her chest; she asked where she could find young Mistress Chu. Well, I cocked my head a second or two, then I said, 'Chu? You mean like a pig*? No, you must have the wrong place. This is a school. We don't have any Mistress Pig or Mistress Dog around here.' I told her to go try other residences, but she wouldn't budge. She just hugged her little bag of clothes, pleading for me to go ask if Mistress Chu was around. I said, 'Do you think we'd hide your young mistress in a closet or something?' Then this old woman got this really pathetic expression on her face. She said 'It's the second master in our family, he's so afraid his new wife will catch a cold coming home, so he rushed me over with these clothes. If I can't deliver them, I'm going to catch such a scolding when I get home.'"

Little Chou broke in, "You all hear that? Come on, own up. Who is it that has such a romantic 'hei-ch'i pan-teng'†? Who is it? Don't be embarrassed. Just step forward and collect your clothes."

"Wait a minute," Little Liu interrupted, "I haven't finished my story yet. I was there talking to this old lady; I thought maybe I could have a little fun with her. So I started to bring her upstairs. And would you believe it? She just looked at those stairs and her legs started to shake, and she asked me in a quavery voice, 'Couldn't you please inquire for me, miss?' So I was forced to in-

---

*The Chinese word for "pig" is *chu*, homophonous with the surname *Chu*, though they are written with different characters. The homophony is exploited here for a pun.

†"Hei-ch'i pan-teng" is a clever play on the English word "husband." The four syllables in Chinese are pronounced like "heycheebahndeng," a transliteration of the word "husband," and they mean "a black painted bench," something stiff and dull.

form her, 'Ma'am, the truth is, we don't have any mistresses or daughters-in-law coming to school here. No, we're all unmarried girls here, and if I were you, I'd be careful about saying things like that. You had better advise your love-befuddled young master he should dote on his mistress in the privacy of his own home. The young ladies at this school are all very pure and innocent and easily embarrassed. If they heard you asking around for a Mistress it would embarrass them all to tears!'"

"So did the old woman finally leave?" Little Chou asked, laughing.

"You're so concerned about her; maybe it was *you* she came looking for," Little Liu threw it back to her.

"Bah! You punk!" Little Chou jumped up in protest; everybody broke out laughing.

"And did the old woman say anything else?" Little Liu had assigned me a couple of lines to say, so I said them, but I said them in a really stupid awkward way. I could see Little Liu giving me the reproving eye, but luckily for me, she just went on with the charade.

"Well, since this old lady was sitting there looking so pathetic and hopeless and stubborn, I asked her what her young mistress looked like, so I could go look for her." Little Liu flashed a mischievous smile around the room. "So she said, 'My young mistress? Well, she's not tall and she's not short . . . she's got a duck egg-shaped face that augurs good fortune . . . and a pair of dumpling-like bound feed that are neither fat nor thin . . . and a pair of long slender delicate hands . . .'"

"Oh, stuff it, Liu!" Hui-sheng shouted out amidst everyone's laughter. "That doesn't sound like the way an old lady would talk. I say you're making it all up."

"Don't interrupt. What else did the old woman say?" Big Wu had been assigned a couple of lines too, and she recited them as flatly and awkwardly as I had.

"I'm not going to tell anymore! You think I'm lying?" Little Liu really sounded furious—but it was all part of the act. "Some of you want to hear what happened, and some of you think I made it all up. It's none of our business anyway. Why would any Mistress Pig or Mistress Dog go putting aside her domestic responsibilities to come attend this chaotic school? It's crazy and absurd." Finished, and smug, she sat down.

"Hmph! Even if they wanted to come here, they'd have to get *our* consent first," Little Chou shouted.

"Well think about it." Hui-sheng who wasn't half bad at making speeches, took the floor. "At home they've got housework, fathers-

and mothers-in-law to serve, those with children at their wit's end coddling them and trying to keep them happy; those without, trying to coddle their husbands and keep *them* happy. Don't you think they're busy enough as it is? Why should they try and pretend that they can come to school and study too? Come exam time, they'll be out of their minds with everything they'll have to do. Their whole act will fall apart. The jig will be up.''

That was a good speech but it was too serious, we were all sitting there trying to think of something funny to say when Little Liu cut in. "Did you hear what she said? It's so funny . . . husbands being the same as *children* . . . needing to be coddled too . . ." Everybody broke out in gales of laughter again.

"I don't know what's gotten into you today, young ladies!" Little Chou turned and sat on her desk. She swept a righteous look around the room and admonished, "Maidens! Unmarried girls! Talking about husbands in every other sentence . . . you ought to be ashamed! This is a school for maidens! Such shameless talk!"

At this, some of us felt the joke was cutting just a little too close to the bone. Our laughter somewhat subdued, we turned around to sneak a look at "Waddles." She had her head lowered, pretending to be occupied with her sewing. You could see her fat round cheeks were flushed.

Just then, the Imperial Tailor Li stepped into the room, bag in hand. Little Liu gave a hurried cough, everybody put on a grin and stood up.

"Teeeaa-cherrr," Little Liu drawled out in the singsong voice we always used with good-natured teachers.

"Yes, what is it?"

"We would like to make something for a baby. Do you think you could give us some ideas for that next time?" Even before Little Liu finished, the room chuckled.

"How big a baby?" Mrs. Li asked.

"Oh, about a month old," Little Chou was laughing so hard she almost couldn't get that line out.

"How come everyone has to make one?" the Imperial Tailor asked. As usual, she was strolling up and down the aisles, bending over now and then to examine a student's work.

"Teacher doesn't know we'll all soon be aunties?" Little Liu said in a coy and delicate voice.

"Don't go stretching the relations too far," Hui-sheng snickered. "You haven't even seen the brother-in-law's face to know whether it's long or round, and here you are calling yourself 'auntie'!" Everyone broke up again.

"Of course our brother-in-law's face is long. Everybody knows that!" Even before Little Liu finished, peals of laughter rose.

"So what if it's long, what's the difference? And what's so 'of course' about it anyway?" somebody cut in.

"Well think, pea-brain. If our brother-in-law is so romantic and doting that he worries about his darling wife getting cold long before the weather has even turned, his face can't possibly be round." We were all about to let loose another gust of laughter, but the serious look on Little Liu's face promised better things to come, so we held ourselves in.

"But actually, we're all just stumbling around in the dark, wouldn't you say? I mean, we haven't even gotten a close enough peek at our own *sister's* face, to see if it's round, or if it's flat, and here we're debating about our *brother-in-law's* face? Now I call that silly. So who *is* this sister that we're making these gifts for?"

We all put down our sewing and started looking around the room, our heads revolving this way and that, hardly able to suppress our giggles.

Little Liu added with a snicker, "We've got to know who it's all for, don't you think?"

I went along with the others and feigned confusion. But naturally, as we were just kids, we were terrible at hiding what really caught our attention—all eyes made a beeline to Waddles' face. It burned redder than ever. Her hands, fumbling in her needlework, were visibly shaking. Pretending to be oblivious to what was going on, she stared down at her work, not daring even to sneak a peek at us. The corners of her mouth twitched, as if she tried to laugh along with us, but clearly she was trembling and having difficulty breathing.

The Imperial Tailor had to leave the room to take something downstairs. Little Chou took the chance and immediately jumped up yelling:

"No need to look around girls! It's got to be the one whose face is the reddest!"

In unison, all eyes turned to steal sly glances at the young wife. Her hands were shaking worse than ever, her head so low her face was nearly hidden in her sewing.

"Little Chou, you're being illogical," Little Liu put on a sober tone. "How can you use a red face as the decisive factor? There is the saying, 'Face is blushing, happiness gushing.' How can you be sure that a blushing face alone is the sure mark of a young wife?"

"What do young ladies have to do with 'happiness gushing' anyway? Isn't it all just 'paying respects to Heaven and Earth'*? They're just doing what they have to: 'having honorable sons one after the other,' right? So you're being even more illogical."

---

*In the ceremonial portion of a traditional Chinese wedding, the bride and groom kowtow to Heaven and Earth.

By this time, this witty exchange had pretty much loosened us up, and everyone was laughing complacently. We had long abandoned what little reserve we had, and began staring unabashedly at the young bride, not worrying anymore if we were embarrassing her or ourselves.

Then suddenly she raised her head, threw the needlework she had in her hands on the floor, and in an agitated voice cried: "What are *you* all staring at!" Big round beads of tears rolled down her cheeks, and her face was flaming red. She ran out of the classroom and clattered down the stairs.

We were stunned, the laughter froze in our mouths, and there was a moment of silence. Then, Little Liu broke it with a snicker. "Little Chou, she's gone to tell the principal on you."

"Aah, so what," Little Chou said defiantly. "You think I'm afraid of being told on? Anyway, don't get excited Little Liu. If there's a catastrophe we'll all bear it together."

"So who's scared? This is exactly what our strategy of 'building the walls and clearing the fields' is supposed to accomplish, isn't it? Isn't this what we planned for? I mean, if we were afraid, we shouldn't have started anything in the first place," Little Liu said cockily.

"You've got to be awfully stupid to be afraid of old Waddles," Hui-sheng laughed. "Ha, a married woman and all, and she thinks she's got the face to go reporting to the principal!"

We all began to get over being stunned. Just as we were feeling pretty smug about our success, someone suddenly shouted, "It worked! 'Building the walls and clearing the fields' was a great success!"

"Hooray for General Little Liu!" Little Chou cheered, putting her arm around Little Liu's shoulder.

"Hooray for General Little Liu, hooray for Little Cow!" The room resounded with jubilant schoolgirl voices.

And as we cheered, we gazed on Little Liu, our leader, our idol. She looked so beautiful, her chubby doll cheeks flushed bright and adorable, her two little dimples, her two big round eyes flashing sparks—"Hooray for General Little Liu!"

It was twelve or thirteen years later, and I was living in Wuch'ang at the time. One day, after lunch, my husband rushed off to class as usual, leaving me with the endless boring routine of keeping house. Out of the blue came a knock at the door. It was the postman with a letter. It was from Big Wu—since we had attended the same college after graduating from high school, we had stayed more or less in touch.

The last paragraph of her letter read, "What you were saying in your last letter—that you feel vacant and listless —I had expected as much. But I think I just might have some good news for you. Just now I was having dinner with some friends, and I got to talking with this woman. To my amazement, I discovered she was Little Liu's sister-in-law. And would you believe, she told me that Little Liu is living in Wuch'ang, on Big Well Front Street, No. 4—the Chin residence—only one street away! She's practically next door to you. You two can get together and have heart-to-heart talks day and night! There's so much life in her, I just know she'll pull you right out of your doldrums. How I envy the two of you."

That piece of good news couldn't have been more timely. I was really going crazy with boredom lately. The only time I ever got to escape the house was when I taught English, two hours a week; and that was so easy I could switch off my mind and still teach it perfectly. And the rest of the week? I just sat at home. Wuch'ang is not a very pleasant place, with high walls around the houses and shallow courtyards. Being new to the city, I found it really hard to take. If you sat quietly and raised your head to look around, all that you could see were dim high walls pressing in on you from all directions. I remember waking from a dream one afternoon, jerking myself out of sleep. I looked around me in panic, desperately trying to remember what crime I had committed that I should be locked up in this dungeon.

Nothing amused me in the town. I had no refined enthusiasm for sights like the Yellow Crane Pagoda, nor had I a taste for window-shopping at the foreign stores across the river. And as for going into town—the streets there are so impossibly narrow that every time a car passes you have to fling yourself quickly into the nearest store, or be crushed. And then you look up at the clerks and they're laughing right in your face because you have no business in their store. And as the sparks fly out of their hookahs, if you don't watch out, you might end up with little burn holes in your clothes as souvenirs of your excursion to town.

Well it wasn't five minutes from the time I received the letter until I was walking out the door, on my way to see Little Liu. As I thought about my own weariness and boredom, I remembered all the more Little Liu's sharp vivacious manners. I thought of a thousand things that we would talk about. I envisioned her nimble birdlike gestures, and those sassy quips that came to her so quickly. It was the perfect sunshine I needed to melt away my dreary mood.

At Front Street I scanned the long row of walls, all so high it hurt your neck to look up at them. I counted the doors; No. 1, No. 2, . . . finally No. 4, the Chin residence. Impatiently, I knocked.

And I knocked and knocked. No one seemed to be answering. Only when my knuckles had begun to sting did I finally hear the dala-dala sound of slippers approaching the door. I quickly called out my name. It was probably my woman's voice that gave me the edge, and the door opened.

The maid standing in the doorway yawned with a kind of insolent weariness as she inquired who I was. Any other day I probably would have been annoyed, but I was in a bouyant and generous mood and didn't think anything of it. I even answered her with a smile.

"Oh, so you're here to see the missus. Please come into the parlor."

I followed her four or five steps into the parlor, and there I saw a little boy about three or four years old, and a little girl who looked just like him. The two of them were fighting over a dish of peanuts on the coffee table. The boy greedily popped whole peanuts into his mouth—skin and all. He ate so hurriedly that when he spat out the skin, along came bits of half-chewed peanuts. There were filthy little piles of chewed-up peanut skins all over the grey tile floor. The kids stared at me with big black eyes. They bore a shadowy resemblance to the Little Liu in my memory. Could these be her children?

"The missus will be here in a moment. Please have a cup of tea." The maid handed me a cup. I took a sip. It tasted like medicine. I put it down again.

The maid went to a doorway on the right and pushed aside a light green printed drape. You could make out greasy handprints all over it. Behind the curtain the missus and the maid said a few indistinct words. Suddenly, "waa—waa—" came the racket of a baby crying. Then followed the sound of a baby being patted. The drape lifted, and out came a woman of about thirty with a thin face and a yellow complexion. She wore a grey printed linen Chinese gown; the collar shone with grease and the flaps at the slits were pulled all out of shape. This had to be Little Liu, but my memory did not allow me to believe it.

"Sorry to keep you waiting." The smile on the woman's face was shallow, awkward.

"We haven't seen each other for a long time." I couldn't think of any other way to keep the conversation going. My smile was strained too.

My God, can this woman really be Little Liu? Her cheeks weren't rosy and shining like apples anymore—now they were yellow and waxy. Her eyes were no longer clear and sparkling with life, but were muddy and lackluster. And her laughter? . . . Her trim figure?

. . . As these thoughts raced through my mind, I just stared at the person in front of me, stupified.

"When did you come to Wuch'ang?" she asked me listlessly. My stare didn't even raise a blush in her.

"It's been over six months." I felt unbearably stiff. I coughed up some phlegm in my throat and thought to spit it into the spittoon. It was a nervous gesture, anything to ease the awkwardness between us. But when I turned toward the spittoon, a rancid odor rose up out of it, nauseating and overcoming me. I quickly turned away.

"It was only today that I found out you were in Wuch'ang. Big Wu, who was in our class, told me in a letter." At first, I thought I'd tell her how I rushed over as soon as I received the news, but when I looked up again at this woman who bore no resemblance to the one I had envisioned, I faltered in embarrassment.

"Big Wu?" Her brow knitted in puzzlement. "Which Big Wu?"

"You know Big Wu. Wu Yü-ch'ing. She met your husband's sister in Shanghai, and that was how she found out you were living in Wuch'ang."

"Oh . . . She's our Fourth Sister." As she spoke, she kept glancing over at the two children eating peanuts.

"How long has it been . . . eleven years, isn't it? Even your kids are so big now . . ."

"Oh you mean him?" she said, pointing to the boy. "He's not even the biggest, there are two girls older than he."

"When did you get married? And why didn't you even tell us?" I asked, smiling.

"Let's see, I was seventeen . . ." She counted out the years on her hand. "Big Pao is seven this year . . . that's right . . . I had her the year after I got married."

"How many little ones are there now?"

"Four girls and one boy."

"I heard Little Chou is married too. Do you know where she is?"

"Little Chou? Oh, she died a long while back. It was a tragic death. I heard she carried a freak baby; it couldn't be born. They operated; she couldn't bear the pain and she died on the table. A couple of my relatives were there—they saw it with their own eyes."

Perhaps because it had been too long since we were together last, and the thing was already past anyway, neither of us felt particularly grieved. We were silent for a moment, and nothing more.

"Have you been in touch with Hui-sheng?" Her mind was recalling the past now.

"We wrote a few times the first year. I heard she got married. But I haven't heard a word for the past couple of years." I unconsciously sighed.

We were silent again. On the way over, I had a million things in my mind to talk over with her. But they had all vanished. Now I couldn't think of a thing to say to her.

The awkward spell was broken by the little boy, who pulled up his gown and yelled, "Mama, poopoo."

"Sun Ma," Little Liu called out to the maid, "come help the young master go poopoo."

The maid rushed into the room. She pulled forward the spittoon—into which someone had just spat—and sat the child on top of it.

"Now sit still; I'll get some tissue." As Sun Ma left the room, Little Liu called after her, ". . . and bring two plates of sweets too."

The child sat on the spittoon and groaned. Instantly the odor filled the room.

Absent-mindedly I glanced over at the child sitting on the spittoon—The face shaped like a water chestnut, the delicate mouth, and the bright black eyes, these features were endearing in themselves. If only his nose didn't look like a piece of stepped-on dough, and his cheeks were a bit rosier, he would have been a perfect miniature of Little Liu.

"He looks like you. I imagine he's a smart little thing, isn't he?" I said.

"Ai! He's horribly obstreperous. Everyone in the family spoils him."

I smiled indulgently. "Well, I'd bet he knows just how to find everybody's soft spot. That's how he gets so spoiled."

"The two before him were both girls, so naturally everyone fusses over him a bit too much."

"The other older sisters are in school?"

"They've gone out with Grandma. Since we've come to Wuch'ang, we haven't had time to look for a school for them yet." As she spoke, her brow tightened for an instant.

Sun Ma came into the room, two plates in one hand, and some tissue paper in the other. As soon as the little boy saw the candy, he started yelling that he wanted some.

"You can't have any until you finish going poopoo, precious," the mother admonished gently. "Don't yell or our guest will laugh at you."

"I WANT IT!" he yelled, his little mouth stretched wide open.

"I'll give you some after you get up. If you eat and go poopoo at the same time people will laugh at you. Now precious, be a good little boy," the mother kept coaxing him in a gentle voice.

"I want to go poopoo and eat at the same time!" The child raged, he was so irate that his face was flushed red. His mother didn't get angry, nor did she say anything.

"Give ME! I hate you, mama, I hate you!" He screamed again.

His mother still said nothing, but placidly, without a trace of anger on her face, got up to coax the child and wipe his behind.

"I want this!" The child jumped over in front of the coffee table and reached out toward the dish. But his mother rushed over and pushed the dish out of his reach, saying in a mild voice, "Our guest hasn't had any yet. I'll give you some. Just be patient and don't grab."

"I want a lot! Give it to me! If you don't, I'll hit you!"

She gave him two handfuls. The child kept ranting, at the same time stuffing candy into his mouth. He ate so fast his breathing became labored, and snot began running down over his lips. He swiped it on the back of his hand and smeared it on his mother's dress.

"Now why did you wipe it on my dress?" his mother asked softly, as she helped him wipe his face.

"You're hurting my nose!" He twisted away from her and ran out the door, slamming it with all his might. A crash sounded outside. In the inner room, the baby began to wail. The mother hurried in to look after her, and emerged with the baby over her shoulder, humming and patting it softly.

"Maybe it's time for some milk?" I suggested, seeing that the baby kept on wailing. The mother nodded and called to Sun Ma to bring a bottle.

"You're not nursing her?" I asked.

"No," she replied, wearily, "I don't have any milk. The last four all grew up on cow's milk."

"How's your health? Have you seen a doctor?" I asked, looking at her sallow complexion and thin cheeks.

"No, no, I'm not sick, just weak . . . I had a miscarriage at the end of last year, and this July I had her . . ." The baby's wailing drowned out the end of her sentence. She called out anxiously, "Sun Ma, hurry with the bottle. Baby can't wait anymore!"

"The bottle was broken by the young master," Sun Ma replied from outside.

The mother looked sadly at the boy and sighed. "What's to be done, I just can't seem to manage him at all . . ." She patted the wailing baby and called out, "Sun Ma, hurry up with the milk — never mind the bottle."

The baby nestled in her mother's bosom, sobbing as if aggrieved, refusing the milk offered her on a little spoon. The mother patiently slipped the milk into her mouth, drop by drop.

The little boy, meanwhile, took this chance to run to the coffee table. He pulled the whole plate of walnut candy to the edge of the table and began wolfing it by the handful.

"Careful you don't make yourself choke," I said, unable to stand seeing a child behave like that. "Eat slowly—we don't want any, you can have it all."

Just then, the next youngest child, a little girl about two years old, toddled in from playing outside and complained to her mother that she was hungry. Little Liu told her to wait a bit, so she sat down on the doorsill, now and then stealing pathetic, yearning little glances at the coffee table. I went over and got her a small handful. She smiled with delight and was just about to put the first piece in her mouth, when her brother dashed over and snatched it away from her. Unable to defend herself, she opened her little mouth and began to wail helplessly.

"What a bad boy!" The mother couldn't hold back anymore. "Why did you have to grab your sister's too? Now give it back to her—I'll buy you some more tomorrow."

"No! I don't care if she cries." He stared belligerently at the little girl. "Go ahead and cry; I'll tell Dad to hit you."

Little Liu smiled apologetically at me. "He knows his daddy dotes on him—he bullies all his sisters."

"Is there anyone at home he's afraid of?" I asked, smiling.

"He's not afraid of anybody. His daddy never disciplines the children. And me, my health hasn't been too good— well one day but in bed the next. I just haven't had the energy to discipline them." Even as she said this, she seemed short of breath.

"They're still young. When they get older they'll be better." I said the only thing I could.

"The child *is* a little rough, but he's a smart little thing, much smarter than the others. When he's in a good mood, he can charm anyone he wants. It's just that his health isn't too good, and it makes him irritable." As she spoke, her tired eyes cast a tender, loving look at the boy.

That's just what a mother would say, after all—so I thought to myself.

With some effort, the maid finally coaxed the little girl out to play. The baby too finally quieted. The mother brought her back into the inner room.

The boy came over, grabbed hold of my wrist and smiled boldly at me, his head tilted. I smiled back and made some small talk, humoring him as he tugged at my hand and began leading me around the room. Then a clutter of photographs on a desk caught my eye. As I stopped to look, the boy pointed to a young opera actress in costume. "This is Pi Yun-hsia, see?" Then he pointed to another, one that looked like a movie star, very fashionable. "This is Yang Ai-hua! Daddy says she's some sort of star." As he spoke, he noisily sucked back the snot in his nose.

"And what about this one—who's this?" I pointed to one of a girl in some exotic outfit.

He shook his head, then said, "That day daddy went to the movies. Yang Ai-hua came out and sang."

"Did you go see it?"

"Daddy wouldn't take us. Big sister started crying and mommy hit her." As he talked, he lifted his outer gown to wipe the snot that had begun to drip again, revealing an even dirtier padded jacket underneath.

I was just about to examine the other photos of female beauties, when he pulled away from me and ran toward the door, calling loudly, "Daddy's home, Daddy bought some bananas."

I looked up to see a man of about thirty with a wan, yellow face and a skinny build walk in the door. The boy, catching sight of the bag he carried, immediately grabbed at his legs and clung there, reaching out for the bag.

Little Liu came out of the inner room and introduced me. "This is Ms. Lin, an old classmate of mine."

The man smiled slightly, nodded, then scrutinized me for an instant through his glasses. The expression on his face repelled me. It reminded me of the looks the store clerks gave me when I would dodge into their shops to get away from the cars. I understood that look—it was a look men reserved only for women. Though it makes one feel humiliated, I knew they didn't mean any personal harm by it.

"This isn't bananas!" The child was making a pest of himself, clinging to his father, pushing the bag roughly away from him.

"Don't get my gown dirty! Look how filthy your hands are." His father pushed the boy over to his mother. "Give him something to eat," he said curtly. He turned and left the room.

"He just finished off a whole dish of candy. How can he still be hungry?" The mother tried to restrain the boy, as he jumped up and down yelling that he wanted bananas, nothing but bananas.

But seeing that no bananas were about to materialize, he dashed to the long table in the middle of the room and knocked the goldfish bowl onto the floor. The bowl shattered, water splattered everywhere, and the little goldfish flipflopped on the floor.

The mother was transfixed for a moment at the sight. Then she said with a sigh, "You've broken your sisters' favorite goldfish bowl. There's going to be quite a scene when they get home."

I already had my purse in my hand. "I'm afraid I have to go. If you ever have time, come see me; I'm on Back Street, No. 10 . . ."

"Stay awhile, it's still early." She stood up slowly. "I'll come visit when the children are better."

I walked toward the front door. Mother and son followed behind me, and when I reached the door and said goodbye, the child piped out, "Goodbye, Auntie!" The word "Auntie" rang out crisp and delicate. I must have heard a voice like that somewhere before. I searched my foggy mind as I walked homeward.

T'IEN T'AO

Very little is known about T'ien T'ao. He was actively writing in North China before and after the War of Resistance. The author Pa Chin admired his writing from this period and apparently helped to publish his works. Since Liberation, T'ien T'ao has had one novel, one collection of short stories, and several single short stories published, all in the 1950s. His writings center around oppressed peoples of China, all in the pre-Liberation period, and usually in the countryside.

"Parting" (Li) was most likely written in the 1940s. The original used for this translation is drawn from the collection Hsiao-ch'eng yeh-hua, published in Hong Kong in 1961.

Parting

Translated by Clara Y. Cuadrado with Vivian Hsu

I

KUAN, A CHILD who was by nature incurably strong willed, was lodging at her maternal grandmother's house, keeping the "young mistress" company. This "young mistress" was only two years younger than Kuan and was her cousin, the daughter of her Big Uncle. Although Kuan did not enjoy the favors of Fortune that were her little cousin's lot, she was spurred on by an inborn willfulness, and she often got the better of the "young mistress" and sent her off in tears, rubbing her eyes and seeking consolation from her mother. Then Kuan's aunt would dash out of her room, her pent-up anger ready to explode, and her eyes flashing and bulging like those of some ferocious animal.

"You just wait, you'll get what's coming to you! Go back to your own home! Get out of our house! Let your father give you a taste of his iron palm!"

With these familiar words sounding in her ears, Kuan would crawl onto a soft dirt mound in the yard. Almost every day she would hear such expressions over and over—whenever she made her little mistress cry, or, out of carelessness, dropped a porcelain bowl during a meal.

During these outbursts, her grandmother could only pretend to be deaf, and the unfortunate Kuan, who had since very young had the bad habit of whining whenever someone touched or scolded her, would burst into a vibrant, full-throated whine that lasted on and on, driving everyone in the household to distraction.

"Go on crying, go on, and I will kill you with these scissors." Mother, fully aware that she and Kuan were unwelcome guests, always cautious, always afraid of making anyone angry, glared at Kuan with a face pulled so tight that it looked like a wooden block. The incurable disease she had contracted during childbirth was aggravated by her rage. She angrily grabbed a pair of scissors and held them tightly in her withered yellow hand. Trembling, she raised her dry, skeletal body from a pile of old clothes in a dark corner of the brick bed, opened wide her lusterless eyes, and threatened Kuan in a weak voice. But her threats had absolutely no effect, and the whines continued like an old refrain, broadcasted from Kuan's throat as from a loudspeaker.

"You wait and see. Little Kuan, you won't be able to come with me the next time," Mother said in a low, tremulous voice.

Grandmother was the kindest person in the world, with a patience acquired through experience, and though she was sad at heart, there was still a smile on her sun-parched face. First she soothed the young mistress until she stopped crying, then she came over to console Kuan. When an atmosphere of peace was restored to the household, quiet and desolation once again descended upon the patient's room.

"Do you feel the pressure in your belly again? Here, let me give you a massage." Grandmother reached out one hand to stroke Mother's belly.

Mother's thin, sallow face was always filled with sorrow. Kuan had never once seen her smile. Mother's chin was pointed to begin with, and now that her cheeks had sunken in, it looked even more like the narrow end of a funnel. When she was sullen, she would curl up her fever-ridden, purplish lips, showing her dingy teeth, while sad and bitter creases furrowed her forehead.

"Ah, she will not last long. She is going to die." All the neighborhood women who were knowledgeable about childbirth diseases agreed. It was "blood-sucking consumption," and it would go on until all the flesh on her body was burned up, then she would die.

Kuan did not understand death. She only felt that having such a mother limited her freedom and subjected her to severe discipline. Threats like "I'll take these scissors and kill you," "I'll throw you into the well and drown you," "I'll call in a tiger to eat you up," and

"I'll send you to your Father to be beaten up" meant little to Kuan's jaded ears. But Mother's withered, yellow arms were really to be feared. Whenever Kuan came near her, whining, those thin arms would suddenly come to life and pick up something — anything—with which to beat Kuan over the head. Sometimes when she could not find anything around her, she would take off her shoes and hurl them at Kuan. Mother was so cruel! She could die, and Kuan would not care less. Without Mother, perhaps she would be freer; perhaps she would suffer fewer beatings and reprimands.

But whenever kind Grandmother went to the Buddhist temple to pray, she would drag Kuan along, and stroking Kuan's hair with her calloused palm, she would make Kuan kneel beside her, kowtow and pray in front of the clay image of the Madonna Bodhisattva. And what was hardest to bear was that Grandmother forced her to recite in front of the Bodhisattva the words, "Good, kind Madonna Bodhisattva, please cure my mother of her disease," again and again.

Kuan never believed that the Madonna Bodhisattva had any efficacy. She had seen the urchins in the neighborhood run into the temple and play pranks on her, and once a naughty boy even took a stick and clubbed her on the head. The goddess submitted herself to the insult without even making the slightest protest.

But Kuan had to listen to Grandmother, so she knelt down and prayed. Grandmother carefully lit the incense, then she burned the paper money. As the ashes rose towards the ceiling of the temple, Grandmother silently looked into the dirt-smeared face of the Bodhisattva. Kuan became very impatient. Her knees were pressed against the brick floor of the temple, and they hurt. She jumped up, "Grandma, I wet myself." And, as she was speaking, a big patch of wetness appeared on the brick floor.

Grandmother grabbed her and dragged her out of the temple hall. Outside the red temple door, Grandmother slapped her and glared with an anger Kuan had never seen before. This time Kuan did not whine; she only sobbed quietly. But Grandmother felt ashamed of herself for having hit her. As she thought about her daughter's illness, sorrow and confusion filled her heart. Two large, hot tears rolled out of her eyes and tumbled down her thin, parched cheeks.

II

Mother's skin was all shriveled from her fever, and Grandmother's hands rarely left Mother's belly. Although she devoted most of her time to caring for Mother, her hands simply could not undo the lumps inside Mother.

One day Grandmother brought in a pair of scissors. Kuan suspected that Grandmother would give them to Mother, and Mother would use them to kill her. She was so scared that she backed away several steps, and stared wide-eyed at Grandmother, but Grandmother did not hand the scissors to Mother. Instead she pulled up Mother's clothes and exposed her belly.

"Good heavens, how skinny you've become!" Grandmother said, scraping away the dried out, dead skin of Mother's belly.

"Have you gone to burn incense before the Bodhisattva again?" Mother asked listlessly.

"Yes, but your Little Kuan behaved very badly. She wet herself in front of the Bodhisattva."

"That little devil! She really puts the curse on me!" Mother painfully moved her skeleton-like head around the pillow, as though she were looking for something to strike Kuan with.

"Don't move. Look how badly scorched your belly is." As Grandmother spoke, she pulled up a large, thick layer of shriveled dead skin. Suddenly her hand started to tremble and she released the skin, not daring to lift it any further. Then, as Grandmother resumed cutting away the dead skin with quivering scissors, Kuan saw her face turn pale as death, as if the gravity of her daughter's illness had dawned on her for the first time and she could not quite believe it.

Kuan heard her speak to Mother in a low weak voice: "Do you feel sad?"

"No, mother. I feel relieved and at peace." Mother shook her head. Her lusterless eyes fluttered shut, as if she did not wish to see anything.

"What would you like to eat? I'll go and fix it for you."

Mother was silent for a while, then she said, "You can make some buckwheat dumplings for me."

Grandmother took out the little stove, set a small earthenware cooking pot over it, and lit some firewood. When the dumplings were cooked, they turned a greyish color, and Grandmother mixed in some cabbage leaves, sprinkled on a little salt, and added a few drops of sesame oil. When Kuan saw the dumplings in the little pot, her whiny refrain began in her throat.

"Your sick mother has not even eaten yet! What are you whining about?" Even the kind Grandmother couldn't tolerate it anymore, but Kuan, to whom whining had become a habit, continued to whine even after her throat had become dry from the effort.

Mother was covered with a mess of clothes and quilts. Grandmother set down the bowl of grey buckwheat dumplings by her pillow. A pair of red lacquered chopsticks was sticking out of the bowl, as though the food were being offered to ancestral spirits. Mother numbly watched the steam swirl up from the bowl. Kuan's whines reached her ears, annoying her and driving away what little appetite she had.

"Mother," she called out to Grandmother, "bring Little Kuan over here. I'll give her a good beating. How dare she bully me like this, thinking that I don't have any strength now, that I can't do anything any more."

"Don't be angry. After all, she's only a child. Finish eating first."

When Kuan saw Grandmother's protective stance, her whines became even more shrill. In the next room her aunt coughed loudly, grumbled and scolded ruthlessly. Mother, hearing the message in those words, found it even more difficult to swallow the dumplings. She stretched out a jaundiced arm, picked up a couple pieces of cabbage with the red chopsticks, and put them into her mouth, but as soon as the wearisome smell of the buckwheat dumplings hit her, she felt nauseous. Her eyes filled with tears, she quickly set aside the chopsticks to lie down. She groaned, and the two pieces of cabbage that she held in her mouth flowed out with a flood of yellowish fluid onto her pillow.

"Mother, I don't feel like eating," she moaned, swallowing her saliva. "Give the food to Kuan's cousin." Moaning, she pressed down on a lump in her stomach. She felt that many such lumps were stuffed inside of her, and she often had the urge to cut open her own belly in order to find some relief.

Grandmother's eyes were wet with tears. She wiped off the yellowish fluid and cabbage that Mother had spat up, then she slowly divided the buckwheat dumplings remaining in the pot into two bowls, giving one to Kuan, and taking the other over to Kuan's aunt for her to feed to the young mistress.

Kuan ate up everything in a hurry, then, as if still hungry, she started to whine again.

"I'm getting you out of here tomorrow!" Mother looked at Kuan sullenly, then turned to Grandmother and said, "Mother, tomorrow, let my younger brother take us back to my husband's home."

When Grandmother heard these heart-rending words, tears immediately brimmed over from her eyes. She could see that her daughter's condition was getting rapidly worse. Returning to her husband's family and eating that coarse food would make her recovery even more unlikely.

"Going back to your in-laws? They have so many mouths to feed, and how could you survive on the kind of food they eat?"

"No, Mother, it's best for us to go back. Little Kuan harasses people here every day."

"Ah—if only your father were still alive, who would dare to raise any objection? I am old now, and I cannot control my sons and daughter-in-law any more. It is my fault." Grandmother's tears rolled down like a spring. She continued: "But as long as I'm alive, you can stay here and let me nurse you back to health."

"In that case, let's send Little Kuan away." Mother was still sullen; her forehead creased with worry. Her sparse, straw-colored hair was tied into a small topknot, and her temples were sunken, pulsing weakly and slowly. At that moment her eyes seemed bigger than ever. Her face was paler too, covered only by a thin layer of dried-out skin. Her lips had grown more purplish, and her eye sockets were only two deep holes, which made her nose look even more prominent.

Grandmother picked up the corner of her smock to wipe her tears. Then she combed Mother's hair and returned to massaging her belly again. She had tacitly consented to send Kuan away.

"Tomorrow tell my little brother to take her home." Mother repeated these words, then she started to moan again.

I I I

Kuan's youngest uncle often caught frogs in the fields for her, but he also hated her whining. This bad habit of Kuan's annoyed even the neighbors. She was born ugly to begin with. Her head, her eyes, forehead, face, belly, thighs—almost everything—were round. When she cried, her mouth opened wide as a ladle, and although there were no tears, her throat gave out an extraordinary vibrating sound, "Hhhho—hhhooo—," as if she were not really crying, but merely putting human tolerance to the test; as though she knew that no one could do anything about her.

Little Uncle caught a cricket in the fields, tied it to a green sorghum stick and lifted it high, deliberately provoking Kuan. He wanted to see just how great her capacity for crying was. Kuan started out sobbing, then warmed up to whines, but finally she broke out in loud wails.

"Take her away quickly, Little Brother." The patient's weak voice came from her room.

"Let's go, Little Kuan. I'm going to take you to your father!"

At that, Little Kuan wailed even louder. Her uncle took her arm, and dragged her out. As they went out the gate Kuan's tears really came. She remembered how Father's strong palm had landed on her back, and how it left an imprint there for a full five days. Such a terrible Father—she would rather die than go back to him. She dropped to the ground and refused to move. Her little legs kicking, she screamed with all her might, as if someone were going to skin her alive. Many children gathered to watch her. Yet, the louder she cried, the more force the determined uncle used. He grabbed her arm tight and dragged her through the dirt as though dragging a log.

"Let's go. Still crying? Look, your father is coming. He's going to beat you up." He dragged her quickly along.

"Er-shun, Er-shun," from behind them came the trembling voice of Grandmother, "If she doesn't want to go, don't force her."

As soon as Little Uncle let go of her arm, Kuan dashed back like one possessed. She clung to Grandmother's legs, wailing and screaming.

Grandmother took Kuan inside. She picked up the cricket, still tied to the sorghum stick, and played with her until she stopped crying. The ashen-faced grandmother then slowly walked into the patient's room and found her eyes filled with hot tears.

Auntie walked in, a cold snicker on her face. In her arms was the young mistress.

"Why bother sending her away? Let her stay!"

"This child really drives me out of my mind!" The patient dried her eyes and forced a smile. "She's been a real nuisance. She pees in front of the Madonna Bodhisattva; she makes your little girl cry all day long, and then there is her bad habit of whining. I want to send her home for her father to straighten her out."

"Why bother? Just let her stay on. Heh-heh." The aunt, still wearing that sarcastic smile, still holding her little girl, slowly moved towards the door. When she finally went out, Grandmother lifted her lapel and wiped the cold sweat off her forehead.

IV

"Mother, I've been meaning to talk with you about something for a long time. It's been on my mind for several months now. When we went home for New Year's, Little Kuan's dad talked to me about selling her to a wealthy family in our neighboring village. They say that in this family there's an old lady who wants to buy a little girl to be her maid. I figure, if we sell Little Kuan to them, she will be able to eat better, and she will not be treated badly. Her dad is very much for it. What do you think, Mother?"

Grandmother lifted her troubled face in silence, and sniffled, not giving an immediate reply. She just stared vacantly at the jaundiced face of the patient. Finally she said, "She is so small, what can she do when she gets there? All she knows how to do is cry."

"They promised not to make her work in the first two or three years."

Grandmother hesitated. Ashen-pale, she fixed her gaze on the floor, like a motionless cat watching a rathole, waiting for some animal to crawl out from under the floor.

The patient was drained from having talked so much. Trembling, she lay down again, sighed ever so slightly, and fell into her private thoughts.

After talking it all out, everyone agreed to have Kuan sold. Mother, who had watched Kuan grow up since she was an infant, was naturally distraught. The image of that little bundle in her arms, gazing up at her with those innocent eyes, remained fresh in her mind. Yet, in order to get some peace and quiet for herself, to take some of the burden off her own natal family, and to reduce the insinuations from her brothers and sisters, she forced herself to pretend happiness about the decision. The compassionate grandmother became even more somber, and she watched her daughter closely, as if probing her true feelings. Is she really willing to give up her own child and let her become a maid to a total stranger? She is ill and has to lean on others for support, so she is forced to such a decision. But, like all parents, she must love her child. The little girl is only six years old. Hai, Heaven's will did not permit her to enjoy love and comfort. Instead, she was born to a poverty-stricken father and a bed-ridden mother.

Grandmother again took Kuan to offer incense and say prayers at the temple, but this time Kuan behaved as if she understood. She knelt straight down in front of the Bodhisattva, keeping her little knees close together, and quietly watched Grandmother finish burning the incense and paper money. She even knocked her head on the floor three times, together with Grandmother. After they returned from the temple, perhaps owing to her recent traumatic experience, Kuan became somber and more compliant. Grandmother borrowed a bit of white flour from a neighbor and made some dumplings for Kuan's farewell meal.

Mother lay in a dark corner of the brick bed, moaning. She saw how Kuan had become somber these days, and felt a boundless pity for her. The child had never enjoyed happiness, and now she was soon to become a maid in another family. Mother felt guilty and distressed. Tears welled up in her eyes again. "Little Kuan, come over here."

When Kuan heard Mother call her, she was afraid that Mother was going to beat her over the head with something again. So timidly, she walked over. Mother reached out to her with her bony arm. Her trembling hand held Kuan's small arm, and she stroked Kuan's two little braids. She did not hit her but was very gentle. Kuan had never seen her so loving before. She noticed how Mother's wrist showed many blue veins, and her sparse lusterless hair was disheveled. Her dried out, flat chest was exposed, her nose and chin seemed unusually pointed, and her sunken eyes were lying in little pools.

Why? Kuan wondered. Why does Mother look like this? She seems to be crying, yet she is not really crying. Only—why does she have these tears in her eyes?

"Mother, there's a flea crawling on the edge of your quilt."

Kuan, so innocent, so unaware of the suffering in this world, reached out her small hand and caught a flea as big as a grain of wheat. She pinched the little creature with her nails.

"Little Kuan, do you ever think of me?" Mother suddenly asked.

"Yes, I think of you, and Daddy, too."

Mother's face turned white, and she fell back on her pillow. "Tomorrow you can go with your Big Uncle to visit your Aunty."

"Going to visit Aunty?"

Mother could not speak. Her face was pale and quivering. Her lips turned purple. Kuan loved visiting relatives, for she could put on new, colorful clothes, ride the oxcart, and eat good things: pork, white flour, white rice, chicken, duck, and fish! When she heard that she was to go visit her Aunty, her somber manner vanished. She became sprightly, and her two little feet jumped up and down. But she noticed Mother's eyes were filled with tears, which rolled over her nose and down her cheeks. Kuan concluded that Mother was again being attacked by the lumps in her belly.

The next morning, as soon as Kuan heard the first crow of the cock, she jumped out of bed, put on her new colorful clothes, and ran all over the yard. She was so excited that she could only eat half a dozen of the dumplings made of white flour; a rare treat which was her farewell meal.

Big Uncle had already yoked the ox to the cart. Kuan blithely called out to him and asked him to lift her into the cart, but she heard Grandmother call her from behind.

"Little Kuan, Little Kuan, go let your mother give you a kiss before you leave."

Kuan ran back to let Mother, who lay ill on the brick bed, kiss her. She also let Grandmother kiss her. Both of them were very somber, but Kuan hardly noticed. She ran out again and got on the oxcart. As she was leaving, many people came to see her off. Her braids, tied with pieces of red yarn, fluttered in the wind, and when the oxcart had traveled some distance from the fence, Kuan turned around and looked back. She saw her Grandmother in the crowd, her hands covering most of her face.

They arrived at a strange village, and the oxcart stopped in front of a big brick house.

"Is this Aunty's house?" Kuan wondered. As she remembered, Aunty's house had two large poplars filled with crows' nests in the front yard. So she asked, "Did you come to the wrong place, Uncle?"

"No. This is your Old Aunty's house."

Oh? Is there also an "Old Aunty?" Perhaps this was the first time she had ever visited here, but she never remembered even hearing of this "Old Aunty" before and she couldn't picture her face. She felt a mysterious sort of curiosity and wanted to see just how old this "Old Aunty" was.

Big Uncle brought her to an old woman, and Kuan concluded that she must be the "Old Aunty." Why, she was really old! Her hair was white as snow, her face was full of wrinkles and her bound feet were smaller than the rice dumplings wrapped in lotus leaves. She smiled warmly at Kuan, and Kuan, without thinking whether it was proper or not, called her "Big Aunty."

She felt that this old aunt was kinder and nicer than anyone she had known. Now that she was going to be settling down with this aunt, life would be peaceful and quiet. The old woman had no family except for an adopted son. She owned many houses—lonely, sleepy houses. After breakfast, when her son had left the house, the old woman and Kuan were the only ones at home. The old woman's favorite pastime was praying. In a quiet room she would put down a large, thick, round cushion woven from wheatstalks. Then she would kneel on it, reverently keeping her knees together. In front of her, in a small incense burner, a short stick of incense was burning. She would close her wrinkled eyelids, and count the beads of the rosary in her hand.

Kuan went out to play every day. She was much happier now than when she was living at Grandmother's. She could now eat white noodles and white rice. She also had a little boyfriend to play with. He was called "Little Pillar" because of the tuft of hair which stood on his head. All day long Little Pillar was out in the fields, a basket on his back, cutting grass and bringing it home to feed the cows.

One day Little Pillar took Kuan out to the weedy ditches with him to catch crickets. Near an embankment, Kuan heard a cricket chirping, but she suddenly lost all interest in catching crickets. She began thinking of her grandmother and mother, and her throat started vibrating. Finally long wails broke out.

"What's the matter? Why are you crying?" Little Pillar asked. Kuan shook her head and just stood there, with her little legs buried in the grass. Little Pillar quit paying attention to her and quickly turned to cut the grass with a sickle. Suddenly he saw a cricket jumping out of a little ditch, and he deftly caught it in his small hands.

"Kuan, Kuan, I caught a cricket. Here, you can have it."

But Kuan kept on crying. She looked up at the boundless sky, the fields filled with verdant growth, and the trees, villages, and mountains far away. She missed her grandmother and mother even more. Little Pillar took her hand and put the cricket in her palm, but as Kuan would not hold it, the cricket jumped out and disappeared into the grass.

"Look, it got away! It got away!"

Little Pillar parted the weeds to look for the cricket, but couldn't find it. Finally he picked up the sickle and resumed his work.

After a while, Kuan stopped crying. She had rubbed her eyes red, and she now wanted to go home. Little Pillar brought her back to the village, right up to the door of the wealthy old lady. Kuan walked in, still plunged in grief.

"Little Kuan, Little Kuan, do you like peaches?" The old woman pulled Kuan to her and stroked her hair. But Kuan's eyes were glazed, and she said not a word. She was on the verge of tears again, and her brow contracted.

The old woman took two big sweet peaches from a drawer and offered them to Kuan, but Kuan wouldn't take them.

"What's happened?" wondered the woman, "Did someone bully her?"

Kuan pouted, staring at the old woman's white hair. Although she was kind and good-natured, Kuan had suddenly lost interest in her. The woman seemed in many ways to be no substitute for Mother and Grandmother. Kuan's anguish mounted, and she finally opened her mouth wide and bawled.

V

A few days later, as Kuan was out in the courtyard gazing up at a date tree full of ripe red dates, she heard shrill voices calling her from behind. "Kuan! Kuan!" When she turned around she saw a group of bare-bottomed urchins carrying fish nets, on their way to catch fish at a ditch outside the village. Among them was Little Pillar who asked her to come along and watch them catch fish. Kuan just shook her head.

"How come? You don't want to come with us?"

Kuan shook her head again.

"If you come with us, when we catch a big one, we'll give it to you, and you and the old lady can have fried fish."

Kaun was touched by his surprising fervor. How could she turn him down? So she followed the pack of bare bottoms out of the village.

Just as they reached the outskirts of the village a familiar-looking man walked towards them from under a willow by the roadside. As the man came closer, Kuan recognized him with a start. Why, he was her very own father! And as soon as she saw Father's face she was reminded of his strong hand, which, when it fell on her back, made her hurt for five days. But not knowing why, she was now brave enough to walk up to him and ask, "Where are you going, Daddy?"

Father was sad at heart for he had come to take Kuan to see her mother for the last time. He had walked a long way and his face was wet with perspiration. He stopped, and when he saw his child, with her two little braids tied with red yarn, he pulled her into his arms. Kuan thought that she was about to be beaten again, and her heart beat aloud. Her entire body quivered, yet she did not dare to cry. Father did not hit her, however. After a moment he set her down, held her hand, and asked her, "Little Kuan, do you miss your Mom?"

"Sure, and I miss you, too."

Only then did Kuan dare to lift her head to look at Father's face. He was so hot that his whole face was red, and his eyes were watery. She couldn't imagine her father crying, so she thought to herself, "Why, do Daddy's eyes sweat, too?"

The bunch of bare-bottomed urchins watched them with curiosity, but after a while they all went down to the ditch to catch fish.

Kuan walked along holding her father's hand. She felt that she was being fooled. Surely Father will beat me up when we get home, she thought, but she did not dare resist, not even a bit. She only dared to look up sometimes to see if there were changes in Father's expression.

At dusk, they finally arrived at their village. Kuan was baffled. She saw many people in front of Father's house, each wearing a white band on his head. A bunch of white paper was hung on the door. What was happening? She wondered why all these people were gathered there.

Then suddenly she caught sight of her grandmother and her uncles in the crowd. Grandmother, with tears brimming in her eyes, scooped her up and carried her into a bamboo shack. She wound a long strip of white cloth around Kuan's head and carried her into a white canvas canopy. Tears tumbled down her cheeks; she couldn't suppress her sobs as she said, "Kuan-kuan, take a look at your mother." She pointed to Mother, who was neatly dressed and sleeping quietly on a door board.

Kuan felt dizzy. She raised her hand and grabbed the white cloth band that bound her head tightly, wishing she could tear it off.

"Ma-a!" she called.

Mother did not respond, nor did she pay any attention to her. Kuan called to her again. Still there was no response. Mother did not even reach out her yellow, skinny arm to her.

Kuan's mouth widened, and loud wails came out.

And once she started, louder wails followed.

TENG YU-MEI

(1931–)

Teng Yu-mei is a writer from a proletarian background who began to mature in the mid-1950s, but was nipped in the bud during the Anti-Rightist campaign, and further humiliated during the Cultural Revolution. Teng was born in Tientsin in 1931. His education lasted only five years. He joined the revolution at age fourteen and did "cultural work" in the army. In 1953, as a fledgling writer, he was sent to Ch'ang-hsin-tien to "experience life." There he became a Party branch secretary. He was a representative to the National Conference of Young Writers and Artists in 1956.

"At the Precipice" (Tsai hsüan-ai-shang), published in 1956, catapulted him to national fame. Although, as literature, the story is imperfect and somewhat immature, it immediately gained popularity at the time, especially among the young, and it elicited public praise from Teng's mentor, Chang T'ien-yi. However, because of its frank and "decadent" view of love and marriage, the story became quite controversial within a few short months. By the end of 1957, "At the Precipice" was branded a "poisonous weed" and Teng a Rightist as a result. He fell into obscurity until the Cultural Revolution, when he was dredged up for further castigation for his alleged association with an antirevolutionary play about a madman presented in Tientsin. However, apparently the "drowning dog" was not beaten to death, for he has resurfaced as a writer in the era following the fall of the Gang of Four. An essay vindicating himself and Chou En-lai's views on literature, and a short story about a hero in the Post-war civil war have appeared in People's Literature *(Jen-min wen-hsüeh, 1979, no. 3, 1979, no. 7).*

At the Precipice

Translated by Hua-yuan Li Mowry

IT WAS A SUMMER night—hot and humid—with mosquitoes buzzing around. Since none of us could have gotten to sleep anyway, even with the lights turned off, we began to talk, each one taking a turn at narrating his love life, and all of us agreeing to be completely candid. A technician from the Design Institute was sitting at the far end of the room. He was generally a high-spirited person, but when it came his turn to speak he said nothing for a long time. Finally, what with all our prodding, he heaved a sigh and began his story.

My wife and I got married of our own free will.

It was year before last. I had just graduated from college and was going to go to work as a technician at a certain work site, but I messed up the very first day—I forgot to get the expense statement for the train trip. I was really upset because I knew for sure that they would not settle my account without that expense statement. Even if they did, there was just no way I was going to avoid being chewed out. I bit my lip as I went in to the accounting office.

Sitting there behind the desk was a trim-looking girl with bobbed hair; the blue blouse she had on was faded to almost white from repeated washings. She pulled up a chair and asked me to sit down.

"But how could you have forgotten to request the expense statement?" she asked seriously. "We've got to have it for our accounting system."

Wiping off sweat, I answered, "Yes, well, I, uh, I've just graduated from college, and I'm still a bit new at . . ."

"I see." She smiled. "Well, in that case I'll write you a note and you take it to the train station and get the expense statement."

I took the note and had just walked out the door when she came rushing out after me. "This is your first day—you must have a lot of things to attend to—so how about filling out a short application for the expense statement, and I will take care of all the rest for you?"

This was out first meeting—I was greatly impressed.

At that time I was applying for membership in the Chinese Communist Youth League, and she was the local secretary, so three days later she interviewed me. She had delicate features and a very attractive smile. I was glad to have such a secretary to guide me, but I never thought I would fall in love with her. I felt that we were of two different kinds—she was on a higher plane than I.

A few days later I learned something of her past—not much schooling, graduated from a junior high school, stayed home for a while. After Liberation she had gone to a vocational school and then started working. She had taught herself Russian and could now read the Soviet Communist Party history. She had joined the Party in the spring of the same year I arrived. Well, when I learned all this, I respected her all the more—as did everybody at the work site.

Then—and I have no idea how it happened—I fell in love with her. I would look for all sorts of opportunities to be with her. On Sundays when I would ask her to go out with me, and she would readily accept my invitation, I always felt greatly honored. And it seemed that when I was walking with her, even my character improved—after all, wasn't she a leader of youth?

When I proposed to her, she thought it over, then said gently, "You might want to consider it some more. I am two or three years older than you. It might not work out too well."

"How can you say that?" I shot back. "I love you, and what's that got to do with our ages?"

From that time on she showed even more concern for me. Not only did she urge me to keep moving forward in my thinking, but she also took care of the many lesser details of my life. I had never learned to budget my money: the first few days of the month I would go out to eat, buy all sorts of things, and then by the fifteenth I couldn't even afford cigarettes. So she volunteered to manage my accounts for me. Thereafter, not only did I make it quite comfortably through the whole month, but I even managed to put away some money regularly every month. Again, in the past I hardly washed my socks and handkerchiefs once a month. When a Sunday came and I was going out with her I would always have to rush out to the store and buy new ones. When she found out, she kidded me about it. "Do you really think that putting on new socks will make people like you more?" She then asked me to bring out all my old, worn-out things, and she proceeded to wash and mend them.

I was embarrassed, and I said, "Isn't everyone going to laugh at you for doing this for me?"

She answered seriously, "Why should they laugh? Don't you agree that it is better for two people to do some work together than to roam about the streets aimlessly?"

Sure enough, none of our comrades laughed at her. They only remarked about me, "The wild horse has been bridled." When I heard this, I was secretly quite proud.

Several times she asked me what my opinion was of her. When I could find no answer to that question, she would say, "See, you never pay any attention to other people politically. You don't even have an opinion of me, not to mention of the other comrades." I would blush and promise to change, but I never did.

It was in the fall of that same year that we got married, and I suggested that we buy a spring bed. She replied, "But isn't sleeping on a wooden bed the same?"

Then I wanted to get a decorative marble lamp, and she said,

"Let's just buy an ordinary lamp—it looks simpler, more attractive."

"But you only get married once in a lifetime, and if there's not enough money we can always borrow some."

"But," she answered, "getting married only marks the beginning of a new life—afterwards you've still got a long way to go."

After we were married, we got along just fine. Mornings we would go to work together, and in the evening we would come home at the same time. We hardly ever took the bus. Instead we would walk, chatting all the while. We always had more than enough to talk about, and any everyday trifle we would discuss with the greatest interest. At home after work, we would study together. At first she studied Russian and I read my technical books, but later on, to correct my shortcoming of not being interested in reading political publications, she began to study Russian in the morning, then at night she would ask me to read something political aloud to her. Sometimes we would study separately, and I would keep looking up at her face, gazing intently at her dark eyebrows or her slightly pale cheeks, and the more I looked at her, the more I wanted to look at her—I just couldn't believe she was now my wife and would live with me for ever and ever. Then she would notice me staring at her, but she wouldn't raise her head—just keep on reading as before, but blushing, a smile appearing at the corners of her lips. Unable to restrain myself, I would jump up and hug her, kissing her with abandon and telling her she was all I'd ever need. "Now," I would say, "the only thing I've got to do is work, work, work—diligently!"

She would laugh, and lean on me for a while, her eyes closed, then she would say, "Now, it's time to study again. Let's make a rule—we'll take a break only every half hour, and whoever breaks the rule will be punished. Otherwise we're just going to go downhill."

After I was transferred to the Design Institute, we were able to see each other only once a week, so Sunday became a festive day for us. We would go to exhibitions or movies, or go dancing. She bought a small charcoal stove, and on those days when we didn't feel like going out we would invite some friends over for dinner. She knew how to cook just about anything, and on cold days she would pack the food she had prepared into glass jars so I could take it with me to the Institute. I was her kitchen and laundry assistant, and she would always accept my help even though it made more work for her.

We would always talk about our work, our thoughts, and the other events of the week, and it was from these talks that I gradually discovered her many unusual qualities, the most impressive of which were her truthfulness and simplicity—call it "down-to-earthness" if you will. Me, if I did not exaggerate some aspect of a certain matter, why, I could never even begin to describe it. Whenever I had finished designing something, for example, I'd always say something like, "By gosh, I worked like nine oxen and two tigers, and I finally finished it, and it sure wasn't easy!" Her, she would always state it simply: "I've finished the monthly inventory," perhaps adding, "I still have to doublecheck one item."

And we would often talk about the future. Sometimes I would say, "During the next couple of five-year-plan periods, perhaps I can design us an ultra-modern home. There will have to be a balcony, a bathroom . . ." But she would counter, "From next month on we'll have to be more thrifty; we ought to save up a little money. If we have a baby next year, then we won't all be able to squeeze into this house."

Unconsciously I was influenced by this aspect of her character, so that when I was designing an office building, I would find, inexplicably, that I was disgusted with my former pursuit of superficial beauty and luxuriance, and I now had my eyes on practicality, on a kind of simple grace. As a result, my designs were commended, and in the antiformalism seminar the leadership even asked me to make a model report. In everyday life as well, I gradually changed my bad habits of exaggeration and ostentatiousness, and my comrades all agreed that I was now much more down-to-earth. It was under such circumstances, then, that I joined the Communist Youth League.

During this period I was happy with both my work and my life. I frequently thought that if I could continue to study, work, and live in this manner—continuously elevating myself, step by step—it would certainly not be difficult for me to become a good party member and a red expert.

But I never expected that halfway down the road, just like some participant in a marathon race, I would get distracted by an exotic wayside plant, would come to ignore the direction on my road sign, and would take up a deviant path.

A new sculptress, one Chialiya, a girl just graduated from the Arts Institute, joined the staff at the Design Institute. Her father was a professor of music, her mother was German. Chialiya spoke fluent Pekingese and Berlin German. It was a day in autumn when she came. That first day she had on a light gray skirt and a beige sweater; her hair was brown, but her eyes were black, with long, long lashes; and ever since that day, the three syllables "chia-li-ya" stuck to the lips of all the young men at the Institute. Whenever there was a meeting, there would always be someone to pull up a chair for her or to hand some tea over to her. During the work breaks, again, there was always someone to ask her out for a walk or to invite her to a ball game. She was always in good spirits and her happiness was contagious. Needless to say, I was not like all those bachelors—constantly flattering her, trying to ingratiate themselves with her—but quite frankly, I did very much admire her looks and bearing, and very much desired an opportunity to take a walk, or to chat a bit, with her.

It was the Mid-autumn Festival, and the Institute had organized a tour to the Summer Palace. When Chialiya declared that she was going along, many young fellows from the Institute rushed in to register. On the day of the tour, some carried her fruit for her, and others saved her a seat on the bus. That day my wife had to take part in the cultural activities at her unit, so I went on the trip alone, and as a bystander in the bus I observed the younger fellows and felt quite amused.

Then Chialiya got on the bus, pretending not to have noticed those beckoning her to sit down, and quite unexpectedly walked up to me. "Excuse me," she said with a smile, "would you move over a bit, please?"

I moved over, watching her out of the corner of my eye. She looked straight ahead, feigning dead seriousness.

As the bus was passing the park in the western suburbs, it suddenly made a sharp turn, and she bumped into me. As she was settling herself back in her seat, she nodded to me and said, "I'm sorry."

"Oh, that's quite all right," I said. "No need to be so polite!"

"With you, I wouldn't dare not to be." She looked at me, then laughed. "You always look so solemn—it's awful!"

"Oh?" I burst out laughing.

Immediately we started up an animated conversation, with me complimenting her on her outfit and figure. Not only did such talk fail to embarrass her but, on the contrary, she moved straight to the subject of the various aspects of a girl's figure, and how to dress so as to complement it. I enjoyed this unpretentiousness, this straightforwardness, and candidly expressed my own opinions as well. After that we talked about college life, about our common interests, and . . . and the more we talked the more congenial we became, so that by the time we got off the bus, it seemed as if we had long been friends.

"How good are you at rowing?" She looked at me so coquettishly.

Well, now, what guy, when still in school, hasn't felt the girls' eyes on him? And who, when he is in a group of his peers, hasn't hoped, to some degree or another, that he'd come out on top? Chialiya, it seemed, was pulling me right back in time to three years ago. So, looking proudly and nonchalantly at all the young fellows staring at me with envy, and taking Chialiya by the hand, I said to her, "Come on—let's go get a boat!"

After that she and I became good friends. Whenever there was a good movie or concert we would always go together.

Once we went to see "Dubrovsky." On our way home she commented to me that the two stars were really very beautiful.

"The two of them were well matched," I said.

"They chose them on purpose," she said, seriously. "With love—aside from considerations of a couple's temperaments, ideas, and interests—there should also be a union of beauty. If both the man and the woman are beautiful, their love will then bring happiness not only to the couple themselves but also to those who look upon them." Just then, a couple walked toward us from the opposite direction. The man, perhaps twenty-seven or twenty-eight, looked young and energetic; the woman was laughing at something just then, revealing deep wrinkles on her face, which made her look four or five years older than the man. At this, Chialiya nudged me with her elbow. "There, see. Maybe they get along just fine, but seeing them together makes others uncomfortable. Don't you think there's something regrettable about that?"

Glancing back at the retreating couple, I was quite pleased at first, for I took Chialiya's comment to be a hint that we were "well matched," but then I thought of my wife. She was two years older than I, and not as attractive as Chialiya. Were Chialiya to see us two walking together, what would she say? The thought was rather depressing.

It so happened that the very next Saturday there was a dance at the Institute, and I took my wife along. As we were sitting in one corner of the dance hall, I had a feeling that someone in the back was poking fun at us. I turned around and saw that it was none other than Chialiya. She noticed that I was looking at her and called out, "I was just talking about you." Tossing back her hair, she walked over to us, winked at me, and said, "Aren't you going to introduce us?"

I blushed and introduced my wife to her. Good heavens! I simply couldn't believe how awkward, homely, and pale my wife appeared beside Chialiya, and now I deeply regretted having brought her along and invited such embarrassment. When the music resumed, I just ignored her; instead I asked Chialiya, and some other comrades as well, to dance with me. "You're letting your wife sit there all by herself?" asked Chialiya. "Won't she be mad?"

"She doesn't like to dance much—doesn't really know how to," I answered. When I finished a waltz and at last returned to my wife, she told me a bit angrily that she wanted to go home right then. "You go ahead and stay—dance some more."

"Why?" I asked hurriedly. "It's still early."

"I'm tired," she answered.

So of course I had to acquiesce and take her home. We didn't say a word the whole way, but when we were almost home, I pretended to be joking. "I bet you're mad because I didn't dance with you."

"Well, why did you drag me there—to be some sort of exhibit? Wouldn't it have been much better if I had stayed at home and read?"

"Nobody had any ill intentions in wanting to meet you—and it was only polite for me to ask other people to dance," I argued.

"I can't stand that sort of contemptuousness. I respect others, and I'd like to be treated the same way," she said.

Once home, we sat in silence for a while, then we went to bed. As I lay in bed the thought struck me that if only the person lying at my side were Chialiya rather than my wife, then this whole unpleasant incident wouldn't have happened. Yes—had my wife also had the looks, the bearing, the fine tastes of Chialiya, then how happy and content I would have been!

To avoid undue friction, I didn't go to any dances for several weeks, but then one Saturday night, as I was getting my things ready to leave for home, Chialiya walked in. "Your wife must be quite a disciplinarian—we never see you at the dance any more," she smiled.

"I'm the one who chose not to come dancing," I said.

"Well, such a nice way to put it!" she said. "Oh yes—the famous dance expert! Except he is not allowed to move around as he wishes!"

I was miffed. "All right then—I'll dance all night tonight and prove it to you!"

"If you get a scolding when you return home," she said with a smile, "don't expect any sympathy from anyone. There is a party tonight," she added, "and they've been talking about selecting a few good dancers to be leads. What do you say?"

"Great!" I said. "We're partners then—it's all settled!"

"In that case," Chialiya kept prodding me, laughing all the while, "you'd better hurry up and telephone for a leave of absence."

"Who should I ask for a leave of absence?" I retorted. "I am a free man!"

But despite what I had said, I actually felt anxious, and was wondering whether my wife would be at home worrying. Nevertheless I was too embarrassed to telephone.

I hadn't been to a dance hall for quite some time, so the moment I heard the music and saw the lights I got excited and forgot about everything else. Chialiya had changed into a beautiful outfit and as soon as the music started the two of us, like a whirlwind, went round and round over the entire dance floor, drawing admiring glances. Chialiya was proud and satisfied.

"It's been a long time since I was as happy as I am now," she said. "To dance is a pleasure; to be admired is also a pleasure. Let me tell you a secret: although young girls like to pretend in front of other people to be sacred and inviolable, in their hearts they nevertheless want people to admire them."

I laughed and asked her whether young men were any different.

"Are you that way too?" she asked. I laughed again.

"Unfortunately," I said, "I am not good looking and draw no admiration."

"Oh, come on, don't be so modest, she said smiling, "I'm always your first admirer."

We danced on, teasing each other this way, constantly bumping into others. "Don't worry about that," she shrugged. "When I am happy I pay no attention to the existence of anyone around me."

"Nor do you pay any attention to your own existence, right?" I asked.

"Exactly. That is what 'forgetting oneself' really means!" Whirling round and round she laughed again. "I can reach the stage of 'forgetting oneself,' but you never can."

"Why?"

"Even if you could forget yourself, there would still be someone who would not forget you."

I'd already forgotten what had gone on at home, and now that she had reminded me my enthusiasm immediately sank. "Let's not talk about other someones, OK?" I said to her.

Just then someone at the door called me. "Telephone! Your wife is calling!"

"Now what do you say?" and she pushed me away, laughing. "You know what they say: 'Life indeed is valuable, and the price of love more so; but if for the sake of freedom . . .'"

I ran angrily to the communication room and picked up the receiver. "I'm leaving for home right away!" I roared into the phone. Nobody answered. I was surprised. "What's the matter? Are you there?"

There was a dry cough, then a low voice: "I only wanted to ask you if you were coming home for supper, and whether I should wait—I wasn't demanding that you rush right home."

When I heard that injured tone of voice my zest for dancing disappeared altogether, and I felt that I had indeed lost my freedom. I went back into the hall to say goodbye to Chialiya. She was dancing with some young guy in a blue Western-style suit, face still glowing with happiness, talking animatedly about something, and when they danced past me, she just gave me a little nod. I was so irritated that I didn't say a thing to her, but left for home immediately.

I found my wife sitting at the table, supper spread out, already cold. When she saw me walk in, she turned her head away.

"No wonder people say that women comrades are all petty-minded," I said. "Yes, I am a bit late, but that shouldn't make you act like that."

"What did I say to make you shout at me like that as soon as you picked up the phone?" she asked angrily. "Was I interrupting something—bothering you somehow?"

I sensed that her words implied something more, and shot back, "All right, all right. Let's forget about this—from now on I won't ever leave you, not even a single step, OK?"

"I wasn't suggesting that!" she cried out, but immediately closed her mouth; then glancing at me mournfully, she said in a low voice, "This is terrible. Now you don't even want to come home on Saturdays, and we are starting to quarrel with each other."

"Don't go imagining things," I interrupted her. "It's inevitable that a couple should quarrel once in a while."

"Well, but once it starts, who knows when or where it's ever going to end?"

After this stormy dispute, she went to bed and fell asleep. Lying in bed, I again thought of the dance, of Chialiya, of the envious glances we got in the streets and at the dance. I involuntarily cast a look at our wedding picture and discovered for the first time that the age discrepancy between us was indeed striking. A bit apprehensively I wondered whether I might not have married somewhat too hastily.

She rolled over, woke up and, seeing that I still had the light on, asked, "How come you are not asleep yet? Are you angry?"

I shook my head.

"Don't be angry. Maybe we still haven't learned how to handle all the problems in our life . . . but you really should have remembered to give me a call." She kissed me. "You can't imagine how long I waited, standing by the door . . . then when the food got cold, I went in and heated it up, and after that, when you still hadn't come back . . ."

"It was my fault," I said, stroking her hair, but then I started to think about Chialiya again, and I felt shamelessly hypocritical—yet I could not help myself.

The initial excitement aroused by Chialiya's arrival quieted down considerably. The many young men who had flocked around her dispersed on their own; and now more and more, whenever her name was mentioned people were turning their earlier appreciation and praise into reproach, saying that she was "frivolous," that in handling her emotional affairs she was "engaging in guerrilla warfare," and so on. As for me, I'd observed that when a guy fails in pursuit of a girl, he frequently declares her to be sour grapes; hence, not only did I not change my opinion of her but, on the contrary, I felt indignant for her. It was clear that she was somewhat distressed by the talk, and therefore she became even more intimate with me. Every day after dinner we would go to Lake of the Ten Monasteries for a walk, or to ice-skate. Her head was so full of wonderful fancies—looking at the ice, she would imagine some day in the future when all the sidewalks would be paved with ice and all the pedestrians would wear skates. Then, she said, "On Sundays we could skate all the way to Tientsin." Or looking at the water, she would imagine someday building a two-layered glass studio and filling the space between the two layers of glass with water.

I said, "One of these days I'm going to design a house for myself, and I'll certainly prepare just such a crystal palace for you, put you inside it, and take care of you as if you were my gold fish."

With that, I stole a glance at her, but she wasn't angry—on the contrary, "You are indeed a person who understands me," she said. "How wonderful it would be if I had an elder brother like you!"

"Well, why don't you just be my younger sister then?" I said. Ever since then, whenever we were alone, we would address one another as brother and sister.

Once, we were strolling around the Lake of the Ten Monasteries, she holding a bough of plum blossoms in her hand, softly singing a tune as she pinned some of them in her hair. "Oh, young maiden . . ." She stopped short, saying to herself, "'Maiden'—yes, what a tinkling sound it has, a word of gold! I will never let it leave me."

I laughed. "According to what you just said, once a maiden marries, the gold depreciates . . . so I assume that you're never going to marry?"

"Not necessarily." She burst into laughter. "It's possible that some day in the future there might be someone whose love I wouldn't be able to resist, that I will have to trade this golden appellation for—but who knows where he might be now!"

I felt feverish inside, assuming that she meant me.

In winter Chialiya always wore a gray, sheepskin Cossack hat, the kind of fur hat that I liked very much and wanted for myself. At the hat store they had informed me that it would be a month before they would have one in for me, so there I was still waiting. Noticing me still hatless in such cold weather, my wife went out and bought me a thick knitted woolen hat. "Don't be too frugal with yourself. When our circumstances allow, you ought to pay a little more attention to your own appearance," she said.

On the second day I wore the woolen hat, Chialiya looked me up. "You like that fur hat I have, don't you? Well, now the store has gotten in some more, so let's go get one." I had had no qualms about taking off with her, but halfway to the store I began to feel a bit uneasy about the way things were turning out, so somewhat hesitantly I said, "Just a minute—I may not have enough money . . ."

"Let me buy it for you," Chialiya said unhesitatingly. "There is only this one of mine in the whole Institute, and it's so lonely—it needs a friend."

She really did buy me a hat, and she wouldn't let me pay for it. Not only that, but she tried it on me right in front of all the shop clerks and customers, and examining me with my new hat on, she clapped her hands, saying, "Snappy! That's really snappy! I'm going to carve a bust of you—you, wearing that hat!" And she gave no heed to other people's laughter or to my blush.

I was careless and wore the fur hat home that Saturday night. As soon as my wife saw it, she asked in surprise, "Did you buy it?"

I blushed and mumbled, "If I didn't, who would have given it to me?"

"But I just bought you a new hat, didn't I?"

"I . . ."

"You never like anything I get you," she grumbled. "I was really stupid—I thought that you weren't buying a hat because you were trying to be thrifty! Now I see you just hadn't yet found one good enough. Hmph! You're getting more and more fashionable all the time, that's for sure!"

Boy, what does she know about aesthetics, I thought to myself. Chialiya is different—she's got artistic cultivation.

"How come you're so quiet now?" she asked, eyes wide open. "Are you mad? Well, just think, wasn't it wasteful? A person's worth doesn't lie in his appearance, but in his soul!"

"Just listen to you carry on!" I said to her. "You are the one who tells me to go buy a hat, and now it's you who's blaming me for buying it!" To arrest her suspicion I joked a bit more with her, then helped her set the table.

After supper, I sat on the bed and leaned back to rest. Unconsciously my thoughts wandered to Chialiya again. I went over in my mind all the things we had done together; I remembered every word we had spoken which could be interpreted in more than one way; and time slipped by, until gradually I sensed something was wrong. How come so quiet? I got up to look for my wife, and found her at the table, face buried in her arms, her shoulders heaving.

Of course she had been crying. Irritated, and growing more and more impatient, I walked over to her. "I didn't do anything, so why all this crying?"

She didn't say a thing.

"Well? What's wrong?" I asked, exasperated. "Is there anything you can't tell me? Is it because I bought that hat—is that what's bothering you?"

"You are hiding something from me! Ever since you came home you've been absorbed in your own thoughts, paying no attention to me!"

"My gosh! I'm tired from working all day! You are not a child—I don't have to humor you!"

She started crying again. "Neither of us is a child. We ought to know by now how to live together as man and wife. There must be some reason for you to act so cold."

"Don't talk such nonsense, OK?" I snapped.

"I'm not blind. You don't even feel like coming home Saturdays now . . . I call you on the phone only once, and you blow up at me . . . Well, you've forgotten I even exist!" I tried various dodges, but my laughter and words sounded hollow even to myself.

From that time on shadows of grief and suspicion hid in her eyes. I became even more short-tempered, and it seemed that everything had changed. Before, when I came home, my heart would always fill with a blissful feeling at the distant sight of my wife waiting for me by the door, but now as soon as I saw her waiting, I'd get irritated. "Hmph! So she can't stand to turn me loose for even a moment— look at her there, spying on me!" And when I got inside, if she hurried me to supper, I would answer in an angry voice, "Could you please just let me catch my breath first!"

She would give a cold, half-hearted smile, then, "Well, say what you please, but let me just say that when a person heads down the wrong between us, let's pour it all out and talk it over, OK? Don't torture me like this!"

Naturally I couldn't "pour it all out," so I would blame it all on her: "The problem is, you're so petty. Why, you blow up and dis- tort every little thing you hear, so how could anybody get along with you?"

She would give a cold, half-hearted smile, then, "Well, say what you please, but let me just say that when a person heads down the wrong path, he's not always aware of it at first, and besides—it always starts with some trivial, insignificant matter."

"Oh, you're always right," I would argue angrily, "and whoever doesn't go along with you is then 'heading down the wrong path'. That's brilliant logic!"

So it was that hardly a week passed that we didn't quarrel. Whenever I had a phone call from her, I immediately felt despondent, as if someone had hung a lead weight from my heart, and whenever I found out that she wasn't going to be able to come home on Saturday, I would feel relieved—absolutely bouyant.

Going home came to be the thing most painful to me.

As my relationship with my wife deteriorated, my feeling for Chialiya increased, and as my feeling for Chialiya increased, my relationship with my wife deteriorated. Which was the cause, and which the effect, I had no idea.

One thing was clear: whenever I noticed something lovable about Chialiya, I would secretly contrast it with something loathsome in my wife. I'd even imagine Chialiya behaving like my wife, and then in my imagination all her loathsome words and acts turned into something lovable, so that the Chialiya of my imagination came to be even more lovable, more perfect, than was the real Chialiya—and the wife who lived in my imagination became even more difficult to get along with than the one in real life.

I couldn't deny that my wife had some admirable qualities— in her character, in her thinking—and I felt that those qualities made her valuable as a revolutionary comrade, but they didn't necessarily make her suitable as my wife. That being the case, why shouldn't I have someone else?

So I began to think about divorce.

I made up my mind many times to mention it to her, but when the time came, I couldn't open my mouth. I knew that she loved me, that it would be a terrible blow to her if I suggested that we divorce, and so I simply couldn't bear to mention it to her. I racked my brain trying to find some way that would enable me to accomplish the goal of divorcing her, yet not cause her any pain. I would seize every opportunity to mention other people's divorces to her, praising these people for their straightforwardness, for their matter-of-fact approach. In order to hint at my determination to leave her, I secretly even separated our clothes into different trunks. But, good lord! When she finally realized my intention, and her face turned terrible with grief, I panicked and tried frantically to soothe her, telling her not to be suspicious, that everything I had done was unintentional. Consequently, not only did the problem remain unsolved, but relations between us became even more strained, even more painful, so that I suffered from insomnia several nights running, while she clearly was losing weight. I swore at myself for being so hopelessly softhearted, yet I could never get my courage up to act decisively.

At the Institute I managed to get through each day only with difficulty, for people had now begun to gossip about Chialiya and me, and even criticized Chialiya in my presence, saying that she was a decadent, immoral person, or that she was behaving just like some "capitalist." And there were those who pointed out, half-jokingly, half-seriously, that I was being "giddy-headed."

But how could I give up being close to Chialiya? She was so extremely capricious. One day she would be painting an oil portrait for this person, another day collaborating on some cartoons with that person. And the man in the blue Western-style suit (but nowadays he was wearing a fur-lined, hooded coat, also blue)—the one who always liked to dance with her—*he* was still constantly at her heels! If I were to lose Chialiya now, I'd be a loser on both ends, wouldn't I?

My affairs eventually came to the attention of the Youth League. Advice was formally offered to me during a section meeting, and the branch secretary had a private session with me in which he indicated clearly that I had breached the discipline of the League. Now I had no choice but to rein myself in a bit.

And Chialiya? The little devil, she showed not even the slightest consideration for me, once inviting me right in front of everyone to accompany her on a shopping trip. Well, I mumbled something, at which she tossed back her hair, turned and walked away.

I caught up with her, tried to explain. But she said, "If you don't want to go with me, someone else will. It's no big deal!"

"I know we are close friends, but why show it in front of everybody?" I asked.

"Oh, is there something between us you think we can't show others? I'm not afraid of loose talk, so if you don't want to be involved, then simply keep away from me!"

"Chialiya, you don't understand . . ."

Seeing that I really was upset, she burst out laughing. "Gee, you are so absorbed by what other people are saying that you can't even pay a little attention to your own neck! Look at that scarf—it's worn out! Can't you even get yourself a new one?"

"Do you think I have time to worry about that kind of stuff?" I grinned helplessly.

"If you don't even pay any attention to your own looks, then how can you talk about appreciating what other people look like?" She took off the camel-colored scarf she was wearing and wrapped it around my neck. It emitted the scent and warmth of her body, intoxicating. Still, it was more pain than joy. I had never before realized that a person's brain could be so jumbled up, and I was desperately attempting to sort out everything that was on my mind, but I just couldn't do it.

The Institute handed me the assignment of designing a hospital, and I was overjoyed, thinking that now, at least, I could forget—for the time being anyway—all things extraneous, inasmuch as I would have to be concentrating on my new assignment; but no sooner had I settled myself at my desk than my thoughts turned involuntarily to Chialiya and to my wife. When I was trying to design the psychiatric ward, I would imagine the unbearable pain my divorce proposal would bring upon my wife, and I would become fearful of my own cruelty; while I was attempting to sketch the sun-bathing room, I would think of Chialiya's glass studio, of her loveliness, and I would ask myself whether I could ever give up this happiness which was practically within arm's reach. No! If I could bear the pain of a guilty conscience for but a brief moment, then I could enjoy happiness for the rest of my life. With my mind wandering here and there the days passed by, and I hadn't even finished the first draft of the hospital.

Suddenly I couldn't delay anymore—they were pressing me from above for the blueprint. When I finally did complete the work, it became clear that I had actually done it all with Chialiya in mind! When I was designing the patient's room, I had imagined Chialiya—Chialiya lying there wearing a soft nightgown; in designing the balcony, I again thought of Chialiya and imagined her painting some water-color in the sun. I was amazed to discover that I had paid too much attention to appearance, to comfort—that the whole design, in fact, looked too luxurious—but there was no time for revision.

Not long after I had handed in the design they sent it back to me with comments. They criticized me for being impractical, for being a "formalist." On top of that, they wrote: "One's design style is inseparable from his thinking process, from his emotional make-up. You are losing your simple, plain style—that is something you should think over seriously."

That was quite a blow, and it aggravated my distress even more. So, I had been unfortunate in love; now if I were to be denied a future in my career, then what hope remained? I became extremely pessimistic, unable to pinpoint the cause of all my misfortune, nor able to put an end to it.

The League then held a special criticism-and-discussion meeting, to help me analyze everything. Some of them said that it was my "capitalist mentality" that had caused all my problems, while others maintained that I was "morally inferior," and although their com-

ments greatly irritated me, I hadn't the courage to counter their
arguments. I told them that there was nothing unusual going on
between Chialiya and me, that at most we shared some common
emotional inclinations. Then they began to criticize Chialiya for her
emotional inclinations, saying that she exploited people emotionally. Those who leveled the sharpest, most severe criticisms turned
out to be the very same young men who had constantly flocked
around Chialiya in the past—just imagine, then, how could *they*
convince me?

After the meeting there remained in my head but a single
thought—all this had to be ended, now, and the longer I procrasti-
nated the messier it was sure to become.

That day after supper, I secretly asked Chialiya to go to the lake
for a walk and, as luck would have it, we bumped into my de-
partmental supervisor—an old cadre, well-respected, very
influential in the department. He scowled at the two of us, then
turned to me. "Would you please drop by my place for a minute
tonight?"

"Surely." I could guess what he was going to talk to me about,
and began to feel nervous. Clearly Chialiya guessed it too. She
looked at me, and curled up the corners of her lips as if she were
laughing at me, or perhaps at herself.

We were absorbed in our own thoughts as we walked for a long
time beneath the straight poplars by the lake. At last she sighed
softly, "It's really hard to know how you're supposed to behave
around here, especially for unmarried girls." She frowned, but her
tone of voice carried no sorrow at all. On the contrary, she sounded
as if she were rather pleased with the situation. "If you're the least
bit attractive, it will be turned against you: people will gather round
you, chase after you, and if you are congenial or act the least bit
intimate with them, they'll say you are emotionally cheap; but if
you pay no attention to them, they'll feel hurt, and then they'll accuse you of being unfeeling. So it's not all my fault after all, is it?"

"There are some things you just shouldn't pay any attention to," I
said.

"I do have my shortcomings—I'm somewhat of a sentimentalist,
and I like to have fun with the guys—but that's no reason for them
to say I ought to marry just anyone. If someone wants to get herself
a husband, fine, go ahead and get one—but why meddle in my
business?"

I smiled. She glanced at me, then whispered: "They also say I've
ruined you and your wife's relationship . . ."

"What nonsense!" I interjected nervously.

"I have been treating you just like an elder brother, and I have never had any other intention, so if you're being criticized just for being seen with me, you know you can simply quit seeing me."

"Chialiya, have I made you so mad that . . ." Suddenly it dawned on me that a girl might often say things which were the opposite of what she actually had in mind: say, if a girl were afraid of losing you, she might say instead that she was quite willing to see you no more, when actually, deep down, she really loved you but simply couldn't express it directly, especially when everybody could see everything.

"Oh, my!" She tapped her trouser leg with the twig in her hand. "Of all the distressing things, nothing is worse than when no one understands you."

"Chialiya." I squeezed her hand and whispered, "Believe me, I understand you."

We stood close together. Several times I had an impulse to kiss her, but I restrained myself. We stood there for quite a long time before turning around and heading back. At the thought of having to go see the supervisor shortly, I took each step more slowly than the one before.

The supervisor was sitting on the sofa in his office. He moved over a bit, inviting me to sit down. "Before, I asked you to consider the changes in your style of design. Have you done that?"

"Well, yes, I've given some thought to it, but I haven't been able to think over everything thoroughly."

"How did you do it? In isolation—considering your design ideas from the perspective of design ideas?"

I slurred an answer.

"One will never get anywhere by considering a problem that way!" he said to himself, raising his head. Then after a minute's thought he became quite direct. "Tell me, what is it that's been weighing on your mind recently?"

"It's my everyday life." I, too, was candid. "I'm not getting along very well with my wife."

"*Why* are you not getting along well?"

I told him briefly of our situation and of my intention.

He was silent for a long time, then he sighed. "Some people say that the issue of love is a trivial thing in life, but I disagree. I feel that the issue of love is the best test of a person's class consciousness and his morality."

Then he went on to tell me in detail of an incident in his past, about how he had once intended to get a divorce, then changed his mind. He'd been married back home, before the War of Resistance against Japan. Once married they got along very well, until after the war, when he went to the city and began to have contact with intellectuals, as a consequence of which he developed the notion of divorcing his wife. After repeated petitions, the leadership granted him permission to return home in order to settle all the legal procedures entailed in divorcing his wife.

On the train going home, he noticed a pregnant woman in labor, on the verge of giving birth. All the passengers in that particular compartment hustled around: some unpacked their own baggage and got out their bed sheets to tear into strips for diapers, some hurried from one compartment to another looking for a doctor. And the conductor had such beads of perspiration on his forehead that one would have thought it was his own wife giving birth—all of which had deeply touched this old supervisor. In recalling his past he said, "I then thought to myself, isn't all of this—the caring for others and the caring about the group—precisely the moral spirit that our society is striving for? Being responsible for others, being responsible for the group, everyone taking another's pain as his own—quite frankly, isn't this the core of the Communist spirit? As for my intended divorce—how much have I tried to see things from my wife's perspective? After she's waited for so many years, finally her husband is coming home—and he's coming home to divorce her! It would not be hard to picture the effect that this would have on her thought, on her spirit. Is there anything more tragic than denying one's own spiritual character? And even if I could find a beautiful and suitable new wife after the divorce, could that compensate for a loss which would be, in fact, irretrievable? In this keen struggle with my self, if I should submit to failure, I would never again be able to convince myself that I sincerely want to be a true Communist."

His story and his choice of words moved me, and at several points in the story I had unconsciously thought of my wife's painful situation, but I was more afraid that my will would weaken, that I might take the supervisor's advice and give up this idea of divorce, and then nothing could be changed in the future should I come to regret having given Chialiya up. "Be tough!" I urged myself. "This will all be over in no time at all." And in order to strengthen the ill feeling I had for the supervisor, I kept telling myself that what he was saying was nothing but grand, empty words—that he'd never been in a concrete situation like the one I was in now. If there were a Chialiya at his side, then what?

I therefore questioned him hesitantly: "If what you're saying is true, then all the differences between a couple's personalities and life-styles are not really the main factor determining whether or not the two can live happily together, right?"

"No, of course, they are important factors—that's why we should all have the right to look around a bit before we become seriously involved and get married. Why was it that you loved your wife while you were going together, and even for a while just after you had gotten married, but now no longer do? Why did you change your mind after you were married?" He wouldn't let up on this inquiry, and added immediately, "I've heard that you like Chialiya, right?"

I mumbled something or other.

"When Chialiya was at the Arts Institute, she had a record of bad conduct—so you find her style and character suit you well, huh? Have you ever considered that her conduct might be contrary to the healthy thought and emotions we advocate? Well, have you ever talked about this with her?"

I was shocked to hear this about Chialiya, but I immediately began to think up excuses for her. Sure, since she had spurned so many guys, how could you expect them to say anything nice about her? And as for her Arts Institute record, who knows? I simply couldn't believe all that talk about Chialiya's "bad conduct and inferior character." After all, I reminded myself, if the supervisor's intent was to change my mind about Chialiya, was he going to sing her praises to me? And besides, wasn't I the only person who could really see Chialiya's many good points?

The supervisor, seeing me hang my head in silence, assumed that he had convinced me. He told me to go on home and think it over carefully.

How was I supposed to "think it over"? To tell the truth, everything he said was right except for one thing—Chialiya was a living person, someone I loved, someone who I believed could love me too! I had imagined and pictured so many scenes of our living together in the future, and of the requisite one hundred steps I had already taken ninety-nine, so how could I bear to sever all our relations at a single stroke?

I knew that if I were to ruminate seriously upon the supervisor's words, my conscience might begin to gnaw, and I might eventually wind up wavering back and forth, which would only postpone indefinitely my putting an end to the whole thing. And now that everybody from top to bottom was aware of my situation, I simply couldn't put off making a decision any longer. I made up my mind to go home, tell my wife everything, then sever our relations once and for all.

The thought of an immediate confrontation, however, cowed me. And then my wife's many lovable traits rose up before my eyes— our first meeting when she had impressed me so favorably, the tolerant attitude she had shown in our most recent quarrel—these things all began to flash through my mind, even more vivid, more clear than the one before, so that I couldn't help asking myself whether I wasn't in fact being reckless, perhaps, doing something I would regret once I had lost her.

"Be more decisive!" I told myself aloud. "If you go on wavering like this, you'll never get anything accomplished!"

Yet I still couldn't decide. Oh, Chialiya, Chialiya! Had you never come into my life, I would now be leading a quiet, peaceful existence, with never a dissatisfaction. Chialiya, you have ruined me!

But no! Good fortune strikes a person perhaps only once in his lifetime! Had I not met you, Chialiya, I might never had experienced the kind of pleasure I've had with you. Ah, Chialiya, it was fortunate you came!

Then I thought of something. Although Chialiya had been quite nice to me, she had never indicated unequivocally that she loved me. What if she had now changed her mind? I had better find out first.

I walked stealthily up to Chialiya's dormitory and knocked timidly on her door. Footsteps inside, then the door opened. Her hair hanging loosely down, Chialiya stood before me, smiling. "It's past midnight. Is something the matter?"

"No, nothing," I answered. "I . . . I've never been in your room, so I just thought I'd come and . . ."

"Well, come on in!"

Two oil portraits of Chialiya—one from the waist up, the other a full view of her leaning against a great stone pillar—and a caricature hung on one wall. The artist's initials appeared at the lower edge of each. On the opposite wall hung a photo of a group of people in skating costumes, with Chialiya standing in the middle surrounded by a flock of young men.

She pulled up a chair for me. I saw an unfinished clay bust standing before a lamp on her desk. "Is that mine?"

"No, but yours is done," she said, turning around to take a cardboard box from the bookcase. She handed it to me. "Go ahead—admire yourself!"

I opened the box. It was I sure enough, in my fur hat, but so much more handsome than the real person that it didn't resemble me. I couldn't restrain myself. "It's great! It's really great!"

"That's just because the model was so great—it has nothing to do with my skill," she laughed. "If I'd been the model, then not even the best sculptor could have turned it into a piece of art."

"If you'd been the model, there would've been no need for anyone to sculpt a bust—you're already a piece of art!"

We joked around for a while, and then just as I was about to lead the conversation to my intended subject, there came a knock at the door.

"Who is it?" Chialiya went to open the door, and who should come in but that fellow who'd been wearing the blue-hooded coat (except that he had changed again, and was now wearing a Chinese-style, padded satin jacket, but still blue). He nodded to me, and then sat down next to the desk.

I silently cursed him for having chosen to come at this hour, but thinking that he must have come for some reason, I decided to wait until he left before continuing my talk with Chialiya; so I picked up a book at random from the desk and flipped aimlessly through the pages.

But, good gracious! He too picked up a book and began turning the pages! I looked at Chialiya hoping she would somehow get rid of him.

She looked first at me, then at him, and burst out laughing. "It's absurd! Surely you didn't both come to my place just to put on a pantomime?"

I couldn't keep from laughing, and neither could he.

To break the ice, Chialiya suggested that we play cards. "Whoever loses serves tea for the winner," she said.

My brain was in a whirl; playing cards was the last thing in the world I would have imagined myself doing at that moment, but I was unwilling to leave and let that jerk stay. I regretted not having thought of visiting Chialiya at her dormitory before. This fellow —why, he must have been visiting her here all along . . . so I began to play cards with them.

I must have been hexed, for no sooner had we started the game than I began to lose; I had to pour tea for him. On top of that, I couldn't really see that Chialiya was any more friendly to me than to him; so when it came to the third game I finally pushed the cards away and said that I wasn't going to play anymore, that I was too tired.

"Oh, come on! Don't take it so hard," Chialiya said to me half-jokingly. "You know what they say: unlucky at cards, lucky in love."

I sensed that Chialiya's words meant a great deal more than they seemed to on the surface, and immediately felt soothed all over. Glancing at the "blue-jacketer" triumphantly, I said, "Very well, let's play some more."

But just then the bell signaling lights out rang.

Carrying my clay bust, I walked reluctantly out of the room. Chialiya saw us out and on the way whispered to me, "When you get home, take a look inside the bust and see if you find anything."

"You mischievous imp!" I said to her, and walking on air, I

headed back to my dormitory. But I couldn't wait until I got back to the dormitory, so I opened up the box as soon as I reached a street lamp. Feeling around inside the hollow bust, I fished out a note. It read: "This does resemble the real person somewhat, but I wonder what his heart is like. I'm going to North Lake Sunday afternoon, three o'clock. Want to come along?"

A warm current rushed up to my brain, making it difficult even to breathe. Elated, I took out a pen and on the spur of the moment, alongside Chialiya's message, wrote, "Chialiya, Chialiya, soon you will see my heart!"

After painstakingly considering everything for several days, I decided to test my wife for the last time to see if there was still any hope of separating without hard feelings; and if indeed there proved to be no such hope, then I would have no choice but to let her hate me. And perhaps this would actually be a better way out, for if she were forced to leave me while she still harbored some affection for me, the separation would almost certainly prove unbearable for her. My conscience probably wouldn't come out unscathed, either.

Saturday night rolled around—an exceptionally cold night—with a harsh north wind roaring through the all but deserted streets, forcing the few remaining pedestrians to pull their heads down into the collars of their overcoats, and causing the hanging street lights to shake crazily.

When I got home that night, my wife was already back, cooking something on the stove which made the whole room sweetly redolent. With a pair of chopsticks in one hand, she was staring straight into the fire.

"Is it cold outside?" she asked when she saw me come in.

I made some reply and put the bust down on the table. She went over to the table, opened the cardboard box, and immediately cried out, "Wonderful!" Then, after a closer examination of the bust, she said, "Unfortunately the sculptor is not first rate. The bust somehow doesn't look quite like its model."

Pulling a long face, I said to her: "Art needs a little highlighting. You don't understand!"

"But why highlight just the fur hat and scarf? Look, the hat is even on crooked! He really is a decent person," she laughed, "except that he now looks like a capitalist dandy."

"Well, I beg your pardon. I don't come from a proletarian family anyway."

"Don't get all worked up," she said, still laughing, "I'm not going to quarrel with you any more from now on—I've made up my mind!"

I noticed that she did seem somewhat different, and this puzzled me. Meanwhile to escape my chagrin, I faked a laugh and said to her, "So you are not going to quarrel with me anymore, huh? But wouldn't crying be an even better way to get under my skin?"

"Nor will I cry anymore. Only a fool would pick a fight or cry," she said with a smile. "No, I've thought it all out. Can quarreling and crying solve any problems? No. It only shows one's weakness and incompetence, and since we have to go on living together, why not find a way that will help us solve our problems? Emotional outbursts are no use at all."

Is she planning to cling to me all her life, I wondered to myself, feeling somewhat at a loss. I took off my coat, pulled a chair over to one side, and sat down. While talking and plotting to myself, I carried on a superficial conversation with my wife on some topic or other—I was afraid that she might otherwise notice my absent-mindedness and again break down.

"What are you cooking?" I asked her.

"Hawthornberry jam. Recently I . . ." she continued with a smile, "I've had a craving for it. You like it, right? After it's done we can each take a jar to the office."

I wasn't interested. "We better not," I told her. "The jars will be hard to wash clean."

"I'll clean them."

I didn't say anything more. Nor did she press me—as she usually would have—for an explanation of my silence. She just stared into the fire, absorbed in her own thoughts, all the while stirring the hawthorn berries in the pot. I thought she was acting a bit strange, but didn't feel like pursuing it, so after sitting for a while longer, I told her I was tired and went to bed.

At midnight I turned over and felt the bed trembling slightly. Pricking up my ears, I noticed she was sobbing under the quilt.

"How disgusting!" I thought. "Living with someone like this would make even a deaf-mute burst out in anger!" I was in no mood to pay any attention to her, so I turned my back to her.

But a long while later she was still sobbing, so I turned over and shouted at her, "If you've got something to complain about, would you please speak up? All this crying! Do you think I came all the way home just to listen to you cry?"

She said nothing but started crying even louder. I felt that if I lay there any longer, I would explode from irritation, so I pushed aside the quilt, threw on my coat, and got out of bed. I pulled out a novel from the desk and sat down by the stove to read. My eyes were fixed on the characters in the book, but my mind was wandering somewhere else. I told myself, well, it looks like a divorce is the only way to release myself from this kind of misery. What kind of lousy life is this? And every Saturday is spent this way! The supervisor only knows how to preach high-sounding words. Ha, I would like to see him spend a couple of days in my shoes.

Much later I was cold and tired, and by then she had calmed down, so I went back to bed, covered myself up, and said to her angrily, "Just remember: there is more than one person here in this room, and if you throw your temper tantrums any old time, how is the other person going to bear it? We are supposed to be equals— it's not as if I've been oppressing you."

She said nothing. I lay there a while longer, then fell asleep.

When I opened my eyes the next morning, she was already up, sitting there sewing something. The underwear I had taken off the night before was now placed around the stove to be dried, and there were some clean clothes by my pillow. Contemptuously I thought to myself, what a phony! It's quite clear that inside she is unhappy with me, yet outwardly, she's still doing all this. Chialiya would never act this way.

Putting on my clothes, I asked her, indifferently, what she was sewing, and without even raising her head, she answered, "Gloves, yours."

"Why don't you stop, give yourself a rest—I'm planning to buy some anyway."

"I know you'll never wear them, but since I've already started, I might as well finish them up." Then her tone of voice abruptly became sorrowful. "One should always finish everything one begins, right?"

I got out of bed and saw that her eyes were inflamed and swollen. "Just look at yourself!" I said. "Last night you were the one who said that you'd never cry any more—then you went and cried more than ever before!"

"Don't worry about it—from now on I'll never let you see my tears again." She sighed softly.

I fumbled despondently about, trying to find anything to talk about, and she calmly kept up her end of the conversation. Now that she's quieted down, maybe I'll get a chance to lay my cards on the table, I thought.

At breakfast she said abruptly, "I've got to go back to my office this afternoon."

"Fine, because I have a meeting this afternoon at three."

"Oh, what a coincidence," she remarked with a vaguely sarcastic smile. "But I may not come home next weekend."

"In that case . . . shall I come visit you?"

"No, that's not necessary," she said—another sarcastic smile. "I have quite a few friends over there too, and this home of ours . . .

it's really depressing!" She began staring out the window, again wrapped up in her own thoughts.

Her sad, painful expression made me feel very bad too. "To cut tangled hemp, use a sharp knife," as they say—I'd better get this over with quickly, I thought. Softening my voice, I spoke deliberately. "Let me ask you a question—and please don't get all emotional. After you've thought it over calmly and rationally, you can then give me your answer, OK?"

At this she gave a shudder, but she immediately composed herself, and with eyes fixed upon the floor she said, "OK, go ahead."

"You are a good comrade, and I do love you, but do you think we are compatible, our personalities? Will we really be happy if we keep on living together? Now please don't get mad, just think it over calmly, and . . ."

"I knew you were going to raise this question," she said, as if prepared for it, "but first let me ask you a question, all right?"

"Fine."

"Tell me frankly what is it about me that you are most dissatisfied with, most unhappy with?"

My face got red and I stammered, "Well . . . well, our personalities, our temperaments are different—I mean, I often hurt your feelings, upset you . . . and I'm ashamed of . . ."

"Don't beat around the bush!" Quite pale now, and looking me straight in the face, she continued, "After all, we've lived together for quite some time now; we certainly know each other pretty well. What do you mean, our 'personalities' are different? Didn't we get along quite well in the beginning? Let me say it for you. I'm older than you are, I'm not so pretty . . ."

In an attempt to explain myself, I began, "You . . . you . . ."

"Don't try to explain, and don't be concerned about whether I can take it—I don't need any sympathy or pity!"

"Now don't misunderstand me," I blurted out. "I've already told you that I was only raising a question, and that you shouldn't get emotionally excited."

"There isn't any misunderstanding. I'm not a baby . . ." She stopped, blinked a couple of tears from her eyes, then whirled around so as not to face me and continued. "Let me just ask you one thing—before, when ! mentioned that I was older than you, and when I asked you to think about this thoroughly, why did you say that you *had* thought it all out, and that you *had* made up your mind? Well . . . I guess there's nothing more to say. It was all my fault—so weak, so useless . . ."

"Now don't get all excited!" I told her. "I'm just asking you a *question*. Did I say anything about divorce?"

"You are afraid to shoulder your responsibility, afraid that I might resent you—so you don't dare suggest it." Then she turned around, facing me squarely, and said calmly, "It doesn't matter. Let *me* suggest it to you, because I am not asking for just any old husband—what I want is real love. To keep on dragging it out like this won't do either of us any good. Before, I kept hoping we could somehow come back together again, but now I gather that there's no such hope, so I'm not going to keep dragging it out," and with that she picked up her handbag from the chair and marched out of the room without turning her head. Then she turned around and closed the door lightly—just as she always did when she went back to her office—showing not the slightest trace of anger.

Staring numbly at the door, I was suddenly faced with a whole slew of questions. Now that my bridges had been burned—now that her heart was completely broken, now that there was no hope at all of our coming back together again—was the road in front of me really as beautiful as I had always imagined? Was it true that I could never again return to her, even if I should have regrets in the future? And what if Chialiya . . . ? Oh, my God! And I had thought that as soon as I solved the problem of separating from my wife, then everything would be so simple, so easy—and I could settle down, relax. Who would ever have imagined that things could become even more tangled and confused than before!

The room was stifling, it was hard to breathe. I had to hurry out to meet Chialiya—she said she would wait for me at North Lake at three o'clock. But it's only eleven now. "Eleven! Oh, you, watch—why aren't you running?"

I threw on my overcoat, locked the door, and went out into the street, where the wind had now subsided and large flakes of snow were falling from the sky. I didn't take a pedicab nor a streetcar but instead, in my confusion and giddiness, I set out walking, from the Lungfu Monastery to Tungan Market, and on to the south entrance of the Wangfuching district, everything in a blur. Several times I was shoved out of the way by pedicab drivers, who pointed their fingers at me, jeering, but I didn't agrue or get angry with them, I simply moved on, along with the other pedestrians.

Finally it was two-thirty. I jumped in a pedicab, and pounding on the seat, shouted to the driver: "North Lake, please. Hurry!" He was going to put the cover up. "No, no," I said, "it feels good—leave it open."

The pedicab took off and flew over the snow-covered ground, but I felt like hopping off and running, running on my own. The snow was falling more and more heavily; the golden roofs of the Imperial Palace were all turning to silver; the palace river and its white-marbled river banks became nearly indistinguishable. I kept wiping the melting snow from my face and gazing in the direction of the front gate of North Lake.

And then I saw her!

A splendid flower in full bloom, Chialiya stood amidst the white snow wearing a purplish-red woolen coat and white felt boots with red trim.

"Chialiya!" I yelled.

She raised a hand in a yellow and black glove and jumped up and down, calling my name. Before the cab had come to a full stop, I had jumped off. Holding her hands, I felt that I must at once pour out the hundreds and thousands of words I held for her in my heart.

"How do you like this place I chose?" Her eyelashes were fluttering; her face, red from the cold, glowed with smiles. "The snow-covered North Lake—how enchanting it is! Let's go to the back hill—we'll play around and build a snowman, all right? No, no— let's not take the bridge—let's slide over across the ice!"

So hand in hand we half walked, half slid across the ice, and as I pulled her this way and that, in my head I was drawing up my plan, intending to lay the whole thing out before her as aesthetically as possible.

And Chialiya? She was laughing loudly, talking to me about the snow, about the plum-blossoms, the birds . . . everything but the matter of my "heart."

I couldn't wait any longer. As we were climbing up the bank and I was carefully steadying Chialiya, I finally managed to say to her with a laugh, "Hey, didn't you want to see my heart? I've brought it with me!"

"What?" she gave me a puzzled look but immediately burst into laughter. "Well, bring it out and let me take a look."

"I'm divorcing my wife." I suddenly shivered and nervously scrutinized her face.

"Really?" She halted, stockstill. After a minute's thought, she said, "Well, since you're going to divorce her, perhaps I can say something to you. I always felt that you got married too early. Just think, diapers, bottles, a stove, a family . . . Oh, my God! All this vulgarity can ruin the imagination of any genius. Love is poetry. But once you get tangled up with those things, then the poetry flies right out the window."

I looked at her blankly, not knowing what to say.

"Furthermore, it takes time to discover an ideal mate." She tossed her hair and continued, smiling. "Before you get married, you have the right to love all five hundred ninety-nine million, nine hundred and ninety thousand people in China, and the right to be loved by any of them. Once you get married, that's finished. Then you have to cling to that one person. If you tie yourself to a particular person too early, then when you meet the ideal person, it will be too late for regrets."

"Chialiya, let's not just talk about all that." I drew near her. "If there's no new love to compensate me, I'll go crazy instantly!"

"You are free now. You can love anyone you like," she laughed.

I plucked up all my courage. "Well, I love you, Chialiya."

She turned her head to one side, picked up a damp rock from the ground, and threw it at some crows in a pine tree. The crows cried out, "Caw, caw!" Turning to face me again, she said, "I have no right to keep anybody from loving me. But remember, if you ever decide to change your mind, don't go around telling on me, saying Chialiya has ruined me!"

I hurriedly interrupted her. "Chialiya, it's true. Don't you understand my situation?"

"Well?" She shut her mouth, glanced briefly at me and swallowed her smile. Biting her lower lip, she stared down at her boots. When she raised her head, she was once more wearing her usual expression, and said in a casual tone, "So you want me to marry you, huh?"

I was startled. I mean, how could she have failed to see that? "You should know my heart, Chialiya!" I said.

On her face there was an expression of satisfaction mixed with disdain, her cheeks even redder than before. "To tell the truth," she said, "I've never even considered getting married yet. It's still a long way off for me. I told you before that I wouldn't give up the status of maidenhood so easily. I'm really sorry."

"What!" It was as if I'd been stunned by a rock. I suddenly felt weak in the knees, and gasped out, "But Chialiya, it's for you that I'm getting divorced . . . how could you? . . ."

"What?" She cried out. She thought for an instant, then pointing at herself and bursting into tears she began to stamp her feet. "For *me*? You're trying to scare me. You are blaming *me* for the divorce and trying to blackmail me into marrying you! But I am not afraid. Oh, God! What am I going to do? Everyone picks on me!" She was crying and rocking herself against a tree, oblivious now of her fine clothes.

I walked up to her and, laying my hands on her shoulders, begged her, "Chialiya, Chia . . ."

"Go away, go away! I thought I'd got to know you, but I only knew your face, not your heart. I've treated you like my own brother, and you—you've been scheming against me! Have I ever asked you to get a divorce? And now you'll spread the story, and everybody will use that to attack me. There's just no way I can stay at the Design Institute any longer!"

"Chialiya! Please! Calm down! Chialiya . . ."

"Go away, just go away! If you don't, I will!" and she pushed me aside, turned around, and took off. I ran after her, calling out her name at the top of my voice.

Just then two people came over the hill and stopped short, seeing us the way we were. I turned crimson and shouted after Chialiya, "Take it easy—I'm not as base and mean as you think." I turned away from Chialiya and walked off towards the hill.

My legs carried me forward mechanically. I walked and walked, with an urge to smash everything around me with my bare fists. I walked and walked until I felt the snow-covered ground under my feet was sinking, soon to pull me down into a deep hole.

What was happening to me? What had I done? Was all this real? Or was it all just a hallucination?

My legs were now so heavy that I couldn't go another step, so I went into one of the pavilions and sat down. I leaned against a pillar, attempting to sort out the tangle in my head, but I couldn't sort anything out. Only a few words flashed back and forth in my mind: "My wife has gone; Chialiya doesn't really love me; I have been left all alone to myself."

It was getting dark. Some fog was settling down silently. It was very quiet in the park, not a single soul to be seen. Coming from the top of a tall building to the west, I could see a thin curl of black smoke. I could vaguely hear the bustling sound in the streets outside the park, and I could see the sparks from the streetcars. It was cold, and I was shivering all over. Not knowing what else to do, I finally walked out of the park, called a pedicab, and went back home.

Our room was locked. I remembered then it was I who had locked it. Then, everything that had happened in this room—everything from the day we were married—rushed before my eyes. Somehow I began to reconsider it all from my wife's standpoint. I imagined myself in her shoes. I would be thinking about her all day long, every day. When Saturday arrived I would come home as early as possible, get everything ready, then I'd be waiting for her outside in the wind. I would wait for a long time, and then I would call her on the phone. And what sort of answer would I get? Angry reproaches, cold indifference. Only then, for the first time, did I see my own cold, heartless face. So . . . I was just such a selfish, mean person—cruel, unfeeling. Yet she had put up with all that!

My eyes smarted. I yearned painfully to find her right away, to tell her everything, to ask her to punish me in whatever way she willed. I wouldn't ask for her forgiveness. I had committed a moral crime—I had injured her.

The door was locked, and I didn't want to open it, fearing that I couldn't bear to see the inside. I staggered away and headed toward the Institute.

"It's all because of Chialiya—she's cruel, evil!" Staggering on I gritted my teeth. Then I heard a dissenting voice in my own head. "But there are so many other people in the Institute, some married, some not. How come it is only you that she has victimized?"

Then my first meeting with Chialiya, our subsequent conversations and walks . . . everything was reenacted in my mind. Now for the first time I considered impartially every "poetic" expression we had uttered, saw again every "impassioned" encounter we'd had. My face was burning. How base, how mean! What was this "poetry"? Wasn't it simply flirtation? And what sort of "passion" was it, if not mere self-intoxication? Clearly, those youthful "fancies" of mine, which had gradually, imperceptibly, faded away during my married life, had all been rekindled by Chialiya, and they had blinded me!

"Ah, you went all muddleheaded because of your indulgence in bourgeois emotional interests—even though you've been married for a long time, you've never appreciated your wife's really valuable traits because it wasn't for those worthy qualities that you fell in love with her."

All the old criticisms casually offered by my comrades, all the old words spoken by the supervisor, again they all rained upon my heart like stones.

But why was I thinking of all this now? Nothing would help me any more—it was too late. How was I to spend the rest of my days? By sinking forever into loneliness and regret? I was only twenty-some years old! Ah! Hadn't I been perfectly normal before? Hadn't I also seen my future clearly? How did I ever throw myself off the track of a normal life?

I stumbled over a rock and was jolted out of my thoughts. Before me stood the gate of the Institute. When I saw the gate, I could see even more clearly what had happened today. So, everything *was* over. There remained now only this trivial, petty person whose true form lay completely exposed, to whom no one would offer sympathy.

In her total and painful disillusionment, my wife would certainly not come back to me; as for Chialiya, she was concerned only with the harm I might have brought or might yet bring to her, and she naturally would no longer pay any attention to me. And my comrades? Yes, my comrades . . . what about them? My eyes were blurred again.

"Comrade! Here's something for you!" It was old Li, the gatekeeper, shouting to me as soon as he recognized me, still quite a distance away. I wiped away my tears and went up to him. He went inside, fetched a bundle wrapped in a piece of cloth, handed it to me, and said, "Your wife brought this some time past four o'clock. She said that she was in a hurry to catch the train and couldn't wait until you returned."

"Catch the train?" I shivered all over and began awkwardly to untie the bundle. A glass jar came tumbling out from the bundle, dropped on the ground, smashed to bits, and splattered jam everywhere. Inside the bundle I also found the clothes I'd taken off that morning and among them, an envelope. I opened it up, and the first thing I saw in the envelope was the note that Chialiya had earlier stuck inside the bust. Puzzled, I hurried on to the long letter. It was from my wife.

". . . I felt very bad and quite confused. I can only hope that you'll read patiently through this letter.

"Yesterday morning I went to the clinic to have a check-up. The doctor congratulated me, informing me that I was pregnant. At that moment I thought immediately of our recent life, because recently we hadn't been getting along too well. If we let life go on in the same way, I thought, then we'll be unable to live up to our original hopes; and also, it would be unfair to the baby, who's not even born yet! I thought to myself that it was all partly my fault. I asked too much from you emotionally, but I didn't pay you adequate attention ideologically.

"In the clinic then I made up my mind that from now on I would never cry or quarrel with you any more; I would discuss everything patiently with you, helping you to distinguish right from wrong.

"But before I had a chance to tell you all this, I inadvertently discovered this note while I was cleaning up the room. Previously I'd only heard some rumor about a rather unusual emotional entanglement between you and another girl. But I never dreamed that the relationship had already gone that far. It was indeed a tremendous blow to me. I was greatly hurt; I was also scared, completely at a loss. I agonized over the matter the whole night, and I felt sorry for the child—what crime had he committed that he should be born into such a difficult situation? It was all our fault; we were not fit to be parents.

"A while ago when you raised the question of divorce, I was determined to maintain a clean, "dry" approach, not asking for your pity. However, after I spoke out, I began to feel bad, and even regretted what I'd said. I just couldn't stay in that room any longer—I didn't want to appear weak before you—so I walked out.

"Starting tomorrow I will be on leave. But now I feel that it would be an unbearable torture to live in that room all by myself, so I have decided to leave for my home in Tientsin right away. Let's separate for a period of time so that we can consider our problems more objectively, more rationally.

"I don't know what the other person you love is like. Although I could never approve of her, I certainly won't say anything bad about her. I only hope that you'll consider this: Can a person who doesn't respect other people's happiness bring you happiness?

"Darling (please allow me to still call you this), I love you. I am really worried that you might get completely off track. This is the one part of you about which I never felt at ease; recently you have changed in almost every respect, and the change in your attitude towards love in part reflects the changes in your ideological consciousness. Before, I wasn't vigilant enough in reminding you to pay special attention to this, and now I will have no chance to remind you of it any more. You really ought to be more aware of this yourself.

"Perhaps all these words of mine will just create in you more ill feelings for me. Don't interpret what I say as a threat, intended to keep you with me. No. Although I love you (and even feel that now I need your love much more than ever before) and shudder like crazy at the very thought of being separated from you, I will never beg for your pity if you no longer love me and prefer not to rebuild our mutual affection.

"Ah, well, there's no way to tell you all I want to say . . ."

I had read through the letter once, but somehow didn't understand what she was saying; I hurriedly read it over once again and vaguely felt that she still loved me, that she would probably still forgive me. I rushed out of the gate of the Institute and jumped into a pedicab just passing by. "East Station! Hurry, hurry!"

Old Li, the gatekeeper, was shouting after me: "Comrade, your things, your . . ."

The technician had told his story and noticed that there hadn't been a single stir in his audience. "What happened? Did everyone fall asleep?" he inquired.

"No, no."

"Please go on!"

"Umm." He sighed with relief and satisfaction, and said after a moment of reflection, "I'm finished. As you all know, I didn't get a divorce."

"But was she there when you got to the station? What happened after you came back? There is still a lot more. What do you mean you're finished?"

"After we came back," the storyteller continued, "it took us both quite some time and effort to rebuild our love. But hey, this is going to turn out to be another long story! And we *do* have to get up for work tomorrow."

After a brief silence, he laughed and said to us: "The best thing would be for all of you to come to my home for a visit next Sunday. You know what they say—it's best to see for yourself!"

TS'AO MING

(1912–)

Ts'ao Ming (born Lo Ts'ao-ming) originated from Kwangtung province in South China, but she has spent most of her adult life in the north. In the late 1920s and 30s, many writers gravitated to the coastal city of Shanghai. Ts'ao Ming moved there in 1931 and subsequently married the famous writer Ou-yang Shan. Following the War of Resistance, she joined the Communist Revolution in the Northeast. She went "among the masses" by becoming a "cultural worker" in various factories in Changchiak'ou, Harbin, and Shenyang. Her association with a hydroelectric plant in Harbin provided the background for her novel Motive Force (Yüan-tung li), which gained her national renown as a writer in 1948. In the same year, she moved to Shenyang and, using her experience with the Shenyang Railroad Factory, wrote The Locomotive (Huo-che-t'ou). These two novels established Ts'ao Ming as an important "industrial writer" in China. She had been the Vice Chairman of the Northeast Federation of Writers. Today, at age sixty-eight, though in poor health, she is hard at work on a novel about industrial workers during the Cultural Revolution.

Aside from the two novels mentioned above, Ts'ao Ming has to her credit the novel Riding on the Wind and Waves (Ch'eng-feng p'o-lang, 1959) and two collections of short stories: Short Stories by Ts'ao Ming (Ts'ao Ming tuan-p'ien hsiao-shuo chi, 1957) and Love (Ai-ch'ing, 1959). "Spring Is Just around the Corner" (Ying-ch'un ch'ü) appeared in People's Literature (Jen-min wen-hsüeh, 1958, no. 5) at the beginning of the Great Leap Forward.

Spring Is Just around
the Corner

Translated by Vivian Hsu

AT A FURNACE in Anshan, the entire team waited anxiously for the next batch of steel to emerge. Hopes were high that this batch would turn out to be high-speed tempered steel, for thus far the process had gone most smoothly, all the way from the mixing of ingredients to the smelting. If the entire process for this batch could be shortened to less than six hours, they would be able to complete it before going off shift. This would mean they could turn out two batches within the eight-hour shift. Although this would not break a new record, it would still be an event to celebrate.

Yao En-t'ai had noticed for some time the tension on the face of his team leader, Sun Yao-wu. His eyebrows were drawn up tightly, and the corners of his mouth pushed downwards in a powerful, authoritative fashion. His temper could be quite imperious at a time like this, although Yao En-t'ai knew his mood was only temporary. Yao En-t'ai was accustomed to Sun Yao-wu's behavior at such times: the team leader ran madly around the furnace checking every item after the smelting had gone into its crucial stage; he became irritable, and his voice often boomed with authoritative demands. The team members dared not slack off their pace; they didn't even dare breathe aloud. They knew from experience that the more tense their team leader became, the more assured they were of getting high-speed steel. The moment the steel came pouring out and the process was over, Sun Yao-wu would undergo a complete metamorphosis and become a congenial, relaxed person, someone you could joke with or even slap on the shoulder. Although no one particularly enjoyed seeing Sun Yao-wu in his imperious mood, his team was fully behind him, and Yao En-t'ai was especially proud to work with him. His reputation for sternness as well as for confidence and vigor was known throughout the factory. He was a person who was put off by easy jobs, but if asked to exceed a target or to experiment in producing a new kind of steel, he could be counted on to rise to the challenge. Yao En-t'ai was convinced that without Sun Yao-wu's severe temper and discipline, such extraordinary accomplishments could never be achieved.

It was the afternoon before the Chinese New Year, and every furnace was competing to see who could make the most high-tempered steel and take the least time off. On this day Yao En-t'ai felt more keenly than ususal that they couldn't do without team leader Sun and all his vigor. He followed Sun's every movement and expression. Even a twitch of an eyebrow was enough for Yao En-t'ai to know exactly what it was he needed; there was no need for Sun to motion or call out.

This was only the first New Year since the start of the second Five Year Plan, everyone was already working with a furious zeal. Actually, every New Year in the recent past had been an occasion for all the furnaces to compete in producing high-tempered steel. But in past years, the competition had not been so clamorous, workers had just quietly applied themselves. Those who did well were lauded, those who did not do so well slipped by without anyone taking notice. But now, what with the Great Leap Forward and the Productivity Competition, everything was laid out in the open. And this new openness was a phenomenon that took getting used to.

"How can our furnace fall behind others? We must produce three batches of high-tempered steel, or we won't celebrate New Year." The more Yao En-t'ai thought about it, the more fired up he got. When it came time to add the magnesium, he tossed it more evenly than ever into the cauldron.

The assistant just returned from delivering some steel samples and brought along a letter addressed to Yao En-t'ai. When Yao first saw the letter he was indignant, wondering who would have written to him, knowing how busy he was.

"Hmpf, who's got time to read this," he muttered to himself. He shoved the letter into his pocket and prepared a long ladle to extract a sample from the ore. But with a second glance at the envelope he realized it was from his wife. "What is she up to now? You think I can just drop everything at the factory and come home to spend New Year with you?" he admonished his wife mentally. Although he refused to read the letter, it seemed to grow heavier and heavier in his pocket, until he couldn't resist taking a peek at it. On his way to the laboratory with a steel sample, his curiosity got the better of him and he finally stole a few extra seconds to read the letter. Then he quickly thrust it back into his pocket. From that moment on, his mind was flustered. His feet dragged him back to the furnace, his head hanging dejectedly.

He had always found it exhilarating to watch the boiling molten steel. Gentle ripples would rise from the fiery red surface; those ripples would smile and communicate a thousand feelings to him. But this afternoon he felt he had let those ripples down; it seemed as though the ripples were laughing at him, mocking his confusion. He didn't know how to vent his frustration, on whom to put the blame for his dilemma.

"I simply can't ask for a leave. Didn't the Youth Corps Branch repeatedly exhort us to keep up the full shift straight through New Year? How can I take a leave and become a backward element? I'm even a member of the Youth Corps too, just like Feng-jung."

But the next moment, he was again moved by his wife's words, "We are determined to struggle for three months in order to complete the irrigation ditch. From now on we will work in three shifts. We'll have just New Year's Eve off, and on New Year's Day we'll be back to dig the ditch. Why don't you come home, I'll only have this one day to be with you."

Yao was tormented by an irresistible conflict. Was she a good Youth Corps member, or was she a good wife?

The troubled expression on Yao's face did not escape the assistant, who came up and patted him on the shoulder. "What's the matter? Does she want you to go home for New Year?"

To avoid answering, Yao picked up a broom and began to sweep up some mineral dust. But the assistant did not let him get off so easily. He went straight to the point.

"Don't listen to that female prattle. They are always trying to tie us to their apron strings. Hey, man, why don't you wait until your next shift change to go home? You'd get more time off then. Why bother with all the hassle of going home at New Year and holidays. Take me, for example. Tomorrow's my day off, but I've decided to come work with you guys for the day. To tell the truth, I think fifteen years is too long to wait to catch up to England. I'd like to see us do it in twelve."

Just these few words renewed Yao's strength. With a resolute expression on his face and a wave of his hand, he indicated to the assistant that nothing was bothering him at all. Just then the bell rang—the steel was ready to come out of the furnace. The two stepped up briskly to their respective stations to receive the high-tempered steel, which was ready at 5:55.

Having changed out of his work clothes, Yao En-t'ai strolled out of the factory gates, bouyed by his team's small success. This last batch of high-tempered steel had brought them considerable glory. New Year was truly something to celebrate now. But the strange thing was, his feet did not take their usual path north toward the dormitory. Instead he found himself walking involuntarily straight toward the train station. And, as if by reflex, he bought a ticket for a nearby suburb. It was only as he was sitting with the ticket in hand on a long bench in the waiting room that he realized with a start what an absurd thing he had just done.

"You haven't asked for a leave. How can you go home, just like that? And isn't taking a leave without permission even more shameful than asking for a leave?" These questions sounded in Yao's mind. In a bit of a panic, he turned to look at the travelers around him. His gaze fell on an old fellow nearby.

"Pardon me, sir, where are you going? Have you bought a ticket yet? I've got a ticket here for T'engaopao, but I don't want to go after all."

The old fellow raised a hand clutching his own ticket. "Ah, I've already got my ticket too. Perhaps you can find somebody else who can use yours."

A rugged young man nearby caught the last bit of their conversation. He turned to them and asked, "Where's the ticket to?" But when he heard Yao's reply, he shook his head and said cockily, "If it's just T'engaopao, why bother taking the train? By the time you've waited in line and bought the ticket, you could have walked there!"

Yao ignored that last comment, thinking that the young man was being capricious. After all, T'engaopao was a good forty *li** away. Who says you can walk there in the time it takes to buy the train ticket? Besides, he had just put in a solid day's work at the factory and couldn't possibly walk that far without collapsing from exhaustion.

As if out of spite, he refused to return the ticket, and he didn't intend to walk back to the singles' dorm either. He just leaned comfortably back, and with a long sigh closed his eyes to rest.

Suddenly visions of his wife Lü Feng-jung began to dance in his mind: she was nodding deliberately and glaring at him from the corner of her eye, as if to say, "If you don't come home, you'll never touch me again." But Yao smiled and congratulated himself. That vision couldn't get the better of him; he was no pushover. He felt perfectly composed as he reassured himself, "I won't pay any attention to her. I'll just explain to her later that the Youth Corps initiated the idea, and we all resolved to stick by it. What can she possibly say to that?" He knew that she was a reasonable person, so he wasn't afraid that she would make a scene. But when he suddenly thought of her playful teasing ways when they were in bed together, a wave of longing gripped his heart, and he wished he could fly to her side immediately.

His wife Feng-jung was a woman of many guises. Sometimes she seemed like a kid, but in front of her in-laws, her behavior was impeccable. When she came home from working in the fields, she got right to the housework—fetching the water, fixing the meals: her father-in-law and mother-in-law never had to fret about a thing. When she was with the other girls, she could be as rowdy as the rest of them; but in front of her elders, she had always been a model of propriety.

Yao En-t'ai's mom bragged about her daughter-in-law every chance she got. "My in-laws really know how to bring up a daughter right. Why she just stands out from the crowd. The grown girls, the young daughters-in-law, all the boys—big and small, they all squabble and make rackets all the time, driving us old folks to distraction, but Feng-jung is not a bit like them."

---

*A *li* is equivalent to approximately one-third mile.

The old lady was especially fond of bragging about her daughter-in-law in front of her son. En-t'ai for his part couldn't help but chuckle to himself whenever he heard her talking this way, knowing full well Feng-jung could play up this image of herself in front of the elders. Only he knew that as soon as the lights were turned out at night and the old folks had lain down on their brick bed to sleep, the young couple would get under the quilt and she would squirm her way into his arms, like a fawn into its mother's bosom, not even bothering to notice whether her hair clips were poking him in the chin and neck. What really got him was the way she loved to tickle his waist. At some point, he'd forgotten when, she had discovered that he was particularly ticklish at the waist; and knowing full well he didn't dare burst out laughing with his parents within earshot, she'd take advantage of him and tickle him mercilessly in the dark. He'd strain to suppress his laugh and, at the same time, wrestle himself out of her clutch. Only when he had grabbed hold of her hands would she relent and snuggle her face up to him.

As he was reliving this scene in his mind, the train pulled up to the station. His feet followed the orderly crowd, although in his heart he wished he could hop onto the train in one leap. As the train started with a jerk, he closed his eyes, thinking that he would catch a few winks. But moments later he found himself sitting straight up with eyes wide open.

Where the train was passing, a thick stream of smoke wafted through half the town. Then it would be caught by the wind and scattered into the atmosphere. The huge trunks of nine tall furnaces gradually came into view. Day in and day out Yao En-t'ai had walked past the base of these tall furnaces and had never taken note of them. But at this moment for some strange reason, they appeared extraordinarily grand and imposing. The yellow fumes surging out from the nearby chemical plant encircled the tall furnaces, creating a mobile pattern of light and shadow, intensifying their aura of dauntless strength. A row of ten smokestacks, lined up in perfect formation, caught his gaze next. His thoughts were drawn to the eighth. It was under this one that he, with his twenty comrades on three different shifts, had sweated together, panted together, and rejoiced together. He recalled a time when the smokestack had been plugged up. He remembered well their anxiety and the mad running around. Two shifts were held up, which meant they missed two or three batches of steel. Not until it was finally fixed, and smoke surged evenly up the stack again, did they relax and smile. He stared at that smokestack, entranced; ah, how majestic, it's slender gray torso standing perfectly erect, wisps of black smoke floating from its top, like the locks of a young girl's hair blowing about her forehead. The wisps of smoke seemed to be waving goodbye to him. He smiled complacently to himself. "Five hours and fifty-five minutes. Not a record, but certainly impressive enough." He was lulled into contented reverie, and his little leave without permission for a time escaped his conscience.

After Yao En-t'ai got off the train, he had to walk another six or seven *li*. It was a snowy evening. By the time he reached home it was already pitch dark. His family had finished making New Year's dumplings and were all sitting around waiting for him. In her most proper tone of voice, Lü Feng-jung greeted him, "How many days do you have off?"

Even though he caught the subtle smile at the corner of her mouth, he didn't like her question. Somewhat annoyed, he lectured her in his mind, "Hmpf, don't you know steelworkers don't take vacations? If we all took a few days off, the furnaces would burn themselves to ruin. I told you a long time ago that we can only rest in shifts, didn't I?" However, he didn't let these words slip past his lips. And how could he? He couldn't exactly play the righteous role. Today wasn't even his day to take a break!

Lü Feng-jung was no dimwit. She understood as well as anybody the shift system at the steel factory, and she knew perfectly well that En-t'ai had come home without leave permission. But seeing En-t'ai in high spirits, she thought she'd tease him a bit.

She hurriedly took his outer jacket, brushed off the snow from it, and hung it up. Then she went right to the stove, stoked up the fire, and got ready to cook the dumplings. Meanwhile, En-t'ai's dad went on in a steady stream about the accomplishments of the village.

"Hai! Even if you don't have time to come home to spend New Year, you ought to take a look at our village. On New Year's—ah—that's right, we used to call it New Year's, you young folks call it Spring Festival now—well, on New Year's, we go on digging the irrigation ditches and building the reservoir. Not to mention the young folks, we old fogies pitch right in too, even your mom does her bit now and then. In all my sixty-one years, I've never seen anything like it."

The old man handed the first bowl of dumplings to his son, while taking a puff or two on his pipe. Then he went on, "In the days of land reform, we poor peasants and hired hands did our fill of hard work. But compared with these days, that was nothing! The difference is, back then, only the poor peasants and hired hands worked their tails off. Nowadays everybody's in the act. Ever since the cooperative was established, when there's work to be done everyone pitches in. This thing about taking time off at New Year's, the commune cadres thrashed it out for hours, and finally decided that we old folks should take a four-day break, the rest would go on with the ditch digging. Now take Feng-jung here for example . . .''

Presently, En-t'ai's mom walked in with a bowl of steaming dumplings, catching her husband mentioning Feng-jung, she gave him a sharp look and cut him short with these words, "Come on old man, let your son rest for a while. He must be exhausted. Let him eat in peace."

Only then did En-t'ai's dad realize that he had been talking his son's ears off. Chuckling to himself, he conceded, "Right! Right! Go ahead and eat." But in fact he couldn't suppress the fervor bubbling up in his mind. In no time at all he started up again.

"En-t'ai, people may think that the country lags behind the cities in everything, but in this case, I think the country's in the lead. Last month when you came home, you told us about your factory's fifteen-year plan to catch up to England in industry. Well, we in the countryside have done you one better. We're going to have an all-out, three-month struggle to end droughts. Now wouldn't you say we peasants are ahead of you factory workers?"

En-t'ai couldn't suppress a laugh. How could digging a few irrigation ditches and building a reservoir be in any way comparable to catching up to England in steel and other major industrial products in fifteen years? What they were aiming at was a momentous target, an all-encompassing target. And digging irrigation ditches? Why, that only involved a single village, or a cooperative at best. He wished he could explain the difference to his father, but he was afraid the old man would be too simple-minded and stubborn to understand, so he just let out a laugh.

At this, the old man's proud expression turned to one of annoyance. Looking askance at his son, he said, "So you laugh. Well, when we say three months, we mean three months. We old folks don't want a four-day holiday. We've made a secret pact. We'll take just two days off to visit a few close friends. Hmpf, you just watch and see what we peasants can do."

En-t'ai didn't want to be at loggerheads with his dad, so he gave up trying to explain anything. Instead he just went along with the old man, "Right you are, Dad. I even read in the papers that irrigation projects are going on in all the villages on both sides of the mountain pass."

When the last dumpling had been dropped into the pot to boil, the two women—En-t'ai's mom and his wife—joined the men at the table. They ladled them out of the pot as they ate. The room was filled with their jovial banter and the appetizing steam from the dumplings. Their talk went from dumplings to the supply of pork, from the strategies for meeting the demand for pork in the industrial cities to their cooperative's program for pig-husbandry, then on to the cooperative's project to increase annual production. As one might expect, En-t'ai's dad got more and more wound up as he talked. But even En-t'ai's mom and Feng-jung interjected excitedly whenever they could get a word in edgewise. An impartial observer of this scene might think that the three of them were converging on this one factory worker, trying to mobilize him to come home and join in agricultural production.

Around three a.m. En-t'ai woke up with a start: this often happened to people used to working on three shifts. But also something was weighing on En-t'ai's mind, and he couldn't sleep anymore. Suddenly he wondered to himself whether the team in the shift before his was putting out high-speed steel at this very moment. He pictured the eight o'clock shift going on without him the next morning. Who's going to run the steel samples to the lab, remove the dregs, adjust the gas valves, so on and so forth? En-t'ai made up his mind to walk the forty-odd *li* back to work. The cocky expression of that rugged young man at the train station resurfaced in his mind, "If it's just T'engaopao, why bother taking the train? By the time you've waited in line and bought the ticket, you could've walked there!" That's right! I can walk there by seven o'clock, the sun will be up then, just in time for me to go on shift.

As En-t'ai sat up and was about to get dressed, he impulsively bent down to kiss his wife on her rosy cheek. She stirred slightly. "Oh, no," En-t'ai thought with alarm: "What if she wakes up and gives me a bear hug? How will I ever get away then?" So he quietly slid back down, kept his breathing soft and even, and peered at her from under his eyelids.

Meanwhile Feng-jung had been awake for quite some time, thinking that her husband was fast asleep. She was about to sneak out of bed. But when he kissed her cheek, she dared not make a move, and just pretended to be asleep. After En-t'ai had lain there quietly for a good while, Feng-jung decided that he must have fallen asleep again. Hesitating no more, she crawled up, put on her clothes, and slipped off the platform bed. En-t'ai distinctly heard her getting off the bed, followed by a creak of the door; he concluded that she had gone to the outhouse. At this point he became anxious. "If I have to wait for her to come back, and then wait until she falls asleep again before taking off, I'll never get to the factory in time." He took a look at his watch. In the dark he couldn't make out the time too clearly, but it looked like three-thirty already. He waited and waited; what seemed like an eternity passed, but there wasn't even the shadow of Feng-jung returning. Now En-t'ai figured: "I bet she ate too many dumplings and is having a bout with loose bowels. I might as well take off before she gets back. She won't be able to catch me then even if she tries." He sat up and hurriedly put on his clothes.

As it turned out, the two old folks had been awake for quite some time too and had heard the two of them moving about. En-t'ai's mom said to her son in a muffled voice, "It's early yet. Sleep a little more."

En-t'ai didn't answer and went right on putting on his socks. His dad raised his head and spoke straight to the point, "If you're going out to look for her, don't bother. She told me beforehand. They were supposed to have a day off, but the Youth Corps kids refused to take a rest. They agreed among themselves to start work in the middle of the night. Feng-jung was afraid you'd be upset, so she told us to keep it from you. Well, she's gone already. You might as well get a little more sleep."

En-t'ai was relieved and delighted. Now he could walk straight out the door without worrying about anybody. He answered the old folks lightheartedly, "No, I've got to get back to the factory. I didn't take a leave you know."

His mom grew uneasy; she fretted, "There's no train now. There won't be a train until eight-thirty! You'd best get back to sleep."

"No, I'm walking back. I can't make it if I take the train."

En-t'ai's mom became really upset. She got up and pleaded with her husband, "It's forty-some *li* . . . and we just had a blizzard . . . and God knows there may even be wolves lurking in that wilderness."

En-t'ai had hopped off the bed, he grabbed a wooden club by the stove and gave the floor a couple of whacks. "With this in hand, I can go anywhere and be safe from wolves."

En-t'ai's dad hesitated a moment, then decided to get dressed too. In a commanding tone, he said to En-t'ai, "Son, wait a minute. I'll walk with you a ways. With two of us, no wolf would dare come near."

En-t'ai wasn't about to be held back by anybody. With a couple of strides, he bounded out the door and headed straight for the main road. Good Lord! Was it cold! It had stopped snowing, but there was at least half a foot on the ground. En-t'ai strained with each step he took, but he was already on the road back to work, he was no longer on leave without permission. This feeling of pride and relief gave him extraordinary strength, the night breeze cleared his head and invigorated his whole spirit.

Old man Yao, clutching a staff with one hand and buttoning his jacket with the other, rushed up to his son with a limp. Gasping for breath, he remonstrated, "En-t'ai, wait up, you're such an impetuous kid."

En-t'ai slowed down for a few steps, letting his dad catch up with him. When the old man had caught his breath, he started up, "There really may be wolves. Before Liberation, that's when they were really ferocious. People were hungry in those days, and the wolves were even hungrier. From our own village, one of the Li kids was dragged off by a wolf."

After they passed the outskirts of the village, the scene grew barren. There was just a large expanse with nothing but the glimmer of the moon's rays on the snow. The old man kept talking, but En-t'ai wasn't paying any attention. He had his mind on something else. Being escorted by his sixty-odd-year-old dad really bothered him. Later on when the old man had to walk back home, who would keep him company? En-t'ai made up his mind, and said in a determined tone, "Dad, you can turn back. I can walk perfectly well by myself. I walk pretty fast you know, you're really holding me back. If I have to keep in step with you, I'll be late for my shift."

The old man wasn't about to be turned back so easily. Puffing up his energy, he rejoined, "What's the big rush? I'll only walk with you through this stretch. Once you are on the highway, it'll be perfectly safe. This is my own small way of contributing to industrialization." He picked up his steps, refusing to fall behind his son.

The two were still some distance away from the Village of the Seven Peaks when sparks of light appeared in the open plains. For a minute, En-t'ai thought his eyes were deceiving him. Rubbing his eyes, he wondered to himself, "What? Have the stars fallen from the sky? Or have I walked into the sky in my sleep?" When he gathered his wits and listened, he caught sounds of hubbub and laughter through the night air. As they got closer, they could hear folks singing.

"Dad, what's going on here?" When the old man didn't answer, En-t'ai asked again, "Are they building a factory here and getting ahead in the night too?"

At this the old man could no longer hold back his proud laughter. He spoke half through his nose, "Son, I told you we had resolved to put up a three-month struggle, and you thought we were kidding? We in T'engaopao are out to do away with droughts. And the other villages? They are all out to do the same thing too! Otherwise, how would I have had the nerve to brag about us peasants getting ahead of you high and mighty factory workers?" He gave a dry cough, deliberately rubbing it in just a bit.

En-t'ai didn't need to turn his head to look at his dad. He could well imagine the complacent expression on his face. As on the previous evening, En-t'ai couldn't help laughing out loud at his dad's views, but he felt it was useless to try to explain or argue with him. When the old man heard his son laughing, he grew indignant. He wasn't one to be bested by his son; stepping up to En-t'ai he grunted, "So you laugh, huh? You think you can have a revolution without us peasants? Never!"

These words struck En-t'ai as being even more ridiculous, but he couldn't help but be touched by the staunch spirit of this old peasant stubbornly shouldering responsibility for the revolution, so he decided to make a conciliatory gesture.

"What you say, Dad, is absolutely right. To catch up to England in fifteen years, we need to have you peasants working right along with us."

Father and son trudged on in silence, each immersed in his own thoughts. They approached another village, and it too was crisscrossed with rows of lanterns and torches as if the great earth were laced with strands of golden lights. Sounds of the young folks' songs and laughter were carried by the cold wind, filling the black night with a festive, exhilarating liveliness. Instinctively En-t'ai halted to gaze at that shimmering fiery-dragon of a crowd. He remembered now that passing on the train in broad daylight the day before, he did see all along the way people hauling earth in baskets. So it was these very same people, moving mountains and filling in seas!

Suddenly, visions of the flames from his steel furnace beckoned him. The urgent, imperative, and yet confident voice of his team leader, Sun Yao-wu, sounded in his ears. Under the dim light of the stars, he stole a glance at his father, then in a gentle but spirited tone he pleaded, "Dad, go on back, with so many people working along the road, what wolf would dare come out?"

The old man squinted his eyes to gaze at the crowd in the distance. "What wolves? None of them has dared to come out in a long time. It's just that if I go home now, I'll get a scolding from your mom. She still thinks of you as a seven or eight year old. Well, okay, I'll let you go on your own; I'll go and haul a couple of basketfuls with Feng-jung and the crew. We'll see the New Year in together . . . and welcome in the God of Wealth . . . Hey, that's not a bad idea." With these words he turned and left.

En-t'ai picked up his steps and began to whistle a tune, echoing the songs from the distance. In the next moment, he flung the club aside. With both arms swinging by his side, he took brisk strides in the direction of Anshan, toward his factory.

The night was still bitter cold, but spring had surely arrived in people's hearts.

AI WU

(1908–   )

Ai Wu (born T'ang Tao-keng) was born in 1908 in the province of Szechwan. He graduated from a government-sponsored normal school in Ch'eng-tu in 1925. Then he drifted to Yunnan and Southeast Asia, maintaining himself with various jobs, sometimes as a manual laborer. He tried his hand at writing at this time. Returning to Shanghai in 1931, he began his life as a writer. The War of Resistance took him to the interior. After Liberation in 1949, he returned to Szechwan, where he taught in Chungking University and served as a moving force for the Southwest Federation of Writers. As of 1973, he was reported to be alive and well.

Ai Wu's most productive period as a writer was the decade before Liberation, during the War of Resistance and the subsequent civil war. He had demonstrated great promise in the five novels, two autobiographies, and two short-story collections published during this period. His output since Liberation has been more limited, but, more fortunate than most writers active before 1949, he escaped the rectification campaigns in the 1950s and continued to write until the Cultural Revolution. He produced numerous short stories, some of which are collected in Homeward Journey (Yeh kuei, 1958) and Going South, II (Nan-hsing-chi hsü-p'ien, 1964), and the novel Steeled and Tempered (Pai-lien ch'eng-kang, 1958), which has been acclaimed as the best "industrial" novel since 1949.

"Rain" (Yü) was published in the collection A New Home (Hsin-te chia) in 1955. It follows the formula promoted at that time, but it also demonstrates subtlety and keen insight into a young woman's psyche.

Rain

Translated by Vivian Hsu with Katherine Holmquist

"GOOD DAUGHTER, your clothes are drenched! Take them off immediately! Why are you standing there in a daze?"

Mother was impatient, worried. She couldn't refrain from helping her daughter peel off her rain-soaked clothes, half scolding, her heart reaching for the daughter.

"What's the matter? Aren't you feeling well?"

"Ma, I'm okay, I feel fine."

Hsu Kuei-ch'ing snatched her wet clothes and hung them up, then stood before the window, silent, absorbed in the sound of the rain. Lightning flashed through the black sky; the buildings opposite were revealed starkly for a moment, then were smothered by darkness. A blast of thunder; windows shivered, stammered; the eaves surrendered a splattering of rain, which beat the ground. Layers of storm sounds settled upon each other and reverberated with increasing intensity.

Mother glanced through the window and sighed: "The weather has gone wild—it's raining harder and harder." She turned a happy, thankful look to her daughter. "It's lucky you ran fast—any slower and you'd have been soaked through. Quickly, go eat. Aren't you hungry?"

Hsu Kuei-ch'ing did not answer. She stood entranced, motionless; her eyes would not be coaxed from the scene outside the window. It was as though something out there had possessed her.

Mother put Hsu Kuei-ching's dinner on the table, looked at her daughter and, somewhat perplexed, asked, "Kuei-ch'ing, what's with you today? Did something happen?"

"Ma, nothing's happened." Hsu Kuei-ch'ing hurried over and sat on the k'ang.* She picked up her bowl and chopsticks, then said ruefully, "Why does it have to rain so much?"

"Why are you concerned about the rain now? No matter how hard it rains you've made it home. Go ahead and eat."

Yet as she said this, the mother lifted her head to examine the ceiling for evidence of the rain seeping through. When she heard the rain falling harder still, she too became concerned.

"Ma, don't you realize that at this very moment there are lots of people who are still walking in the rain?"

Kuei-ch'ing was clearly disturbed. Her thin, curved eyebrows drew together and her small eyes glistened anxiously. Another terrifying roar of thunder shocked Kuei-ch'ing—she could no longer eat—and unconsciously she muttered, "Couldn't have been struck by lightning . . . could that happen?"

"Hurry up and eat. Don't worry about them, they would find shelter in people's homes."

---

*A k'ang is a raised platform that serves as a bed. It is heated by the flue from the stove running across its length underneath. The Chinese also sit on it by day to sew, read, eat, etc.

Hsu Kuei-ch'ing's face was filled with disappointment. She put down her bowl and mourned: "What homes? There are no homes on that road." Even as the words left her lips, she realized she shouldn't have uttered them. She ducked her head and began to eat vigorously.

Mother surveyed her quizzically—then, triumphant with insight, she said: "You should have asked Little Chang here to sit out the storm. Then, when the rain stopped, we'd have let her go."

"Ma, Little Chang doesn't concern me. Today is her day off so she didn't come to work." Hsu Kuei-ch'ing answered with annoyed impatience, then added, "I *am* worried about those who live in the country."

"Aiya, why be worried over nothing? There are three hundred and sixty days in a year, it's got to rain once in a while." Mother lectured: "Do a good job on the train and you'll have nothing to worry about. Sometimes you really go out of your way—you're good to everybody. You become concerned about things that you have no need to be concerned about. Other times you couldn't care less about people—you lose any sense of propriety—for instance, when Little Chang visits here and stays a bit too long, you actually become annoyed."

"Ma, don't talk about Little Chang anymore. I don't like her—all she likes to do is play cards; she has no desire to study at all." To show how much she disapproved of Little Chang, Hsu Kuei-ch'ing punctuated her remark with the shaking of chopsticks.

Hsu Kuei-ch'ing was a conductor on a commuter train that circled the city. The steel company operated the train primarily to transport workers to and from the factory. Many workers lived in villages surrounding the city and depended on the train. A few of the young workers had taken an interest in Hsu Kuei-ch'ing. The pretty and slightly aloof way in which she carried herself attracted them. Sometimes they would plan pranks to play on her. Each day she made her rounds with a ticket puncher in hand, and as she arrived beside the young workers she would say in a business-like tone, "Ticket-check." Her admirers would hand her their meal or vegetable coupons, along with very serious expressions, and act as though there were nothing amiss. Other young men would pretend to be so deep in slumber that even a clap of thunder could not awaken them. These antics annoyed Hsu Kuei-ch'ing and sometimes she would curse them in her mind, "I wish these devils would go to hell." But she never let these words escape her lips.

There was one young worker who was unlike all the others. On boarding the train he would immediately lean against the train window and, with the utmost concentration, read his book, sometimes pulling out a small notebook in which he would make calculations with a pencil. The summer sun, in its twilight position, sparkled through the fields of sorghum, slanting its rays through the train window and across his face, but his eyes did not once shift their attention from the book. In the winter, the sun would have set by the time the young worker boarded the train. He would swiftly find a seat near a light. If the light was weak, he would stand up and lean against the seat, trying to be as close to the light as possible. This young man began to attract Hsu Kuei-ch'ing's attention. Other young workers read on the train, but none pursued their reading with such unfaltering dedication.

Hsu Kuei-ch'ing's father had been a locomotive engineer. When he was afflicted with severe arthritis two years ago, he was hospitalized and, finally, sent to a convalescent home. Since then, he had received a long-term disability salary that was, according to regulations, somewhat reduced from his previous salary. Therefore, the family's financial situation had become difficult. The daughter was forced to look for work as soon as she graduated from elementary school, so that she could supplement the family's income. Hsu Kuei-ch'ing became a ticket-checker on the train. At the time, she had a good cry about not being able to go on to middle school. On her way to work in the morning, she sometimes ran into former schoolmates with handsome book-satchels slung from their shoulders. She saw them striding along willow-lined avenues toward the middle school, their faces, flushed with excitement, lifted toward the fresh-risen sun. Hsu Kuei-ch'ing's eyes would fill with tears on such occasions. Her ticket-checking job was on three alternating shifts, scheduled according to the needs of the commuting workers. The first week of the cycle, she would report to work in the morning, the next week in the afternoon, and the third week she would go to work at midnight. This made it impossible for her to attend evening school regularly, and she grieved over the lost opportunity, feeling that it was her last chance to learn. She asked the leadership to transfer her to another job, but they could not find an appropriate job for her within a short time and told her to be patient.

From the moment she took notice of him, the young worker became a symbol of perseverance for Hsu Kuei-ch'ing. When she noticed the pencil or the book in his hand, she felt a surge of courage within herself. She would reason: "Don't I have a lot of spare time myself? Why should I play cards with Little Chang and the others when I can get books to read?" She was inspired by his example, and her pocket soon bulged with books. In the evening, as she read beneath a light, she would sometimes become so exhausted that her eyes could not stay open and she would doze off.

But awaking with a start, she would see the youthful, glowing face of the young worker bathed in sunlight or lamplight, concentrating with characteristic intensity, and she would urge herself to read on, brimming with self-encouragement. She would tell herself: "He works eight hours a day in the factory, and when he boards the train he reads without resting. At this very moment, he's probably at home, and I bet he's still reading. My job is nothing more than checking tickets—that's not tiring work." By telling herself this, she was able to persevere in maintaining a consistent study schedule.

It had been a year since Hsu Kuei-ch'ing noticed the young worker for the first time, but she still didn't know his name. There was one thing about him that she was absolutely sure of: the young worker always left the train at the Willow Village Station. Yet several times she was puzzled when he rode past Willow Village and disembarked, several minutes later, at the next station, Clear Water. Each time the young worker missed his stop, Hsu Kuei-ch'ing noticed that he was so intent on mathematical calculations that he refused to put away his pencil. She decided that his village lay somewhere between the two stations. However, one day, by chance, she overheard his conversation with two other young workers as they left the train at Clear Water: "Little Ch'en, now you must walk three or four extra *li*." And he said, "It doesn't matter—I had just enough time to finish a math problem."

Hsu Kuei-ch'ing was certain then that the young worker's village was closer to the Willow Village Station. She pondered about which village it was. Four or five *li* past Willow Village Station, by a green sorghum field, there was a village surrounded by willow trees, revealing patches of white wall that could be seen from a distance. In the winter, the village bared itself and could be seen in detail from the train. Glittering snow blanketed the fields, threads of naked willow branches patterned the dark grey roof-tiles which appeared to be closer than in summer. Unconsciously, she imagined it to be a beautiful village. More people board and disembark at Clear Water that at the other stations, and the train stops there longer. From this station two broad roads forge across the fields, each flanked by rows of young willow trees. One of the roads stretches toward Willow Village.

Hsu Kuei-ch'ing stood in the doorway of the train, gazing into the distance, and fantasized about how it would feel to walk that road—it became a dream—she could imagine nothing closer to her heart than to be walking toward Willow Village. This fantasy danced through her head for an instant, then disappeared. But ever since then, she felt sorry for the young man each time she saw him leave the train at Clear Water Station: why did he make himself walk three or four extra *li* just to finish a math problem? She questioned his behavior but, at the same time, admired his determination. At times, when she reached the young man in her ticket-checking routine, she would feel an urgent desire to say: "Don't make yourself walk farther than you need to—get off at the Willow Village Station." But since they had never spoken before, she would suppress what she really wanted to say, and instead just come out with a "Your ticket please." He never uttered a word, nor did he look at her. He merely fumbled for his ticket, eyes never straying from the book, and absently held the ticket within her reach. She would clip the ticket and hand it back to him saying, "Here's your ticket," and he might extend his hand to accept it. Sometimes he was so intent on his reading that he would absent-mindedly leave his arm in the same pose that had offered the ticket, casually waiting for her to replace the punched ticket between his fingers. He simply did not see her.

This daily encounter became a source of frustration to Hsu Kuei-ch'ing. How could she turn the process of transferring a train ticket into a relationship that would accommodate sincere advice? She could not possibly suggest that he disembark at Willow Village when she was not even in a position to say "Good day." Often, after puzzling over such a small dilemma, she laughed at her own vexation and realized that the source of her anxiety was mostly her own imagination. With such laughter she dissipated the whirl of thoughts and feelings that bewildered her, and her encounters with the young worker became no more significant than the scenes that swept past the train windows: like an apple orchard, or a cottage enveloped in a haze of blossoming trees, images which flowed past the window panes, then vanished again in the wake of the train. But strangely, the young worker's glowing face, and those eyes all intent on a book still appeared to her from the farthest corner of her mind whenever she had a novel idea. Try as she would, she could not escape the image of that face, nor did she really want to.

Little Chang fanned the playing cards in her hand and called out, "Little Hsu, come play a round or two." Hsu Kuei-ch'ing, without thinking, skipped to the card table. But as she picked up the cards she began to look introspective and uncomfortable, then quickly she pushed the cards away and left the table, pulling a book from her pocket. Little Chang tried to tease her into playing, but Hsu Kuei-ch'ing would not budge.

Some mornings, she would still pass her old schoolmates with their clever bookbags, but now she would quip proudly to herself: "Now let's see who learns the most." At times like these, she discovered how bright she felt as a result of her disciplined reading, and she admired the young worker even more.

The burgeoning basic-construction program began to employ

many young village women to work in the factory. Women workers began to ride the beltway train. As she checked tickets on the day-shift, Hsu Kuei-ch'ing noticed two or three young women sitting with the young worker. They were also reading, and she observed that they too disembarked at the Willow Village Station. She gradually became aware of a keen anxiety within herself but did not know the cause of it. Sometimes she assuaged her anxiety by telling herself how ridiculous she was to be bothered by a guy she didn't even know. She would turn her back and say to herself "Why worry about someone else's business? They're not your concern." But if Hsu Kuei-ch'ing caught sight of the young worker sitting alone, without the two or three young women workers, she felt a surge of satisfaction. She smiled, without knowing why.

On the day of the storm, black clouds were gathering in the sky as the train pulled out from the factory station. Dark swirls engulfed the sun before it dipped into the horizon. Expansive fields clutched the bending, shivering trees that bordered the irrigation ditches. The sorghum grain outside the train windows was like shimmering waves on a turbulent sea. Gazing at the swollen sky outside, the workers feared that when it came time to walk home they would be drenched in a torrent. Hsu Kuei-ch'ing sensed the workers' tension as she was checking tickets. At last she came to the young worker and saw that he was spellbound by some diagrams drawn in pencil: circles, squares, an ellipse, rectangles, all manner of shapes that made him unaware of the storm threatening outside the train window. Kuei-ch'ing peeked at the diagrams with great interest, but was unable to decipher what he was doing, and moved on after checking his ticket. She wondered how the young worker could be so absorbed that he was unperturbed by the impending storm, but then calmly accepted this behavior as being part of the core of his nature.

The rain was still waiting to be released when the train reached Willow Village Station. At Clear Water Station the tempest broke loose. Workers raced from the train to the station seeking shelter. Hsu Kuei-ch'ing caught sight of the young worker, the last man to leave the train, dashing towards the station. Scolding him, she muttered to herself, "You deserve the wrath of this storm—why didn't you get off at Willow Village?"

A thick mist swathed the fields and the rain fell more densely. Sky and earth melted into a darkness that obscured even the row of poplars in front of the train station. Hsu Kuei-ch'ing decided: "It's just as well that he found refuge in the Clear Water Station: if he had left the train at Willow Village he'd be on the open road now." She no longer worried when she remembered that the summer deluge would spend itself quickly and that in a short time the young worker would be strolling home.

Clear Water is the largest station: it marks the halfway point on the beltway railroad, and trains moving in opposite directions meet there. There is a large waiting room with a candy and cigarette shop. By the time the train reached Clear Water all the home-bound workers had reached their destinations, and people traveling to work began to board the train. As the train collected workers along the route to the factory, the rain kept on at a manic pace, dashing raindrops against the train windows. Many workers boarded the train dripping with water; small puddles formed in the carriage corridors. Each time Hsu Kuei-ch'ing passed a soaked young man, her fear revived and she thought to herself, "I'm sure that young worker is almost drowned in the rain by now." She hoped that the rain would stop but it persisted.

Hsu Kuei-ch'ing's shift ended when the train arrived at the main station. She rode the trolley home. As the rain pelted the earth with renewed force, lightning shattered the sky, and explosions of thunder seemed to penetrate each crevice of the land. Obsessed with the vision of the young worker huddling within Clear Water Station, trapped by the storm, Hsu Kuei-ch'ing asked herself, "How will he sleep tonight? He may lose his senses and try to brave the storm to walk home—that would be his end." This image twisted her heart, tormenting her until, as she reached home, she felt dazed, as though she had lost her soul.

Hsu Kuei-ch'ing finished her dinner, then repeatedly ran to the window to watch the sky. She saw nothing but the dark swallowing the earth, until a jagged knife of lightning illuminated the street in eerie detail. Thunder spilled across the sky. The rain grew sharp. Now Hsu Kuei-ch'ing felt calmer: the storm had become so violent that the young worker certainly could not have attempted to walk home. He certainly was not stupid; he was certainly in the Clear Water Station at that moment waiting for the warring elements to subside.

These "certainties" lightened her heart, and she began to envisage the waiting room at Clear Water Station. The beltway train stops at Clear Water to wait for the train from the opposite direction to pass. Hsu Kuei-ch'ing often had time to run into the station to see what new political posters had appeared on the walls. Consequently, she was familiar with the layout, of the station. She imagined the young worker sitting beside the glass counter, reading in the light of the shop, and occasionally munching on a roll, perhaps stopping to make diagrams with a pencil. Hsu Kuei-ch'ing began to smile at this vignette—she thought he must be an amusing sight, studying with absolute concentration as he absent-mindedly chomped on the roll. Swiftly Hsu Kuei-ch'ing pocketed her smile; pulling out from her drawer volume one of the Middle School literature books, she spread it out on the table and began to read.

Mother was upset to see her getting ready to sit up late and said, "You've been through a lot today, you should go to bed early tonight."

Hsu Kuei-ch'ing kept reading as she replied, "I must use every spare minute to read—some people even study in the train station—I would be ashamed to give up now after seeing their example."

This reply confused Mother, who asked, "Who in the train station are you talking about?"

Hsu Kuei-ch'ing felt her face swelling hot and red, she lowered her head farther into her book. Mother waited for her to explain herself, but the daughter only continued reading, lost in concentration. Mother decided not to disturb her, and took out her needlework.

The tempest continued to thunder and howl outside the window.

HSI JUNG

(1923-)

*Hsi Jung was born in the province of Shansi. As a teenager he joined
the communist wing of the War of Resistance against Japan, serving as a
"cultural" worker. He became nationally known in 1949, the year of
Liberation, with the publication of the novel* Heroes of Lüliang
(Lüliang yinghsiung chuan), *written with his fellow provincial Ma
Feng. Since Liberation he has been associated with the Shansi Federation
of Writers and Artists, serving as the editor of that association's literary
journal* Sparks Monthly (Huo-hua yüeh-k'an) *since 1956. In 1957, he
again collaborated with Ma Feng and produced the movie script* The
Unextinguishable Flame (P'u-pu-mie-de huo-yen). *He has to his
credit three collections of short stories and several others published in the
journal* People's Literature (Jen-min wen-hsüeh). *During the Cultural
Revolution, Hsi Jung experienced some setback when he was criticized
for "portraying middle characters."*

"Corduroy" (Teng-hsin-jung), originally published in People's Literature *in 1961, portrays a woman's struggle between loyalty to her
family and loyalty to the state.*

Corduroy

Translated by Julia Fitzgerald and Vivian Hsu

I

ACCOUNTANT MA SHOU-JEN was at his desk working away at his
accounts. There was a sound at the door; then someone tiptoed up
to his desk. "He's not here?" a woman's voice asked.

Accountant Ma raised his head and pushed the heavy, thick-
lensed glasses up to the bridge of his nose. Ah, it was Aunt Ch'ien,
the Old Cooperative Chief's wife. She was probably just looking for
her husband, he thought, and, going back to his accounts, he replied: "That man never sits still. Who knows where he may have
run off to now."

He worked for a few minutes more finishing up his accounts; then he closed the account book and said, "So what's up?"

Aunt Ch'ien took a quick, furtive glance around the room. No one there. Gleefully, her tone confidential, she leaned forward across the desk: "Did you know the Supplies Coop has just gotten in some red corduroy cloth! It's just the most wonderful corduroy, heavy and thick as a rug; I held it in my hand between my two fingers," she went on excitedly. "I've never seen such corduroy. And what a dazzling red! I've just got to get several feet of it."

Under this deluge of enthusiasm, Accountant Ma teased, "Well my goodness, Auntie! Who would have suspected? A respectable old woman like you—still young enough yet to be fashionable, is that it? Could you be looking for a husband or something?"

"You old devil!" Aunt Ch'ien broke into a great, good-humored laugh. "It's my *son*, Yü-pao, who's looking for a wife. And *I'm* going to sew up some clothes for Yü-pao's little fiancee. You know all about Yü-pao's little romance, don't you Uncle? With Tung-hua, this year's model pig-raiser? They were both very quiet about it. And she's quite a girl, quite a girl. If you want to talk about figures, she has got a *figure*. If you want to talk about beautiful faces, well just take a look at hers. But imagine! We didn't send her a single penny of dowry money and she's *still* willing to follow our son into marriage.

"But, you ask, what about the duties of a parent in this affair? Of course we don't need to follow old customs anymore. But we can't be so stingy that we wouldn't spend a penny on our own son's marriage. Why just the other day I ran into Tung-hua's mother. We got to talking. And then Tung-hua's mother let slip a valuable bit of information: that young lady *loves* red corduroy! Now, can you imagine, what should arrive at the Supplies Coop only today but this very commodity! Well I just have to get a piece of it and sew up a pair of trousers or a jacket for that young lady. After all, I understand my position as mother-in-law, and no one could ever accuse me of neglecting my proper obligations.

"And," she continued, though poor Accountant Ma had attempted quite a few times to interrupt, each time succeeding only in being swamped by her flood of excited words: "And you see, the timing is just perfect too! On the twenty-eighth of the third month, the Temple Fair is being held. What better occasion for her to show off a new outfit!"

The way she talked sounded like a frying pan full of hot beans. Pip pop! pip pip pop! On and on . . . he couldn't get a word in edgewise.

"Well, that's all very interesting," he finally asked, "but I still don't understand what you want the Old Chief for."

"Well, *you* should understand this problem of mine; you're an accountant. If you don't have any money, no matter how good the stuff is, the Supplies Coop isn't going to let you have it for nothing, right?"

Accountant Ma finally understood what she came for. He opened the account book and glanced into it. Then he looked up, puzzled. "What about that hundred and ten dollars your family got last year?"

"That's been deposited in the Savings and Trust Cooperative. And you know how the commune's all caught up with capital investment now—that old man of mine won't let me take out a penny. And he has the checkbook with him all the time, so there's nothing I can do . . . Ay!" Auntie Ch'ien gave a long sigh.

"Doesn't he know Yü-pao's planning to get married?"

"Him? Hah! No, when it comes to his family, he practices total 'laissez faire'. He never ever thinks about his own family. The only thing that matters to him is his precious commune. It's commune this and commune that. It's the only thing that comes out of his mouth! 'This year the commune *must* buy a water pump' and 'soon we'll have to get some chemical fertilizer.' But when *I* ask to buy this little something, he won't even give me a penny. When I made the suggestion that we take out some of the savings, what do you think he said? 'No, the term isn't up. You can't take any out.'"

"He won't let you take it out? Then you should lock up the door at night and not let him come home," Accountant Ma teased.

Auntie Ch'ien was serious. "Not even that will work! He doesn't even come home at night anymore, not for the past two weeks. I can't even catch his shadow to talk with. The other day he came home to get his cotton-padded jacket. I asked him whether we couldn't borrow a few dollars from the commune. He just pulled a tight face and said, 'No, the commune has a regulation. Before pay-days, no one is allowed to borrow or draw advances.' Now I ask you Uncle, is that the truth? Are the commune regulations really as strict as all that?"

"That's the way the system's been set up. But you know, when important things come up, we have to be flexible too."

"That's right; for important things we have to be flexible," Aunt Ch'ien went on. "But my husband is so unreasonable, so difficult—everyone in the village agrees . . . he's the most difficult cadre member in the commune to get past. You have something that involves a tiny sum of money—nothing to get worried about, really—and he thinks it's as huge as a millstone! If he had *your* job, handling money all day long, why, he'd be so anxious and tense he'd hang himself!"

The accountant was never one to turn a deaf ear to flattery. Nothing pleased him more than being high up on a pedestal. So whether Auntie Ch'ien had come for that purpose, to give him a good buttering up; or whether she had come just to fill his ear with her marital complaints; or whether, in fact she truly admired the way Accountant Ma handled himself and his duties in the world—it did not really matter to the accountant. The flattery was all he heard, and it made him feel good all over.

"Well," he said, "That big brother in your household, that husband of yours—he's all right. He's all right—but he's just too niggardly about money. And he's so serious! And of course it's terrible the way he's so stingy and restrictive with you. He's pressed me between the boards many a time, too. The commune gets a little bit of money, and he can't get it off his mind. What's he so uptight about? When I worked in Tientsin for a big business there I handled eight hundred to a thousand dollars *in cash* a day and even then I was more tranquil than he is now. But Auntie, you can put your mind at rest. This little problem is no problem at all!"

Auntie Ch'ien beamed. "I *knew* you could handle this." After she had praised Accountant Ma, she saw him fumble with the keys to his drawer. Was he getting the money out for her? She waited expectantly. But all he did was take his account book, place it in the drawer, and lock it back up.

"About that money," he said, "I'll see that you get it. But I'll have to talk to the Chief first."

"What for?" Auntie Ch'ien frowned. "His job is commune leader, not accountant. He's got nothing to do with money."

"That's the rule," the accountant replied. "The resolution of the commune council was: if commune members have emergencies or run into difficulties they didn't expect, and they need to take out a loan, it's got to be approved first by the chairman."

"So where is he?"

"Right now he's probably at the horse stable. Better go quick or you'll miss him—he'll have gone to the fields."

Aunt Ch'ien seemed reluctant to leave. She sat for awhile on the bench without moving, her eyes on Accountant Ma. Finally, she said, "Uncle, it's just no use for me to talk to him. Every time I open my mouth he tells me my thoughts are backward. But you're a cadre member, and you're a leader in the commune. You've got real authority in our community, and I know you can work this matter out for me. It will probably be some trouble for you, but don't think I'm ungrateful, oh no! When my son Yü-pao gets married, *you'll* take the seat of honor. And there'll be a few extra cups for you to drink as well."

Accountant Ma was on the spot. If he didn't go, it would seem as if he didn't have the power to deal with this little problem. But if he did go . . . well, he knew the old Chief's temperament and he was reluctant to get in a tangle with him. He could talk with the old Chief about some things, but when it came to money, there was no one who could block a request more skillfully than he.

But, maybe this was a different situation. Maybe there was a chance. Because this wasn't just any old commune member asking for a loan, this was the Chief's own wife. And the cloth was for the soon-to-be wife of the Chief's own cherished son. So maybe he wouldn't be so stubborn, maybe not in this case.

Weighing all this, Accountant Ma agreed to give Auntie Ch'ien's request a try. He took off his heavy glasses, put them in a box, lit up a cigarette, and went to look for the old Cooperative Chief.

II

The old Chief Ch'ien Chü-fu was already over fifty, but the years had not slowed him down. His energy and high spirits flourished magnificently. He was not an educated man—he knew only a few characters and had been a hired hand most of his life. His memory, however, was exceptional, and no detail of the thousands he dealt with daily ever slipped his mind.

He had joined the Communist Party in the year of the Land Reform. It was only then—so he told people—that he began to do revolutionary work. After organizing the mutual-aid team, the people elected him to be the team's leader. The team soon became a low-level agricultural cooperative, then a high-level cooperative. In all these changes, Ch'ien again and again accepted the responsibility of being leader. Then, in 1958, when the People's Commune was formed, he was elected the district's Party Branch Secretary and concurrently, the chairman of the Commune. But the people still fondly called him the old Cooperative Chief.

He was not a great orator; his public speeches were awkward, but in the fields, when he was talking heart to heart with his fellows, everyone listened. Aphorisms and folk wisdom seasoned his talk. Every other sentence began with "Well people often say . . . " or "You know, as the saying goes . . . " His favorite sayings were: "Well you know what people say—if you want to be full, eat plain food. If you want to be warm, wear coarse cloth." and also, "Like they say, wealth grows from little bits and pieces. Best be frugal, son," or "As the saying goes, the earth is like a board from which one can reap gold. If you are hardworking and diligent, the earth will not be lazy." These he used to inspire the people of the commune to follow the directives and to work with patience and enthusiasm for the commune and themselves, to be frugal and disciplined.

But in a commune of a hundred people, there will be a hundred personalities, and in spite of the Chief's teaching, there were small problems, There was, for example, the accountant Ma. It had always been Accountant Ma's opinion that the Cooperative Chief was timid in his leadership and had no poise or flair. The very sound of the Chief's habitual "as the saying goes . . ." made the accountant throw up his hands in disgust. "Forget it!" he would say to the old Chief, "Forget it! You and your sayings! All you know how to do is to recite dusty old proverbs. I think you must have been poor to the point of starvation in the past. Now you've got your life turned around and have even become the commune Chief, but everywhere you go, you still carry this poverty-stricken cloud around you."

They seemed like harsh words, but the old Chief wasn't offended. Later, however, there were two misdemeanors on the part of Accountant Ma that really roused the leader's anger. Fortunately, in both of these cases, Accountant Ma finally did listen to the old Chief.

The first incident concerned an irrigation project. In the spring of 1957, in a cadres' meeting, someone had suggested that, as an irrigation method, they fill in all the wells that were currently being used—innumerable small wells—and in their place, dig a row of deeper, larger, more efficient wells near the major water source. Pumps would be installed, a large drainage ditch would be dug, and, using this system, all the cultivated land could be irrigated.

"Not a bad plan," the old Chief had replied, "not bad at all. But there's one factor we all have to keep in mind. Machinery costs money. It's true, it's true. The production of the cooperative has been increasing yearly; it's something to be proud of. But still, we don't have much capital. If we use it all to buy machinery, nothing's going to be left for our other investments, our other projects. "And," the Chief continued, "think of how many cooperatives there are in the country. If every one of them went out and bought themselves heavy machinery, would there be enough to go around? And if there were enough machines would there be enough technicians?" These were practical, pragmatic questions. But several of the younger cadre members did not agree. In their opinion, the situation demanded bold, decisive action, and, as usual, the Chief was being slow, over-cautious, backward.

In a cleverly sarcastic tone, Accountant Ma stood up and addressed the Chief. "Big brother," he said, "you've been around for a long time. You've seen a lot. Now tell me, have you ever, in your whole life, seen a situation where it is possible to accomplish something without spending a single cent?"

There was more debate. The old Chief put forward reason after reason why it was impractical to buy the machinery. No one at the meeting was being receptive. So in the end he had no choice but to shrug his shoulders and say "OK. So let's give it a try."

The next day, Accountant Ma went to the bank, took out a substantial loan, got on a cart, and went himself to the capital of the province to purchase the machinery. Back at the homefront, people were ready to begin work, to fill up the old wells and dig the drainage ditch. But the old Chief stopped them with an aphorism. "The saying goes," he said, "those who are impatient never get to eat soft rice. And in doing things, you know, you've got to make sure you leave a footprint with each step you take. You can't work on thin air. Let's not be hasty, hmmm? Why don't we just wait until Accountant Ma drives up the road with those machines before we start filling the wells. Because it only takes one man-day of work to fill up a well. But to dig a new one? nine, ten, even eleven man-days."

Despite his words of caution, several people began filling the old wells. Then Accountant Ma returned with his news: at present, there weren't enough machines to fill the demand; the supplier was out of stock.

"It's not eating that leads to poverty," was the old Chief's reply, "and it's not putting clothes on your backs that leads to poverty. It's poor planning that leads to poverty. It's poor planning, . . . poor planning leads to poverty. Or so the saying goes: It's not enough just to look in front of yourself. You've got to look to the right, to the left, behind, beyond—you've got to use your eyes and look around. This is called planning."

So the wells that had been filled in were dug out again, and, under the old Chief's direction, ten more new wells were dug. It was not a program of total irrigation; nevertheless, the amount of land that was under irrigation that year had increased by one-third over the previous year.

The second matter over which Accountant Ma and the old Chief nearly came to blows was the purchase of office furnishings. Over the past several years, the economy of the commune had been progressively improving. Production was increasing, they had received awards and pennants and had been mentioned in the newspapers. They had acquired quite a reputation. And yet, the commune office was still squeezed into the hall of the Dragon King Temple. When the party leadership arrived for business or inspections, there was nowhere for them to sit. They were offered water in nothing better than old ceramic bowls. This pained Accountant Ma; it embarrassed him to have to receive guests with such miserable hospitality and so little splendor.

He began attempting to remedy the situation. Where there was paper covering a window in the office, he decided glass must be installed. And a thick slab of glass for the desk top too. And on the glass-topped desk, a brush container, an ink bottle, a bowl to hold the wet sponge, stamp pads in a variety of colors, a box of paper clips, a container of tacks. And, for those long evenings in which there was some work to be done, a kerosene lamp was needed, a kerosene lamp on a stand, with a lampshade. On the four walls there would have to be hanging framed portraits, and of course a tea service would have to be purchased. Carefully, Accountant Ma considered all these details and then drew up a list. When it was complete, he handed it to the old Chief for approval.

The old Chief held the list before him for a long time, his eyebrows involuntarily twitched, but still smiling, he asked, "Do we really need all this?"

"We certainly do," the accountant replied. "We've needed them for a long time. You should go look at the other communes' offices. They really look like something. You step in and you *know* you're in an office," he said enviously.

"Are offices the same as dumplings you sell on the corner, that there has to be a standard model?"

The old Chief's question put the accountant on the spot, but he also could not help but laugh. The old Chief continued, "So, you think other people's offices are better than ours. *I* think ours is all right. You know, Secretary Lü of the County Party Committee tells the story of Chairman Mao during the campaigns—he had to use his own knees for a desk. He would write documents, send out orders, and even without a desk, didn't he still defeat the enemy? Now Ma, you know the saying, 'Eat according to what food is available; cut your clothes according to the measurement of your body'. You're the one in charge of the money; you should know how much capital we have. You can't just gawk at the way other people are doing things and imitate them like a monkey."

Accountant Ma did not move. The disappointment was apparent on his face. He said nothing, unable to find an argument to counter the old Chief. But of the entire list he had drawn up, to be denied every single one! He could not be more dissatisfied. In a tone of both complaint and resentment, he said, "You want the horse to run well, but you won't feed him even a handful of grass. Who is it, when every three months the members get their wages, who is it has to burn the midnight oil calculating and recording? Who is it has to suffer then? I do. If I light the wick low on that old, useless kerosene lamp, I can't see a thing; and if I light the wick high, I get a headache from the smoke. So all I ask for is a kerosene lamp with a glass cover, and what do I get instead? A big long lecture."

Seeing how unhappy the accountant was, the old Chief tried to reason with him: "Comrade, comrade, we'll buy what we have to buy. All I'm saying is that when we spend, we should keep frugality in mind. I'm not objecting to you buying a lamp with a shade, not at all.'

So, since there was no objection, Accountant Ma sent someone off to the city to buy a new kerosene lamp, one with a glass shade. When it arrived, he lit it with great joy. It was *much* brighter than the other! he noted with satisfaction, and wrapped another piece of white paper around it.

In the evenings, then, in his free time, Accountant Ma took to reading his newspaper under the pure snowy light of that lampshade. Other times he'd call in a few friends and they'd have a card game. He was having a marvelous time.

One night, however, Accountant Ma had come into the office and was about to light the lamp, when he noticed the lampshade was missing. Ma, grumbling and cursing, began searching about the room, when the door opened and someone came in. "Why haven't you lit the lamp?" a voice asked. Ma looked up and saw the old Chief.

Ma said hurriedly, "The one we bought only a few days ago . . ."

The old Chief laughed. "No, nobody's broken it. I just took it and hung it on the wall. Our capital is too small; we can't afford to support that hungry god of a lamp."

"Well, we may as well not light any lamp at night then," Ma replied angrily.

"Now now," the old Chief said placidly. "Of course the lamp has to be lit at night. But the way you've been lighting it, it blazes brighter than the sun. I would think you'd be blinded by it. And besides, you only used less than an ounce of kerosene before; but now, to keep your sun blazing, you've been feeding him more than *twice* that, more than two ounces of kerosene a night. Figure that up in the long run, and you've got quite a supply of kerosene frivolously gone up in smoke. Now if you've really got something to do, go ahead. Use the lamp with the shade. But if there's no business —light the small lamp."

From that moment on, the glass lampshade hung on the wall. Whether from spite, or merely because he found it too troublesome to take down, Accountant Ma let the shade hang there gathering dust, and he refused to touch it, even when doing accounts late into the night.

III

The courtyard of the Animal Husbandry Team seemed unusually vast and deserted. The animals had all been taken out to the fields to work. Under the eaves of the horse stable, on the west side, sat the old Chief.

He was repairing saddles, taking bits of cotton to work with from a loose pile on one side of him; and while he worked, he talked with members of the Animal Husbandry Team. "Whenever you use a piece of equipment," he was saying, "always take a good look at it first. Examine it from top to bottom, and underneath as well. If it's broken, fix it. This way, the animals don't get hurt from accidents, the equipment doesn't get ruined. Take a look at this saddle, for example. It's unbalanced. Put it on a horse, ride him for a day, and what does the poor beast end up with? A bruised shoulder. But does the horse speak up? Tell you his shoulder hurts? No. So you pay no attention to what you do to him; you think you can do anything. It doesn't hurt you, that bruised shoulder. But Yu-hsi," he went on, directing his lecture toward the head of the Animal Husbandry Team, "if I gave you a tight pair of boots and made you walk around in them all day, I think you'd yell soon enough."

"I suggested a long time ago," Yu-hsi replied self-righteously, "that we buy some new saddles. But Accountant Ma refused us the money."

The old Chief laughed, a dry, cold laugh. "Oh, that's just dandy. Now you've all learned how to open your mouths and eat. And to stick out your hands and ask for money. As soon as the first paint chips or the first thread breaks, you're thrown into helplessness and all you know how to do is buy a new one. You just take the lazy man's path and ask for the money to buy a new one.

"Have you ever given any thought to the question of where the commune's money comes from? Do we print our own? Or maybe we're a bank? No! we don't have much money at all. And if we grab those few dollars in both our fists and toss them extravagantly into the wind, how are we going to manage production? You know the saying, 'Even the household with ten thousand strings of cash still has to make patches half the time'. When you guys worked for yourselves, you could make a saddle last ten, twenty years. But now? Saddles fall in pieces in five, in *three* years. The spirit of living collectively is not a lot of big talk at big meetings. Collective living is how we deal day to day with concrete details."

Yu-hsi and the two other Animal Husbandry Team members, shamefacedly joined in on the saddle repairs.

Two women, who had been waiting on the side for quite a while, now glanced at one another as if to say, "look at him! the minute he starts working, he forgets everything."

"Ay! Old Chief," the younger of the two women began, plaintively, "Can we resolve the difficulty I brought up with you?"

The other one, a woman of about fifty, also started in, "Old in-law! And what about me? The Temple Fair is almost here; my daughter needs a new pair of trousers. And the Supplies Coopera-tive has just gotten in a shipment of corduroy. Can you see to it that I get an advance of a few dollars?"

"That's right! A shipment of corduroy has arrived! In every color of the rainbow; and sturdy, quality-made cloth. A girl in a jacket or in trousers made of this cloth would be as beautiful as a bird."

No one noticed Accountant Ma's entry into the scene. By the time anyone noticed him, he was already there, standing next to the two women. As soon as he heard Tung-hua's mother mention the cor-duroy, he quickly wedged himself in for his own request. If the old Chief listened to her, then his request would be granted too, and his promise to Aunt Ch'ien would be fulfilled.

Raising his head, the old Chief caught sight of Accountant Ma. "Ah, you've come in the nick of time. Go, give her an advance of twenty dollars."

"Give *me* twenty dollars?" Tung-hua's mother said, flustered and excited.

"Hold your horses, in-law!" the old Cooperative Chief laughed. "Why are you in such a hurry? You and I have to talk a little more about this matter you've brought up. The twenty dollars is for Ts'ui-hsiang to take her child to see a doctor in the city. But for a piece of corduroy . . . well, I'm sorry, but your need really isn't urgent enough."

"Well that's just great," the woman grumbled. "You have to fall sick before you're allowed any money around here, and those of us who are unfortunate enough to be healthy . . . we go away empty-handed."

The old Chief's voice was quiet and patient. "It was announced very clearly at the last general meeting that it was not possible for anyone to borrow money before the pay date. It was a resolution agreed on by everyone. Weren't you there? Didn't you agree to it too?"

Tung-hua's mother persisted obstinately. "Those meetings are all a lot of talk. We're a big commune; if I borrow a few dollars, no one's going to feel it."

"If that's the case," the old Chief replied, "Shall I give money to everyone that comes to me and requests it? Anyway, about the Temple Fair—if everyone's clothes are clean and their rear ends aren't hanging out, I think that's good enough."

"Well listen to you! We're talking about young girls—not rough unmannered hayseeds like you." She did not disguise her con-tempt.

"My hayseed appearance may not be real pleasing to you, and I apologize for it, but I sure haven't let anyone go hungry or bare-assed. Take a look at the accounts at the Savings and Trust Coop. Every single family's got eighty to a hundred dollars."

"Well I don't even have a dollar saved."

"You've let your family's entire hundred and ten dollars slip away already?"

"My old man's got it locked away. He says he's going to buy a Flying Pigeon bicycle."

"You people!" the Chief said in despair. "You people are like a carpenter's axe—you know how to chop on only one side. You sure know how to handle your own money—buy yourselves a brand-name bike, got it all planned out. But when it's the commune's money, you suddenly get easy and careless. Borrow a little here and there. There's plenty where that came from . . . No, no, when we manage the commune's money, we've got to be just as careful. Why don't you use some of the money you're saving up for the bike to buy the corduroy?" The old Chief gave the woman a sly glance.

"If we use that money we won't be able to buy the bike!" the woman answered seriously.

"Well now, the commune has two big necessities on its list: a water wheel and fertilizers. They're as precious to us as your Flying Pigeon is to you. Now do you think we should use up all our money?"

She was driven into a corner and could think of nothing to reply. She stood at a loss for a moment; then, catching sight of Accountant Ma standing in the corner, she appealed to him. "Old Ma, what do you say? What can I do?"

Ma had listened to all the arguments, and his first impulse was to reply with two simple words: "Can't do." But he was afraid of spoiling his own case, and then he wouldn't be able to keep his promise to Aunt Ch'ien. So he hedged, hesitated, and smiled. "Well maybe we should look into it."

"Wonderful, that's just wonderful," Tung-hua's mother said irritably. "You two look into it. Fine." And she left.

The old Chief stood up too. He brushed the dirt from his pants and shook his head. "Concepts, concepts," he said wearily. "There's nothing harder than to try and reform concepts." He was moving toward the door of the horse stall with his purposeful, long-legged stride, and was nearly out when he heard Accountant Ma calling behind him. He waited. "There something on your mind?"

Accountant Ma had been waiting to be alone with the old Chief to bring up the business of Auntie Ch'ien; but now suddenly his heart warned him it wasn't the moment, so, deftly, he changed directions and said: "Oh nothing much. Just that the commune called and wanted to know how many catties of chemical fertilizer we wanted."

The Chief, surprised, said, "Didn't we do that chart a long time ago, and send it on? Three thousand catties."

"That's right, that's right," Ma answered sheepishly. "I don't know why I asked." He had only made up that little white lie, but when he saw the Chief was taking the question seriously, he dropped it, and turned to leave.

"Ay!" the Chief caught him by the shoulder and stopped him. "Go tell the Savings and Trust Cooperative to pay out the money for the fertilizer today. Tomorrow we'll send around some carts to go collect it."

"Fine, fine," Accountant Ma was afraid the Chief was going to start asking questions, so hurriedly he stepped out the stable door.

IV

Aunt Ch'ien was still there, in his office, waiting, when he returned. He had been gone a long time. "Well," she asked anxiously, as soon as he stepped in the door, "yes or no?"

What answer could he give her? That the Chief had said OK? That lie would force him into handing over the money, against the rules, without the required authorization. Not a risk the acountant wished to take. But he couldn't tell her that the Chief had refused the loan either. In the first place, he hadn't even raised the issue with the old Chief, so he couldn't know if the Chief would have approved. And second, to admit he had failed would have made him look impotent. So the accountant just answered evasively, "The old Chief will have to look into it."

"Look into it with whom?" Aunt Ch'ien asked again, nagging him, he thought, worse than a horsefly.

Accountant Ma shook his head. "Who knows, who knows?"

"Well, you're the accountant; can't he look into it with *you*? This is pitiful," she said contemptuously. She would not stop complaining. "That old bag of ours, that backward old fuddy-duddy—you can't teach *him* any new tricks. His thinking is about as lively as the thinking of a dead grey rock. He's the *Chief* in this commune. Shouldn't he have enough authority to deal with family matters without having to worry that someone might object? But you're someone in charge too, Ma; why can't *you* make decisons?"

Aunt Ch'ien had unsettled Accountant Ma. He now became agitated and critical toward the strict, sober, inhuman way the old

Chief insisted on doing business. He was uneasy too at his own recent cowardice; feeling a few pangs of regret, he began to reason that, after all, it was a matter of *marriage*, not simply money, this affair over the corduroy. It was domestic trouble Aunt Ch'ien was asking his help in. And she was the one in the right, the accountant reasoned, her arguments were sound; it was her husband's attitude that was narrow and unjust. So, putting on an easy, confident tone, he said, "Aunt, set your mind at ease. The loan's yours and I'll take full responsibility. So how much do you need?"

She was not slow to see that she had persuaded him. She grew animated. "Oh not much at all, not much at all. Certainly not eighty or a hundred dollars, no, no. Just enough to cut a nice swatch of cloth."

The accountant turned the lock, pulled the drawer open, and took out a stack of bills. But as his hands nimbly flew through the bills, counting them out, doubts began to assail him. Auntie Ch'ien's request was clearly worthy; but the old Chief had not been consulted. That was a pitfall, and could be quite a nasty one too. Ma counted and re-counted the money. Finally he put it in her hands, but as she was just about to disappear gratefully out the door, Ma, in haste called out: "Aunt, I'm giving you this loan, but it would be better if nothing were said to the old Chief. Do you understand my meaning?" he asked uneasily. "It's a matter just between you and me?"

She nodded, she understood well. Her face was jubilant. "Rest easy, Accountant," she said. "I won't sell you out." Then she turned and went directly to the Supplies Cooperative.

Even before she got to the counter, she saw the sales clerk pulling out that precious bolt of red. He was talking with some woman and showing her the cloth. It was Tung-hua's mother.

"Ah, it's you, in-law!" Aunt Ch'ien cried in a warm, cheery voice. "So you've come to cut a piece of cloth too—great stuff isn't it? I've never *seen* such a dazzling red . . . Wouldn't it just look charming on a young girl? Trousers, or a jacket . . ."

Tung-hua's mother, nodding, asked, "And what did you come to buy?"

"Me? Why, several feet of the corduroy."

"For whom?"

"Guess." Aunt Ch'ien's heart danced with delight. Then she leaned toward Tung-hua's mother's ear and said in a low voice, "Our daughter's got a small frame: I think eight feet should be enough, don't you?" She didn't wait for an answer. "Seven feet wouldn't quite cover—she *has* gotten a little plump. Eight feet should do it. Better to have more than not enough. Good, sturdy fabric, isn't it? I'll bet it lasts more than a year without fraying. She could wear it while she's living with you, and then, when she comes to live under my roof—why, she'll *still* be wearing it!" Aunt Ch'ien stretched her wit to appear as generous as possible in front of her future in-law.

Tung hua's mother did not, at first, quite understand who this young girl was that Aunt Ch'ien was referring to. But as it gradually dawned on her, she became somewhat peeved. "Well, if I had only known," she was thinking, "that this was in my future in-law's head, I wouldn't have had to go through all that teeth-grinding with the old Chief today." So she too, in a tone of extravagant generosity, said: "Aunt, you are just too kind. She hasn't crossed over to your house yet; why worry your head about her? And young people to-day, why, they spend all their time in the fields falling into mud and water and calling it manual labor. They can't wear beautiful clothes—they'd ruin them. Why bother cutting such fine cloth for Tung-hua?"

"Oh, just listen to you!" Aunt Ch'ien pushed her future in-law playfully. Then, taking hold of her arm, she pulled her close to herself again. "Your daughter has every right to wear whatever she chooses, even if it were a dragon robe. She's a model worker; look how many work days she earns in a year! She's going to be attending conferences, visiting the County Seat—she's going to have to dress properly. If she's not decent, we'll both lose face."

This exchange of course did not displease either of them; still Tung-hua's mother felt it necessary to hide her jubilation and pride in her daughter and continue her pretense of discontent a while longer. "Young people just aren't the same these days," she said. "Good food, elegant clothes—they claim none of this is important to them. All they talk about is frugality, building socialism. Tung-hua is even behaving as if she were already drinking water out of the same vat as the old Chief, as if she had already crossed over into your household!"

"Aiii!" Aunt Ch'ien leaned her head to the side in a gesture of helplessness. "The young people today! They're all like that. My own son, Yü-pao, sends letters home from the army criticizing me! You can just imagine how angry it makes me—someone you've given life to, treating you like that! But of course he's your flesh and blood, so your heart softens. But this building up socialism—I think it's the young people's business entirely. We old people don't have to bother our heads about it. But what we *do* have to do is to stick together and keep our traditions alive, don't you think?

"Now, I've had this little plan in my mind for a long time, but there was never any cloth in the Supplies Cooperative. The cloth finally comes—and I don't have any money. I have to run here and there dealing with this person and reasoning with that one—oh what an exhausting day I've had!—before I finally get together the money. So here I am at last, with the goods in my hand."

"Where did you manage to get the money from?" Tung-hua's mother asked sympathetically, remembering all the frustration and irritation she had had to suffer in her pursuit of a loan.

The question cast Aunt Ch'ien into a gloom again. She thought with dissatisfaction about the old husband she was saddled with. "He put our entire bonus under lock and key in the Savings Bank and wouldn't let me touch a penny of it. So I have to go begging all over the commune. He really drives me mad!"

"I couldn't agree with you more. That old bag of yours is terrible! He doesn't recognize any of his responsibilities to his relatives or family." Tung-hua's mother gave the whole angry report of her attempt in the afternoon to get the old Chief's permission to borrow money.

The attack alarmed Aunt Ch'ien. Would the discontent of Tung-hua's mother affect her son's marriage? Aunt Ch'ien hurriedly began to defend her husband: "He's just getting old lately—too old to manage all the affairs of the commune. I've been telling him to quit for months. But everyone says he's a good leader and they support him, so he won't step down.

"But everything is getting out of hand these days. There are so many rules! The commune votes in more and more rules! All that trouble you had today—it was because of those silly rules. *I* couldn't even get around them. If it wasn't for Accountant Ma, I would never have been able to get this piece of cloth cut . . ." Suddenly, Aunt Ch'ien caught her tongue. Her secret with Accountant Ma had almost slipped out! She wavered a moment more, then could not resist. She leaned toward Tung-hua's mother's ear. "I'm really not supposed to tell anyone. Accountant Ma is afraid someone might report us," she whispered. "But it's all right to keep it in the family. I know I can trust you."

Tung-hua's mother was a little upset. So the old Chief had approved his own wife's loan, she thought mistakenly, and had turned her down! But of course she could say nothing to Aunt Ch'ien's face. So she nodded once or twice and smiled a bright but bland smile. "That's very nice," she said. "I myself was thinking of making Tung-hua an outfit—now you've saved me the trouble!"

The sales clerk was done with all the paperwork. Now he handed the bolt of cloth to Aunt Ch'ien. Aunt Ch'ien took the soft material into her arms as if it were a newborn baby. "Look at this color!" she said reverently. "It's so bright it hurts your eyes!" She could not find enough words of praise. "Feel how thick it is. Take it," she said generously, thrusting the cloth at Tung-hua's mother. "Take it home to your daughter."

"Me? Oh no, you should give it to her yourself. After all, she should understand that it is her mother-in-law and no one else who's giving her this fine gift."

"You're right, you're right! You think of everything. Well, send her around to see us soon, then." And, full of the animated chatter of old ladies, the two women left the Supplies Coop.

V

Aunt Ch'ien had never been very good at keeping things to herself. She could not stop thinking about what a rare and beautiful piece of cloth she had come into possession of; she could not stop marveling over its hue and texture. And she could not keep from sharing her happiness. By afternoon, everyone in the neighborhood had heard about the daughter-in-law, and the jacket, and the bright red cloth.

In the evening, the old Chief broke off work at an unusually early hour and came home. He seemed delighted at something too. He came into the center of the room, saying, "Great day, great day! At last this thing's worked out."

It was an easy leap for Aunt Ch'ien to assume he had heard about her red cloth and her good fortune; an even easier leap to assume this was why he was in such good spirits. So, in a righteous tone, she began to upbraid him. "You never lift a finger to help me. I have more luck getting a nail to ferment in the pickle bin than I have in getting *you* to help me."

The old Chief chuckled. "You know, people often say, 'The flower doesn't bloom before its time; and you can't ripen a gourd with impatience.' Yes, we've been waiting and working and waiting and finally our commune has bloomed. Our strength and our finances have developed and things that should be done are being done!"

What the old Chief was thinking about, of course, was a big white Berkshire boar the commune had purchased that afternoon. It would be a substantial asset: the pig-raising business would leap forward. He had been dreaming of this boar for more than a year. In the afternoon, Tung-hua had walked the boar home. It was a huge creature with great meaty flanks, as big as a calf. In one meal, it ate a whole bucket of food. The old Chief had stood by the pigpen happily, lost in thought, gazing at the boar. Such moments were good for the soul.

Then he called Tung-hua over. Together, they went over the care and feeding instructions meticulously. "And we'll have to have a pen for the boar," he added. "Call the wood and mortar work team and tell them to get on it. He'll need a separate pen definitely, a pen all to himself."

Only after every detail had been arranged would the old Chief allow himself to walk home. He walked happily, he whistled; feeling alive and excited, he told his wife the whole story, from beginning to end.

Contrary to her usual habits, Aunt Ch'ien listened patiently. On most days, her husband's reports of commune business bored her. But today her face beamed, as he wound patiently and lovingly through all the details on the great white-flanked boar. The moment he paused, she jumped in with her own tale. The entire tale of the red corduroy cloth came tumbling out, and she unfolded and displayed the prized material itself without skipping a beat. "And I *knew* how the young lady wanted it, but she was too shy and reserved to say anything. Take a look at what a dazzling red that is! And Tung-hua's mother herself mentioned to me that Tung-hua needed a new jacket. I understood what she was saying! It was impossible not to buy it, not under the circumstances. What a shame on our household if we were to ignore the requests of our own future in-laws! And it was a great bargain, quality material at a low cost." She fibbed to convince her husband that what she had done was both reasonable and proper.

The old Chief looked at her coolly. He did not praise the material. In a stern voice, he asked if she had gone to the Savings and Trust Cooperative for the money.

"Now how could I take out the money?" she replied. "It's in your name." Her gaiety of only moments before quickly dissipated.

"Then where did you get the money from?"

She did not dare tell the truth. "It's none of your business," she said. "I didn't steal it, so don't worry about it. I took care of it all. I can manage very well without your help, thank you. Look at you, grinding your teeth and worrying your hair grey over commune affairs. And what do they call you? The 'household manager'? What a joke! You don't manage your household. You don't give your home three seconds of your time."

The attack, of course, was a defensive maneuver. She bombarded him with a lecture in the hopes that she could get him on the floor before he saw what was happening. It worked. The old Chief, his mind still dreaming about the big white boar that now snuffled and rooted quietly within the confines of the commune, had no patience for a shrew's domestic warfare.

"OK, OK, you're right. I don't know anything about what goes on here, it's terrible. I leave it all to you, and the only one who knows how to manage things is you." And, noticing the water vat was empty, he picked up the buckets and went outside. Out there, someone called to him. Something had happened, he'd better come quickly. What? The old Chief dropped his buckets and rushed over to the office courtyard.

There, by the foot of the east wall, a group of people had gathered, each mouth putting in its own opinion, so that when the leader arrived, he could make out nothing but chaos and babble. Some outrage had occurred, some scandal.

"Isn't it fine," they said sardonically, "the way the hand is so conveniently attached to the wrist? The ones closest to the money boxes need only reach inside."

"Oh, I understand," threw in another. "Now that they've become cadre members, they are no longer bound by the rules, is this it?"

It was pointed out that the character poster was not signed. "Who wrote it? Who was it that wrote this?"

"I'd say Tung-hua," one man pointed out. "It's her handwriting."

The old Chief approached the clamor and the crowd. He peered forward at the character poster plastered across the wall. It was too dark to make anything out. He went into the office, lit the lamp, and returned carrying it. He peered again at the poster and finally realized what the uproar was about. Even though it didn't mention his wife by name, he knew it had to do with his wife and the accountant and the illegal funding. It was a clever and pointed poster. Before he even finished reading the characters, the old Chief realized what the long lecture he had just received from his wife was all about.

Accountant Ma had been strolling happily through the courtyard, whistling a tune.

"Hey you! Ma! Come here, I've got something I want to see," the Chief shouted at him angrily.

Accountant Ma ran over. He raised the lamp and stared up at the poster that spread above him. His jaw dropped, a muscle in his cheek twitched. He became speechless as a gourd.

The old Chief, in his fury, did nothing but jab a finger at the accusing characters. Then finally he said, "Oh Ma! How can you have lived for decade upon decade and still do something so stupid? Haven't I told you a thousand and ten thousand times that the most important thing to being a cadre is to have a selfless, public-minded attitude? Now look what you've done!" In his anguish he raised both fists above his head and shook them at the poster. "Your own ass is sitting in shit. And you think you can raise a voice of education and criticism in this commune?"

Accountant Ma stood numbly under the abuse; he felt the critical eyes of the people around burning tiny holes in his body. All the arguments he had constructed in his defense fell down dead inside him, like sparrows in winter. He lowered his head; he could not reply.

V I

The next day, the wood and mortar team were hauling the bricks and mud for the construction of the boar's pen. The old Chief approached and singled out Tung-hua.

"Tung-hua," he said in a low, demanding voice, "did you write that poster?"

Taken aback by his ferocious manner, she hesitated. Had she written something wrong? Had she been wrong in writing it?

"Yes there was a defect in it," the old Chief said. "It was not thorough enough."

She was confused; what did he mean? "There was a defect?" she asked.

"Accountant Ma certainly committed a crime and you were right to expose that. But why only Ma? Your old Aunt was as guilty and her name should have been scrawled across the paper in characters just as bold."

"But Accountant Ma is a cadre, " Tung-hua objected, "and my Aunt is just one of the people. It seemed to me that in a situation like this, it was the cadre we should assign the primary responsibility and blame to, wouldn't you say?"

"That's true, that's true," the old Chief agreed, "but things with your Aunt have just gone too far. She is stubbornly backward in her thought. What she needs is a good shock to wake her up, otherwise she'll just get more and more backward. She won't listen to me— maybe if you young people and everyone in the commune were to take this opportunity to make her ways clear to her, we might be able to bring her around."

He was right. Admiration of her leader's insight and regret for her own shallow thinking rose up and mingled in Tung-hua's heart. "You're right; I didn't think to the bottom of it," she replied.

"I've got a job for you then," the old Chief said. "Now you must make sure you do it well."

"What job?"

"Go talk to your Aunt and help her. Point out where she's gone wrong. Help her write up a statement and post it on the wall. As you know, one sentence from you will be ten times more effective than all the nagging I might attempt."

"Old Chief, I . . . " Tung-hua hesitated, feeling that she was in an awkward spot.

"Is there a problem?" he asked, suspicious. "Tung-hua, I heard it was you who wanted the corduroy cloth and that you had suggested to your mother that she might be able to get Aunt Ch'ien to buy it. Is this true?"

"No, not at all! I didn't even know about the business with Aunt Ch'ien and Accountant Ma until yesterday when my mother began talking about it with me."

"And what did your mother say exactly?" He wanted to get to the bottom of the matter.

"She was criticizing you. She said you were a hypocrite. She said that you really didn't have a selfless public heart at all. She was telling me how she asked you for a loan and you turned her down; and then when your wife asked for a loan, she received it. She said Accountant Ma must have gotten the OK from you, since that was standard procedure. So I think it was you she was most unhappy with—I said the accountant probably had made an unauthorized loan. that's what I thought. So that's what I wrote on the poster."

"What you did was right," the old Chief said. "But we've still got a few messes to clean up here. Let's go to my house—come with me."

He led the way to his home. As soon as Aunt Ch'ien caught sight of the two of them, she beamed. "How well things are going now! The old man seems to be coming over to my way of thinking," so she thought, "yesterday he saw the piece of cloth I cut for Tung-hua, so today he brought her, our future daughter-in-law."

Hurriedly she got off the brick bed, went over to the closet and got out the red piece of cloth. She pulled Tung-hua over to her and said affectionately, "Tung-hua, I have a son but not a daughter; so you must be like a daughter to me. Now I know you young folks like this color: just look at that rich, thick texture."

"Auntie," Tung-hua said smiling, "these days it doesn't matter what I wear, as long as it's clean and covers me decently. I think we can wait until the work on our socialist society is completed before we begin wearing fancy clothes. It won't be too late then. But this is not the time. Auntie," she continued, "I heard you got an advance from the public funds. When I heard it, I hoped it wasn't true. You know it wasn't an honorable thing to do."

That Tung-hua addressed her as "Auntie" pleased Aunt Ch'ien enormously. She felt herself growing warm. But at the same time, the content of what Tung-hua was saying! Why, it was the same old garbage that worthless husband of hers handed her. She shook her head. So the old man had poured his lies into Tung-hua's young head, what a shame. She glared at her husband, then, turning back to the young girl, she said, "Well, now, I just had the notion that I wanted to do something for you and I couldn't think of anything appropriate."

"Didn't you tell me it was Tung-hua who wanted it?" the old Chief demanded. "I want to get this story straight. Maybe I'll have to get the real story out of the girl herself."

Aunt Ch'ien's face twitched. How could he do this to her? Not only did he not support her as a husband should, he actually took pleasure in humiliating her in front of a guest! She was sick and furious but there was nothing she could say, not with a guest still in the house. So she could only reply, "You don't need to concern yourself with my business. You take care of the commune and I'll take care of the home. Even if I decided to buy a dragon robe for our future daughter-in-law, there would be nothing you could say about it. It's not your concern!"

Tung-hua hurriedly intervened, "Now, now Auntie, don't get mad. Nobody's saying you shouldn't have bought the gift. You just shouldn't have asked for an illegal loan. If you had just waited until payday, the money would have been yours; you could have bought the cloth, and everyone would be happy. But reckless advancing and borrowing will ruin our production plans. Everyone will suffer."

The old Chief saw Tung-hua's words were making an impact. His old wife sat there speechless. So he caught the girl's eye. "Why don't you sit here and chat with your old Aunt for awhile? I've got some business to take care of." Having said this, he took off.

The girl and the old woman talked on and on until dark. When Tung-hua finally emerged from Aunt Ch'ien's home, she had the piece of red cloth under her arm. She went directly to the Supplies Cooperative and exchanged what Aunt Ch'ien had spent so much effort obtaining. With the money in her hand, she made her way to Accountant Ma's office and laid it before him on the desk. Then she found the old Chief. "Everything is straight now," she said. "Give me a piece of paper. Aunt Ch'ien and I have something to write."

The next morning, two fresh character posters hung on the east wall of the office. One was signed, "Ma Shou-Jen" and other other: "Chia Ch'un-e" or, in parentheses, "Great Aunt Ch'ien."

VII

Three days later there was a meeting of the commune representatives. At the meeting, the old Chief discussed the whole matter. He mentioned Accountant Ma and Aunt Ch'ien by name. Accountant Ma, before the whole council, stood up and made a self-criticism.

Then, just as the meeting was about to conclude, someone

brought up the fact that although payday was still some time away, the Temple Fair was rapidly approaching. He said the majority of the members wanted to advance some money. He said there should be a vote, some uniform policy should be made. Arguments were heard on both sides. It was a special day, people should have money, some said. If they had no money, they would spend less, others argued. The old Chief sat back, hearing the debates, mulling it over. Finally, he gave his opinion in a firm confident voice. "I agree with the loan," he said. "It's only once in every long year that the Temple Fair comes around. It's an occasion for happiness. Let everyone have a little spending money; if you're happy, your spirit is whole and healthy, and in everything you do, you will be more alive. People will be more joyous in their work. Let's be frugal where we should be frugal, but let's not be stingy with celebration."

A vote was taken, the holiday-loan policy was approved. Accountant Ma took down the glass lampshade which had been untouched for more than a year. He lit the lamp. He burned the midnight oil; and at the end of two days, he passed out a small sum of holiday money to every member of the commune.

The old Chief took his share of the money home to his wife. He suggested she go to the Supplies Coop and retrieve the corduroy. "This time," he said with a smile, "no one will say that you are in the wrong."

But Aunt Ch'ien had not completely come to terms with the matter yet. In a cantankerous voice she said, "When I run into an obstacle and have to take out a loan, it's considered a crime. But when other people suggest borrowing money, well then all of a sudden it becomes honorable and public-minded! I don't think your name is Ch'ien at all. Your loyalties certainly aren't to *this* family."

The old Chief felt the old wave of weary impatience. Instead of arguing with her, he said with a smile, "Well, you know what people say about raising up a tall, multi-storied building, that it starts from the ground up. The construction of a collective society is no easy matter."

Aunt Ch'ien angrily snatched the money from his hand. "Back and forth! Back and forth! I feel like a pebble bouncing down a stream. I don't even know what's right anymore, you've given my head such a spinning! It makes me sick in my heart."

She was angry, but still, she went back to the Supplies Coop and retrieved the bolt of material. When she unfolded the cloth to show the old Chief, her anger had long vanished.

"Have you ever seen a brighter red?" she kept saying admiringly.

SUNG SHUN-K'ANG

In an era when China encouraged literature from the ranks of workers, peasants, and soldiers, many hitherto unknown writers, who were in fact not writers by profession, came on the scene, saw publication, then disappeared into oblivion again. Apparently, Sung Shun-k'ang belongs to this category, for he is all but unknown except for the one story "Old Team Captain Welcomes a Bride" included in the New Collection of Short Stories (Hsin ku-shih-chi) *published by Writers Publishing House (Tso-chia ch'u-pan-she) in 1965. This story, listed in the "peasant" section of the collection, is an interesting reflection of the ideal role promoted by the Chinese regime for young women in the countryside, and for this reason, has been included in this anthology.*

Old Team Captain Welcomes a Bride

Translated by Dale Johnson

I. ESCORTING THE BRIDE

IN THE AUTUMN of 1963, everywhere the fields were golden and hopes were bright for a rich harvest. Members of the Ho Village production team in the Victory Brigade were in a gay, high-spirited mood. But, they were not complacent. They had resolved to meet the party's challenge to produce in 1964 a record crop of a thousand catties of grain, a hundred catties of cotton, and a hundred and fifty catties of rape seeds. But, because fertilizer was an essential factor in producing such a high yield, the production team, following the directive from the brigade party branch, had quickly organized a task force to collect fertilizer.

At the crack of dawn, team members were out in force busily gathering water plants, dredging mud from the river, and pulling up weeds. On the team was a former poor farmer named Ho A-huo. Everyone called him Old Team Captain because he had served for the past few years as the leader of the fertilizer-collection team. The

Captain at fifty-eight was a man of forthright character who freely spoke his mind, and if he undertook a task for the collective, his loyalty and fortitude could be counted on. At present, he was responsible for collecting water plants. Every morning before the break of day, he set off in his boat and never returned before dusk.

The Old Team Captain's nephew, Ho Pai-ch'ing, was to be married on National Day, which was fast approaching. His bride-to-be was a girl named Cassia from the Lu Village production team in the Red Star Commune to the west. Pai-ch'ing, who had been just a boy when his father died, was now head of the production team of the Ho Village.

"Trees bear fruit but once a year, and a person marries but once in a lifetime," mused Pai-ch'ing's mother to herself. "It's a great event affecting one's whole life. But my son is of the new breed. I wanted him to hold a banquet, but he just shook his head. And, when I suggested that the bride's family get together a bit of dowry, he didn't want that either. Well, if he doesn't want it, then forget it; but there is one custom that can't be disregarded. When the bride enters our gate, she mustn't be allowed to do it on her own two feet. A boat will have to be sent to fetch her, and Eldest Uncle is the man for the job. Eldest Uncle is the head of the clan and the head of the fertilizer-gathering team in the village. Only by having him go over in a boat to fetch the bride can we welcome her with the proper ceremonies, thereby demonstrating our sincere affections and enhancing our status in the village."

Pai-ch'ing's mother talked it over with the Captain's wife, Pai-ch'ing's aunt, and she was of the same mind. "When the bride enters the household, of course she should be escorted," she replied. "It's all right for in-laws to come on their own, but not for the bride. Furthermore, Pai-ch'ing is the last young sprout in our two households. Although things are often different these days, we can't allow the custom of escorting the bride to be reformed too. As for that old man of mine, I'll go and talk with him and insist that he personally undertake the job."

It was September thirtieth, the day before National Day and Pai-ch'ing's wedding. At dusk, the Captain finished unloading the water plants and went home for supper. As he set out his rice bowl and began to eat, he was thinking to himself: "Today while I was gathering water plants by Victory Bank, I discovered a small stagnant stream filled with plants and rich mud. They would make fine fertilizer. I'll take my boat there tomorrow. In fact, there is so much that I'll probably need two boats to handle it all."

He was interrupted by his wife who chimed in, "Old man, is everything settled for tomorrow?"

"Everything is settled."

The wife chuckled when she heard this and asked again, "Tell me, old man, how have you decided to manage it?"

"I thought I'd go over with two boats to save a little time."

When his wife heard this her heart leaped. "What?" she puzzled. "He's taking two boats to fetch the bride? That's a bit much! It's just like him! Yesterday when I asked him to go over in one boat to fetch the bride, I talked my tongue dry and he wouldn't give in. Now, he says he's taking two boats."

"But I haven't talked it over with Pai-ch'ing yet," replied the Captain.

When she heard that he planned to mention it to Pai-ch'ing, the old lady became flustered. "We must keep it from Pai-ch'ing," she thought to herself." He is sure to object if he hears about it."

She spoke up quickly, "Old man, Pai-ch'ing has a meeting. His work keeps him very busy. There is no need to discuss it with him. You're the eldest uncle, and the head of the family should decide."

"Well," responded the Old Team Captain, "I may be head of the family, but the head of the fertilizer team takes orders from the head of the production team, so I should ask his advice about it before I set out."

"This has nothing to do with work," said the old lady. "Why do you need his advice?"

"This old woman doesn't understand," thought the Captain. "Since when has fertilizer gathering not been considered work? It is important work!" So he countered, "If gathering fertilizer isn't work, what, then, do you call work?"

"What!" The old lady realized with a start that they had their signals crossed. "He's going off to gather fertilizer? He's not going to fetch the bride? No wonder he planned on two boats. My ropes are really tangled up this time. Collect fertilizer! Collect fertilizer! It's affected his head. He can't even remember his own nephew's wedding. What kind of flesh-and-blood uncle is he?"

Becoming upset, she leaped to her feet and shouted at the Captain, "So! So! I knew it all along. You don't pay any mind to the family anymore! You can't even remember Pai-ch'ing's wedding!"

Only after hearing the word "wedding" did he realize that he had confused the issue, and that his wife was talking about fetching the bride, not fertilizer. "Didn't I tell her about that yesterday?" He was getting annoyed with her now. "When we are so busy with the fertilizer, old customs have to give way," he thought. "These old-fashioned people won't be turned around. She's like a stone that can't be shattered. And yet she's finding fault with me and getting all heated up."

He blurted out, "If you've nothing to do tomorrow, you can come with me to gather water plants and see a bit of the outside world."

The more the old lady thought about it, the angrier she became. "Pai-ch'ing is the only sprout in a two-acre bamboo grove. We have no son or daughter, and the day will come when we will have to depend on the young couple to lay us to rest. Gathering fertilizer may be important, but you can't just put aside Pai-ch'ing's wedding."

In the midst of the argument, Pai-Ch'ing's mother came running in. Remonstrating with the Old Team Captain, she said, "Brother-in-law, try to put yourself in my place. I'm a person who is open to the new ideas. This is an important event in Pai-ch'ing's life, but I didn't invite the bride's relatives. I didn't even give a banquet. All I'm asking now is that you go over to escort the bride. Can't you even do that for us?"

"Sister-in-law, this is the ideal time for collecting fertilizer. In another few days, when the autumn harvest begins, there will be no time to spare. Pai-ch'ing told me a few days ago that the two of them had already made up their minds that the bride would come over on foot on the day of the wedding. So why bother to fetch her?"

"I've no intention of holding up the fertilizer gathering," said Pai-ch'ing's mother, "you're the head of the family, and a cadre too. You understand better than we do the principles of things. But did you ever hear of a bride walking to her new family on her own? You know the old saying:

> Going alone to the husband's gate is improper;
> A bride who would do so isn't worth a copper.

What's more, I already sent a message to the Lu Village yesterday to say that we would send someone to fetch the bride. We can't break faith with the bride's family."

At this point a young man came running up to speak with the Captain. "The party branch secretary sent me to inform you that tomorrow, our National Day, has been declared a holiday. He asked me to tell you especially to take a good rest and look after yourself, because of your advanced age and poor health, and because you've worked so hard these past few days." The young man then added with a chuckle, "If you don't rest tomorrow, we will call a special meeting to criticize you." Having said this he was off. It was clear to the two old ladies that their opportunity had come. Tomorrow was a holiday. The branch secretary wanted him to take the day off. He couldn't claim now that he was too busy with the fertilizer. The two chattered animatedly about how the Captain must go in person to fetch the bride.

"They will pester me until they get their way," the Captain reasoned to himself. "If I don't give in, they will never give me any peace, and the branch secretary is concerned about my health and wants me to take the day off. On the other hand, I find it hard to sit around idly with nothing to do. Why not combine both jobs, collecting the fertilizer and escorting the bride? There are plenty of water plants in the river around Lu Village. I can bring back the water plants and the bride in the same trip."

So he gave in to the old ladies: "All right, all right, enough of this babbling. I'll go tomorrow." Thus he finally set their minds at ease.

II. THE ENCOUNTER

The Old Team Captain was up at the first cock crow, before his wife was awake. Feeling chilled and a bit uncomfortable, he drank a glass of hot water and put on some extra clothes. He took a chair along for the bride to sit on and placed it with great care in the boat. Then he pulled up the bamboo punt, plied his paddle and set out. As he paddled past Victory Bank, his eyes were fixed on the stagnant stream choked with water plants. Instinctively he steered his boat off the river and entered the smaller waterway, and as the eastern sky began to show traces of white, he was already within two or three *li* of the bride's house. He knew that the water was thick with plants by the sound of the constant thumping on the bottom of the boat. The morning was young. He arranged some of the floor boards to partition off the back of the boat for the water plants, leaving the front section for the bride. She was one of the new breed, so it would not make any difference to her. When the preparations were complete, he began to load the boat with water plants.

By the time the sun was up, he had the boat half-loaded. Since it was well into the morning by this time, he thought he should paddle over and pick up the bride, but when he leaned his weight into the bamboo punt, the boat did not move. He could not budge it at all with his punt. He was more than a *li* from the bride's house, and he did not know what to do.

The Old Team Captain was not in the best of health, and he had been loading the boat all morning. As he strained, feeling anxious about the situation, he suddenly felt a chill come over him and there was an aching sensation in his heart. Then his knees weakened and he toppled over into the stern of the boat.

Luckily a young girl had seen him from the river bank. "Uncle, uncle," she called out, but the Old Team Captain did not respond. Slipping off her shoes and rolling up the bottoms of her pants, she crossed the sandy shoal with shoes in hand and jumped down into the boat. She placed her shoes, her straw hat, and the bundle she carried in the front of the boat and assisted the Old Team Captain to a sitting position. The old man's face was deathly pale, his teeth were clenched. He could not speak, all he could do was nod in her direction. "Uncle," her tone of voice was urgent, "what's the matter?"

The Old Team Captain responded, his voice quavering, "It's an old ailment . . . the pain . . . will soon . . . go away."

The old man had been captured during the War of Resistance by the Japanese devils and beaten until his entire body was lacerated. Afterward, they threw him into a dungeon without even so much as water to drink for four days and nights. Pai-ch'ing's father had sold everything in the house and borrowed money at high interest rates. He had to make a thousand promises and beg on hands and knees before his brother was finally released. After he came out of prison, the Captain's house and land were confiscated by the landlord, and the family was thrown into the streets and forced to beg for food. Exposed to the weather and not always having enough to eat, the Captain developed a serious stomach disorder. After liberation, life gradually got better for him, and his ailment flared up much less often. For several years he had consistently been among the hardest workers in the brigade. But because of the hard work he had just put in on the fertilizer project, his stomach had been acting up for the past few days. Now he had a serious relapse.

Seeing him suffer wave after wave of pain, the girl grew worried: "Such an old man coming out here by himself to gather fertilizer and getting ill, and no one knowing about it. I just can't go off and leave him."

"Uncle, where do you live?" she asked. The old man simply pointed to the east. She got into the water and gave the boat a tug. Then, pushing with all her might with the bamboo pole, she finally managed to free the boat from the sandbar. Turning eastward, she began to paddle.

As she paddled, she noted something very strange about this boat. The back half was loaded with water plants, but in front, stark and empty, there was only a chair, which had been placed there with deliberate care. She could not imagine its purpose.

The Captain's stomach had somewhat recovered, and when he realized she was paddling the boat he said, "Many thanks comrade, but don't paddle any farther. After I rest up a bit, I have another matter I must attend to."

"You aren't going to gather more water plants, are you?" asked the girl. "Uncle, you aren't well. You shouldn't try to collect any more. I think I'd better take you home."

"No, no, it's not water plants. I have to go fetch someone."

"Uncle, who are you supposed to fetch?" she inquired.

The whole business of fetching the bride made the Captain a little cross again. He blamed his predicament on his wife's old-fashioned insistence that he go fetch the bride. "I have to meet a cadre," he said in a weak tone of voice.

Hearing this, the girl thought it strange that a chair should be necessary for a meeting with a cadre, so she asked, "What kind of cadre are you meeting that you have to use a boat?"

"An important one."

She persisted, her curiosity mounting, "Uncle, I thought cadres didn't have ranks anymore. Don't they all serve the people equally?"

"There is no point in going on with this topic," he thought. "I'd better get back to the real thing." Without allowing her to finish, he interrupted, "Comrade, thank you. I'm feeling a lot better. You can be on your way now. I must go to meet someone." At this he tried to stand, but his legs were too weak and his body began to tremble, so he sat back down again.

Quickly restraining him, the girl replied, "Uncle, you are ill. I'm going to take you home. If you really have some important cadre to meet, I'll go pick him up for you after I deliver you home."

"This will never do," thought the Captain. "How can I permit a stranger to go meet the bride? When the women hear of this, heaven only knows what they will do." But unable to stand again, he could do nothing but sit back and listen to the sound of the paddles.

Old Team Captain observed the girl's healthy, glowing face, her strong body, and her kindly manner and asked, "Comrade, where do you live? Where are you going today? I don't like to detain you."

On hearing this, the girl's face flushed from ear to ear and she felt too embarrassed to reply. She was, in fact, the very person the Captain had set out to meet today, the bride, Cassia. She and Pai-ch'ing had agreed long ago that their wedding should exemplify the new customs, and they decided that she should go by herself today. Her mother was a very open, receptive person. They had only to suggest it and she agreed. The bride was puzzled yesterday when her neighbor Lin Sheng delivered a letter saying that a boat was coming to fetch her. Pai-ch'ing was not a man to change his mind, and this was clearly inconsistent with what she knew of his nature. They had reached the decision on this issue together, so she decided that it would be better to follow their original plan and go over by herself. She could leave early and arrive before anyone from Ho Village started out to fetch her. Having made up her mind, she combed and arranged her hair, changed into clean clothes, packed her clothes and other belongings into a small bundle, and set out following the river.

It was here that she caught sight of the old man falling over in his boat. When he failed to respond to her calls, she realized that he was sick, and went down to the boat to help him. Now, when the old man asked her where she was going, although she embraced the new ideology, she still felt hesitant about admitting that she was a bride on her way to her husband's home, so she simply replied, "Uncle, I live to the west in Lu Village. I am on my way to visit relatives."

Hearing that she was from Lu Village, the Captain was quick to ask, "Comrade, there's a girl in the village named Cassia. Do you know her?"

Cassia's heart skipped a beat. "Why does he mention Cassia? Is this boat the one that's coming for me? He asks if I know Cassia, but, I am Cassia." And she blurted out, "It's I who . . ." But, she regretted the words even as they came to her lips, and broke off in mid-sentence.

The Captain interpreted her half-finished phrase to mean, "It's me." "Oh!" he burst out with an air of surprise and great delight. "Then, you are Cassia!"

By this time Cassia was almost certain that this boat was intended for her. After all the small complications of a while ago, she found herself too embarrassed now to make a clean breast of it. Bending the truth, she replied, "Cassia is one of my closest friends in Lu Village. This morning she left early for Ho Village on foot."

When the Captain heard that the bride had already gone on foot; he was very relieved and his stomach began to feel much better. In another few moments the small stream, which was connected with Victory Bank, came into view directly ahead. The Captain, noting that he still had half an empty boat, grew animated again. "Well," he reasoned, "since the bride has already gone by foot, I may as well turn in here and gather a few more water plants and take back a full load."

"Comrade," he addressed her, "I can paddle the boat now. You go on back up the bank. Don't let me delay you any further. I have another matter to attend to."

"Uncle, what is it you have to do?" asked Cassia. "I can lend you a hand."

The Captain quickly declined her offer, saying, "No, thank you kindly, you have relatives to visit. Don't let me hold you up. It's nothing important. I just thought I'd go by way of that stagnant stream and gather a few more water plants and fill up the rest of the boat."

Cassia considered how he had been attacked by stomach pains

only moments before, and now he was about to work again. "Uncle," she said, "you aren't well. You should be resting. Actually my relatives don't live far from here. Let me give you a hand." And, even as they talked the boat was entering the small tributary. When they reached the stagnant stream, there were plants growing on both banks. Cassia abandoned the paddle, picked up the bamboo pole, and began hauling in the water plants. The Captain was very moved but was at a loss to think of how he could repay her kindness.

After a while, she noticed that the water was shallow. Rolling up the bottoms of her pants, she slipped down into the water and began to gather plants by hand, dumping armload after armload into the boat, and spraying water in all directions. This made the Captain very uneasy. He could not sit still with idle hands. So, ignoring the fact that he had only just begun to recover, he took up the bamboo pole and began to pull plants into the boat. In no time at all the boat was loaded to the brim. Cassia poled the boat out, and the Captain, taking up the paddle, steered homeward.

III. WELCOMING THE BRIDE

The Old Team Captain watched the girl as he paddled along. Smiling, he mused to himself: "This girl is clever and capable. We think a lot alike. Whatever comes to my mind, she seems to know it instinctively and she carries it out. A fine girl like this speaks highly of the caliber of leadership at Lu Village. Cassia must be a capable girl too. She came over twice during the past six months, but I was always out spreading manure and never saw her. I'll soon meet her for the first time. We left some of the water plants in the stagnant stream today. I'll bet if I ask the bride to go with me tomorrow to get more, she'll do it." As Old Team Captain paddled along with these thoughts running through his mind, the boat was nearing the village.

At home that morning, the Captain's wife rose early. Seeing no trace of the Captain, she went down to the river behind the house; but as his boat was gone, she knew that he had gone to fetch the bride. She ate a quick breakfast, fixed her thinning white hair at the mirror, changed into a new light cotton jacket and went over to Pai-ch'ing's house. As she reached the corner of the front court, she could hear Pai-ch'ing reproaching his mother.

"Shame on you for being so stubborn," she chipped in. "Everything else has been done the way you wanted it! What's so old-fashioned about having your uncle go over in his boat to fetch her? Enough! Enough! Go get yourself ready now."

Pai-ch'ing, realizing that there was no way to stop the boat now, simply shook his head and went down to the office by the river. The two old ladies continued, with renewed vigor, to busy themselves with the preparations.

When everything was ready the two old ladies waited at home for the bride. They waited and waited, but there was no sign of her. They began to worry. After lunch was over in the village and there was still no sign of the Captain and the bride, they began to feel anxious, and neither sitting nor standing seemed to help. By this time all the neighbors had arrived, and some of the older ones began to ask to see the bride. The younger boys and girls started helping themselves to the wedding sweets, and in no time, the house was bubbling over with excitement. Suddenly a shout was heard from the back of the house, "The Captain's coming with a boatload of water plants."

Auntie jumped to her feet mumbling, "The old fool's lost his senses. We sent him to fetch the bride, and he went off to collect water plants!" Pai-ch'ing's mother was upset too.

By this time, everyone had crowded down along the riverbank. When the Captain saw the throng waiting on the bank he assumed the bride had arrived, and in his excitement he said, "Where is the bride? I heard that she came over on foot early in the day. I would like to get a look at her. Tell her that I've brought her a whole boatload of dowry. When we harvest a thousand catties of grain next year, this dowry will have made a considerable contribution."

When the crowd saw that there was no bride in the boat, they began to wonder. And, when the Captain asked where the bride was, they lapsed into an awkward silence. All were utterly baffled. If the bride came on foot early in the day, then why wasn't she here? All eyes were fixed on Pai-ch'ing's mother and aunt.

When the two old ladies saw the Captain back with a boatload of water plants, along with a stranger wearing a big straw hat, they were ready to burst with anger. It wasn't enough that the old man had gone off to gather plants, but he had even taken someone to help him! As the boat touched the bank, the girl helped the Captain onto the shore, cautioning him, "Uncle, be careful, be careful now."

At this moment Pai-ch'ing came running over from the office shouting, "Cassia, Cassia. You're here!" The crowd was mystified. Where was Cassia? Then, they noticed an embarrassed blush on the face of the girl assisting the Captain. She kept her gaze lowered and was smiling.

Only then did the Captain realize who she was. "Oh! Young lady, so you are the bride, Cassia!"

The two old ladies looked again closely. It was the bride. They hadn't recognized her in her straw hat and mud-spattered clothes. All they could manage was a happy, "Oh! . . .," accompanied by wide smiles of welcome.

"Welcome to the bride! Welcome to the bride!" chanted the villagers. "Instead of being escorted, she brings her own uncle home. She's added a touch of 'new' to the 'new' customs. From now on, who needs to escort brides anymore!" Speak of the "new" and she made it new. Speak of "well done" and she did it well. The bride escorted her uncle home and, with him, a dowry of water plants. But what was more, early the next morning, the bride, Cassia, went again with the Captain to the stagnant stream to collect water plants; and thereafter, the Captain had a new hand to help him collect fertilizer.

PAI HSIEN-YUNG

(1937-)

Pai Hsien-yung was born into a prominent mainland family in 1937, the son of the famous warlord-general Pai Ch'ung-hsi. He spent his childhood in Kweilin and later in Shanghai. He received his high school and college education in Taiwan, graduating in Western Literature from National Taiwan University in 1961. He received an M.F.A. from the Writer's Workshop at the University of Iowa, after which he taught Chinese at the University of California at Santa Barbara. In 1960 Pai founded the literary journal Modern Literature (Hsien-tai wen-hsüeh) with the help of his contemporaries and, with minor interruptions, has been its publisher ever since.

Pai Hsien-yung has been recognized by critics as the most talented Chinese writer of his genration. His promise as a writer was established while he was still a college student. His first story, "Madam Chin" (Chin ta-nai-nai), was published in 1958, after he had completed only one year of college. Pai Hsien-yung exhibits extraordinarily keen insight in his portrayals of characters, especially of women, and their mutual relationships. His most moving stories are to be found in Taipei Residents (Taipei jen, 1971), a collection of stories about the demise of Chinese mainland exiles in Taiwan. Most of Pai's other stories are to be found in the collections A Celestrial in Mundane Exile (Che-hsien chi, 1967), Wandering in the Garden and Awakening from a Dream (Yu-yüan ching-meng, 1968), and The New Yorkers (Niu-yüeh k'e, 1974). Since 1974, a few stories have been published singly in newspapers and magazines, and the serialized novel Outcast Son (Nieh-tzu) appeared in Modern Literature (1977–78, nos. 1–5). A collection of his stories in translation, Wandering in the Garden, Waking from a Dream: Tales of Taipei Characters, is forthcoming.

"A Day in Pleasantville" (An-le-hsiang te i-jih) was first published in 1964 and was included in the collection The New Yorkers.

A Day in Pleasantville

Translated by Julia Fitzgerald and Vivian Hsu

ON THE OUTSKIRTS of New York City, there's a suburb called Pleasantville, inhabited by six or seven thousand upper-middle-class commuters. These commuters bring home quite a bit of money from the City, so, accordingly, they've got one of the highest property taxes in the nation. In the mornings, early, about six o'clock, all kinds of beautiful big cars pull into the parking lot of their train station. Men, thirty to fifty years old, step out, wearing Brooks Brothers suits with shiny tiepins and cufflinks. In one hand they're carrying a black briefcase, in the other, a local newspaper, rolled up. They see each other, they exchange a pleasantry or two, a few tidbits on the latest Harlem riot or who hosted the Democratic campaign cocktail party in Washington . . .

The train pulls up, they slide in the doors like a school of minnows. Then off to the heart of the City, Manhattan; riding in their climate-controlled cars like a billion other businessmen.

Pleasantville's like any big-city suburb, designed by an architect who must have learned his style from hospital operating rooms. The air is clean, the streets are clean, the houses and trees are clean. Not a pinch of dust. It looks almost as if the health department had come in and disinfected everything, killed every last little bit of bacteria.

On both sides of any street are lush green lawns, trees full of green leaves. An unusually beautiful and healthy green. Probably this is because of the way they soak the ground with chemicals. In fact, their leaves are so green and so shiny and so healthy looking, they sort of look like the plastic flowers and leaves that people sell in dimestores. And the lawns are neatly trimmed and each so exactly the same height as the next one, that you'd swear everybody had bought their lawns in the carpet department of Macy's.

And of course, at one end of the town is the standard shopping center with its A&P (We Have Branches Throughout the Nation!), Woolworth's, a barber shop with two barbers, and a small theater that only shows old flicks. So, while the breadwinners are all off in the City, the housewives of Pleasantville drive up in their late-model, luxury cars to run an errand or two. Now, Pleasantville is a very small town, but still the housewives take care to dress well and don't forget to make up before appearing in public. At the shopping center they push their baby-carriages, carry their bags full of detergent, milk, peas and Coca-cola, and chat in the parking lot about their sons' summer camps, their daughters' sweet-sixteen birthday parties, or last night's TV shows. Then, after a few minutes of such pleasantries, they disappear again into their shiny Fords or Chevrolets.

In Pleasantville, on White Pigeon Hill, at the end of a cul-de-sac, live Yi-p'ing and Wei-ch'eng. Their street connects the small hill of the neighborhood with the highway that runs into New York City, and of course their street is quiet, wide and clean. The pavement is a light grey. A sort of odd light grey that, if you ever bothered to examine it, you might notice that it looks a lot like a dried-up river, full of stagnant grey water.

White Pigeon Hill has a special quiet to it. You can't hear wind, you can't hear people, only now and then, the sound of a car door shutting, like a pebble thrown into the dead river. An instant of noise and then the quiet comes back. Though, very far away, you can hear the sounds of cars on the New York highway speeding back into the City. They make a sharp noise, the tires on the pavement. But it's a twenty-four-hours-a-day noise and always the same, so even if it's sharp, it's monotonous, and has long become a part of the quiet on White Pigeon Hill. Yi-p'ing hears it, now and then. To her it means that outside of White Pigeon Hill there really are people who run around and have things to do.

Now, it's mid-winter, December. There's no snow yet, but soon. The quiet is deeper than ever. It looks as if everybody has rolled up their green summertime carpets and brought them inside. What's left of the lawn is dried yellow earth. Leaves are gone, elms in front of every house are just black skinny branches, and the slope becomes more spacious and desolate. The new-looking houses on both sides of the street all stand exposed: uniformly grey wooden structures. Roofs and sidings are of the same color, approximately of the same size. Registering the current trend, the houses are all split-level. The large windows, with white curtains trimmed at the borders, are closed all year round (climate control, of course). In fact, if you climbed to the top of the Hill and looked down, you'd see that there seems to be no one living in these houses. They look more like kids' playhouses.

The playhouse that belongs to Wei-cheng and Yi-p'ing is on the right side, very close to the dead end. They could never be accused of being old-fashioned. In their living room they've got the most fashionable of arrangements: a sofa in the half-round, a kidney-shaped table, some small tables and stools of irregular shapes, with a wonderfully refreshing color scheme, chiefly orange and white; long-necked lamps, looking like luxuriant tropical plants, weave in and out among the tables and chairs. The set-up is cute and colorful, but looks a little unreal, like something made with children's blocks.

In the kitchen, all the most up-to-date built-in appliances are uniformly white: electric dishwasher, electric eggbeater, electric can-opener, miscellaneous electric pans of all sizes. Against one white wall are the switches, all black and arranged row on row on row. Most of her day Yi-p'ing spends in this laboratory of a kitchen.

The morning is easy to while away. She prepares breakfast and gets Wei-Ch'eng off to the stockmarket, and then gets her daughter Pao-li off to school. She then goes shopping for this and that, washes vegetables and fruits; and then it's noon. The first half of the afternoon slides easily too: letter writing on the dining room table to Wei-ch'eng's friends and relatives; the month's accounts, income and expenses; phone calls about the meeting dates of the PTA, or some church group, or other help-your-neighbor clubs. But every day around five o'clock, things start slowing down. It's like the train's coming into the station, and it's on the track and moving and everything, but it's going so slowly you can't help but get mad and impatient. It seems as if it's never going to get there.

So, between five and six every day, Yi-p'ing's train is crawling. The housework's all been done, the electrical gadgets are all switched off, dinner's ready. What's there to do? She'll sit for a minute and smoke a menthol, stand up and take a taste of her ox-tail soup; maybe move the bowls around on the table she's already arranged, move them here—no, move them there—well . . . move them back. Walk to the picture window and watch the quiet grey white street, count the neighbors' cars coming into White Pigeon Hill in the twilight. She's waiting for Wei-ch'eng to get off work and pick up Pao-li from a neighbor's home. It's only when they come home that she can start the second half of her day.

It was when Pao-li was three that Wei-ch'eng began his run of luck, making a fortune in the stock market. When this happened, they moved from their New York apartment to a house in Pleasantville (bought, not rented). It was Wei-ch'eng's belief that the small-town environment was simple and clean and appropriate for a child's education.

They are the only Chinese in Pleasantville. Yi-p'ing doesn't know how to drive, so most of the time she stays home, or stays within the neighborhood. Because of this, over the five years that they've lived here, she's gradually lost contact with all her Chinese friends in the City. On weekends, Wei-ch'eng says it's family time and refuses to go into the City. He says he needs to rest. In the summer he takes Pao-li to the amusement park near Pleasantville to go swimming or boating. In the winter, father and daughter put on snow-suits and go shovel snow or make snowmen. Yi-p'ing doesn't like sports, doesn't like the outdoors either. So whenever Wei-ch'eng and Pao-li go romping, she usually doesn't join in. Sometimes she'll go along, but just to stand off to the side and watch their jackets.

Wei-ch'eng tells her, try and get into the swing of the neighbor-hood social life. So she tries; she joins the bridge club. But her game's no good. She tries joining a reading club, but what can you expect? She can't read very fast in English, and she can't keep up with the conversation.

On Sundays, the neighbor ladies used to ask Yi-p'ing to go to church with them. Yi-p'ing wasn't religious, but Wei-ch'eng said to her, "You see how the housewives of White Pigeon Hill get all dressed up and go to church? You are the only one who doesn't dress up and who stays at home. When people notice this and talk about it, it doesn't sound very nice."

So Yi-p'ing bought herself a white gauze hat, and on Sundays she puts it on and goes to church.

They're the only Chinese in Pleasantville—Yi-p'ing and her family—so the American housewives of White Pigeon Hill are al-ways falling all over each other trying to be nice to her. They'll call her up on the phone and talk about this and that, speak in their must bubbly tone of voice, try to treat her like a special guest. They really do want to please her, so they pretend they're fascinated with everything Chinese—what the Chinese wear and live in and do and eat. And then some of the ladies are afraid Yi-p'ing won't know what's going on in American life, so they take her under their wings and point out all the subtleties of American customs, as if they were the official foreign hostesses.

And all of it makes Yi-p'ing even more aware that she's Chinese and different. So she moves with even more care, subconsciously playing the role of a stereotyped Chinese. At parties, she puts on her Chinese dress, hangs a slight smile on her mouth, and, in a gentle tone of voice, adds her part to the conversation, politely an-swering the same questions over and over.

After a while, when the ladies would come over and invite her somewhere, she'd give her grateful regrets. She didn't like playing the Curious Chinaman; it exhausted her. And she was tired of com-ing home from parties and needing an aspirin to get to sleep.

In China, Yi-p'ing had studied home economics. She had wanted only one thing: to be a good wife and a good mother. But when she got to the United States and married Wei-ch'eng, she started to dis-cover that the golden rules of conduct she had so carefully learned in China were pretty useless for White Pigeon Hill. Like the dictum that the wife should aid the husband: Yi-p'ing's husband was so capable, she felt there was nothing at all she could do to help him. He was a wizard at the stockmarket; nine times out of ten he would win big, so he had plenty of clients and business was always running smoothly.

Yi-p'ing, on the other hand, didn't know a thing about stocks and wasn't even interested in learning, though, whenever Wei-ch'eng began showing off his expertise, she would sit there and pretend to listen with enthusiasm.

Wei-ch'eng was awfully Americanized, and this sometimes made Yi-p'ing uneasy. But whenever he saw her uneasiness, Wei-ch'eng would start into his lecture on the need to adjust. So even in her own territory, the housekeeping, Yi-p'ing had to listen to Wei-ch'eng's criticism. Was this right?

And Pao-li didn't make things easier. She was a real daddy's girl, and had been since she was a baby.

"Wei-ch'eng, don't do that, you'll spoil her," she often had to shout, in a tense voice.

But Wei-ch'eng would just say, "Don't worry, Pao-li's a good kid," and he'd smile and seem completely unworried.

Pao-li would seize the opportunity to scold her mother, saying "Mother's bad," in a perfect New York accent.

Up until Pao-li was six, Yi-p'ing insisted on her speaking Chinese; but after two years in school, the mother lost control. Pao-li rebelled, refused. Her friends all talked in English, even Wei-ch'eng when he was at home often spoke English with her. Yi-p'ing struggled and scolded and worried; but after a while Pao-li couldn't even remember her parents' names in Chinese.

Yi-p'ing was the product of a traditional upper class family in China; hers had been the strictest of educations. So she wanted to do the same for Pao-li, to train her to become a well-bred Chinese lady like herself. But things have not turned out that way at all. The year before, when Pao-li came home from summer camp, she stepped off the train wearing the jeans Wei-ch'eng had bought her and sucking a lollipop. She ran towards Yi-p'ing and called out in a loud voice "Rose!" which was Yi-p'ing's American name. Yi-p'ing was stunned, and rebuked her on the spot. Pao-li said that in summer camp lots of kids called their parents by their first names. Yi-p'ing answered, "In a Chinese family, this never happens."

But Pao-li was Daddy's little girl and not Mother's. This was a joke when Pao-li was a baby, but it had become less funny and more real as she grew up. There always seemed to be some sort of a secret pact between Pao-li and Wei-ch'eng. The two seemed always ready to give moral support to each other. They had the same interests, like sitting in the living room on the carpet every night after dinner, watching TV, and talking about the programs. Yi-p'ing thought most of the shows were childish and meaningless, but they liked them, and laughed and talked together. Usually Yi-p'ing sat up on a chair behind them, watching vacantly. She wanted to join in the chatter, but didn't have anything to say.

So here she was, at the dead hour of the afternoon, staring out the kitchen window at the grey and white street, listening to the sharp noise of the cars on the highway to New York, and waiting impatiently for Wei-ch'eng and Pao-li to come home, to end this hour of vacuum, and to start the second half of her day, the half in which daddy and daughter shared their secrets, the half in which she, Yi-p'ing, would sit looking vacant and left out.

"How come the light's not on?" Wei-ch'eng came in the front door at six-o'clock sharp. Pao-li followed him, hopping and jumping, and carrying Wei-ch'eng's briefcase. Wei-ch'eng was wearing his new high-fashion coat; his hair was just cut (two sharply cut hairlines running behind each ear), and on his face, he was wearing an appreciative expression for the wonderful smells that came from the kitchen. Pao-li wore her bright red corduroy suit and white wool hat, the one with the red pompom. She wasn't a very pretty girl—she had a big mouth and her nose was a little flat—but her eyes were big and round and very black. Bright eyes, that darted back and forth, almost like a monkey's; lovable eyes.

She came in the house, threw her daddy's briefcase on the couch, and her own bookbag too, and climbed up on Wei-ch'eng's lap to share a few secrets. He stroked her cheeks; "What's up, sweetheart? Why's your face so red and cold?"

Yi-p'ing was dishing out the food. "Pao-li, go wash your hands and get ready for dinner," she said.

Pao-li didn't move. She played with Wei-ch'eng's tie and said to him quietly, "I was playing hide and seek behind the hill."

Yi-p'ing turned her head sharply, "I heard you. You were playing outside again. I told you you can only play indoors; your cold's not better yet."

Wei-ch'eng pinched Pao-li's red nose and laughed. "Mother sure has sharp ears. Let's not talk about it any more. Go wash your hands."

Pao-li jumped down from Wei-ch'eng's lap and ran into the bathroom. Wei-ch'eng opened up the evening paper to look at the stock reports and said to Yi-p'ing in a soft voice, "What'd you do today, Rose? Did you play bridge at Mrs. Jones's?"

"They asked me to go, but I didn't want to."

"Northwest closed at 34, Delta 28, G.E. 40.3 . . . they're all up. I just bought two hundred shares for the Chang family, the ones on Park Avenue. They sure made a big haul. I guess their fortunes are on the upswing. Mmm, what delicious smelling ox-tail soup."

He threw down the newspaper, went over to the bowl of soup, and breathed in deeply. Pao-li came in and yelled, "I don't want ox-tail soup!"

"Children should learn to eat everything that's given them and shouldn't be picky," Yi-p'ing said severely. She remembered when she was little, she had hated the awful bitter melons. Every day her mother had fixed them, just to train her to eat them. She didn't stop until Yi-p'ing said she liked them.

"I don't want to eat ox-tail soup!" Pao-li sat in a chair and yelled loudly.

Wei-ch'eng said, "It's OK, darling. This is a democratic country and we believe in freedom. You don't have to eat the soup if you don't want to. You could have a bottle of Coke or something." He got a tall glass and poured her some Coke. "What'd you do in school today? Tell Daddy, won't you?"

"Well, this morning our class had an addition competition."

"How'd you do?"

"I was Number One!" Pao-li said proudly.

"Really?" Wei-ch'eng was proud too. He had always said Pao-li had a scientific mind. "When she grows up, she'll be a female math Ph.D." he always said. "Tomorrow Daddy'll go into town and buy you a reward, OK?"

"We also made Valentine cards at school," Pao-li said, blushing.

"Oh, who was your Valentine?"

"I'm not telling."

"Is it that fat boy, David?"

"No, 'course not."

Yi-p'ing smiled and said, "Oh, Mother knows. Is it Daddy?"

Pao-li blushed, squirmed; her big eyes were bright and happy. Wei-ch'eng laughed, took Pao-li's face in his hands and gave her a kiss. "Oh, Daddy's your big Valentine, you're Daddy's little Valentine. Isn't that right, sweetheart?" he said.

Yi-p'ing broke in harshly; "Pao-li, Lolita's mother called me this afternoon and said that at school you pulled Lolita's hair and made her cry. Now why did you do that?"

"Oh, Lolita's a dirty pig," Pao-li said, gritting her teeth.

"Pao-li, you mustn't call your schoolmates that kind of name. How could you pull someone's hair?"

"Well, she said I'm Chinese," Pao-li blurted out, and both her cheeks turned red.

Yi-p'ing put down her chopsticks and said in a softly strained voice, "Pao-li, Lolita is right. You are Chinese."

"Well, I said I'm an American and Lolita said I'm lying and she calls me Chinaman."

"Listen, Pao-li, you were born in America; you're an American citizen, but Daddy and I are both Chinese. You are our child, so you are also Chinese."

"I'm not Chinese!" Pao-li screamed.

"Pao-li, you mustn't talk like this. Look at our hair and skin. It's different from Americans'. Daddy, you and me, we're all Chinese."

"I didn't lie. Lolita lied. I'm not Chinese, I'm not Chinese!" Pao-li screamed and stamped her foot.

"Pao-li," Yi-p'ing's voice began to shake. "If you keep this up, I'm not going to let you eat."

Wei-ch'eng broke in; "Rose, let's finish dinner and then we can talk with Pao-li about this."

Wei-ch'eng stood up and walked toward Pao-li. He wanted to comfort her, but before he could, Yi-p'ing stood up, pushed herself between the two, grabbed Pao-li by her hands and picked her up from her chair.

"No, I want to give her a lesson now," she said. "I want Pao-li to always remember that she is Chinese. Pao-li, listen; you say this after me: 'I am a Chinese!'"

"I'm not Chinese, I'm not Chinese!" Her feet were kicking and her struggling body was twisting.

Yi-p'ing turned pale and shouted in a tremulous voice, "You must say after me: I-AM-A-CHINESE!"

"I'm not Chinese! I'm not Chinese!" Her screams sharpened.

Yi-p'ing let go of one hand and slapped Pao-li on the cheek. Pao-li stood stunned, then shrieked, hopped up and down, and started crying hysterically. Yi-p'ing raised her hand and was about to hit Pao-li again, but Wei-ch'eng grabbed Yi-p'ing's arm and released Pao-li.

Yi-p'ing jerked her arm away from Wei-ch'eng. She was dazed for a minute or two, then a feeling of faintness rose in her. She hunched over the sink and threw up all the ox-tail soup she had just eaten. Wei-ch'eng helped her into the bedroom, laid her down gently. He sat by her and said in a muffled voice, "We have to educate our child, but this isn't the way. Pao-li's only eight, how can she understand the difference between Chinese and Americans? All her schoolmates are American. Of course she feels she's an American too. Rose, to tell the truth, Pao-li *was* born in the U.S., she *is* growing up in the U.S., after she grows up, all her living habits will be American. The more she can adjust to her environment, the happier she'll be. I know you're afraid of her becoming American because you yourself don't want to be one. But do realize that's your own psychological problem. If you transmit this problem to the child, it's not fair. Certainly you want Pao-li to grow up to be a psychologically healthy person who can adjust to her environment, right? OK, so don't be too upset. I'll go get a tranquilizer for you. After you take it, have a good sleep."

Wei-ch'eng poured her a glass of water, gave her a Compoz, then turned out the light, closed the door and went out. Yi-p'ing lay in the darkness. Her whole body felt as if it had gone somewhere else. She couldn't move. Cold tears trickled out of the corners of her eyes. And from a crack in the door, Yi-p'ing could barely hear Wei-ch'eng and Pao-li talking.

"Mother's so bad, she's bad."

"Shh, Mother's asleep. Don't raise your voice. It's eight o'clock, our TV program's about to start."

In a minute the sound of the TV came alive, the voice of the Winston cigarette commercial, the same one they heard every day, exactly the same:

> Winston tastes good
> Like a cigarette should

YÜ LI-HUA

(1931-)

Yü Li-hau was born in Shanghai, but received her college education in Taiwan, graduating in History from National Taiwan University in 1953. She was one of the first Chinese students from Taiwan to come to the United States. In some ways, Yü Li-hua's life experience in the United States is typical of that of student-intellectual émigrés from Taiwan. She received her M.A. in Journalism from U.C.L.A. in 1956, married another student-émigré, raised three children, and has been teaching Chinese at the State University of New York at Albany.

What is atypical about Yü Li-hua is that she has remained a prolific writer, in a way unmatched by other émigrés. Her writings reflect an ability to absorb and reproject recent and current events and circumstances, but they are also informed by her rich past experiences. She admits that she herself enters into her writings in the statement: "A piece of writing cannot avoid having in it some shadow of its author. I feel that the distance between myself and my protagonists is shorter than most."

Yü Li-hua is most noted for her short stories and novels about her generation of student-intellectual émigrés. These writings evolved along with the unfolding of their lives. In an earlier period her writings concentrated on the student life, careers, and marriages of the new arrivals and on their rootlessness and problems of adjustment. Now they depict the generation gap, mid-life and mid-career discontent, the degeneration of youthful aspirations, and the second generation. Yü Li-hua's writings also encompass the greater Chinese world, as in the story "In Liu Village" (Liu-chia-chuang shang, *translated by the author and C. T. Hsia in* Chinese Stories from Taiwan: 1960–1970), *and in the following story, "Nightfall"* (Mu).

Yü Li-hua's better-known publications include the novels Dream of Returning to Green River (Meng hui Ch'ing Ho, *1963),* Change (Pien, *1965),* Again the Palm Trees (Yu-chien tsung-lü, yu-chien tsung-lü, *1966), and* Sons and Daughters of the Fu Family (Fu-chia-te erh-nü-men, *1978), and the short story collections* Autumn (Yeh-shih ch'iu-t'ien, *1964) and* An Inside View of Conferences (Hui-ch'ang hsien-hsing-chi, *1972).* "Nightfall" *appeared originally in a magazine in 1969 and was reprinted in* An Inside View of Conferences *in 1972.*

Yü Li-hua received the Samuel Goldwyn Creative Writing Award in 1957 for her story "Sorrow at the End of the Yangtze River" written in

English, and Taiwan's Chia-hsin Award for the best novel in 1967 for
Again the Palm Trees.

Nightfall

Translated by Vivian Hsu and Julia Fitzgerald

I. FATHER

FATHER HAS ARRIVED. His face is sallow and gray, his body lean and
shriveled. How defenseless he seems—like a tree in winter. People
still tell stories about him, how in his younger days he was irresistible to women. I was just a child then. What was meant by a man's
attractiveness? I did not have the slightest idea. Now that I understand it, I can only think of him as a tree in the wintertime. But a
tree, in the spring, should break into bloom again. And my father?
. . . They say old people are always anxious at the changing of the
seasons, and especially at the change from winter to spring.

Now a still, pale dawn floats in the window past the curtain. Too
early to get up—but from the living room comes a ragged burst of
coughing that jars awake the lightly sleeping dawn. The coughing
crashes through the air; it sounds like raucous, spiteful hands
slamming notes out of a piano. I tie the sash of my robe and get up
to see if it is, indeed, Father. Stepping out of the bedroom, I see
him standing there, a cigarette in his hand, facing the window that
opens out onto the vast pale stillness of dawn. He looks as if he's
been sketched in black ink with a few deft, bold strokes: the two
black eyebrows, the cheekbones, the high bridge of his nose, the
locked lips. Standing in the half-light, I have time to examine all of
this in detail. Can he really have been handsome once? It would be
hard for anyone to imagine. But I do know what his life was like
before he reached fifty, the glamor and the women, and all the plea-
sures that he savored in those years.

I cannot remember what year it was or where it took place, but
that incident over Gold Flower—or was it Silver Flower? Oh what's
the difference? But I can remember it vividly. It was a beautiful
spring day with the delicate fragrance of flowering vegetables in the

air. The sun shone down on our bodies and mellowed us. Gold Flower bent over, washing clothes at the water spigot near the front gate, and I stood near her, nagging at her and begging her to take me downtown. I wanted to buy some sesame candies. She ignored me, frowning and scrubbing strenuously at some clothes on the washboard. Her full breasts inside her short blouse jiggled so much they began to irritate me. Then I looked up and saw that Father had come up behind me. Immediately, I dodged away. There was no reaction from Father: he continued to watch Gold Flower pound the clothes. I don't think he even noticed that I had been there, or that I had darted away.

"Gold Flower," I heard him say, "Go into my room and see if you can find my grey sweater-vest."

Gold Flower raised her head with some surprise. Her red, glossy lips were parted slightly, and between them shone the dazzling white of her teeth. Her eyes were large and filled with the bright spring sunshine.

"My wife has gone out to play mahjong, and I don't know where the vest could be," Father said.

I had always been afraid of Father. I seldom looked at him directly. I did not see the expression on his face at that moment, but I could hear the urgency in his voice. Gold Flower obediently stood up and followed him into his room.

I squatted in front of the water spigot, fishing the clothes one by one out of the bucket. I took off my shoes and socks; I stepped with the soles of my bare feet on the clothes, squeezing out the chill fresh water. The bottoms of my feet were refreshingly cold, while the tops of my feet bathed in sunlight. I must have played for hours. It was only when I began to shiver from a cool wind that I noticed that the sun had long ago sunk below the horizon. The clothes under my feet were one solid flattened slab. I ran into the house and yelled, "Gold Flower! Gold Flower! Why aren't you coming out to wash the clothes?"

Out came Gold Flower from the inner room. Even though the sun couldn't possibly have projected its rays into my parents' room, her face was flushed red. It was past dinner time: my stomach was beginning to rumble and I was getting irritable and snappish. And Mother was out playing mahjong. I was just about to scold Gold Flower, when I saw Father emerging from the inner room; so I held my tongue. Father had the grey vest under his arm. He walked past me; then turning his head halfway, he said, "Go get your little brother. It's getting late."

One night, a week later, I woke up with a violent start. My head spun: I thought I was on a battlefield, or at the edge of one. There

was something terrifying me but I wasn't sure what. I sat on my
bed and put my head between my arched legs, with only my ears
exposed to catch every noise. I was terrified, but still I wanted to
catch every word.

"... and you still consider yourself a decent person? You do it
even with servants ..."

"That's cheap slander and you know it; and that's all you know
how to do. What could you possibly know about my behavior at
home? When you yourself are never here, not morning, not noon,
not night—*never* here. You have eyes in the back of your head?"

"... I may be out during the days, but I *am not dead*! How dare
you accuse me of not being home, when you are off doing this
shameful thing? I think you're the ..."

"... will you *control* yourself? Watch what you're saying! You're
saying I've no sense of shame; and what exactly do you think you
mean by that? ..."

"I mean exactly what I said. If a man doesn't have a sense of
shame, he just doesn't have it. *You* don't *have* it! You are nothing
but an animal."

Now, outside the window, the day is breaking in the sky. There's
no life in Father's eyes. They stare out at a branch that shows not
the slightest stirrings of any greenery. In the corners of my father's
mouth you can see loneliness. No, I can't believe this is the man I
heard that night. That raging man who beat my mother with his
fists, who howled like a dog, who took Gold Flower roughly by the
arm and left in a whirlwind. He was gone three days. And when he
came back, everyone in the household went mute. Even the regular
weeping of Little Brother was swallowed and silenced.

Not long after, Gold Flower was sent back to her village. The war
between Mother and Father subsided. Only I held a grudge; every
time I had to face Father directly, I would stand like a defeated
soldier in front of an enemy too strong to oppose. I hated him, but I
did not dare stand up to him.

In the years that followed this incident, the war never broke out
again into actual violence. Nevertheless, hostility was built into the
relationship between Mother and Father. Sometimes things would
flare up over a photograph of a fashionable woman in Father's
pocket or the lipstick mark of unfamiliar, crescent-shaped lips on
the shoulder of his shirt. Mother had never been a warm or tender
woman. Now her voice became loud and harsh. Her expressions
and manner became more severe. I could not bring myself to
understand or forgive Father; but to my surprise, I found I had no
sympathy for Mother either. Because the anger Mother had accumu-

lated came to be like a land mine left on a battlefield: it was always
exploding on the innocent passers-by, us her children.

I hear Father sighing. His sighs are soft and weak, because he
doesn't want anyone to hear them. Then he gets up slowly and
painfully from his chair, his old hand against the beige tabletop, his
arm trembling. He begins to pace around the room. He paces in
stiff, aimless circles the way he did the night Mother left home.

The night Mother left home, that date I *do* remember. It was the
year I entered college, the year Father was promoted to manager,
the year we moved to our new home with our grand front door
made of glass and our lawn as fine and smooth as an infant's hair.
That was also the year Mother found out about Father's "other"
house and the woman who was living in it. It all happened suddenly; one day she just gathered us all together and took us there.
We got into the car driven by chauffeur Chang, the one who normally took Father to and from work. In a short, curt manner, Mother
gave the chauffeur the name of the street. "Drive us there," she
said. The chauffeur, with his short black fingers resting uneasily on
the wheel, hesitated. Mother snapped, "What are you waiting for?"
Then, reluctantly, he set his foot down on the accelerator.

All that happened that day flashed across my eyes like the
wind-blown pages of days flipping up from a calendar. Whenever I
try to piece together that incident in recent years, all that I can recall
are fleeting images that rise and fade in my mind: that woman's
face, red like the Sundays on the calendar, so red that it dazzled the
eye . . . the servant coming to open the door . . . Father's surprise,
then anger, and his shamefaced expression . . . and on that woman's white face, the bright red lips parted in surprise . . . then her
slim and graceful back as she scurried away . . . Father was scolding, and chauffeur Chang, in a weak voice, tried to defend himself.
And tangled up in it all were the hoarse tones of Mother's voice:
"So children, do you see? Do you understand? This is the father you
never see day or night. Do you understand why I can't buy that
American wool fabric at Daisy's for you? Do you see why Mother
can't buy you a Phillip racing bike? And, you, Little Brother, you
need a more qualified tutor, don't you? Why don't you ask your
father where all the money has gone. Go ask your nice father . . ."

I clung to the wall, not daring to meet anyone's glance; not daring
to look myself in the face. My small body throbbed with anger and
shame; at Father, yes, but at Mother even more, because she had
dragged all this out into the open right there in front of the servants: in front of the chauffeur and in front of the maid.

It all flew past me, as speedily as calendar pages blown by a howling wind. By the time I dared lift my head again, we had already reached our own front door. Close behind us, Father had also come home. I locked myself in my room, but through the door I could hear the sounds of slaughter coming from the battlefield. I wasn't afraid, not this time. I was like a scarred and battle-toughened general in helmet and armor. My younger brothers were outside my door, weeping and begging me to mediate. I just put my hands tightly over my ears. Tears? I wasn't going to shed a single drop.

That night, Mother left. Little Brother told me she had left with a gash on her forehead. The maid fixed us some dinner: I put the younger brothers to bed. The horrors Little Brother had seen that day had exhausted him completely; he fell immediately into a deep sleep. But even in his sleep he kept choking and crying without tears, and begging, "Ma . . . Ma . . ." endlessly. I felt myself breaking down then; I was terrified at the thought of hearing myself cry. I turned off the light and groped my way back to the bed again. I lay my face down near Little Brother's throbbing neck, then the tears I had suppressed all day poured out.

I don't know when I woke. Stumbling back to my own room, I passed through the small living room and saw Father there alone, pacing with his hands behind his back. The cigarette he held between his fingers had burned down so low it was nearly scorching his skin. Without thinking, forgetting everything that had happened that day, I cried out, "Father! The cigarette! . . ."

With a vacant expression, Father turns around and says, "Hmmm? . . . What? . . ."

I have to shake myself out of a fog before I realize where I am: Father has arrived. He's my guest; this is my home. "You're up so early Father. I would have thought you would be exhausted from your trip. Why don't you sleep a little longer?"

Father stops pacing for a moment. Massaging the muscles in his jaw, he says, "I've slept enough. I'm getting older, and old people wake up early in the morning. But why don't you go rest a while longer?"

"I've slept long enough. You must be hungry. I'll go heat up a glass of warm milk for you."

What I've just said reminds me again of that scene, of that first morning after Mother left home. I was sitting in the dining room with a bowl of hot rice gruel. My little brothers had all gone to school. I hadn't slept all night and was in no shape to go to classes. When I saw Father, in his robe, walk into the room, I hurriedly put down the bowl of gruel and stood up. Avoiding his eyes, I just rushed from the room, and at the door, I collided squarely with the maid, who was carrying in a glass of hot milk for Father. It splashed all over me. Father leapt forward with a towel in his hand; gently, he wiped my scalded arm. His touch made me tremble. It was a combination of confusion, shock, and hatred.

"Look at you, how clumsy you are. Who would think you were a college student?"

He bent over me, wiping the milk off my lapel. I tried not to look at him, but I could not avoid seeing the white hair at his temples. Unconsciously I recoiled from him. I went back to my seat at the table. My gruel had grown cold. The cigarette that Father had put down in his hurry was already burned out.

"Don't you have classes today?"

"There are classes; but it'd be pointless for me to go."

There was no doubt Father was even more aware than I of the despondency and resentment in that sentence. As he lit a cigarette, he pushed in front of me the second glass of hot milk the servant had just brought in. "Drink this. I'm not hungry just now."

I took the glass and sipped at it. Tears kept falling into the milk and dissolving. Father sat silently, smoking his cigarette. Then he said: "I know what you and your brothers are thinking, but you haven't even tasted life yet: you don't know anything about how the world works. It would be pointless to try to give you an explanation now."

"You don't need to explain. I saw it all myself."

"Some things . . . ," he stood up and began to walk around the room, "you can't just look at what's happening on the surface and think that's enough to pass judgment on. You have to dig out the causes, the reasons, the roots. But, in any case, you don't have to worry: your Mother will return."

"I know." During all those years of bickering, Mother had stayed not out of any feelings of tenderness toward Father; such feelings, if she had them at all, were far too weak to stop her. Rather she had stayed purely out of concern for us, her children. We were the cords of hemp that bound her legs and arms. And twisted around her, too, were the admonitions of the Three Obediences and the Four Virtues. She was a woman bound by tradition, a woman not prepared for independence in a new society. I never worried that Mother might leave for good. What made my heart so sick was that I knew that between Father and Mother there would never be any hope for harmony.

In a desolate tone I had never heard him use before, Father said: "Since you're not going to class, would you mind coming with me to look for Mother? Maybe if you were there, there might be more of a chance that she'll let me apologize gracefully."

I don't know if it was the white hair on his temples or the flagging spirit in his voice; or maybe it was that when he said, "let me
apologize gracefully," all the fierceness of Mother's face and voice
came rushing back to me; or maybe even something had matured in
me, some capacity for empathy . . . But in any case, I had a sudden
urge to put my hand in his and say, "OK, I'll go with you." I took
the glass of milk in both hands, drank it all in one gulp and stood
up.

Mother did return, but that woman never left. The atmosphere at
home fluctuated from beautiful to stormy. When it was fine and
cloudless at home, Mother would sit at the edge of the round table
in the living room with her needlework in her hands; and Father
would rest on the rattan chair near the window. The smoke from his
cigarette looked like a fog swirling and coiling and escaping out the
window. From the living room, the sound of chatter and laughter
spilled into the den where my brothers and I sat doing our
homework. My younger brothers would be in unusually high
spirits, and as for me, doing homework would be as easy as turning
over the palm of my hand. No homework could give me any headaches at those times.

But when it was cloudy at home, the living room was like a sheet
of lead. Mother would light cigarette after cigarette, and with every
one she lit, the sound of the match being struck scratched painfully
at my heart, and at my brothers'. The unoccupied rattan chair was
like an internal organ that had been ripped open and left hollowed
out. Father went off for days at a time. But always it was only after a
bitter and dispiriting argument with Mother.

One time when he left, I tailed him on my bike, following the
pedicab that he had called at the corner of the street. He was going,
just as I expected, to that woman's place. She, looking like a
Japanese geisha girl on a color postcard with her fair skin and crimson lips, opened the door herself. I was far away, but still I could
see the smile on her face when she caught sight of Father. It was
gentle and soft, submissive on the surface, seductive underneath.
She was the kind of woman that could charm and soothe a man—or
a woman for that matter—into a kind of pleasurable state that dis-
armed all criticism. Seeing her, even I could not hate her. My first
reaction was to search in my mind—when had Mother ever smiled
like that? Mother's face was well proportioned, it could even be
called handsome, but somehow it was hard and chilling. If only she
would smile like this woman to soften her severity. In that brief
moment on the street corner, seeing this woman's tenderness, then
seeing Mother's raging face in my mind, I began at last to have
some understanding of what Father had meant on that occasion
when he tried to defend himself.

"You don't need to boil it," Father said. "Just hot is fine for me."

I poured the hot milk into a glass, added two teaspoons of sugar, carried it carefully to his side, and set it down in front of him. Lightly, he took the teaspooon in his fingers and stirred the milk. The fingers were as elegantly round and tender as they had ever been. The only change was that the nail on his index finger had grown discolored to a coffee brown from smoking. I looked at my Father's hands and thought of the women who had passed through them. There were questions I wanted to ask. When I lifted my head, I caught a glimpse of his glassy eyes. Those eyes betrayed his depression, loneliness, and the silence of old age. I took a cigarette from the pack he'd placed on the table, picked up his lighter, and only then, for the first time, did I notice what an exquisite piece of artwork Father's lighter was. It was a delicate perfume jar with an elliptical cap that, when pressed, flew open to let escape a light green flame. Such an ingenious and delicate toy, I thought, could only be a keepsake from a woman. Was this the lighter Father had been using all along? I had been away from home so long I couldn't remember. I fondled the lighter in my hand a long time, contemplating it; that caught Father's attention.

"It was a gift from Yoshiko, more than ten years ago. It's had to go into the shop for repairs a few times, but it's still good."

His words startled me; the exquisite lighter slipped from my hand and hit the floor with a crisp "bang," shattering the half-awakened dawn. My surprise was not so much at the discovery that Japanese goods could last such a long time: it was at hearing Father mention the affairs that had always been taboo. He saw the look on my face. "Now that you're a mother and a wife yourself, your understanding of the relationship between husband and wife must have matured. I don't need to hold back in what I say anymore, do I? But I'm not trying to make any pleas for myself." He stopped talking, stirred his milk. The hot vapors that had been rising at the mouth of the cup had already cooled, weakened, like the smoke from my cigarette, which I had lit and not yet smoked. The smoke and the steam from the milk, which Father had not touched, rose up and mingled together, then dispersed into the air.

"What's the point of explaining things that are long past?"

"You're right, what's the point? I'm not even going to try. I just feel like getting it off my chest. It's been bottled up for too many years. It would be good if you could understand. But if you can't, don't worry about it. It doesn't matter." His voice was hoarse, the way it used to be when he came home drunk in the middle of the night. It was the gutteral voice I remember hearing when he had thrown up or had been chain-smoking, sitting in the living room after a quarrel with Mother. But now these memories don't bring back the anger that I used to feel toward him. Now it's compassion I feel, a compassion close to pity.

"So, Yoshiko was that woman? Where is she?"

"She passed away, in the third year after you left home."

"I remember the oldest brother wrote me saying that the feeling between you and Mother had changed. Could it possibly have something to do with . . . " I couldn't bring myself to say her name, as if afraid that if I mentioned it again, that fair and radiant face would reappear. "Perhaps the death of that woman has something to do with it?"

Father shook his head. "The feeling I once had for your Mother disappeared a long time ago. It didn't last very long after that incident with Gold Flower."

The name Gold Flower sent a chill immediately to the soles of my feet; a chill that traveled rapidly through the rest of my body. Now that whole scene played out again in my mind: I was trampling the damp clothes under the water spigot, they lay still and lifeless under me. Gold Flower had been gone so long the sun that had been warming the tops of my feet had already set. I could not hide the accusation in my voice. "How can you put the blame on Mother for that affair with Gold Flower?"

The weary, defeated expression in his eyes returned. "I don't blame her. I could never blame her. In all these years of squabbling back and forth, have I ever let fall one word of blame in front of you children? Your mother is an upright woman. A dutiful woman who can endure hardships. When I was poor, she did not complain. When I was rich, she didn't grow arrogant. There was just one thing: on an emotional level, she was too icy toward me. In the several decades of our marriage, with the exception of the first one or two years, I have always felt that life with your Mother was like a winter that would never pass."

With a pair of hands that were still supple, not yet withered or dry, he gently rubbed his dry, wrinkled jaw. His palms rubbing against his stiff whiskers made a chafing, scratching noise. "I don't blame her. The affair with Gold Flower was my fault. I apologized to your Mother; I admitted my fault to her. But she refused to forgive me. She never did forgive me. It's human to make a mistake. If she hadn't made such a scene in front of you children, my sense of shame wouldn't have turned so much into anger. But making such a scene, kicking Gold Flower out—exposing my failings to the whole neighborhood! And anyway, I was young then. Young men are always getting into fits of anger and going off shouting that they don't give a damn. It's only natural."

He had much of my sympathy. Just remembering Mother's curses made my ears burn. Still, I said, "Do you mean to say that Mother should have tolerated all of this? That she should have let Gold Flower remain in the household after all that?"

"No, that's not what I mean. She was right to get angry. And driving the maid away was only reasonable. But if, after it was all over, she had forgiven me . . . if she had accepted me again, maybe . . . " He fell silent again, stirring the milk that had long since lost all its warmth.

". . . maybe there wouldn't have been a Yoshiko?" I said, so softly it should have almost been inaudible; but it came through distinct and clear. There were other women in Father's life before Yoshiko, but in comparison, none of them was of any significance.

Stirring the milk as if this helped him think, Father said, "That's hard to say, very hard to predict what might have happened. But at least, if your mother had forgiven me, I would have tried to make up for that mistake. Whether I would have been successful or not is hard to say. But your mother's temper drove me thousands of miles from her. And as time passed, the ice grew thicker and more impossible to melt. Later, when I ran into Yoshiko. . . ." He stopped again, staring down at the cup intensely with his tired eyes. "I'm thankful that your mother did reject me so severely. Because otherwise I would never have known how the tenderness of a woman could make me feel so warm."

As if he wanted to veil the fond memories of the woman he had, without meaning to, suddenly revealed to me, he picked up the glass of milk and roughly drank it down. Then he began to cough, coughing so violently that green and black veins stood out near his temples. For some reason my impulse was to stand up and massage his back, pounding on it with my fists. Yet I could not do it; I sat there and could not bring myself to move. It was only when the cigarette ember between my fingers nearly burned down to my skin that I jumped up, looking for an ashtray.

Father's coughing continued violently. His withered face had become as red as a dried maple leaf, a maple leaf writhing as it falls from the tree. He turned to face the window as he coughed, as if hiding his face from me. I don't know why; maybe he didn't want me to see his face in such contortion. From my angle, I could see his profile clearly. He was coughing so violently that tears had begun to flow from his eyes. His neck was stretched forward and his back bent. He was a helpless old man standing there in front of that window. And outside, a few naked grey-white birches stood in the desolate winter.

I forced myself to do something after all; I approached Father and began to massage his back, gently pounding on it with my fists. I wanted to pound the forgiveness I felt for him into his heart. My brothers and I had always felt Mother was the one who had been mistreated, even though during those days when Father was absent from home, Mother never wept in front of us. We had made a secret pact that as soon as we finished school and got jobs, we would rescue Mother from her pit of misery.

In less than six months after the oldest brother got married, he and his wife took Mother in. And the other two, the next younger brother and the youngest, also began their careers, so Mother could take turns staying in three different homes. Occasionally she came to visit me too, in my little world. I don't know whether it's because I inherited some of her strong will, or because all along I reserved some small part of my heart for Father, but whenever Mother and I were together, things were never completely comfortable between us.

Then Father abandoned the solitary lifestyle that he had followed for so many years and unexpectedly came to live with me, his daughter. Was he possibly trying to find some thread of family warmth in those few, pitiful strands of empathy I could offer? Oh Father!

"Father, if you and Mother didn't feel any love for each other, you should have gotten a divorce a long time ago."

He was gradually recovering from his fit of coughing. From the pocket of his robe, he took out a white handkerchief that had been folded neatly into a square. He dabbed his eyes; then, putting the handkerchief discreetly to his mouth, he removed the clot of mucus that had been coughed up. He folded the handkerchief slowly and put it back in his pocket. Without turning to look at me, he said, "Divorce is the privilege of your generation." Then he went on, "At that time, even if I could have gotten a divorce, and even if I had wanted to, I wouldn't have done it. But if your mother raises this with me now, I'll not hesitate, because I don't have to worry about her livelihood anymore." He picked up his cigarettes and the lighter, lit a cigarette and took a drag from it. "But why bother with a divorce now? Our lives are almost over."

When a man in his forties or even earlier says "life is almost over," there isn't the least bit of sorrow in his heart. He knows very well that forty is the prime of life. When he reaches fifty or so, he may say it again, but he still doesn't believe it. But when he gets up to sixty or over sixty, like Father, and when his past has been a glorious one; when a man in this situation says life is almost over, I wonder what kind of feeling he has in his heart. His career days and his warm-natured women are all things of the past. Even his wife now belongs to his sons. And his daughter? Well, she does offer him an ounce of acceptance, but just the minimum that arises out of pity. Is this all that remains of a whole lifetime? All I can find, when I study his face, are these few pathetic remnants, and the memories and images of the past.

Facing the window, he finished smoking his cigarette. Then, at last he said, "I'm a little tired: I think I'll go lie down for a bit." His tone was almost as if he were pleading for my approval of that remark. Suddenly a fit of pathos gripped my heart.

"Go rest," I said gently. "I'll make sure the kids aren't too noisy." He put the lighter in his pocket and turned to go. I was afraid to look at his face. In a voice as calm and unstrained as I could manage, I said, "Father, we're all very happy that you came to live with us."

II. MOTHER

"Father's been living with me for about a month now."

"I'm aware of that. He wrote me."

"Really? About what?" Suddenly I felt hurt. It was as if my children had been bullied on their way home from school and had gone running to strangers before they came to me.

"When have I ever lied to you?" she said sharply, her eyebrows raised in reproach. All of a sudden she had pushed me back to those days, more than ten years ago, when I had to stand there and be lectured after I had said something wrong. "Your father says nothing special in the letter. Just that he's staying at your place."

I waited for her to ask about Father's health, but she just went on knitting the sweater in her hands. It was a pale pastel color, probably for my brother's child. She was always knitting in the old days, when she was left alone too often, as if she were pushing away the solitariness with every stitch. When we used to come home from school in the late afternoon, we would see that ball of yarn rolling around like an unsettled heart on the spacious, but soundless parquet floor. When she concentrated, she frowned, contracting her eyebrows, all her attention fixed on the two metal needles. In those days, she had to be solitary. Father didn't give her any other choice. And now? She herself chooses solitude.

"Father's health is OK. He does cough a lot, especially at night. And it seems he sleeps very little. He always gets up early in the morning."

Mother did not reply. Father's hair hasn't gone completely white yet, and still hasn't thinnned out. Only the hair at his temples is gray. His old age is all revealed in his lusterless eyes. But Mother's hair is not only more than half white, half of it has already fallen out as well. Now she combs it into a knot at the back of her head. Her face is wrinkled, but it hasn't lost its oval contour. What most clearly shows her age are the loose folds of skin hanging from her jaws. Could it be that the skin sagged from the way she had drooped her head over her unhappy, endless knitting? She has used her hands to kill so many lonely hours.

"Why do you keep knitting? I thought the doctor told you to rest your eyes."

"It makes me panicky when I just sit here idly."

"Come stay with me for awhile. Little P'ei only goes to school for half a day: he can chase away the boredom for you."

"It's too much trouble going back and forth. And anyway, they need a helping hand here. Your sister-in-law's never done any housework before. At least when I'm here, I can teach her something."

"Who's ever done any housework before they're married?" I caught myself and suppressed what I was about to say next. Instead, I shifted, "I get bored myself sometimes; there's no one home for me to talk to. Come and keep me company."

"Isn't your father there? You always seemed to have a lot to talk about with him; at least much more than your brothers ever had."

"Father has become more taciturn than ever. He can sit by himself for hours; he's already thumbed through the few magazines we have in the house so many times that they've fallen apart. He takes Little P'ei to the store sometimes to buy ice cream or a toy, but aside from that, he never sets foot out the door. I guess living by himself so many years with nobody to talk to, he's gotten used to it."

Mother did not reply. She ripped apart the row of stitches she had just finished knitting; then, putting the stitches back on the steel needles and carefully counting the number, she knit it over again.

"Mother, let bygones be bygones. Father is very sad, I can tell. Give him another chance. You two living apart like this makes all of us uneasy."

"Us? Who's 'us'? Your brothers all think this is the most reasonable arrangement. Your father isn't short of money. When he lived in the country, he had a maid to take good care of him. Now that he's living with you, he's looked after even better. What could possibly be wanting?"

"What's wanting is someone for him to talk to. An old companion."

"Did it ever occur to him, in all those years, that I might also need someone to talk to? All day long I used to sit like a mute, and my mind would run in circles, thinking of where he was, talking and laughing with that low-class, shameless woman. And in my agony, I imagined to myself: maybe they are talking about *me*, and laughing at *me*. Did he ever give it a thought, that I sat there alone all day long? I didn't want money; I didn't demand good food and expensive clothes. All I wanted was someone to be there so at least I could open my mouth once in a while and say something. Do you think he ever thought of that?" Her hands were moving quickly over the yarn; her words, too, seemed to skitter out nervously. Her needlework had gotten into a mess. At last she gave up, put down the yarn, and simply sat facing me.

"We all know Father wasn't fair to you. But . . ."

"It's good that you realize that. No use trying to plead his case in front of me. No matter what you say, I'm not going to live with him."

"I didn't say I want you to live with him. I just want you to come visit; because the younger brothers don't welcome him here, he can't come see you. I see him sitting there by himself sometimes and not saying a word all afternoon. It makes me so sad, Mother . . . I feel so sad for him . . ."

"And what about me? Didn't you ever feel sorry for me?"

"I did, I did. But you're tougher than Father. So . . ."

"Oh I am? And how can you tell? What makes you think that?"

"Look how many years you've managed to endure. You raised us single-handedly, and now we're all grown. That in itself must have taken incredible strength. And through all those years, you've never cried in front of us, not once."

She stood up abruptly. The yarn in her hand fell to the floor, but made no sound. "Haven't you heard of swallowing tears into the stomach? Ai! You're still a child, you still don't understand." She turned her face to prevent me from seeing it, but from where I was sitting, I could see the trembling of her loose chin.

I wanted to go to her, hold onto her shoulders, stroke her back, kiss her graying hair. But I could only sit there motionless. When I was younger, once after she and Father had had a vicious fight, Father had shouted violently and left. Mother, with her hair disheveled, just sat there and gasped in the living room littered with broken china. My heart had been full of sorrow and sympathy for her. I had rushed forward to hug her; but she put out one hand and pushed me away. "Go away!" she said. "Go away. Don't touch me." I will never forget the icy expression in her eyes.

"Oh Mother," I said sadly, "I came here to cheer you up and look what I've done. I've upset you."

"Your father sent you here to plead his case."

"No, he didn't. Father's never said anything about wanting you to go see him; he just asks about your health. This is all my idea; it just seems to me that after fighting for a lifetime, it's time to think about a reconciliation . . . especially since Father's health is so bad."

"So he's finally begun to think about my mealth, has he? When I was giving birth to Little Brother, you couldn't even catch sight of his shadow. When I screamed out, neither heaven nor earth responded. I was in pain until midnight. Then, in the middle of the night, I had to beg the Changs next door to take me to the hospital. It wasn't until three days after Little Brother was born that your father came crawling home, soused as a pile of soft mud. You should really ask that pitiful father of yours whether he remembers this incident."

"Even I remember it. How can Father possibly forget?"

"Well I suppose now that his health is getting bad, he must be looking for a nurse who won't cost anything. How did his health get bad in the first place? He used to spend handfuls and handfuls of money on those women of his—why can't even one of *them* come wait on him? Would that be too much to ask? What about that one woman, the one he kept in such fine style in that house . . . ?"

"Yoshiko? She passed away a long time ago. Cancer of the throat."

Mother picked up the yarn that had dropped on the foor. She put on her glasses and concentrated again on her knitting. She knit two rows, then ripped them out, knitted and ripped, knitted and ripped, again and again. In the past, she had been able to knit without even using her eyes, without a single flaw, without ever dropping a stitch.

"Mother, you must have known about it, her death I mean."

Dusk had begun to fall; the room was darkening. I couldn't see Mother's expression very clearly, but her voice seemed to have softened, to have grown more feeble, like the voice of an aging person. "I knew about it. For a week after that woman died, your father couldn't swallow one grain of rice. He tried to hide it, but I saw him break into tears more than once. I knew about it."

I could not imagine a man crying. Father, crying? I could not imagine it.

"Mother, consider it for awhile."

She shook her head and went on counting her stitches. "You might as well go on home now. It's getting late. Little P'ei will be looking for you."

III. MY PARENTS

Father became ill. A cold, a stomach ache, rheumatism, old age, and loneliness all converging on him at once. He slept fitfully, feverish, talking in his sleep. He seemed to have called out Mother's name; or maybe it was Yoshiko. I couldn't make it out. I called Mother on the phone; she had nothing to say, and of course she wouldn't mention the idea of coming.

That night, when I came home after filling a prescription, I found Father huddled next to the phone, wearing a thick blanket around his shoulders. He coughed and talked at the same time. I don't know if it was because he was talking, but his hands trembled and he had to pause often to gasp and wheeze.

"It's OK . . . just an old problem . . . I know . . . I've already tried those . . . I know . . . yes . . . It is done . . . too much . . . That's right . . . why bother . . . Hui-chen, you're right . . . you've always been right . . . I know. I know. They're all fine! . . . I feel ashamed . . . No no, please don't rub it in . . . OK. Don't worry. She'll be right back . . . No, that's not necessary, that's not necessary . . . How about you? Take good care . . ." A fit of coughing made him unable to continue. I steppped forward and held onto him. I helped him back to his room and into bed. The telephone receiver that was left hanging seemed like an exposed scar. I could hear Mother's voice coming out of the receiver. It sounded far away, but at the same time urgent and shrill, saying, "I am coming. I am coming," or was it "I am not coming. I am not coming."?

I really couldn't make it out clearly.

CH'EN YING-CHEN

(1936–)

Ch'en Ying-chen (born Ch'en Yung-shan) is one of the earliest and most prominent native Taiwanese writers educated in post-1949 Taiwan. He was born and raised in a town near Taipei, and in 1960 graduated in English from Tamkang College. In the 1960s he was active in the then young literary movement that was beginning to fill the literary void of the 1950s. His writings appeared in several literary magazines at the time, The Pen *(Pi-hui),* Modern Literature *(Hsien-tai wen-hsüeh), and* Literature Quarterly *(Wen-hsüeh chi-k'an), and for a time he was the editor of the last.*

In 1968, just before he was to come to the United States to study at the University of Iowa, he was arrested and sentenced to ten year's imprisonment for his allegedly dissident activities. He was granted amnesty in 1975 along with other political prisoners by Chiang Kai-shek's son and successor. His prison experience seems not to have intimidated him, for recently he has again been quite open about expressing his views on Taiwan, China, and humanity in general.

Prior to his arrest in 1968, Ch'en Ying-chen had published numerous stories, essays, and movie reviews, which were collected by Joseph S. M. Lau in Selected Stories of Ch'en Ying-chen *(Ch'en Ying-chen hsüan-chi, 1972). A collection of his pre-prison writings entitled* The First Case *(Ti-i-chien ch'ai-shih) was published in 1975 with a new preface. Ch'en's first post-prison story, "Night Freight" (Yeh-hsing huo-che), was published in 1978, and his latest story is "Clouds" (Yün), which appeared in* Taiwan Literature *(T'aiwan wen-i), no. 68 (August, 1980).*

Perhaps due in part to his religious faith — his family are missionaries—Ch'en Ying-chen's writings are characterized by a deep concern and sensitivity for the oppressed peoples, not only of his homeland, Taiwan, but in all of China and throughout the world. "A Rose in June" (Liu-yüeh-li te mei-kuei-hua), published in 1967, demonstrates remarkable insight into the Vietnam War, the position of blacks in America, and the commonality of oppressed peoples from two entirely disparate societies.

A Rose in June

Translated by Shu-hua Chiu and Vivian Hsu

TIRED MOON

THE DOOR OPENED. For an instant, the white sunlight flashed past into the bar, dark as a cellar. A thin, tall black man walked in. The heavy door closed slowly behind him. He hummed softly a song which he had been humming before he entered the bar, and groped his way to a small table near the air-conditioner. He put his camera on the table and with his thick lips pecked out a long cigarette from a cigarette pack; he lit it. As he puffed out some smoke, he kept on humming:

> Melinda, pretty Melinda;
> Only fourteen,
> Has a white, plump baby . . .

A bar girl came over and sat down beside him. The black man kept on singing, "Melinda, you are happy, never complain." She glanced at the waiter standing to one side, then said to the black man, "Buy me a drink, how about it?"

Stretching himself with eyes half closed, the black man opened his mouth, revealing a row of teeth that glistened in the dark— teeth that occupied almost the whole lower half of his face. "Sure," he said.

"Whiskey and soda," she told the waiter. "What about you?"

Now he took a good look at her, his snow-white horse teeth covered by his thick lips. His hair was thickly kinked like unraveled woolen yarn; it looked as if it were only pasted to the bald pate at the back of his head. His eyes were big and bulging. They took her in earnestly, in a way that reminded her of an overworked old ox in her home town.

"Hey, sweet sister," he said tenderly.

"My name's Emily Huang," she said. "The guys call me Emmy."

"Hey, Emmy," he said.

"He's waiting for you to order a drink," she smiled.

"Gin on the rocks."

The cellar was packed with American G.I.'s in civilian clothes and military uniforms.

The low ceiling was decorated like the upholstery of a sofa; dim lights were inlaid into it like so many tired moons.

Emily Huang dug out a pack of cigarettes from her hand bag.

"Seems like I've met you somewhere before," she said, not very convincingly.

"I can't remember," he said playfully, flashing a toothy smile. She let him light her cigarette. She understood this kind of flirtation. Unmindfully, she let him stroke her bare back. "For example, on the way to your military base," she said.

He let out a hearty laugh, half closing his oxlike eyes. A drunk fat guy was shouting loudly, "God, I tell you, the girls here are a million times better than those in Tokyo—they're delicious and they're cheap."

"Emily, sweet sister," the black man said, "we never met on the way to any military base. I just got here from Vietnam."

His big black palm pressed on her not very white hand. Emily Huang looked at this big black hand: the fingernails were like light brown pebbles which had been scrubbed very clean by the waves on a sandy beach. Emily's whiskey and soda and the black man's gin on the rocks came. He reached out for the drink, brought it directly to his lips and drank it. Squinting his big eyes, he said: "Very thirsty." With his free hand he stroked her back. "No, we never met anywhere before. This is my first time here to spend my seven-day vacation."

"Oh," she said. His touch was gentle beyond her expectation. "Anyway," she said, "welcome, Mr. Soldier."

They clinked their glasses.

"You can call me Barney." Then he announced in a military manner, "United States Army, twenty-sixth regiment, under the direct command of the artillery company, Private First Class Barney E. Williams invites you to dance."

He stood up, like a long-legged ocean spider. Being with this not-very-good-looking black soldier was beginning to make Emily a little happy. She understood very well the importance of this kind of happiness. Girls like them didn't often meet clients who made them happy. Someone rare like this could make them forget their professional nature, or could even give them, from time to time, a kind of intoxicating feeling of being in love.

Although the music was fast and frenzied, they unhurriedly pressed against each other in a corner, oblivious to other people. She strained her neck to look up at him and let him press his face to hers. His black hand caressed her bare, not very white back. She was a sturdy woman, you could tell just by looking at her unusually wide shoulders. Two people of different colors embracing each other, there was something particularly erotic about it.

"Are you very brave when you're in battle?" she asked.

He found her ear with his thick lips and whispered into it, "You'll find out in bed tonight."

She begant to titter. "You're a bad boy," she said. Suddenly she saw, across from them, a handsome white officer dancing the surf with a girl who was pretty enough to make one jealous. The fair-skinned girl had long hair in the style of Suzie Wong. Her dance movements were like the tides under the full moon, icy, yet intense. Emily Huang scrutinized her for a moment. Then she said, "Barney, I want you to see a pretty 'piece.'" She held his head even closer to her face. "But I don't want you to fall in love with her."

The black soldier laughed. "Sweet sister, I won't."

"Promise?"

"I promise," Her fragrant scent began to excite him. He stroked her whole bare back. She pushed him away. He looked over at that pretty "piece."

"Ah!" he said, "Captain Stanley Birch!"

The handsome white officer turned his head and looked around.

"Jesus Christ!" Barney said, "He's a nasty pompous pig!"

"You stupid ass!" The officer saw him. "You stupid ass!" he called out ecstatically. He came over, pulling along the girl with the long hair.

"Captain Stanley," the black man said smiling, "it's really great to see you here."

The officer let out a lusty laugh, revealing a row of straight teeth. His chest was broad. A short-trimmed mustache grew above his thin lips. Blond hair lay neatly pressed on his square head. "You are a stupid ass," he yelped with joy. He was a classic scion of an East Coast, upper-crust family. His face was flushed red—due to either a suntan or the effect of alcohol—and looked full of vigor. He gazed proudly at this lowly black soldier who had suddenly become subdued.

Then he announced, "Do you know? Today is a great day for you." He started to laugh aloud again. Captain Stanley Birch was in fact already a little intoxicated. He lowered his voice and said, "This is perhaps the greatest day in the history of your family." He winked his eyes mischievously, then raised his voice and said:

"Gentlemen, quiet, quiet."

He walked toward the bar. "Gentlemen, quiet," he said. He stood smiling under the light, like a young senator who was about to give a speech. The cellar-like bar quieted down; only the hi-fi, which had been turned down, could be heard. He said:

"Captain Stanley Birch hereby announces the honor that our great government of the United States confers on Private First Class Barney E. Williams."

The G.I.s in the bar all turned their eyes to the black soldier in the corner. They saw him embracing Emily from behind and standing there dumbfounded. Drunken laughter and jovial applause broke out in the bar.

Captain Birch, with his Eastern accent, which sounded peculiarly affected, announced that black private first class Barney E. Williams was by order promoted to sergeant for his courage in annihilating the enemy who had long been hiding in a village. He spoke in a manner reminiscent of some college speech class:

"Barney E. Williams is a great soldier of the United States and a great patriot. He battled in a distant land to defend the principles upon which our United States was founded. In fighting to protect and assist in building an independent and free ally, he has added glory to the traditions of justice, democracy, freedom and peace in which we have had deep and unshakable faith since the founding of our country!"

A rousing round of drunken but earnest applause broke out. Sergeant Barney Williams didn't know when he started to cry. "Oh, Jesus Christ," he sobbed.

"Don't cry, my baby." Emily, overjoyed, was hugging him as if he were a tall, strong tree.

"Jesus Christ, I've never been so happy in my life!" His voice cracked and finally he burst out crying. "Jesus Christ," he kept on saying.

"Don't cry, good baby." Emily's eyes became red. "Don't cry, good baby."

"Don't cry, baby, don't cry," several voices echoed mockingly.

"Jesus . . . oh, good Jesus," practically losing his voice. "My great-grandfather was only a slave!"

"Don't cry, good baby," she said.

"Don't cry, baby, don't cry!" the drunken soldiers echoed in chorus.

GROUNDHOG

Barney and Emily had a wild evening. For Barney, it was as if the doors to everything in the world had been opened for him: success, hope, glory and dignity were all smiling gently and humbly at him. And Emily was completely infected with his glory and happiness. "Do you know," Barney had pinched her flat nose with his fingers and said, "You chatter endlessly like a little sparrow."

She grew sullen. "You don't like it?" she asked with a trace of melancholy. Barney hugged her. His black body was like a wild tropical tree. He kissed her little nose.

"Oh, oh, not at all," he said. "You're the only girl in the world who has shared my happiness." He loosened his hug and knelt facing her. With his left hand half raised and his right hand on her shoulder, he assumed a solemn expression: "I am a king of Africa who rules the hot and dark land and reigns over its forests, surging currents, pythons, fierce lions, ivory and diamonds."

She immediately started to bow to him on the bed. Her breasts dropped onto the sheet like two fruits hanging quietly at harvest time. She hailed him repeatedly, "King, oh, King. . . ."

"You are the King's sparrow, you are the King's beloved consort," he said. "You are the only woman with the good fortune of accompanying the King through his vacation."

The little sparrow compulsively and passionately hugged Barney. She kissed him, like a little, charming white hen happily pecking for food on the black earth. "I'm your little sparrow, the King's beloved consort," she murmured. "I want to wait on you, and take you to another village where the wind blows."

"Another village where the wind blows?"

"Yes, my King," she said. "Like that little village we went to today."

The King said, "Oh it's a village where the wind blows like the one I grew up in."

The black King was lying on the bed. This was a big luxurious bed in a tourist hotel. At the head of the bed there was an exquisite golden carving.

"I wish you'd been to our old, old South," Barney said. "We lived there generation after generation. There we sang, prayed, wept, drank, labored, and then buried our bones."

"If you like, I'll take you to another village tomorrow," the little sparrow chirped excitedly, "a small fishing port; the fishing boats busily drag huge batches of fish and shrimp out of the sea and unload them on that little port."

"Ah, no," said Barney.

"As you please," she said, and got up to pour him a glass of water. Her shoulders, broad and smooth, were like a mountain slope, waiting to be plowed.

The sergeant propped himself on his side to drink. He held the cup with both hands like a baby. She stroked his black stomach; her hand appeared very white against him. And yet she knew she was definitely not a fair-skinned girl. "Didn't you say the sights are all the same everywhere?" he said apologetically.

"That's true," she smiled, "yeah, that's true."

"Yeah, that's true," he said. He peered at the ceiling through the bottom of the glass, squinting the other eye, as if he were gazing at a distant place through a telescope. He echoed in almost a whisper, "Yeah, that's true, it's the same everywhere, the countryside is the same all over the world."

Her hand was traversing his black body. "Is that true?" she asked.

"Today I saw your countryside, large rice paddies everywhere. The sun shone on the grain that rippled in the wind. The only things missing were the roar and smoke of artillery, the dense forest—otherwise, it would be too much like the place where we fought." He suddenly started to giggle, because Emily was stroking his pubic hair. He dodged her and put the glass on the table beside the bed. He giggled again. He grabbed her hand. "Don't do that," he smiled, "You're a little whore."

"Don't you like it?"

"No, not now," he said, kissing the hands that he had grabbed, with a tinge of melancholy. She laughed.

"I mean," she said, "you don't like the way the village is, because . . ."

"I don't know," said Barney. His thick lips, like a suction cup, were powerfully sucking the back of her hand.

"Because of the war?"

"Ah, no," he quickly replied. "My great-grandfather was also a soldier. He joined General Lee to fight the Yankees." He looked over at the table, picked up a pack of cigarettes lying between the cup and a small harmonica, and pecked out a long, white cigarette with his thick lips. She lit it for him. He was just like a soldier.

"Now I am a sergeant," he said, full of self-confidence. "Above sergeant is second lieutenant, first lieutenant, lieutenant, then major, lieutenant colonel, and then colonel."

"You'll make it," she said happily. "You'll make it for sure."

"By that time, people will call me Colonel Williams—then for the rest of my days the young fellows will respectfully call me Colonel Williams, Colonel Williams."

She didn't actually understand what the honor of being a colonel meant. Nevertheless, she faithfully believed that one day he would become a colonel, a devilish and dashing officer, like that Captain Birch who had conferred the promotion on him.

"By that time, people will invite me to be a member of the neighborhood good-will committee, to attend parties with whites, and even to give young white fellows some useful smart advice," he smiled. "What's more, I'll live in a big, clean comfortable house, sheltered by tall southern banyan trees. In the shade of the banyan trees the lawn will always be green . . ."

"Colonel Williams," she whispered," You haven't mentioned Mrs. Colonel yet."

The sergeant was pleasantly startled. His little sparrow was anxiously toying with a silvery barrette. He held out his arms to hug her, saying, "You're my baby, little sparrow." She didn't say a word, but, as tame as a pigeon, let him kiss her. However, her mind couldn't rest. She asked: "Are they all high-class people?"

"What high-class people?"

"The friends of Colonel Williams."

"Of course, they're all high-class people." The sergeant laughed.

"You'll want to marry one of their daughters," she said sadly.

The black sergeant silently stared at the air-conditioning vent. The cold air flowed in steadily and blew against the thick drapes. Because of his new ambition, he was trying, with some difficulty, to maintain a certain stoic mien. But he said: "I won't marry anyone but you: my baby, my little sparrow."

"Really?" she said delightedly.

"Really," he said.

Emily, wriggling, squirmed into the crook of his arm. It reminded him of a groundhog back home.

"Really?" she said again.

"I swear by Jesus Christ, you'll be my Mrs. Colonel for sure," he promised. He began to kiss his groundhog. But he knew she just couldn't concentrate on making love.

"Barney," she said affectionately.

"Yeah?"

"Barney, listen to me." She was nibbling on his black finger. "What you said is enough to make me very happy."

"What do you mean?" he asked.

"What do I mean?" she said with a smile. "I'm just a bar girl. I can't be Mrs. Colonel."

"Emmy!"

"Even if I wasn't a bar girl, I'm a bartered bondmaid—do you understand?"

"No, I don't understand," he smiled. "But it doesn't make any difference, you're my Mrs. Colonel."

"A bondmaid is a girl who was sold by her family as a small child," she said. "My mother was also a bondmaid, her mother too."

"Jesus!" the sergeant sighed, "a hundred years ago we were auctioned off like cattle! But look, I'm a sergeant now . . . "

"Yes, I'm happy for you," the little sparrow said. "I was brought up in those dark dingy huts, the kind you saw in the countryside. But what does it matter? I live more comfortably now than any of them. It's just like you're a sergeant now, but tomorrow you'll probably be a proud colonel."

"You were brought up in those huts?" the sergeant pondered. "I remember the battlefield where I did my distinguished service. It too had those low, dark huts. I walked into one of those huts holding a gun. A little girl huddled in a corner was holding a rag doll with broken arms. She wasn't terrified, nor did she cry. You grew up in that kind of hut too?"

"Tell me that you gave chewing gum to that little girl," she begged earnestly. "That you took that little girl to the camp and gave her lots of canned goods and food."

"Of course," said the sergeant, "of course! O Jesus Christ, I gave her all the chewing gum, canned goods, and food."

"I knew you would," she was relieved. "Just like you did today, when you gave those children that surrounded you pieces of chewing gum."

The sergeant grew silent, then lit another cigarette. He said, "But I don't like your rice paddies here or over there. I don't like the sun, the malicious woods, and those sons of bitches who hide in the jungle. They're as disgusting as leeches."

"The sons of bitches!" she echoed his curse.

"You can't tell who is who. God damn it!" the sergeant said angrily. "But I don't like to see us burn the villages to ashes, really, I was once a farmer . . . "

"But when the war is over, you'll be a colonel."

"That's right!" the sergeant, who had started to brood suddenly perked up again. "Just think, when my great-grandfather joined General Lee, he was only a groom."

Their passion flared again, and afterwards they fell asleep exhausted. At dawn, however, the sergeant suddenly started to scream in his sleep. His voice sounded like that of Homo sapiens in an age before language, yelling in terror.

YOU ARE A DUCK

Sergeant Barney E. Williams became ill. Since that day, he had had long nightmares every night, and just couldn't shake them off. He was sent to a mental hospital in the suburbs. An ambitious young doctor was put in charge of his case. He could speak English very well, but Barney didn't like him, because he constantly asked the sergeant many things about his past that he wanted to forget. However, the nightmares would return like ghosts to terrify Barney at a certain time every night. So he couldn't help but gradually grow to depend on this proud Chinese doctor, although he had always hated and feared these self-assured, arrogant, upper-class people.

"Are you feeling better?" the doctor asked with a smile. He sounded more like a duck than a doc, the sergeant thought. He answered despondently, "The nightmares just won't stop, you know that."

"Eventually we'll find out what's behind them," the duck said. "We are trying to find out what events may have caused you to be like this." He let out a professional laugh. He was really an arrogant duck, not a doc.

"Yeah, duck," the sergeant laughed mischievously, "yeah, duck."

"Very good," the doctor said. "Now, think. Before this have you ever experienced nightmares?"

"Jesus! I've never had them" the sergeant was getting irritated. "Well, once, but that was when I was only a kid."

"You said once when you were a kid. Very good," the doctor said happily. "Do you remember why?"

"I don't remember."

They became silent. The doctor just smiled and looked at him. He was really an obnoxious duck, the sergeant thought. However, he began to feel worried.

"Maybe because I was scared—I don't know," he replied despondently. "My father could sing a lot of pretty songs, especially if someone lent him a good guitar."

"Your father could sing a lot of pretty songs?"

"No one in the world can sing better than him," the sergeant smiled wistfully.

"That didn't seem scary, did it?"

"I don't know." The sergeant covered his eyes with his hands. He kept shaking his head. "I don't know," he said. "Doctor, do I have to tell you everything?"

"You must tell me everything," the duck replied gently. "We want to help you, you see."

The doctor lit a cigarette for the sergeant. Holding the cigarette, Barney's hand trembled faintly. But the doctor deliberately ignored it.

"OK," the sergeant said, giving in. "Often, late at night, he took me out to wander under the street lights. He was very good to me, Doctor." He began to laugh wearily.

The doctor said, "Go on, I'm listening."

"He would drink slowly, and then begin to sing softly in a strong, low-pitched voice," the sergeant said. "In the cold nights, after he'd finished drinking and singing, he'd say: 'Kid, let's go home.' "

"Your father said: 'Kid, let's go home.' Go on."

"We'd go home. Sometimes, sometimes that white man hadn't left yet, then we had to hide and wait for him to leave. Then, my mother would see that white man to the door—he was a dirty pig! And my mother, she would be all naked."

The sergeant began to sob. A glass on the table held a blooming red rose.

"It's good for you to let out your feelings," the doctor said. "All that is over now. It's good for you to let out your feelings."

"I hope so," the sergeant said. He lit another cigarette. "Then when we went home, my father would begin to curse and beat my mother savagely. But she only cried softly and never rose up against him." He dropped the cigarette into the water-lined ash tray, and watched the water slowly soak through the cigarette butt. He said, "It was on those nights that I started to have nightmares."

"This is a sad story," the doctor sighed gently. "But never regret that you told me these things. I'm a doctor. We are already beginning to move in the right direction: it was those emotional experiences of anger, dread, and anxiety that made you have nightmares. Let's keep on in this direction. Never regret that you've told me all these things," he said, "I'm your doctor."

"That'll depend on whether or not you can cure me."

The doctor and the sergeant laughed together. "I feel better now," the sergeant said. "Now I feel more at ease with you."

The doctor smiled. "Very good," he said, "very good. It says on the record that you have rendered distinguished military service. The was hasn't been too terrible for you, I guess."

"Not very," said the sergeant.

"For instance, are you ever frightened?"

"Yes, a little," the sergeant continued earnestly. "In the beginning, yes. But soon you begin to like it—you know, it was the first time in all my life that I was equal with whites: we hid in the same trenches, ate the same food, played cards, and went on missions. There was no difference at all. They could be shot down by the enemy too; there was absolutely no difference. In a war, you become a full-fledged citizen of the United States."

"And before the war?"

The sergeant laughed. "Before the war! Jesus Christ . . . You knew from the time you were a tiny kid you couldn't walk on the same streets as the whites. Ah, those clean, pretty, wide streets . . . Good Lord, you knew, even as a kid, you couldn't play with Dick, Tom and Jimmy. This made you mad, Doctor. Your world was so small, forever disappointing and filthy."

"You must have been a sensitive child," the doctor said.

"One time, I secretly scrubbed my face very hard with soap," the sergeant laughed lustily. "I was hoping to wash my skin white—Jesus Christ!"

"Ah," the doctor said, "so you like the army. You've fought side by side with Dick and Tom, and you could leave your sense of inferiority behind."

"I don't know," he said. "Sometimes I really wish the war would never end. Once I braved a hail of bullets to drag Roger back to the trench. I had known him since we shipped out. An enemy grenade blew away his left shoulder—it was all torn up. The son of a bitch!—he said: 'Barney, I really want to thank you for saving my life.' And then he died as if nothing had happened. He said: 'Barney, I really want to thank you.' It suddenly occurred to me that never before in my life had a white man spoken to me in this way. I cried, Doctor." The sergeant chuckled to himself. "They say Barney is a sentimental guy."

"You are."

"I don't know," said the sergeant.

"You are," said the doctor. "Now, think a minute. Did anything special happen this time just before these nightmares began?"

"The fact is, recently I've been happier than ever before," said the sergeant. "I met a girl."

"You fell in love with her," the doctor was delighted.

"I often ask myself, have I fallen in love with her?" the sergeant said. "She's a bar girl. Have I fallen in love with her?"

"Is she upsetting you?"

"Of course not," he said. "Emily's a nice girl. She's a pitiful good angel."

"Emily is a pitiful good angel?"

"She is a pitiful good angel," the sergeant said. "She's a bartered bondmaid—the kind of girl who was sold as a little child."

"Has she fallen in love with you?"

"I don't know," the sergeant said. "To use your language, she has a kind of 'inferiority complex'—did I say it right?"

"Yes, inferiority complex."

"Emily said she wasn't fit to marry me, because some day I will be a colonel," the sergeant was embarrassed. "That's what she said."

"At any rate, she didn't upset you in any way?"

"Absolutely not—Lord Jesus knows—Emily's a sweet girl."

"You said she is a pitiful good angel?" the doctor asked. "That didn't remind you of anything?"

"She told me she grew up in those small, dark huts," answered the sergeant. "This bothered me, but it wasn't Emily that bothered me—she's a pitiful good angel."

"Those small dark huts bothered you?"

The sergeant was suddenly alarmed. "I guess so," he faltered. "I guess so."

"We've come to a crucial knot, Sergeant," the doctor said gravely. "Keep going."

"Emily took me to visit a little village," the sergeant said with a deeply troubled expression. "The sun there, the rice paddies under the sun, even the lush bamboo thickets reminded me of another village."

"Do you remember that village?"

"I wish I didn't. At that time, the enemy, about four times as many as we, had encircled us from all directions. Those leeches in black shirts, those sons of bitches!" he grew furious. "We were slaughtered. Those sons of bitches!"

"You said you were being slaughtered. Go on, Sergeant."

"I was the only one left alive. After the enemy left, I ran with my automatic rifle all through the night. Then, I think I must have tripped over the root of a tree, and just fallen asleep. Because when I woke up, I found myself clutching the rifle and lying under this tree. Perhaps because of the fierce sunlight, I felt extremely nervous. I grasped the rifle tightly and shot at anything that moved or made a sound."

"So you became very nervous, you clicked off shots at anything that moved or made a sound," said the doctor.

"Then I guess I walked into a small village, just firing off shots like that," the sergeant murmured sadly. "That sun, those rice fields, those hideous woods. I shot without stopping until I walked into a small, low hut."

"So you walked into a small, low hut. Go on."

"In that hut sat a little girl, hugging a rag doll that had broken arms," the sergeant said. "She wasn't scared, nor did she cry, she just looked at me with big open eyes. Then I clicked the trigger . . . O Jesus Christ!"

The sergeant began to sob in terrible sorrow. The doctor poured him a glass of cold water.

"Doctor, I had to do that, you have to believe me," he said.

"I believe you completely," the doctor said. "Here, drink this. I believe you, completely."

"You couldn't tell who he was—they all looked the same: flat faces, slanted eyes, black cotton shirts. And I was all alone. Do you believe me?"

"I believe you, absolutely," the doctor said. "I know that you were in battle."

"I dropped into a groggy sleep outside that small, low hut," the sergeant said softly, "until our troops arrived. They said I had annihilated the whole enemy village."

The sergeant began to sob again. "Good God," he said. "You must know I didn't mean to do it. You just couldn't tell the commies apart."

"Drink some water, Sergeant," the doctor said gently. "Letting out emotions is a good thing for you—a very good thing."

"Ah, Jesus Christ," murmured the sergeant.
Tears slid down his black cheeks, like rain drops sliding down an ancient black rock.

A RED KERCHIEF

Holding a big bunch of red and yellow roses, Sergeant Barney E. Williams got out of a taxi, stretched out his long legs, and walked up to a small apartment. The sweltering July heat surrounded him from all sides of the narrow stairway. Sweat had made his face shine with oil. And beads of sweat gathered at the roots of his curly hair. But the sergeant was singing happily:

> Melinda, pretty Melinda,
> You are happy, never complain

He panted from climbing up the stairs. He opened a small door, and immediately saw her cute, but not very sturdy bed. A silvery hair barrette was lying on the sheet.
"Emily!" he panted happily. "Emily, my little sparrow."
She rushed out of the bathroom, wearing an old robe, her hair all wrapped up in a red kerchief. They rushed into each other's arms, and he kissed her still wet neck.
"Oh, oh," the little sparrow sobbed with joy. "Barney, you're such a bad boy," she said, "bad to the bones."
The sergeant bent down to pick up the red and yellow roses which had scattered all over the floor. "Look," he said, "I got out of the hospital, hopped in a taxi, and came straight here."
"What beautiful roses!" she said, tears flowing down.
"The whole month of June!" He put the roses separately into four wide-necked bottles. "The whole month of June, they didn't let us see each other." He put the rest of the roses into cups, jars, and empty cans. "But you sent me a rose every day—for the whole month of June."
"They told me they took very good care of you," she said. "Is that true?"
"Why, yeah!" he laughed, again revealing a row of snow-white horse teeth. "They treated me like an old friend."
"I was worried the whole time." She unbuttoned his khaki uniform for him and kissed his black, slim chest. "I have an uncle, I remember him, he . . . "
"He . . . ," said the sergeant.
"They locked him up in a dark room. It's been more than twenty years."
"He was mad?" the sergeant said.

"Don't mention him!" she hurriedly cut him off. "I was just worried."

"Don't be afraid of mad people," the sergeant said gently. "They are only wounded in their hearts. It's no different from being wounded on your skin—that's what the duck said." He started to tell her how that doctor was like a proud duck. She hung up the uniform for him.

"I'm not the least bit afraid," she said happily. "Let's forget it, OK?" He hugged her from behind.

The sergeant said, "Now I'm healthy as a contented bull. Emily, you're my bride. Marry me, OK?"

She turned around. They were silent. She started to laugh, her eyes were glittering with happy tears. "I'll be your bride forever," Emily said, her flat nose fluttered happily. "I'm your bride forever, but you can't marry me; I'm only a bar girl."

"Little sparrow, listen to me," the sergeant said solemnly. He was so solemn that he could paint the whole sun black. He said, "Remember? I'm the great grandson of a slave—a slave."

Even if she knew what a slave was, she couldn't really understand what it meant to be a slave. She shook her head. "But you want to become a colonel." She untied the red kerchief. Her short, half-wet hair slid down coldly. "But it's all the same. I'll always be your bride," she said smiling. "As long as you love me before you leave, that'll be good enough."

"You're a silly little sparrow," he said, full of the confidence of a healthy man. "The sergeant says he wants to marry you, then he wants to marry you."

"You don't have to be that way, really." She squirmed happily against his chest like a brown groundhog. "As long as you love me before you leave—completely love me—that'll be good enough."

Sergeant Barney E. Williams began to feel sad. He said, "They told you I'm going to leave soon?"

"You all leave sooner or later," she said softly. "Forget it! Let's enjoy the rest of your vacation. How many more days do you have?"

"Four days," he sighed softly, looking at the red and yellow roses all over the table and on the shelf above the bed. They were silent.

"Four days," she whispered.

"Little sparrow, listen to me . . . "

The little sparrow started to weep silently. "It's OK," she said. She began to take off her robe. Her breasts, which seemed slightly fuller, were trembling slightly. She turned on the fan beside the bed and lay down on her side.

"Little sparrow, listen to me," the sergeant kissed her. "When I was in the hospital, I told myself: for the first time in my life, there is a person who makes me feel important. That person is you, my little sparrow. I also told myself: for the first time, I have a purpose in life that I will fight for."

"I love you," the little sparrow sighed.

"I love you." The sergeant kissed her whole body lightly. "I don't want to leave you, do you believe me? But I want to go back to that battlefield; I want to kill all those black mountain leeches hiding in the woods, those sons of bitches. I want to become a brave soldier, a colonel. I want you to be proud of me."

Several times Emily wanted to tell him that she'd been pregnant with his child for over a month. It must be a pretty little black boy, she thought, blinking a pair of big goldfish eyes, just like his father. But she only said, "I will be proud of you." She smiled happily. The sergeant began to breathe heavily with excitement. The child must be a pretty little boy, blinking big goldfish eyes like his father, she thought to herself.

GLORIOUS SUNLIGHT

It was a foggy night. She came home from work and picked up a handsome white envelope lying at her doorway. She turned on the light and took the elegantly trimmed letter from the envelope. On it was a fierce eagle, grasping a bunch of sharp arrows in its claws, as if it were about to lift its wings and fly off. At once she remembered the certificate promoting him to sergeant. It too had a majestic fierce bird like this one on it. She kissed the letter happily. "Barney, you made it—I don't know what rank, but you've been promoted again," she murmured. "You made it, Barney, you made it!"

She put the elegant letter on the table. Sergeant Barney E. Williams was smiling gently from the picture frame. She took off her clothes and began to take a shower. She whistled his "Pretty Melinda" and thought of his manner as he boarded the ship. His profile in a peaked army hat looked truly like a brave soldier. The glorious sunlight was shining on the huge battleship and shining on his brand new khaki uniform. He was stretching his long arms, waving to her incessantly, and yet, she cried the whole time, as she stood on the pier.

"Sweetheart, I'll be all right," he shouted. "I'll come back to see you, I will." Then the ship slowly sailed out of the harbor. What glorious sunlight! Now her whole face was directed toward the shower head. She grinned.

"Tomorrow, I'll ask the bartender to read the letter to me." She said to herself, "This time, it's at least a second lieutenant. Lieuten-

ant Barney E. Williams!" She couldn't help laughing out loud and
spat out a mouthful of cold water.

   Under the light, the elegant letter was lying in silence.

*   *   *

   "He fought for the irrefutable ideals of democracy, peace, freedom and independence. He gave his life for the sacred principles
and convictions of the United States. In his sacrifice, he has added a
powerful boulder to the foundation for the struggle of the free
peoples of the world against inhumanity and slavery."

*   *   *

YANG CH'ING-CH'U

(1940-)

Yang Ch'ing-ch'u (born Yang Ho-hsiung) is a prominent figure in the native Taiwanese literature of the 1970s. He is unique in not having had a formal education, but he received an extremely rich education and experience from the school of life. He was born in a rural village in South Taiwan, but like many rural Taiwanese in the past thirty years, his family moved to an urban setting. In his case, the move was to the industrial port of Kaohsiung when he was eleven. He has worked at many jobs, most notably in tailoring and in the oil refinery industry. His last job was as a middle manager in a Kaohsiung refinery. Recently he has been involved in political activities outside of the Kuomintang Party. He was arrested along with other dissidents, including the writer Wang T'o, in December 1979, and as of this writing, he is serving a six-year jail sentence.

The stories of Yang Ch'ing-ch'u are populated by the people he is most familiar with: rural folks rooted to the land and those who became urbanized, small-town tailors, city factory workers and bar girls, petty clerks and hawkers. His writings have been criticized for their crudity, vulgarity, and lack of objective and intellectual perspective. But in the opinion of some, those shortcomings are more than compensated for by the immediacy, sometimes raw psychic violence, and first-hand knowledge and empathy for the land and the people that characterize his writings.

Most of Yang Ch'ing-ch'u's stories initially appeared in literary supplements of newspapers. They have since been published in the collections Virgin Boy *(Tsai-shih nan, 1971),* Wife and Wife *(Ch'i yü ch'i, 1972), and* Heart Cancer *(Hsin ai, 1974).*

"Born of the Same Roots" (T'ung ken sheng) was first published in Literature and Art Monthly *(Wen-i yüeh-k'an, no. 13, July 1970) and later in the collection* Virgin Boy.

Born of the Same Roots

Translated by Thomas B. Gold

THE CAR PULLED up to the Imperial City Hotel, and the driver opened the door. Cloud got out, pulling her two boys after her. She tilted her head and looked up at the towering building. Wow! So high, so broad! One, two, three, four—window on window, window by window, windows, windows, windows, all perfectly square. She could not tell where each floor ended. Was it two windows per story? She counted from the top to the ground and from the ground back up to the top. Twelve stories, twelve stories! The spotlights on the edge of the roof illuminated the building from above, and the night shone blue and beautiful. The mercury lamps in the front of the hotel, which were flashing regularly to welcome guests, made the street as bright as day. Cars were lined up at the entrance. The taxis dropped off their customers and disappeared trailing ribbons of exhaust fumes. As one bus left, the next crowded into its place. There was a string of firecrackers hanging from the third story down to the ground, and a big wooden board with large black letters written on red paper. Cloud was illiterate, but she imagined they must say something along the lines of, "The Wu's and the Chiu's: a wedding."

Her father was standing in front of the hotel door, beaming, shaking hands and chatting with all the guests. "Come on in, come on in, it's just about time. How come your mother didn't show up? What? Why didn't you tell her to come along too? Your wife didn't come? Why didn't you bring her?"

The doors were automatic. Whenever people approached them, they slid apart, and closed by themselves again after the people went in. Cloud didn't know where to find the switch. Holding onto one child with each hand, she stepped onto the rubber mat and after a moment the doors slid open. She quickly dragged the children in and when she turned, she found the doors were just sliding back to the center. Before they had a chance to close, the people behind her entered, and they slid back open. What kind of clever contraption was this? Sure was magical. Cloud was dumbfounded. She had never been through an automatic door in all of her thirty years. Her sister, Spring, was standing in front of the counter, laughing and greeting guests. "To the left, just turn left. It's in the Ts'ui-hua Room."

"Hi, Ah-fu, Ah-ts'ai!" Spring bent down and kissed Cloud's two boys.

"Big Sister, didn't your husband come?"

"He doesn't want to come," answered Cloud on the brink of tears.

"Well, I'll be. Wait a minute and I'll go fetch him."

Cloud helped Spring take care of the guests. She tried to imitate her, gesturing and saying, "Turn left please, in the Ts'ui—Room, in the Ts'ui-what Room?"

"Ts'ui-hua Room," Spring put in, telling the guests and answering Cloud at the same time.

"Oh yes, the Ts'ui-hua Room, in the Ts'ui-hua Room. Turn left, turn left, please." Following the sisters' introductions, the guests streamed to the left.

Then it happened in a flash: like a golden Bodhisattva coming down to the world, the bride entered, in a long pink evening gown, moving gingerly with the help of her mother and the matchmaker. Embroidered on her gown was a colorful phoenix of strung pearls with its head pointing at the collor of her powdered neck, its tail stretching down to the bottom of her train. A snow white fur stole was draped around her shoulders. Golden rings, bracelets and arm bracelets wound from her fingers all the way to her armpits. Golden rays flashed from her two golden arms. The most bedazzling of all was a pair of three-inch-wide dragon and phoenix arm bracelets. A pair of golden ankle bracelets shone faintly through the slit at the bottom of her swaying gown. Cloud studied the bride's face and felt that the beautician had worked magic on her homely younger sister, redoing her inside and out. With a face loaded with stage make-up, she looked like a flirtatious singer fresh from the television screen.

In her wildest dreams Cloud never imagined she'd ever live to see such a magnificent bride. Her sister looked like a princess out of a play. Cloud didn't know if she was happy or sad. Ten years ago, on her own wedding day, where was the fortune that could have made her a modern princess like her second sister? She had had nothing more than a new everyday wool dress. By comparison, she had really looked as destitute as a beggar's wife.

As the bride trod slowly with short steps, Cloud and Spring followed behind.

"Sis, take a look at the bride's handbag; it cost five thousand dollars—pure alligator skin. They got a guy to bring it back from America."

"Five thousand dollars?" Her heart stopped beating and plunged into the depths of despair. She couldn't imagine what made that dark brown, wrinkly handbag so valuable.

Mother turned to Spring, winked, and pursed her lips, signaling that she should not tell any more.

Mother doesn't want to let me know, Cloud thought. Because of my second sister's wedding, everyone treats me like a terrifying stranger, as if I'm going to steal her trousseau. Tears welled up in her eyes. My entire trousseau wasn't even worth one of my sister's handbags!

"Auntie's a bride, auntie's a bride!" The two children circled around the bride shouting.

"Don't be so noisy." The bride showed her displeasure.

"Don't be so noisy," Cloud pulled them over and admonished them.

You're the children of a pedicab pedaler. How can you be worthy enough to call her "Auntie"? She blinked back her tears. Second sister has always looked down on her pedicab-driver brother-in-law and on her sister, a pedicab pedaler's wife.

With him pedaling a pedicab we could still get by. But in July, they're going to forcibly abolish all pedicabs. How can he make a living then? He worries day and night.

She rushed forward and sped into the Ts'ui-hua Room and wiped away her tears. The bride was assisted into an upstairs room.

"Come in, come in," Spring was at the door helping people into the Ts'ui-hua Room.

"Spring, how much is Lotus's dowry actually?" The more they wanted to keep the secret from her, the more she wanted to ask. Spring did not look down on the pedicab pedaler's wife the way her other sister did.

"Don't tell it's me who told you; just pretend you don't know. Father and Mother told me a million times not to let you know. All in all, there's five catties of gold; a car; a hundred thousand cash and a house; plus a washer, television, refrigerator, dresser, and fabrics to the tune of about fifty thousand dollars."

Cloud felt her blood course and churn throughout her body. She leaned against the wall in a daze. My whole trousseau wasn't even worth one of her handbags!

"Sis, sis!" Spring shook her to her senses. "Pretend you don't know anything. For God's sake, don't tell how much her trousseau is worth."

"No, I won't, I won't," she forced herself to smile vacantly at Spring.

The Ts'ui-hua Room! As swank as they come. All over, countless decorative chandeliers illuminated the magnificent hundred tables. On the stage, a red velvet curtain hung from ceiling to floor. The walls were covered with a dark blue material decorated with all kinds of patterns, interspersed with famous Chinese and Western paintings. An embroidered carpet stretched down the aisle of the parquet floor. When I got married, they put up a canvas awning in the front yard of our broken-down thatch hut. Five tablefuls of guests were invited. They didn't have a chef, but just recruited two clanswomen to lend a hand.

The firecrackers began to explode and dinner was served. In came the bride and groom. The groom was handsomer by far than the bride. He was tall, with a large head and face, a high nose, and a striking air about him. You can just tell he's been a graduate student in the States! Of course, he's not to be compared with the pedicab pedaler I married. My man's not bad looking either, just a bit timid and not suave enough.

A self-satisfied smile formed on the bride's thick, protuberant lips. Her high cheekbones exuded the haughtiness of a daughter from a wealthy family. What could such a good-looking groom see in her? Could it be that enticing dowry? Or Father's two factories? Ah! Second sister graduated from professional school—although it took her three tries to pass the college entrance examination—not like me with no education. Father is loaded and so he could keep on hiring tutors for her; and after being tutored for three years, she got into a home-ec college to learn how to be a bride. Thus they plated her with silver and managed to catch a son-in-law gold-plated à la America. They say that after the wedding they're off to the States. And me? Still a pedicab-pedaler's wife.

A drum roll sounded from the stage and the music began. The red curtains slowly parted. Although it was a brisk spring day, the singers were wearing chiffon evening gowns with exposed shoulders. It was enough to make you shiver.

"Sis, let's go over to the bride's table. After all, we are sisters." Spring came over to the corner table where Cloud sat.

"No, you go ahead."

"The chauffeur is back. Should I tell him to go pick up your husband?" Spring grabbed the chauffeur and ran out with him.

He wouldn't come, no matter what. As his wife's father's buildings grew higher and higher, the son-in-law became more and more estranged. Then an acquaintance said to Father: "Mr. Yungchi, sir, when you go out you ride in your own black limousine in high style, beep beep beep. I ran into your son-in-law, the pedicab pedaler, on the overpass a few times. He had a customer and couldn't get the pedicab across. So he had to climb down and push with all his might, bent over with one hand gripping the handlebars and one on the seat. He was all out of breath when he got on the overpass. Sweat coursed down from his brow, stinging his eyes, and he kept taking a towel from the back of his pants to wipe it away. Poor guy! A fat cat father-in-law like you should help him out a little bit!" Father began to feel that he was losing face because of this no-account son-in-law, so gradually he began treating him differently.

And hadn't Father tried to help him out? He told him to work at his factory and that he would support the whole family. But the pedaler said, "My limbs are strong, why should I go depend on relatives? I couldn't stand having to be at Father-in-law's mercy to get by from one day to the next. Can't I make a living from my pedicab just the same?"

There was nothing Father could do. Next he found a man who knew the fabric business, and Father put up some money for him to open a shop with the pedaler. His son-in-law promised to learn the business. But the shop went under in less than a year. The man dissolved the partnership and opened his own shop, while the pedaler went back to his pedicab.

Father chewed him out: "You've always been just a no-good pedicab pedaler. That guy took you for a ride and you didn't even know it. I've lost face 'cause of you. Don't even pedal a pedicab anymore; don't do anything. I'll give you three thousand a month to support your family."

"I can't let you support my family my whole life. If you're afraid you'll lose face 'cause I'm a pedicab pedaler, you'd best disown me as your son-in-law." He hung his head and completely refused Father's offer.

He never visited his father-in-law from then on. Was it because he was too proud? Or was his sense of inferiority too deep? When his wife and children went to visit his in-laws, he took them in the pedicab to the corner of his in-laws' street, dropped them off, and pedaled back.

The singers came and went, holding the microphone, singing, twisting and dancing through their incomprehensible numbers. A girl wearing a traditional Chinese gown with a slanted lapel and wide trim came onstage and sang the Taiwanese folk song "Waiting for the Spring Breeze." That old song from Grandma's time has never gone out of style.

> A lonely night, alone beneath the lamp
> The spring breeze blows on my face.
> Seventeen, eighteen, eager to marry,
> Waiting for a young man . . .

The voice was soft and sweet, soaring to the ceiling and circling around and around, drifting back to the luxuriant green fields of home, floating through the bamboo thatch hut, wafting into and gently ruffling the needlelike leaves of the horsetail plants along both sides of the dirt road. Carrying Lotus on my back, with one hand holding a basket and the other hand a rake, sweeping up the fallen leaves, rocking Lotus on my back. "Waiting for the Spring Breeze" was a song of the firewood collectors. I was just at the age that my heart would flutter slightly upon seeing a young man.

One time my shoulders were killing me so I undid Lotus and put her down under a tree on a field divider. That way I could concentrate on raking the leaves and twigs. Lotus had just started to walk and she toppled over, puncturing the corner of her left eye with a branch and bleeding profusely. When I carried her back, Grandma beat me all over with a bamboo switch. Afterwards Lotus had a seven or eight centimeter scar by the corner of her eye. When it was time for her to take notice of the opposite sex, she often held me to blame for her disfigurement. How could she possibly sympathize with her family's poverty then! Mother had to work in other people's fields, and I, her big sister, had to carry her to the fields to gather pig-feed grass, sweet potatoes, and firewood. If I slacked off even a little, there was Grandma's unforgiving bamboo switch.

In the last twenty years, Father's business took off like a skyrocket. Father started out fixing woks and aluminum buckets by the side of the road. He was too poor to ever afford three meals a day. Three years after Taiwan was reverted to China at the end of World War Two, a mainlander who had just come to Taiwan from Shanghai brought a leaky kerosene stove for Father to patch up. At that time there were no kerosene stoves in Taiwan, and Father acted as if he had discovered a gold mine. He asked the man to pick it up in two days, and that night he brought it home and excitedly leaped around and told Mother, "Cloud's Ma, I'm going to strike it rich! I'm going to strike it rich! This kerosene stove from the mainland is the latest thing and it's perfect. Go borrow some money and buy me some aluminum sheets from the city. I want to make one like it and sell it. I'm sure it's going to make a fortune!"

"Let's see the fortune, then talk."

Skeptically, Mother went out to borrow money for Father and brought back the aluminum. Father worked day and night, night and day, hammering and soldering, and he finished the first batch of five stoves. Cloud and Mother took them to sell in the market. They gave a demonstration: lit the fire, cut up vegetables and cooked them right in front of the people.

"Come on! Take a look at this new product, a kerosene stove. It's convenient and practical. It's from the mainland! From the mainland! Cook a complete meal in only an hour!"

Mother and daughter jabbered on, stressing all the good points of the kerosene stove. Sales were beyond all expectation. From the village markets to those in the cities, they sold as many as Father could put out. Half a year later, Father hired five boys to help; after another year, he hired ten. He expanded from selling himself to wholesaling. Production couldn't keep pace with demand. Father ran around scraping up money to buy machines and a lot for a building in order to open a steel plant to produce in large quanities. Cloud happened to get married hastily just when Father was burdened with debts. Right afterwards, Father's fortunes took off rapidly.

When the era of the kerosene stove had ended, gas stoves took over. Father expanded his steel plant's equipment and retooled to make gas stoves. Again, he made a bundle. At present, Father owned a steel plant and a hemp factory, with over two hundred employees.

"Ladies and gentlemen, today we are very happy to attend the Wu's wedding reception. The groom is so handsome and the bride so beautiful. A match made in Heaven! Now let's ask singing stars I Hung and Pai Mei to offer flowers to the bride and groom and wish them a happy honeymoon and eternal marital bliss."

After the mistress of ceremonies finished, the two songstresses, accompanied by the orchestra, offered flowers to the bride and groom. A burst of applause resounded in the hall.

Cloud watched the bride put on her lei, flashing a toothy smile with her thick lips turned outward and cheek bones thrust high. She thought her sister looked ugly. She got goosebumps at the thought of the word "beautiful." By all accounts, Cloud was the prettiest of the sisters. At the age of nineteen, her face flushed from working out in the sun, she was like a bud about to blossom. Everyone who was introduced as a prospective match loved her. The first man's family owned a fabric shop, and he was almost ready to marry her. But when he learned that she had no schooling, he said that she couldn't even help out with the bookkeeping, and that was that. That man owns a small textile mill now. The next two men were also lost because she had no schooling. Grandma began to regret not having let her go to school.

The matchmaker introduced a pedicab pedaler as the forth prospect. Father said, "As long as he's honest and wants to get ahead, even a pedicab pedaler can succeed." Without even seeing the guy, he steeled himself and agreed to it. Well, since she hadn't gone to school, she was lucky that the guy wasn't choosy. It's all fate anyway. It wasn't until the wedding night that she saw his face clearly. He was pretty good looking but straightforward to the point of being slightly doltish.

Now they're going to forcibly abolish pedicabs, so they told him to learn how to drive a taxi. He learned how to drive all right, but after seven tries there was no way he could pass the written test for his driver's license. Every day he had a man who could read come over to teach him: no left turn, pass on the left . . . He memorized the traffic signs so well he'd never forget them as long as he lived. But he couldn't read two-thirds of the test. He knew the names of the signs but not how to write them out. He'd finished six years of primary school but wasn't much better at reading than Cloud.

When she was a child the teacher came to persuade Gradma to let her go to school. Grandma said, "What's the point of having school? No matter how much knowledge she's got, she still ends up getting married, raising children, and doing the cooking."

From the age of eight, she'd never eaten a meal at home she hadn't earned. She carried her first brother on her back till he was grown, then the second brother. When he could walk, the third brother came along. And then she carried the second sister and third sister.

Could she blame Grandma? Whenever she went home for a visit, Grandma would stuff three or five hundred dollars in the childrens' pockets. If any of the kids looked down even the slightest bit on the pedicab pedaler, Grandma's cane would get him. As Grandma lay dying, she held onto her last breath till Cloud came back. And when she came close to the bed, Grandma took her hand and said, "Cloud . . . Grandma's so sorry . . . I didn't let you . . . go to . . ." Without finishing, she died, carrying her regret with her.

If I were a young daughter in my parents' home now, how nice that would be. I'd live in a house with a garden, a maid, and a car. I'd go to school from kindergarten on, all the way up through elementary school, middle school, and college. With all the money in the family, if I could pass the test to study abroad, Father and Mother would surely let me go. At least, if for nothing else but an enticing dowry, I'd never end up marrying a pedicab pedaler. But can the clock be turned back?

Spring returned to the hotel and told Cloud, panting, "Sis, your husband's got me *so* mad . . ."

Spring said that when she got to their house, Cloud's husband had just come home for dinner.

"Brother-in-law, don't eat anymore, let's go to the restaurant."

"No. Your sister and the children have already gone. That's good enough."

"Your sister-in-law is getting married, and you, as a brother-in-law, should come and help out."

"I'll have to work the night shift."

"I'll give you ten times what you can earn in a night. Quick! Go change and let's go." He just mumbled something. Right then, a man on the street clapped for a pedicab, so he put his rice bowl down and hopped onto the pedicab. Dingdong! He rang the bell and pedaled off with all his might.

"Sis, now isn't that enough to really make you mad?"

Cloud choked. She threw down the piece of eel, rushed into the powder room and sobbed, leaning against the wall.

"Are you all right?" Spring followed after her.

"Your brother-in-law is afraid that Father will lose face if he comes. He just can't bring himself to come." Cloud couldn't suppress her grief any longer. "He's always been a no-good pedicab pedaler. They're forcing out pedicabs in July!"

"Sister. You've worked so hard for the family since you were young. You got married just as we started to move up. I'll graduate from college in July, and I'll be getting married soon, too. I'm going to ask Father for a dowry worth as much as Lotus's. And I'll give it all to you."

Spring started crying too. Cloud held her, weeping, her words choking between the sobs.

"No. Father would never go along with it. Anyhow, anyone who marries a girl from a rich family like ours expects a big dowry." A married daughter becomes part of another family. How dare she think of things that don't belong to her? She wiped her tears and eased Spring out the door. "Don't worry about me. Go take care of the guests, and keep an eye on my children while you're at it. I can't eat anymore."

When Cloud walked out of the powder room, a human pyramid was being erected onstage. All the guests held their breath, mesmerized. Cloud slipped out through the emergency exit and walked toward the street.

Taxis scurried along the asphalt road which was illuminated by fluorescent street lights. On the long stretch of road, you couldn't see even one pedicab. Pedicabs will soon be extinct. They're going to forcibly abolish them in July. Well, one thing good will come of that, he won't make Father lose face anymore.

She considered flagging down a taxi to take her home, but thinking about him pedaling so hard on his pedicab, she couldn't lift her hand.

WANG T'O

(1944–)

Wang T'o (born Wang Hung-chiu) is perhaps the most action-oriented writer of native Taiwan literature in the late 1970s. In his view, a writer's duty is to "struggle for the realization of the ideal of a more just, equal, and enlightened society," and contemporary literature should "give its strength for not only life and society, but also for the future."

Wang T'o was born in 1944 to a poor fishing family in the village of Pa-tou-tzu near the major northern port of Keelung in Taiwan. Early experiences of class prejudice instilled in him a strong class consciousness. He came of age in a period when Taiwan had a rapidly developing economy and a relatively mobile society. Wang T'o was one of the few from his home town to receive a college education. After graduating in Chinese Literature from Taiwan Normal University, he taught in a junior high school in the then remote town of Hua-lien. Soon he grew dissatisfied with his destiny as an obscure country schoolteacher, so he began to travel around Taiwan and immerse himself in life. At this time he tried his hand at writing. Wang T'o's consciousness of nationalism and sociopolitical activism was sparked by the Pao-Tiao Movement in the late 1960s, and was further fueled by changes in Taiwan's status in the international arena in the 1970s. As Wang became more active politically, his writing, which had always been concerned with social injustice, became more activist and strident in tone. He has to his credit two collections of short stories, Chin-shui Shen *and* May He Return Soon *(Wang chün tsao kuei), published in 1976 and 1977 respectively; a collection of political interviews entitled* Voices outside the Party *(Tang-wai te sheng-yin, 1978); and numerous essays on contemporary literature.*

Wang T'o also was a lecturer in Chinese literature at the National University of Political Science in Taipei. He is currently serving a six-year sentence following his arrest along with other political dissenters in December 1979. "May He Return Soon" is largely based on his childhood experiences in a fishing village, and as such, is realistic and convincing in spite of its social mission.

May He Return Soon

Translated by Vivian Hsu and David Wank

I

AT NINE O'CLOCK in the morning the sun suddenly disappeared. Gloomy darkness descended on the earth. An aria from the Taiwanese opera "Wang Pao-ch'uan and Hsüeh P'ing-kuei"* blared from the radio in the living room. Grandma Chin sat on a stool by the doorway, listening to the opera while sewing a button on the school uniform for her third-grader grandson, Chia-hsiung. Bending down her head and holding the garment right under her spectacles, she was a picture of perfect concentration.

"Ma, with the sky so dark, how can you see without the light?" Her daughter-in-law Ch'iu-lan walked past her and out the front door, carrying a bucket of freshly washed clothes.

Grandma Chin tilted her head and shifted the garment around to face the light. Holding a needle in her right hand, she groped on the garment for a while, then pulled the needle and thread through.

"Curse it! What kind of September weather is this? This early in the morning and the sun's gone out already, everything's so dark. I can't even see the needle to sew on a button." She looked up. Ch'iu-lan had already carried the bucketful of clothes to the clothesrack in the front yard.

"Aiyo! How can you wash bedding in this kind of weather? They'll never dry out!"

"Who could have known the sky would cloud over? Earlier this morning the sun was blazing like a fire," Ch'iu-lan said, wringing out the wet sheet with both hands. She then spread it dextrously over the bamboo pole and tugged at the corners to smooth it out.

"In five or six days Wan-fu will be home. If I don't wash them now, he'll scold me again for lazing around the house," she said.

"How dare Wan-fu scold you for being lazy? He isn't exactly hardworking himself. I've never seen him pick up a broom or wash a bowl when he comes home, yet he has the nerve to say that others are lazy. He's got a mouth to criticize others but not himself!"

"He works hard all day long on the boat. When he comes home

---

*Wang Pao-ch'uan is a character in a popular romance set in the T'ang dynasty. She is said to have endured stoically in an abandoned kiln for eighteen years, before her husband, Hsüeh P'ing-kuei, came back to be reunited with her after having led successful military expeditions in Korea.

he deserves a good rest. Things like sweeping and washing dishes are best left to us women. No reason why he should bother with them." So Ch'iu-lan defended her husband.

"You're right. What you said makes sense." Grandma Chin felt comforted by her daughter-in-law's words. She tied a knot in the thread and carefully broke it off with her teeth. She then folded up the garment, all the while muttering to herself, "That child Chia-hsiung. He's as wild as an ox. There aren't even two buttons left on his uniform. God knows how he pulled them off." She stood up, holding the uniform in both hands. Then suddenly she turned and asked Ch'iu-lan, "You say Wan-fu will be home in five or six days?"

"That's right. They left port on the seventh. Today is the six-teenth. It's been ten days already."

"That's about right, isn't it?" Grandma Chin turned and walked into the house still muttering to herself, "I'm really getting muddle-headed. I can't even remember how many days Wan-fu's been at sea anymore."

The opera suddenly stopped. A woman announcer came on, speaking Taiwanese in a crisp voice. "Emergency typhoon report. Packing powerful winds, typhoon Zola is three hundred kilometers west of Luzan Island. Due to southwest air currents, typhoon Zola has veered northeastward and is heading for the Taiwan Strait."

Hanging up clothes outside the house, Ch'iu-lan suddenly felt her heart contract. She threw down the wet clothes, ran into the living room, and stood listening intently to the radio.

"The Weather Bureau issued a typhoon warning half an hour ago. Boats in the Taiwan Strait are advised to keep on the alert. Boats should prepare to go to the nearest harbor to avoid the typhoon."

Ch'iu-lan turned off the radio and walked silently out the front door. All around was a deep gloom with not a speck of sunlight. Grandma Chin followed Ch'iu-lan out of the house, then said to her back, "Ch'iu-lan, is the opera over?"

"Another typhoon is coming," Ch'iu-lan said weakly.

"Curse this September weather! A typhoon every three or five days! It's clearly conspiring to make trouble for us people who eke out a living from the sea."

Night descended gradually. Grandma Chin sat with the whole family in front of the radio in the living room listening to the broadcast. Several times she glanced at Ch'iu-lan, uneasily scrutinizing her face. At dinner, Ch'iu-lan had only swallowed a few mouthfuls. Her mother-in-law had urged earnestly, "Eat, you've got to eat a little more." But Ch'iu-lan just brushed her aside, "I'm full. I can't eat anymore." Every time a typhoon came,

Ch'iu-lan was always like this: unable to eat or sleep. Her behavior only deepened Grandma Chin's own anxiety.

After the news broadcast came the weather report. Chia-hsiung yelled out, "I don't want to hear anymore! I don't want to hear anymore!"

Grandma Chin coaxed in a low, wheedling voice, "Chia-hsiung, behave. Don't make a fuss. A typhoon is coming. Let's listen to the weather report." Her little granddaughter, Yü-chiao, had fallen asleep in Ch'iu-lan's lap. Ch'iu-lan pursed her lips and gazed silently at the radio.

"Weather report on typhoon Zola. Strong southwesterly air currents have pushed typhoon Zola to two hundred kilometers southwest of the Banshi Channel, and it is picking up intensity. According to the Weather Bureau, barring unforeseen factors, Zola is due to enter the Taiwan Strait tomorrow afternoon. The typhoon center will land at Heng-ch'un at midnight tomorrow. The Department of the Interior has issued this statement: Regional typhoon emergency centers have been set up. All citizens should keep tuned for news of the typhoon's progress and be on the alert at all times in order to minimize typhoon damage. Now, the fishing industry's report: Typhoon Zola has increased wind velocity in the southeastern Taiwan seas to an average speed of grade twelve to fourteen . . ."

Hugging the child to her bosom, Ch'iu-lan stood up and walked silently toward the bedroom. Grandma Chin gazed after her retreating figure, shook her head, and sighed. She then got up and snapped off the radio. Chia-hsiung immediately began wailing, "I'm still listening! I'm still listening! Why did you turn it off?"

Grandma Chin scowled. "How can you be so naughty! Can't you see that Mommy is upset? Don't be such a nuisance at a time like this," she scolded.

"I still want to listen some more," Chia-hsiung grumbled, looking sullenly at his grandmother.

"The hell with your listening. We don't even know what's happening with your father out at sea, and here you want to keep listening to the radio." Grandma Chin tugged at him. "Come along. Come along. Go to bed. Big people are really worried . . . and you want to keep listening to the radio. Only bad children are like that."

Ch'iu-lan came striding angrily into the living room and scolded him loudly. "You think no one here dares to give you a beating, don't you? You don't listen when people talk nicely to you. In a minute I'm going to beat you until you crawl like a dog."

At this Chia-hsiung finally stood up. He pouted as if suffering from a grave injustice. Dragging his feet he went off slowly to the bedroom muttering to himself, "So I'll go to bed. What's the big deal?"

Grandma Chin followed him with her gaze. Shaking her head she said tender-heartedly, "That child. He just doesn't listen to reason." Then she turned to Ch'iu-lan, "You ought to go to bed a little early too. No need to be so upset. This isn't the first time Wan-fu has gone out to sea. Hasn't he come back safely every time there's been a typhoon? You're just getting yourself all worked up for nothing."

Ch'iu-lan did not respond. She stood stiffly and watched Chia-hsiung's back disappear through the bedroom door. Then she walked after him.

Grandma Chin gazed at Ch'iu-lan's bedroom and heaved a sigh. Then she picked up a bunch of incense from the red wooden table in the living room. Lighting a candle she bowed reverently to the gods on the altar table and prayed quietly for Wan-fu's safety. She then bowed to the ancestral tablets. After she had completed this ritual, she retired to her own bedroom, leaving the two candles burning. Through the wind-whistling night, from their stations on the altar table, the austere countenances of the gods and the dim ancestors looked through the flickering candles into the pervasive silence.

Ch'iu-lan lay on her bed and stared at the ceiling with her wide-open eyes. The distant howling of the wind and the roaring of the waves pounded on her ears. It was already midnight, but she was still being kept awake by an unconquerable anxiety. Over and over again she comforted herself with her mother-in-law's words: "This isn't the first time Wan-fu has gone out to sea. Hasn't he come home safely every time there's been a typhoon?"

And yet, the voice from the radio echoed repeatedly in her mind, "Emergency typhoon alert . . . Emergency typhoon alert."

She turned irritably on her side. Just then she saw that Chia-hsiung, who was asleep on the bottom bunk against the wall, had kicked off his blanket. He was lying flat on his back, with his tummy exposed. His breathing was coming in wheezes. She considered getting up, but her head felt heavy and her limbs didn't want to move. She hesitated. Chia-hsiung's wheezing breath finally got to her, forcing her to get up and go over to his bedside. She pulled up his pants, tucked his shirt in, and gently pulled the blanket up over him. Then she tiptoed back to her own bed.

"You've been married almost ten years already. How come you are still so nervous about this? Wan-fu's no child. Whenever a typhoon comes you go crazy worrying about him. You practically stop eating and sleeping. You're only being ridiculous."

Her mother-in-law had teased her this way many times, but only because her mother-in-law was fond of her. Ch'iu-lan knew that Wan-fu was no child. Since he had been a boy he had been out to sea with his father, and for all his life he had eked out a living from

fishing. There was no reason for her to worry. Yet every time a typhoon came, she felt as if her heart were hung up on tenterhooks.
Wan-fu had told her he didn't like for her to be like this. He teased
her about being so neurotic. But . . .

"Aiee." She lay on the bed and sighed. She thought of the first
time her marriage to Wan-fu was discussed. Her parents had said to
her, "Anybody who chooses the route of a sea fisherman puts half
his life in the clutches of the Sea Dragon God. You are putting your
whole future on the line. Wan-fu's a good man, but you'd better
think this over carefully."

No, it wasn't that she regretted her decision to marry Wan-fu. It
was just that from the outset she had been determined to get him to
change his occupation. But already ten years had gone by and he
was still a fisherman. She was annoyed and somewhat angry with
him. They had argued about it many times. He would always say,
"I've been a fisherman since I was a kid. It's the only thing I'm good
at. You think I can change jobs just like that? Well, it's easier said
than done. We're not kids playing house who can quit whenever
they feel like it. If I leave the sea how will I support the family?
What will we all eat?"

With his kind of reasoning, she could never win. But . . .

Aiee. Why doesn't he show any consideration for those who
worry about him and suffer over him?

Waves of aching swelled in her chest. Tears trickled down her
temples. She felt all alone. In the deep of night with a typhoon approaching, how she wished that Wan-fu were lying safely by her
side. She wouldn't mind it even if they had to endure greater hardship and poverty.

"When Wan-fu comes back this time he'll have to find another job
no matter what." So she told herself as she lay on the bed. The
howling of the wind and the distant roaring of the waves sounded
like a dirge, singing of the bitter life of the fisherman.

II

By early next morning, the wind and waves had intensified. The
tall foaming breakers outside the harbor could be seen from the
window. Ch'iu-lan made breakfast for Chia-hsiung and got him off
to school. Then she did the wash. By now it was already past nine
o'clock. Her daughter, Yü-chiao, was still fast asleep. Ch'iu-lan
looked over at Grandma Chin, who was combing her hair.

"Ma, look after Yü-chiao for me, will you? When she wakes up be
sure to put some extra clothes on her. It's really windy out there.
I'm going to Wan-fu's company to find out what's going on."

"You really are one to worry. Wan-fu's been captain of his boat for almost five years now. Whenever there's a typhoon warning he always rushes back before anybody else. How could anything happen to him?" Grandma Chin cocked her head to one side. Too occupied with coiling the bun on the back of her head to notice that Ch'iu-lan had gone out the door, she continued garrulously, "Since you love to worry, go ahead and ask around at the company, that'll at least set your heart at ease."

Their house was on a mound behind a row of houses right up the street from Wan-fu's company. Directly opposite the company was the fish market, while the Fishermen's Union office was cater-cornered. From the front door of their house one could see the bustle of pedestrians and cars up and down the street and, just a bit beyond, the two breakwaters of Keelung harbor extending out like pincers. When Ch'iu-lan was pregnant with Chia-hsiung she liked to accompany Wan-fu to the docks to see him off when he was putting out to sea. But after Chia-hsiung was born, she stopped seeing him off. For one thing, she had become more tied down; and for another, the fellows on Wan-fu's boat teased them about it, saying that they wore the same pair of pants and that was why they couldn't be apart. She'd always lived in the city, so she felt no embarrassment at this kind of joking and even found it rather amusing. But Wan-fu would get all flustered. He told her that this just wasn't done and that it really put him on the spot. She concluded that Wan-fu objected to her seeing him off. Peeved, she stopped going to the harbor with him. However, she would still stand by the window in her house and watch the boats going in and out of the harbor. When she could vaguely make out the name, "Hua Feng I," on Wan-fu's boat, she would gaze after it as it sailed out of the harbor and faded into the vast sea.

Ch'iu-lan opened her umbrella, but the strong wind blew it around wildly even though she was hanging on to it with both hands. She gave up and pulled the umbrella shut. The slanted weave of the rain beat down mercilessly on her. She smoothed her hair back with her hand and ran down the steps.

When she reached the company's front door, her nostrils were assailed by the odor of engine oil mixed with that of rancid fish. The office was completely deserted. Coils of thick rope were piled on one side. On the large blackboard against the wall was written the name of each company boat with its departure and arrival times. Ch'iu-lan quickly scanned the blackboard for Wan-fu's boat. Only the departure time had been recorded. She looked at the names of the other boats and saw that some had already returned.

Her heart suddenly sank, and a sense of foreboding filled her. But then in the next instant she reprimanded herself, "How can I think like this? Nothing is going to happen. Nothing is going to happen."

She called loudly into the inner office, "Anyone here?" She waited for a minute, but no response came. She felt slightly annoyed and grumbled to herself, "How come there's not a soul here?"

She waited a bit longer. Just as she was about to leave, a tall thin man suddenly emerged. "Who's there?" he asked.

Ch'iu-lan rushed over to him, "Lin, it's me."

"Oh. So it's Mrs. Wang. Come sit down," he said.

"With such a terrific typhoon, fierce wind and waves and all, I wonder what's happened to Wan-fu's boat."

"The Hua Feng I and II should be just fine. They cabled us yesterday that they're already enroute home. You can set your mind at rest. Go home, eat well, and get some good sleep. Everything will be OK," Lin said. "It's well known in Keelung that Wan-fu is very cautious. You can rest assured, Mrs. Wang."

"If it's like you say, I won't worry anymore," Ch'iu-lan said with a short laugh. "I was just afraid he's too stubborn, that he won't think about sailing to safety until the storm is right over his head."

"No way. I can't say the same for the others, but I wouldn't be worried about Wan-fu. He always starts back first when a typhoon is on its way."

"But . . . " Ch'iu-lan looked at the records on the blackboard and felt her worry rise up again. She knit her brows and, pointing at the blackboard, said, "The others' boats have come back already. But the Hua Feng I and II . . . "

"Oh, you're talking about the records on the blackboard. They're not a hundred percent accurate either. Each pair of trawlers works in a different area. Some are pretty close to Keelung harbor and others are far off. This time, the Hua Feng I and II were working in the Bashi Channel. They couldn't have gotten back to Keelung harbor so soon," Lin smiled. "Mrs. Wang, just relax. I'll guarantee that Wan-fu's OK. He's probably in Kaohsiung drinking beer and playing games with the crew right now. Why worry so much about him?" After listening to Lin, Ch'iu-lan felt less anxious.

"I guess you're right. It's too early to start worrying. Everyone should be OK, as you say." She thanked him repeatedly and left.

The street was drenched. Cars cruising by splashed up sheets of muddy water, making the whole street seem even filthier. Small groups of fishermen, wearing knee-high boots and stinking of fish hurriedly worked their way up to the street carrying bundles of rope and boxes of fish.

So this time Wan-fu had gone to work in the Bashi Channel. No wonder his boat was slower than the others in getting back. But didn't the radio broadcast say that the typhoon was coming up from the Bashi Channel? And if the typhoon came up so suddenly, could he have escaped in time?

Uneasiness began gnawing in her chest. If the boat had sailed to Kaohsiung harbor, the company would undoubtedly know by now. The boat company has always kept a watchful eye on the whereabouts of each boat. The radio dispatcher would have cabled back a report. Why hadn't Lin mentioned this?

Ch'iu-lan suddenly stopped in her tracks. But she caught up her own thoughts, and again reassured herself, "If the boat really had an accident, Lin wouldn't have been so offhand about it. He was laughing and joking . . . An accident is a serious matter after all."

She calmed down a bit, but suspicion still weighed on her heart. She considered going back to the company and really clearing this thing up for herself. But she was afraid they would think she was a nuisance and laugh at her for being neurotic. Don't bother then? That too left her feeling uneasy. Her mind seesawed back and forth as she bowed her head and walked slowly on. When she had already reached the stone steps leading to her house, she finally made up her mind: she turned around and walked back to the company.

This time, Lin wasn't there. The only person there was the accounting girl who had just returned from the bank. She said that Lin had gone to the fish market. As for the whereabouts of the boats, she knew absolutely nothing.

The noise of people and cars swirled together in a vast, confused hubbub in the fish market. Fishermen were carrying boxes of fish from the boat at the dock to the auction ground. Some boxes were being transported on conveyor belts directly from the dock to freezer lockers. Competing voices blared from megaphones, quoting the prices, "Eighteen dollars. Twenty-five dollars." Occasionally a loud curse or a vulgar joke rose above the din. Although Ch'iu-lan had been to the market many times before, she could never get used to the thick, fishy smell and the confused uproar. Ch'iu-lan looked around in the crowd, hoping to catch sight of Lin or one of Wan-fu's friends. At the same time she had to be on guard to dodge the men carrying boxes of fish in order to avoid being knocked down by one of them.

The bay was jam-packed with boats. One by one Ch'iu-lan scrutinized the name of each boat, Man Fu, Ch'ing Feng, Lung Ta, Fu Hua. . . . Some boats were right up against the dock. The rest were lined up row upon row extending out from the dock. Thick steel cables, fastened securely to the round moorings on the dock, lashed the boats together.

"Wan-fu's wife!"* Suddenly someone called her from one side. Ch'iu-lan turned and saw that it was K'un-huo, a fellow who had once worked on the same boat with Wan-fu. A towel was tied around his head. He wore cotton gloves as he pulled on a steel cable.

"K'un-huo, have you seen Wan-fu's boat?"

"No. We just got into the harbor ourselves. We didn't see any boats behind us either. The typhoon really came on fast this time. As soon as we heard the alert we pulled our nets in and made a dash for it. We almost didn't make it."

"I wonder if anything has happened to Wan-fu." Ch'iu-lan said.

"No, nothing would go wrong with Wan-fu . . . he's always been very careful," K'un-huo reassured her. "Have you gone over to ask at the boat company yet?"

"They also said there would be no problem, but . . ."

"Well, if the company says so, then you needn't worry. Wan-fu's very cautious."

As Ch'iu-lan left the fish market, her heart felt more troubled than ever. By the time she got home it was almost noon. Holding Yü-chiao in her arms, Grandma Chin rushed out to meet her.

"How come you went off for so long? When Yü-chiao woke up she was crying and calling for you. I couldn't get her to stop. I can't make sense out of her babble. It's driving me crazy."

When Yü-chiao saw her mother she immediately reached out her little arms and cried, "Hug mommy. Hug mommy."

Ch'iu-lan took the child into her arms. Grandma Chin asked at once, "What's happened? Is Wan-fu's boat all right?"

Not a sound came from Ch'iu-lan's throat. Hugging the child tightly to her bosom she slumped into a chair. She looked exhausted. Grandma Chin sat down opposite her, gazing at her intently, waiting for a response. After an uneasy pause Ch'iu-lan finally said, "Everything is going to be all right. Lin from over at the company said they've already gone to Kaohsiung to sit out the storm."

Grandma Chin's face broke out in a smile. Deep wrinkles crinkled up at the corners of her eyes. Her voice perked up. "See. Didn't I tell you? Wan-fu's no child. He's been fishing since he was just a kid, and even studied at the Maritime Institute. He's also been a captain for many years now. He doesn't need you to get all anxious over him."

Ch'iu-lan just sat in the chair, totally unaware of the child wrig-

---

*In the Chinese original it is "Wang-fu *sao*," emphasizing that the speaker regards the addressee's husband as a brother.

gling around in her hap. Her eyes gazed vacantly out the window at the waves and mist being whipped up by the wind outside the harbor. She thought of the typhoon, of Wan-fu's boat, of what Lin and K'un-huo had said, of the boats that had already returned to the harbor . . . Everything fell into a jumble.

The night gradually deepened; the room had grown pitch black, so black that one couldn't even see the fingers of one's own out-stretched hand. Ch'iu-lan clutched a quilt as she sat on her bed, head down on her knees, listening to the wind howling over the roof. The door and the windows shook and clattered incessantly, punctuated intermittantly by the creaking and crackling of the tim-bers. The whole earth was quaking violently under the onslaught of the typhoon.

Even though Ch'iu-lan was exhausted, she tossed and turned about, unable to fall asleep. She heaved a sigh and reached out to stroke the two children by her side. On this stormy night, she was afraid that Chia-hsiung would catch cold if he kicked off his blan-ket, so she made him sleep by her. This boy, who had inherited his father's features, was a little wild. He was so mischievous that he even gave his teachers headaches. Wan-fu often said this was be-cause Ch'iu-lan had spoiled him. She maintained that, to the con-trary, it was because Wan-fu was never home to discipline him. She used this as another argument to get Wan-fu to quit his work on the boat and find a different kind of job. That way, she said, he would be able to spend a little more time bringing up his children.

However, he would always give her the same retort, "My abilities lie entirely in the kind of work I'm doing now. If I left my work on the sea, what do I have to compete with others for a job on land? I have to think about our family. How will I feed five or six mouths?

Aiee. When Wan-fu came home this time, he would have to change his job, no matter what. Ch'iu-lan was lost in thought. She was dead tired. Finally she dozed off into a fitful sleep.

Suddenly she woke up. Still groggy, she thought she heard some-one knocking at the door shouting "Ch'iu-lan! Ch'iu-lan!"

Her heart gave a start. In a flash she sat up in bed. "Wan-fu's back," she thought.

Without even taking the time to light a match, she jumped out of bed. Groping in the darkness she stumbled out of the bedroom and went to the front door. In a tremulous voice she asked, "Who is it? Who's there?"

She pressed her ear to the door and listened. She heard only the moan of the wind. She raised her voice, "Who is it? Who's there?"

She waited. Again no one responded. She hesitated a moment.

Then, trembling all over, she pulled the door open a crack. A blast of icy wind shot straight through to her heart. With a whoosh the candle on the altar table was extinguished. Her heart sank at once. She shut the door and her head slumped against the wood. Irrepressible tears flowed steadily down her face.

III

The typhoon passed over. One after another, most of the fishing boats had gone back out to sea. News that the pair of trawlers Hua Feng I and Hua Feng II were missing spread rapidly through Keelung Harbor and the surrounding area. The families of the missing crew members from such villages as Nantzuliao, Aoti, Shenaok'eng, Patoutzu, and Pachihmen all drifted to the fishing company. Old and young, men and women, all crowded into the main office of the fishing company inquiring anxiously after the fate of their kinsmen.

"Nothing has gone wrong. Everyone please calm down and go home. Get some good food and rest." Lin tried in vain to pacify the families that continued milling about the office, unwilling to leave. "The boats have temporarily lost touch with the company. We're trying to track them down. We've already cabled every harbor. We should be getting some information soon. Everybody please calm down. There is absolutely nothing to worry about."

"What's the use of cabling! How could they have lost contact if they're safely at anchor in another harbor? It's pretty clear they're still at sea and didn't make it to safety, otherwise, the company would surely know where those boats are."

An old man, his face a mass of wrinkles and his head wrapped up in a piece of cloth, said in a voice quivering with urgency, "I've worked on boats myself for half a century. I'm no three-year-old child. You guys had better send boats and planes out immediately to search. That's what you should do. You won't find a goddamn thing by sitting in your office sending cables."

"That's right. God damn it! The lives of twenty-some men are at stake here and you just pussyfoot around sending out cables. You had goddam better send people out there to search right away." A man wearing a farmer's hat, his face contorted with anger, roared out, " You don't give a damn for the lives of other people's sons! You act as though this is nothing!"

"Now, now. How could the company take people's lives so lightly? We've already asked all the other boats in the area to keep a lookout. How can you say no one has been sent out to search?" Lin said.

"What's the use of asking the other boats? You couldn't even fool a three-year-old child! Other people's boats don't eat your food or get your money. Why should they bother to search for you? Even a half-brained idiot can see that!"

"That's right! You've got to send people out to search immediately, not just sit on your ass in the office!"

"Our whole family with five or six mouths to feed depends on our one man to get by. Where's your conscience? You can't just brush the matter off this lightly," Grandma Chin chimed in.

The crowd became stirred up. People began to grumble and clamor. Suddenly a person standing by the door shouted out excitedly, "Yung-fu is coming!"

That caught everyone's attention. All eyes swung to the street outside the doorway. "Where? Where is Yung-fu?"

"There. Isn't that him?" The person by the door pointed out into the street. They saw a sturdy thirtyish man of medium build striding firmly across the street. He approached the doorway of the fishing company.

"OK. Let's wait for Yung-fu to get here, then we'll really talk business with Lin," everyone said.

As Lin glanced through the doorway into the street, his expression suddenly darkened.

Ch'iu Yung-fu was an employee of the Keelung Fisherman's Union. He had joined the Union almost eight years ago, after graduating from the Maritime Institute and doing his stint in the army. When he was in junior high school, his father had been the captain of a trawler that was lost in a particularly severe typhoon. The fate of its crew remained unknown. At the time, Yung-fu's mother and older brother took him along to the boat company. There they joined the families of the other crew members. They all milled about blubbering and weeping. The fishing company put them off by saying that the whereabouts of the trawler was temporarily unknown and that they had to wait until more accurate information was available before a settlement meeting with the families could be convened. In this manner, the affair dragged on, and it had dragged on for fifteen years now. The company had, in fact, not only failed to pay a bereavement settlement but also had not paid any other form of compensation. Out of sheer helplessness the families swallowed their grief and accepted their fate. Unable to collect and galvanize their anger and grief to make any demands on the company, they went their separate ways. Since then Yung-fu's mother had depended on their small sundries store to support the family. Through much belt-tightening she had managed to keep the family together and to raise him and his older brother's whole family. Each time Ch'iu Yung-fu thought back on that affair, deep down in his heart he blamed his mother and older brother for their weakness in dealing with it.

"Goddamn! We let them off the hook too easily!" he would often say.

Ch'iu Yung-fu had inherited his father's sturdy physique and was a born sailor. In studying at the Maritime Institute, he was, consciously or unconsciously, paying a memorial to his father. However, when he graduated from the Institute his mother firmly opposed his going to work on a boat.

With tears streaming down her face, his mother had entreated him, "You and your brother are the only ones left in the Ch'iu family. What if you too have some kind of disaster at sea? I've suffered half my life over your father's fate. How could you take the same route as your father and make me suffer for the rest of my life?"

Thus, Ch'iu Yung-fu was forced to remain on land. When he first started working at the Fisherman's Union, he saw with his own eyes the consequences of sea disasters. The crew members' families, the old and the young, would come crying to the Fisherman's Union seeking help. However, the Fisherman's Union was, for the most part, a puppet of the company bosses. It was the tool by which the bosses mollified the families. When Yung-fu saw this, the anger that had been smoldering in him since his father's death flared up. However, nobody paid any attention to the objections of an inexperienced youth who had just begun working in the Union. At first he could do nothing but swallow his anger. But the more he saw, the more his understanding and wisdom developed. He came to regard the hardship of the fishermen as his own. He exerted himself on their behalf and gradually won their respect and support. This enabled him to become a spokesman for the fishermen and to fight for their rights and welfare. Especially in negotiating financial settlements for sea disasters, he spared no effort in helping the bereaved kinsmen devise strategies. And during negotiations, he often led protests against the tactics of the boat companies. Although he seldom emerged the victor in these struggles, no one could deny that the companies had become much less ruthless in settling sea disasters with the Fishermen's Union than they had been ten or twenty years ago. They could no longer walk all over the fishermen. As a result, there wasn't a single company boss who did not detest him to the bone. Rumor had it that four years ago the bosses of several fishing companies jointly exerted pressure on the president of the Union to fire Ch'iu Yung-fu. However, the Union president was afraid of incurring the wrath of the fishermen and didn't dare fire him. There were also several fishing companies that had wanted to give him the title of "consultant" or some other kind of immaterial office. He would have received a substantial monthly subsidy. They hoped that he would thereby at least not stand against the boat companies. However, Ch'iu Yung-fu could not be budged.

This time a nephew of his was on the crew of one of the lost Hua-feng trawlers. Yung-fu's mother—the boy's grandmother—had been all worked up for the past several days. With a runny nose and tear-filled eyes, she berated him, "He's just a boy of sixteen. His voice hadn't even changed completely. How could you be so cruel? You didn't teach him to study hard. Instead you told him stories about the sea and got him all excited so that he signed on with the crew of a fishing boat. He was a perfectly good kid until you . . . Damn you! You deserve hell for this!"

His grandfather's sea-faring blood had flowed in the nephew's veins. Since he had been a small child the boy had shared his grandfather's passion for the sea, for a life of battling the wind and the waves. Although he was only sixteen, he was already as tough as an ox. He never took a liking to books, but dreamed about sailing on the open sea. Yung-fu and this nephew had always hit it off well. Perhaps out of his own frustrated passion for the sea, Yung-fu had encouraged the boy. He had even gone so far as to help him sweet-talk and convince his grandmother.

Now that something had happened to the Hua Feng I and II, Ch'iu Yung-fu was more worried and upset than anyone else. As everyone watched, he strode ashen-faced through the doorway. People rushed up to him and asked, "What's happened? Is there any news?"

"We don't know anything yet. I hope the boats are safe." He forced a smile to put everyone at ease. Then, glaring at Lin who was sitting behind a desk, he asked, "What the hell is your company planning to do? So far you haven't done a goddamn thing! You haven't sent out a single boat or plane to search. You've got the lives of twenty some-crew members here and you guys are sitting around as if nothing has happened."

"Yung-fu. How can you say such a thing? It's not that I'm unwilling to do something. It's just that the boss hasn't arrived yet. I'm powerless to make any decisions." Lin spread out his hands in exasperation, as if he were a helpless victim, wrongly accused. "What's more, a typhoon of grade thirteen-fourteen . . . Anything smaller than an aircraft carrier wouldn't hold up. What's the use of sending out boats and hiring planes? It would all be for nothing!"

"Hey, hey, Lin. What the hell are you saying? You dress like a man but you're talking like a shit-eating dog." It was Bonshi* the woman fish dealer who spoke. She was built like a tall husky man and had a sharp, resonating voice. At the market, she jostled with

---

*Bonshi is a typical Taiwanese name given to girls at birth. It reflects both the family's disappointment that the newborn is a girl and its reluctant willingness to raise the child.

the men to get the first shot at the newly arrived catch. In bargain-
ing she was second to no man. Her younger brother was also on
one of the Hua Feng's trawlers. Listening to Lin speak, she couldn't
keep from bursting out at him. "There are twenty-some human
lives on those two boats. Their young ones and old ones are so
worried their hearts are about to burst. And you have the nerve to
say that sending boats and planes out to search is a waste of time.
You're not made of flesh and blood! You must have grown up on
shit! Even a pig or a dog is more human than you!"

Her anger aroused now, Grandma Chin pointed a trembling
finger at Lin.

"Lin, how can you say what you just did? You haven't got a conscience! You've always been so chummy with our Wan-fu, and now
you act like nothing is the matter, and you even have the nerve to
talk that way! Heaven and earth won't let you get away with this!"

"Haiya. That's not what I meant. You all don't understand." Lin
wanted to explain but he had no idea what he could say. He was
sitting in his chair, shaking his head, with a nervous bitter smile on
his ashen green face. His exasperated expression was that of a helpless victim of false accusations.

"What's the use of yelling at me over and over? I'm not the boss. I
just work for him and get my pay. The boss hasn't come in yet.
What can I do?"

"There's no point in talking to a lackey of the rich," Bonshi said
to the crowd. Then she knocked on Lin's desk with her knuckles.
"Lin, where's your boss? Get him out here. He doesn't even pop his
head in for something as major as this. That's really going too far!"

"How do I know where the boss is? I was hired to work for him,
not to keep an eye on him," Lin said defensively.

"What nerve you have passing the buck at a time like this.
Everybody knows that your boss has entrusted you with the man-
agement of the company, down to the smallest detail," Ch'iu Yung-
fu said in a sober emotional voice. "Think of your father who made
a living as a fisherman and brought you up. He suffered the same
hardships as all fishermen. Now that you've become the manager of
a fishing company, you seem to have forgotten all that."

Lin's greenish face dodged Ch'iu Yung-fu's piercing gaze. He
said weakly, "I really can't do anything. I really can't do anything."

"Damn it! Talk gets you nowhere when you're dealing with an
ingrate who turns his back on his roots." Suddenly someone
brawled out, "Give the scum a good beating, it's the only thing he'll
understand."

The angry voice had its effect on the crowd. The mood became
ugly. Lin paled and turned to Ch'iu Yung-fu. He asked timorously,
"Why get so violent? We can handle this in a civil way."

"You must know how the families feel. You can't just sit around and wait for something to happen," Ch'iu Yung-fu said. "You can't wait until a house has burned down to put out the fire. You've got to rent a plane and begin searching right away."

"The boss hasn't given any instructions. I really don't have the authority to decide . . ."

"Fuck your mother! You're talking in circles. You're the manager, and yet you say you don't have the authority to decide. You mean your position as manager is all a hoax?"

"Don't reason with him anymore. Beat him up first and then let's see if he'll talk sense."

Tension was running higher and higher. Angry voices, curses, and shouts frothed up like the waves in the ocean. Lin stood up and implored Ch'iu Yung-fu with a timid expression.

"Please everyone, cool down a bit! Cool down a bit please!" Ch'iu Yung-fu faced the angry crowd and shouted over the uproar. He restrained a middle-aged man who was making a rush for Lin.

At this moment, a black sedan pulled up at the entrance to the boat company. Lin looked as if he had just seen his savior. He rushed out, calling out excitedly, "The boss is here!"

All eyes followed Lin as he rushed up to the sedan outside the door. They saw a squat, balding, middle-aged man sitting in the car. Over his round pot-bellied body he wore a spanking Western suit. Sticking his head out the window, he greeted Lin.

"How goes it? Any news?"

"There's still no news, sir," Lin said obsequiously.

The crowd came pouring out the door and surrounded the car. In great commotion they pressed in. "Hey boss. What's happened to the boats? You've got to give us an answer!"

"How's the company going to deal with this? You've got to tell us. This is a serious matter. Putting it aside as if it's nothing is going a little too far, don't you think?"

The boss surveyed the crowd surrounding his car.

"What do these people want?" he asked Lin.

"These are the families of the Hua Feng crews. They've come to inquire about those boats." In a low voice Lin spoke into the boss's ear. "They're making a row because they want the company to hire boats and planes to go out and search. They're getting vicious, even threatening to punch and kill . . ."

"Get a grip on yourself. Here, I'll tell you how to deal with this." He whispered some advice into Lin's ear.

"Yes sir," Lin said obsequiously. "You're not going to come in and sit awhile?"

"There's too much of a crowd. There may be trouble with me here. I'll leave it to you to cope with it."

"Mr. Chen," Ch'iu Yung-fu took several strides toward the car and called loudly, "I've got a nephew on one of the Hua Feng crews too. I represent all the families of the crew members in asking you what the company intends to do. The typhoon has passed, but nothing has been done to search for the missing boats, not a boat or plane has been sent out. What after all . . ."

"Don't worry Mr. Ch'iu." The boss's round, flabby face broke into a grin. In a smooth voice he said, "Just now in Taipei, I telephoned the air force and requested them to send planes out to search. I don't think anything serious has happened. The boats are probably just temporarily out of contact."

"Really?" Ch'iu Yung-fu looked askance at the boss and asked suspiciously, "I've just come from the Fishermen's Union, and I called to ask . . ."

"The planes probably haven't taken off yet," the boss said cutting Ch'iu Yung-fu short. He added nervously, "I'll have Lin call again in a little while to make sure they get moving on it. I've entrusted everything to Lin. If you've got something, talking to him is as good as talking to me."

"OK. You're the one who said it." Ch'iu Yung-fu wheeled about and faced Lin. "Lin, you heard what your boss said, didn't you?"

Even before Ch'iu Yung-fu finished speaking the fishing company boss hurriedly started up his engine.

"Hey, hey! You're going to leave us like this? Nothing has been resolved yet," everyone began shouting.

However, the boss paid no attention to them. Sticking his head out of the window, he exhorted Lin, "Do as I told you."

People cursed after the car as it sped away, "Damn you slick talker! You haven't cleared up a damn thing and you take off just like that!"

All this while Ch'iu-lan was leaning against the wall, with Yü-chiao on her back. Sitting down beside her was Grandma Chin. Throughout the whole confrontation with the boss, Ch'iu-lan had only listened in silence, her eyes red. Grandma Chin kept wiping away her tears, and occasionally she turned to those next to her, telling them how good her son was and what good care he took of his family. "He's our family's only able-bodied man. We all depend on him to live. The goddess Ma-tsu* couldn't be so blind." As she said this tears welled up in her eyes again. But then her faith in Ma-tsu soon restored her strength. She turned her face up to comfort Ch'iu-lan, "Everything will be all right. Ma-tsu will look after

_____
*Worshipped as the patron goddess of fishermen.

him. Whenever Wan-fu goes out to sea, he takes the Ma-tsu talisman with him. He'll be all right."

However, these words of comfort had a contrary effect on Ch'iu-lan. The tears that had welled up in her eyes began to course down her face.

IV

Five days after the typhoon had passed, the sun was blazing a fiery orange in the sky. The families of the boat crews had congregated in the corridor of the Fishermen's Union office building. As before, they were asking each about news of the boats, sighing helplessly, shaking their heads, and consoling each other endlessly. Just then, Ch'iu Yung-fu came walking down the corridor; his eyes were red, and his expression was full of anguish.

Ch'iu-lan immediately felt a sense of foreboding. Her heart felt as if a metal hammer had just pounded on it. A booming sounded in her ears, and her limbs went cold and limp. The walls around her seemed to be crashing down, mercilessly crushing her. By the time she got a grip on herself she could hear the anguished, heart-rending cry of a woman. The sound of muffled sobbing surrounded her. People from all sides surrounded the woman who was wailing uncontrollably, but she was lost in a world of her own, oblivious to those around her. Hugging one of her children she doubled over, shrieking her husband's name, "Ah-huo, Ah-huo!" The child on her back was asleep, but the three boys by her side, frightened by their mother's wails, began to sob fearfully, "Papa. Papa. Papa."

Grandma Chin stood to one side and held Chia-hsiung's hand. She too began a sad, heart-rending cry. "My son . . . Aaahh . . . My own flesh and blood . . . How could you have left this way . . . leaving behind your wife, children and old mother? How will we survive? . . . Aaahhh . . . My own flesh and blood."

Seeing his grandmother like this, Chia-hsiung cried out in alarm, "Granny, Granny." Grandma Chin immediately pulled him into her bosom. "How pitiful . . . So young and already fatherless . . . Who will bring you up? Ahh . . ."

Chia-hsiung had never experienced anything like this. His young and naive heart was confused and frightened. He could only make vague guesses as to what had befallen his father but he had no way of really knowing. Hearing his grandmother carrying on like this, he was unable to control himself and began to howl.

"Don't cry anymore. At a time like this, crying won't do any good."

Ch'iu Yung-fu suppressed his anguish and comforted the woman

with five children who had cried herself hoarse. He then walked
over to Grandma Chin and gently patted her on the shoulder.
"Grandma Chin, get a hold of yourself. Nothing has been
confirmed yet. You mustn't cry."

Ch'iu-lan held Yü-chiao in her arms. Her mind was a total blank
and her eyes gazed vacantly straight ahead—like a lifeless shell.
She walked straight through the crowd, down the corridor and into
the street. Sobbing piteously, Grandma Chin followed, leading
Chia-hsiung by the hand.

When they got home, Ch'iu-lan walked straight to her bedroom
still carrying Yü-chiao. Only then did Grandma Chin suddenly
realize that there was something odd about Ch'iu-lan. She quickly
wiped her tears and apprehensively followed Ch'iu-lan into the
bedroom. Ch'iu-lan was sitting bolt upright on the edge of her bed,
her mouth pursed tightly and her face a deathly pale. She was staring vacantly straight ahead. Grandma Chin reached out and took
over Yü-chiao. She asked timidly, "Ch'iu-lan, what's wrong?"

Ch'iu-lan sat absolutely still, as if she had heard nothing.

"Ch'iu-lan," Grandma Chin raised her voice. "What's the matter
with you?"

She leaned forward and peered intently at Ch'iu-lan. Ch'iu-lan's
lips quivered for a second but, as before, no sound came out.
Grandma Chin gave a start. She tugged at Ch'iu-lan's sleeve and
called out in alarm, "Ch'iu-lan, say something!"

She began shaking Ch'iu-lan and crying out wildly, "Ch'iu-lan!
Ch'iu-lan!" Just then Chia-hsiung also came into the bedroom.
Hearing his grandmother crying he was frightened again and began
sobbing, "Ma, ma!" Seeing the others crying, Yü-chiao began to
bawl. Grandma Chin and her two grandchildren surrounded
Ch'iu-lan, crying in a chorus.

After quite a while Ch'iu-lan suddenly said, "You all mustn't
cry." Her voice was strangely calm.

Startled, Grandma Chin immediately stopped crying. In a tremulous voice she called out, "Ch'iu-lan."

"Nothing has happened to Wan-fu," Ch'iu-lan said. "He's all
right. He's coming back!"

Grandma Chin looked up apprehensively at her. "What are you
saying?"

"Nothing has happened to Wan-fu. He'll be back soon." Ch'iu-lan
spoke with certainty, as if it were true.

"How do you know?"

"Didn't Wan-fu say so when he left?"

Dumbfounded, Grandma Chin gazed at her. Had her daughter-in-law gone crazy from grief? But her words and expression
were too controlled, not at all like someone deranged.

Grandma Chin followed Ch'iu-lan into the kitchen. She watched as Ch'iu-lan washed and boiled the rice and cooked the vegetables. It was just as always.

Could someone gone crazy act like this? She wondered: Wan-fu had always been very careful. Whenever there was a typhoon warning he was always the first to head for safety. How could anything have happened to him? The families of the crews must not have been thinking straight. They may have heard some rumor, and when they saw one person crying, they all started crying. Without having seen a single corpse, they went ahead and believed in some rumor. Curse them! Their crying can bring on real bad luck! When she had gone to the temple to offer incense the other day, the goddess Ma-tsu too had said, "Your son is alive. Rest assured. He will be home in three days." If Ma-tsu had said so, then it must be true. As these thoughts ran through her mind, she felt somewhat reassured.

However, there was still this nagging anxiety in her heart because the three days that Ma-tsu had spoken of had already gone by and Wan-fu was still not back. But then she again reassured herself by rationalizing: Well, actually three days is almost the same as five. In any case Ma-tsu had said he will return, so he certainly will return.

Having reached this frame of mind, Grandma Chin walked into the living room and announced to Chia-hsiung, "Your father is OK. He'll be home tomorrow." Her voice was unnaturally loud, as if she needed to convince herself.

However, the next morning, Tu Shih-hsien from the Fishermen's Union came running to their house. He called agitatedly to Grandma Chin, "The families of the Hua-feng crews are all at the settlement meeting at the Fishermen's Union. Why haven't you come? Hurry, hurry! We're all waiting for you."

"A settlement for what?" Grandma Chin looked at him, her heart pounding wildly.

"You mean you haven't heard?" Tu Shih-hsien glanced at her in disbelief. Then in a suppressed voice he said, "Wan-fu's boat sank."

"Who . . . who told you that?" Grandma Chin's face paled. In an anguished voice she charged Tu Shih-hsien, "How can you say something so sinister! Wan-fu was a good friend of yours. How could you put a curse on him like this!"

"Grandma Chin, you must be losing your wits in your old age. Would I dare lie to you about this?" Tu Shih-hsien continued anxiously. "Some tires, boards, and a water bucket from the Hua Feng were floating on the water; they've been picked up and brought back by other boats."

Grandma Chin turned her tragic, pale face towards Tu Shih-hsien. Tears were already streaming down.

"Grandma Chin," Tu Shih-hsien said as he walked out the door. "You've got to come soon. Either you or your daughter-in-law will do. We are all waiting for you to start."

She stumbled into Ch'iu-lan's bedroom. Ch'iu-lan was busy polishing up Wan-fu's leather shoes. Seeing her thus, Grandma Chin's heart gave a start. A flash of pain shot through her chest.

"Ch'iu-lan," she called out sorrowfully. She could say no more, her voice was too choked up.

Numbly, Ch'iu-lan lifted her head up. Ashen-faced, she stared at Grandma Chin. In a strained voice she muttered, "It couldn't have happened to Wan-fu. He's going to come back. He couldn't have . . ."

As Grandma Chin heard this her tears started up again.

V

By the time Grandma Chin got to the Fishermen's Union, the meeting was well underway. She wiped away her tears and sat down in a vacant chair near the doorway. All around her were women with babies tied to their backs or with toddlers in their arms. Their eyes were red from weeping and occasionally they brushed away a tear. Grandma Chin's eyes were drawn to Lin who stood on the far side of the round table at the front of the room. Slowly and coolly he said, "The company feels as grieved at the fate of the Hua Feng I and II as the families. The boat company is sympathetic to the financial difficulties the families are facing. Even though the death of the crews have not yet been verified, the company will give each family a support subsidy of 5,000 *yuan*.* Upon verification of the deaths of the crew members, the company will pay the family of each crew member a compensatory fund of 25,000 *yuan*, irrespective of the job-rank of the deceased. The 5,000 *yuan* support subsidy may be picked up at nine o'clock tomorrow morning at the company office. Please bring along your family's census records."

Lin finished talking and sat down. Immediately a loud voice piped up. "Hold on a minute. Hold on a minute. I have some questions here!" The speaker was a seventyish, dark-complexioned old man. He stood up and spoke in a quavering voice, "You mean to tell me a human life is worth only this bit of money? Your company is big enough to send out eight or nine boats each time. The crews of the boats are the ones who battle the wind and waves and earn big money for you, while their families depend solely on them for

---

*A U.S. dollar is equivalent to roughly 35–40 Taiwanese *yuan*.

their bare subsistence. But as soon as something happens, you totally ignore your responsibility to their families. The old and the young, all seven, eight or ten of them in each household, have no way to earn a living. The menfolks have given their lives for the company, yet you just fart around and only give 30,000 *yuan*! Isn't this . . . isn't this going a little too far? Aren't you being downright ruthless?"

"So that's it? Go to hell! A human life . . . and the fate of an entire family . . . They're worth only 30,000 *yuan* to you? Don't you have any conscience?"

"Money, what do I want with your money? Human life is what matters. You give me back my son," Grandma Chin said through her sobs. "You were born of a father and a mother like anybody else. You're made of flesh and blood. What nerve you have setting down these inhuman terms!"

The families were filled with grief and anger. The meeting seethed with righteous indignation.

"Please everybody, calm down a little. Don't get all worked up. This is a meeting," the paunchy man in the chairman's seat spoke up. He was a department head of the Fishermen's Union named Chao. "If there is a disagreement, let's talk it out calmly. We're here to resolve a problem, not to squabble!"

"I'm just a roughneck. I've never gone to school and I don't talk as genteel as you do," the old man stood up again and said in a shaky voice. "But I've lived almost seventy years. I've only got this one son; he's worked on the Hua Feng for five years now. Our entire family depends on him for our livelihood. And now he's died at sea for the company, and you can't even find his body. How do you expect me to talk genteel at a time like this?"

"Talk politely? You can talk politely for all anybody cares! Goddam, let's see somebody die in your family, then we'll all see how politely you can talk!" Bonshi joined in.

"Fuck you, you fat pig! Your words are sweeter than songs. You can talk like that just because nobody died in your family."

"You're an officer in the Fishermen's Union and chairman of this meeting. It's your job to speak up for us. For a human life and the fate of a whole family, you'd give only 30,000 *yuan*. Why the company is a downright bloodsucker!"

"I said if you have things to say, you can say it turn. Don't just yell. Otherwise how can we conduct the meeting?"

"What do you mean don't yell? Should we just sit here quietly and let the company trample all over us? Damn the blood-sucking company!"

At this Ch'iu Yung-fu stood up.

"Will everyone please calm down. The time hasn't come yet to bicker with the company about the size of the financial settlement."

Everyone immediately quieted down. All eyes were fastened upon him. The tone of the meeting became somber.

"Now that a city official and Director Chao from the Fishermen's Union are here, I beg them to uphold justice. I charge them to thoroughly investigate who is responsible for the death of the twenty-some crew members on the Hua Feng boats."

"Ch'iu Yung-fu, what's your point in dredging that up at this late stage?" Lin shot back, a tremor in his voice.

"What's my point?" Ch'iu Yung-fu glared at him. Enunciating each word deliberately, he said angrily, "For the twenty-some men on board the two boats, I accuse the Ch'ing-Ch'ang Fishing Company of outright murder."

Everyone was visibly startled. Lost for words, they just stared at the awesome figure of Ch'iu Yung-fu. For a moment the meeting room was frozen in a fathomless silence.

Then in a flash Lin was on his feet. Ashen-faced, he said in a trembling voice, "That . . . that's just absurd! Why . . . you're . . . you're a slanderer!"

As if a stone had smashed through heaven and earth, curses, cries and accusing voices exploded in the meeting room.

"You murderers! You murderers! Damn you, you ruthless pigs! Go to hell!"

"Slanderer? Bah! If you've got a shred of conscience left, if you remember how your father suffered the hardships of a fisherman in order to raise you, you'd drown yourself in the sea to do penance to your deceased father!" Ch'iu Yung-fu's eyes glittered with anger. Gritting his teeth, he pointed at Lin and shouted, "It's been five or six days already since the typhoon passed through. If the boats really did sink, perhaps some of the crew are still floating out at sea, or they could be stranded on some deserted island awaiting rescue. Not only did the Ch'ing-Ch'ang Fishing Company fail to send out a single boat or plane to search, you even lied to the families of the crews, saying that search planes had been sent out. If this isn't deliberate murder on the part of your boss and you yourself, I don't know what is!"

"Hear, hear! Yung-fu is really talking sense now. Just because the Ch'ing-Ch'ang Fishery has money and power on its side, you think you can take advantage of the bereaved families—the old and the young. You think no one dares stand up to you? You think you can just gobble us up alive, don't you?" Bonshi stood up. With one hand on her hip and the other pointing at Lin, she burst out, "It's not that simple. Let me tell you something Lin! You and your boss are responsible for the deaths of the twenty-some men. You're the murderers! We'll make you pay back those lives!"

Like an unleashed typhoon, a storm of curses and accusations rose to a furious height:

"Yeah! Yeah! You owe us those lives!"

"Damn you. You heartless murderers! You'll pay with your own lives!"

Lin's face became as gray as death. Turning to Director Chao and the city official sitting at his side, he forced a bitter smile. As if pleading for help, he said in a trembling voice, "What are they saying? I don't understand."

"Everybody please settle down. Settle down." The director pounded fiercely on the table. "This is the Fishermen's Union!" he bellowed. "It's not a court or a police station. We're holding a settlement meeting to resolve a concrete problem. We're not here to accuse anybody. If you want to make accusations go to a court or a police station."

The city official put down the tea he had been sipping and stood up. "The lives of the twenty-some crewmen are a serious matter. The government will certainly conduct a thorough investigation and arrive at a verdict that is fair to all parties involved. If the Ch'ing-Ch'ang Fishing Company is found to be guilty of negligence in the deaths of the crewmen, the government will deal with it through legal channels. We can all rest assured of that!"

"It is not within the scope of this settlement meeting to investigate who is at fault. Everyone please observe the rules of this meeting," the director said to Ch'iu Yung-fu. Then, turning to Lin, he said, "Please continue."

Lin swallowed a mouthful of tea and took a deep breath. Thus fortified, he stood up. "People. People. Please quiet down, let me have my say. My father was also a fisherman, so I speak from my heart. I have nothing to be ashamed of. I have done nothing that compromises my conscience. In its decision to pay a financial settlement of 30,000 *yuan* to each family, the company has taken into account the adverse circumstances of each family. At a time when the company is undergoing its own financial difficulties, we have decided to squeeze out the money. No other company has ever paid out such a generous settlement. If you ladies and gentlemen want to verify what I say, Director Chao of the Fishermen's Union is sitting right here. He specializes in this kind of accident settlement. You can just ask him."

"What Lin says is absolutely true. I'll vouch for that. The Fishermen's Union wants to see justice done for all involved. We hope that the families and the company will appreciate each other's difficult circumstances and resolve this problem as quickly as possible." Sitting in the chairman's seat, the director spoke in a sincere tone. "In addition to the 30,000 *yuan* settlement from the company, the Fishermen's Union will pay out a mutual aid fund of 10,000 *yuan* per family. There's also over 10,000 *yuan* in worker's insurance."

"The social security office of the city government also has a relief fund of 5,000 *yuan* per person," Lin added.

"Right. There's also the social security relief fund. Added altogether that's more than 60,000 *yuan*. Of course, 60,000 or 70,000 *yuan* is not enough to support a family forever. However, it will meet all your needs for the time being." Director Chao continued, "You can't bring a dead person back to life. There's nothing to be gained by bickering. If the matter is settled quickly, you can get the money and start thinking of your next move, . . . start a small business or what have you. Now that's the right track to be on!"

"To hell with you! We're not here to put on a play. You guys are picking up cues from each other. It sure looks like you've had it worked out in advance."

"What the hell is this, Chao? You toady up to the company just because they've got money."

"We don't need this kind of meeting. I haven't heard a single fair word on behalf of us fishermen."

Grandma Chin sat numbly in her seat listening to others' voices batting back and forth as if Wan-fu's boat had really sunk; she became choked up with anguish. But when she thought of Ch'iu-lan's steely conviction as she said, "Nothing has happened to Wan-fu. He'll be back soon," those words seemed to ring true. She couldn't be sure of anything anymore. She asked herself over and over, Who said that Wan-fu's boat had sunk? Who saw it happen? A few planks and a bucket can't prove that Wan-fu's boat had sunk. Through much effort she finally succeeded in convincing herself that the boats had not sunk and that she had been duped only moments before. Goddamnit! What are these people up to anyway? Even Ma-tsu had promised that Wan-fu would return safe and sound. Why are they carrying on like this? They are just putting the curse on. These thoughts gradually turned her grief to anger.

"Nobody knows if the boats sank or not, or if the men are dead or alive. It's ridiculous that everyone is wrangling about the bereavement settlement. I've gone to ask Ma-tsu, and she said that Wan-fu's boat will return safely. It's only lost now. People should be sent out to search right away!"

"Yeah! Grandma Chin is really talking now. Lin, what in the hell are you guys doing anyhow? The boats have been lost almost a week now, and yet the company hasn't even sent out a single boat or plane to search. And now, on the basis of a few planks and a water bucket you're ready to pronounce the fate of the crewmen. Do you really have a heart?" A woman in her thirties, her eyes red at the rims said plaintively, "Even if the boats really did sink there may still be some survivors floating at sea or stranded on a deserted island, just like Yung-fu said."

"Yeah. We want our men to come back alive! Who gives a damn about your 60,000 *yuan*! You've got to send boats out to search immediately!"

"Hai! How can you all be so irrational? We've already found a bucket, planks and tires floating out on the sea and you people still want to cling to your futile hope." Director Chao had lost all patience. He turned to the city official and muttered with a sigh, as if to himself, "If this keeps up, how will the meeting ever end?"

The city official, wearing a somber expression, uttered not a word.

"It would be most fortunate if they're still alive, however . . . " Lin finally stood up. Looking at the woman in her thirties, he said solemnly, "Remains from the Hua Feng I and II have been found and brought back by other boats. Going by past experience, this is decisive evidence that the boats have sunk. In a typhoon that severe it's not inconceivable that even a hundred lives might be lost. To say that there might be survivors after the boats sank . . . I'm afraid that . . ."

"How can you say that? Did you see any bodies? How do you know for sure that the men are dead?" A well-dressed, middle-aged woman, apparently a distant relative of one of the crewmen, spoke with composure, challenging him. "Even if there's only one chance in a million that some lives can be saved, you should go all-out to organize a search. I don't understand why your company is so unwilling to send boats out to try and save the crewmen. On the contrary, you hastily announce that the boats sank and the crewmen drowned. What does your company expect to gain from this?"

"What does the company expect to gain from this? Not a goddamn thing." Lin eyed Director Chao, then continued, "In fact, the company would be better off if the affair is dragged on. The company could invest the relief funds and draw interest to the tune of 29,000 to 30,000 *yuan* a month."

"For your sake, there's really no point in dragging this matter on," Director Chao backed Lin up.

At this point, Ch'iu Yung-fu, who had remained silent for some time, stood up. In a composed manner he faced the families and said, "Ladies and gentlemen. Today, for my nephew Ch'ing-hua who gave his life, and in the interest of everybody's rights, I'm going to divulge some facts that have been kept secret." His voice betrayed his emotion. He glared challengingly at Lin and Director Chao. Steadily enunciating each syllable, he said, "I've done some investigating and found that the boats have been insured. The crewmen are most likely covered by the company's accident insurance as well. Their identification cards, personal signets, and the signets of the beneficiaries have all been deposited with the company, so even the crewmen may not know that they've been insured. Using the water bucket, the tires and the planks as evidence that the boats sank with all hands on board, the company can collect compensation and replace the boats with new ones. The fishing company won't suffer any financial loss. The company has decided to pay the family of each crewman 30,000 *yuan* in relief funds. On the surface the company may seem charitable, but nobody really knows how much money the company is getting from its accident insurance. Probably the company not only won't suffer any loss, but may even stand to profit from the insurance for the fishermen who lost their lives. That's why the company is so eager to pronounce the boats sunk and the crewmen dead, and that's why they didn't make any effort to organize a search . . ."

"Bullshit!" Lin stood up in a flash without waiting for Ch'iu Yung-fu to finish. His face was red and the veins on his neck were bulging. In a hoarse voice he shouted, "I'll tell you something. The company'll haul you to court for the lies you've told today, for the way you've slandered the company's reputation!"

His stomach bulging, Director Chao also stood up. Pointing a threatening finger at Ch'iu Yung-fu, he said, "Yung-fu, you have violated your responsibility as an employee of the Fishermen's Union to speak from the impartial standpoint of the Union. Instead, you're making groundless accusations, sowing discord between the company and the families with your wild accusations. What the hell are you trying to do?"

"The Fishermen's Union! Hah! The Fishermen's Union has gone to the dogs. They'll work for whoever feeds them. What's the fucking use of the Union?" Ch'iu Yung-fu pounded the table with his fist. He continued with passion, "You can't frighten me. I can stand tall and walk straight. I'm not afraid of your threats!"

The city official stood up. With a solemn expression on his face he said, "This is an extremely serious matter. The government has always been very concerned with the welfare and livelihood of the fishermen. It would never permit any underhanded plots on the part of the fishing company to exploit the fishermen. I will report any allegations against the company to my superiors. The public security office will investigate this matter. It will see justice done for all concerned."

This threw the crowd into an uproar. Shouts, curses, and accusations flying back and forth turned the meeting into a turmoil. Several stalwarts pushed their way to the front, intent on giving Lin a beating. Director Chao pounded on the table repeatedly, exhorting everyone to calm down.

"People. People. The Fishermen's Union stands by justice. We do not know whether the fishing company does in fact have insurance on the boats and crewmen. But if any of you have proof, the Fishermen's Union will fight for your rights. But please everyone, use your sound judgment, don't just listen to unfounded rumors." Chao paused and glanced at the city official as if seeking consent.

"As I see it," he continued, "the meeting will adjourn here for today. Those of you who agree to the 30,000 yuan settlement can go to the fishing company office tomorrow morning and pick up the first 5,000 yuan relief fund. Those of you who don't agree can call for the meeting to be reconvened. This meeting is officially adjourned." Having announced this in a loud voice, he stalked out of the room, along with Lin and the city official.

"So the matter is settled, just like that? Damn it! You call this a negotiation meeting?" people cursed after them.

Grandma Chin walked up to Ch'iu Yung-fu. "Did the boats really sink?" she asked timidly.

"Aiyee!" Ch'iu Yung-fu hung his head and heaved a dejected sigh. "No use talking about that anymore."

Tears welled up in Grandma Chin's eyes and began trickling down her cheeks. Women holding their children wept openly. "What are we to do? A whole family. Five or six kids and not a single wage earner."

Ch'iu Yung-fu surveyed the crowd silently. Finally he took a deep breath and said in a voice taut with determination, "The boats have already sunk. It's no use crying anymore. What's important now is that we stick together. I've worked in the Fishermen's Union for several years now and I'm most familiar with this kind of thing." Gesticulating with clenched fists he continued, "If we don't all work together, the fishing company will just trample all over us. We'll end up having to settle for whatever crumbs the company is willing to give us. How could a human life on which the survival of a family depends be worth only 30,000 or even 50,000 yuan? To hell with all the company bosses! There isn't a decent one among them all!"

"Yeah! We've got to work together. If we allow these bosses to make money off the dead bodies of loved ones, our consciences will never forgive us," Bonshi put in.

"OK. Let's send someone to go inquire at the insurance company.

If we get our hands on some evidence, then the fishing company will be caught with nothing to say."

"No way. The insurance company would never tell us a damn thing." Ch'iu Yung-fu knitted his brows and pondered for a moment. Then suddenly a determined expression formed on his face.

"Here's what we'll do," he said in a forceful, steady voice. "Tomorrow let's all go to the fishing company, but don't anyone pick up the relief funds. Bring everybody, all the young ones and the old. If you feel like crying, cry with all your might. We'll go ahead and raise a big ruckus."

"Yeah, we'll fight it out with them!" Bonshi said. "Thirty thousand *yuan* for a human life and the survival of a family! Shit! They're nothing but black-hearted scoundrels!"

"Let's hear it. We'll fight it out with them. Those goddamn dogs." The crowd voiced its assent.

"OK, everybody, let's stick to our guns!"

The late afternoon sun cast slanting rays on the road. Cars cruised by, kicking dust up into the air. The entire street was a worn-out gray. Grandma Chin walked along, her head downcast and her back hunched up. She seemed a little unsteady on her feet, as if her legs were made of rubber. Her topknot had come undone and was hanging loosely. The hair around her temples was dishevelled, accentuating her aged and worn features.

For the past several days there had been constant speculations, rumors, disputes, and anxieties concerning the Hua Feng I and II. It had all happened so quickly—a confused mass of events—that everyone was at a loss as to what to do. It was a nightmare. One minute things appeared one way; the next minute everything was turned upside down. At first it was said the boats had only lost contact, then it was said the boats were lost, and now it was said they had sunk. As in a dream, nothing seemed real. How Grandma Chin wished that she would wake up from the dream to find everything as it had always been before. Wan-fu would come home carrying a bag of dirty clothes. His voice would ring out, "Hurry up and heat up a pot of water. I want to take a bath!"

However, what had just transpired at the settlement meeting was clearly etched on her mond. The people, the noise, the confusion: it was all too real. Even Ch'iu Yung-fu said that the boat had sunk. So there wasn't any hope for what Ch'iu-lan and Ma-tsu had said after all? Grandma Chin felt a piercing pain through her heart.

From here on, there would just be the four of them, all either too old or too young. She could not help but get all choked up again. As she stumbled along as if in a daze, she repeatedly dabbed at her eyes with her shirt sleeve.

Suddenly she heard an urgent voice calling out behind her, "Mother Chin! Mother Chin!" Grandma Chin raised her eyes and saw a plump fiftyish woman walking up to her. When she recognized her to be her in-law, Ch'iu-lan's mother, she burst into tears. "Ooh, In-law!"

"What? Still no trace of the boats?"

"Uh-uh. The boat company said that . . . the boat already . . . already . . ."

Her in-law's face blanched. She too raised her arm and wiped away a tear. "So, Ch'iu-lan . . . "

"Ooh, Ch'iu-lan, she . . . "

"What's wrong with Ch'iu-lan?" Her in-law pulled excitedly at Grandma Chin's sleeve and asked anxiously, "What's wrong with Ch'iu-lan?"

"Aiyee." Grandma Chin heaved a sigh; then in a choked voice she said, "At first Ch'iu-lan seemed all right, but she's not really herself anymore. She still can't believe that anything has happened to Wan-fu."

"How could that happen?"

"You've got to come and talk her into her senses. After all, the two little ones still need someone to look after them. She has a long life ahead of her." As Grandma Chin thought of her two grandchildren, so young and now fatherless, she was overwhelmed with sorrow.

As the two old women approached the front door of the house they could see Ch'iu-lan's frail, solitary figure standing by the window. Her face was expressionless, her eyes gazed out at the sea. When Ch'iu-lan's mother saw this, she was overcome with sorrow. With tears in her eyes she walked over to Ch'iu-lan and called her name in a voice filled with pity. "Ooh, my poor Ch'iu-lan." She was too choked up to say more.

Ch'iu-lan appeared not to have heard. She continued gazing vacantly out to sea. Her expression was one of intense concentration and anticipation, as if hoping against hope.

Tugging at the corner of Ch'iu-lan's shirt, Grandma Chin raised her voice, "Ch'iu-lan, your mother has come to see you."

Ch'iu-lan slowly turned her head around and looked blankly at her mother. Her mouth trembled. She struggled as if wanting to say something, but no words came.

"Ch'iu-lan. It's me. Don't you even recognize your own mother?" As she spoke, tears flowed unchecked down the older woman's face.

Ch'iu-lan's face twitched suddenly as if in pain. Her mouth trembled silently for what seemed like a long time. Finally in an almost inaudible voice she squeezed out a single word, "Ma-a!" Then she began sobbing uncontrollably.

Her mother reached out her arms and pulled her into her bosom, patting her, as if consoling a sobbing child. "Ch'iu-lan, you mustn't cry. You mustn't cry."

Standing on the side, Grandma Chin too broke down. "Wan-fu! My son! My flesh and blood! Wan-fu . . . "

Ch'iu-lan's mother helped her into a chair as she comforted her, but her wailing grew even more disconsolate. She gave out sounds like a wounded, helpless animal wailing mournfully in the silent, deserted wilderness, "Waaaan-fuuuuu!"

VI

The settlement meeting was never reconvened. Every day the families, with their young and old, congregated at the fishing company and clamored for the company to raise the amount of the settlement. The company pleaded financial difficulties and firmly maintained it could afford only 30,000 *yuan*, not a cent more. After a while even Lin began to shy away from the families. They were left to mill around by themselves protesting aimlessly. Finally the families were forced to go again to the Fishermen's Union and ask them to reconvene the meeting. However, Director Chao's reply was, "Haven't we already had a settlement meeting? It was you all who wouldn't resolve the issues. What more can I do? The company representatives aren't available now, how can we reconvene the meeting?"

"It's up to the Fishermen's Union to call the company representatives to a meeting."

"What's the use of calling them? Even if notices are sent out, they can simply ignore them. I can't tie them up and drag them here. The Fishermen's Union is just a civilian organization. It has no legal authority to make people do this or that. It can only mediate disputes, not give orders. There's not much I can do." Director Chao sat in his desk chair puffing away on a cigarette. Then assuming a concerned, sympathetic tone of voice, he continued, "Of course, 30,000 *yuan* isn't a whole lot of money, but the fishing company really is strapped. It just won't do any good to try to put the heat on them. Fact is, it was only through the intervention of the Fishermen's Union that you got even 30,000 *yuan* in the first place. Of all the sea disasters, it's the largest settlement to date. That's the plain truth. Take the Lung Ch'ang Fishing Company, for example. This July they paid out only 15,000 *yuan* per family. In the case of the Hai

Feng Fishing Company last month, the company at first agreed to a settlement of 10,000 *yuan* per family. But when pressed to pay more, they were forced in the end to declare bankruptcy and the boss ran off. The bereaved families ended up with nothing, not even a dime. You can't go wrong on what I tell you. I wouldn't try to screw you. I know it's only 30,000 *yuan*, but it's better than nothing. You shouldn't let people incite you and get you all worked up, you'll only lose out in the end."

Thus the matter dragged on and on. The whole thing was beginning to wear out the families. But Ch'iu Yung-fu was not about to give in. He remained tireless in encouraging everybody.

"We've held out this long. Why can't we hang in there a little longer?" he said with great emotion. "We can't count on the Fishermen's Union to help us with this. I'll be frank with you, the Fishermen's Union is nothing but a puppet. We have only ourselves to depend on. We've got to hang together till we see this thing through. We'll raise a big hullabaloo. The newspapers will have a big write-up, it might even get some TV coverage. Then we'll see if the company won't give in."

"Yeah. As soon as it gets into the papers, the boss'll hand the money over without a fuss," Bonshi said. "In this kind of situation, the bosses all give you the same story: that they are strapped, they're in financial difficulties, etc., etc. How the hell do they expect people to believe that? A guy who's supporting a wife and three or four mistresses on the side—and he says he has no money? He wouldn't give us a cent if he had his way!"

"You said it! Those damn bosses are all black-hearted sons-of-bitches! The lousy dogs!"

"We've got to fight it out to the end! Otherwise our loved ones will have died for nothing," Ch'iu Yung-fu said with cool determination. "We'll stage a hunger-strike. Let me first get in touch with some reporters, then we'll get all the families together. The more people the better. We won't eat until the company agrees to our demands!"

"Will that do any good? They've got hearts that are hard as rocks. If we don't eat, they'll just let us starve to death. Do you think they'd give a damn?"

"Whether or not we can succeed will depend on everybody's will and determination," Ch'iu Yung-fu said decisively. "We'll fight it out to the end!"

Lin and Director Chao soon heard about this plan. They also received word that the courts were investigating the incident. Evidently the city official had reported to his superiors what had transpired at the meeting.

"If we let this thing evolve, it may really get out of hand." Director Chao clasped his hands over his protruding belly. In a grave tone he said, "Lin, you've got to come up with something. Why don't you give them some token increase to placate them? That'll give me a way out too. I know damn well you guys can afford it."

"If it was possible, I'd be more than happy to give them more money. It's not my money after all," Lin replied apprehensively. "But the boss won't hear of it—there's nothing I can do. I'm just his errand boy."

"How am I supposed to deal with this?" Director Chao's voice grew tense. "This thing is getting out of hand. Even the courts are sending people out to investigate. You're leaving me in the lurch. This will be my ruin!"

"Now, now," Lin said soothingly. "Don't get upset. We'll think of something. There's got to be a way to deal with the whole thing."

"You're good at sweet-talking! Deal with it yourself, if you can! Damn you. The whole thing's already been blown way up, and now this investigation. When the ax falls, it'll be my head that rolls. I'm supposed to be the director . . . well, damn it, I don't need this goddamn job!"

"Hey, Chao, calm down. Nothing's going to happen. You know as well as anybody what it's like between the President of the Fishermen's Union and my boss. If it weren't for my boss's backing, do you think he could have been elected president? Keep your cool." As he calmed Chao down, Lin was hatching a scheme in his mind. "It's all because of that Yung-fu . . . stirring up everybody." He thought for a moment. Gnashing his teeth together, he chopped his hands through the air. "If we get rid of him, it will be curtains for them all."

"Get rid of him? How do you propose to do that?" Director Chao looked at him doubtfully.

"Fire him!"

"Fire him! Man, you really know how to talk! If I fire him at a time like this, I'll be the goat for all the abuse and mistrust! You're only scheming to save your own hide. When things get bad you can always count on someone else to take the blame!" Director Chao fought down his rising temper. In a flat voice he said, "Don't write this Ch'iu Yung-fu off as a petty officer. He's worked in the Union for several years now and is popular with the fishermen. The last time the Union was electing a president, a lot of fishermen wanted him to run. It's a good thing he decided not to. Otherwise you really would have had a tough one on your hands."

"OK, OK, Old Chao, don't get mad at me. We've been friends for a long time. You know that I always have your interests at heart. I'm not trying to make brownie points. It's just . . . just . . . Would I do anything nasty to you?" Lin laughed, putting on his sincerest expression. "If firing him will put you on the spot, I won't press you to do it. I wouldn't want to do a friend a wrong turn. Let's see if there isn't another way out."

Lin cocked his head to one side and cogitated for a few moments. He then leaned over and whispered into Director Chao's ear. As Chao listened, he nodded occasionally, his face gradually relaxing into a smile.

"Good thinking!" He slapped his thigh. "We'll do it!"

That same day Lin sent the girl accountant to the bank to withdraw a bundle of cash. Then he sent her down to meet the bereaved relatives who were milling around the company, and she invited them one by one up to see Lin at his office.

Events of the past couple of weeks had worn the families thin. There had not been a bit of news concerning the missing boats; the relatives gradually gave up all hope. The men were already dead, so what was the point of fighting anymore? Overwhelmed by grief, their will melted into despair.

Yet, in their hearts they still couldn't resign themselves to accepting the 30,000 *yuan* settlement. Even a pig or an ox is worth more than 10,000 *yuan*. How could a human life be worth so little? These thoughts again aroused their deep hatred for the fishing company boss. Ch'iu Yung-fu's words again pounded like the surf inside their heads. "We must hang together. If we stand united we'll see this thing through. If we don't . . . goddamn it, the boat company will just trample all over us."

However, when the families went one by one to see Lin, he spoke to them with the most solicitous expression.

"You shouldn't let yourselves be led around blindly by the nose. Do you really think that Ch'iu Yung-fu is working in good faith for your benefit? You all have eyes. His family has a big sundries store. He doesn't need the 30,000 *yuan*. Of course he can afford to let things drag on. But what about the rest of you? You're all sitting around with empty pots waiting for the rice for your next meal. The longer it drags on, the harder it is on you. If Ch'iu Yung-fu is really on your side, go and try to borrow some money from him. He won't even lend you 300 *yuan*! Now I'm concerned only for your welfare. It's not my company, so why would I want to make this hard for you? It's just that . . . ah . . . if things drag on much longer I'm afraid you may end up with not even one thin dime. Look at what happened with the Hai Feng Fishing Company. It just declared bankruptcy and the boss ran out. When a boat sinks, the boss loses out, too, eh?"

He piled stacks of bright new bills in front of each bereaved family. In a most sincere voice he urged, "This money is all ready for you to take home . . . ah, ah . . . All you have to do is stamp your signet on this agreement form and the receipt. If anyone still has qualms about this, we can call another meeting later."

By the time Ch'iu Yung-fu had the media coverage lined up two days later, most of the families had already stamped their signets on the documents and taken the money home.

"Aiya! How could you all . . . How could you all be taken in so easily?" Bonshi stamped her feet and thumped her chest. Snorting angrily she said, "You might as well have sold the ancestral tablets of your dead loved ones. What is there left to fight with?"

Ch'iu Yung-fu's eyes were shot through with red veins; his normally dark, healthy complexion looked a little haggard. He gazed contemplatively at Bonshi. When he finally spoke, it was in a clear, measured voice, each word being pressed out from behind clenched teeth, "We'll keep up the fight! We've got to fight it out to the end!"

"Fight it out to the end?" Bonshi was astonished. "But there's no one left."

"It's OK to take the money, but we'll still fight on. Why shouldn't the families take the money? Everyone has to eat after all." With clenched fists, he continued, "If we don't fight now we'll never see better days, company bosses will forever tyrannize us. The courts have begun an investigation now. Small wonder the boss is running scared. If we win just this once, we will set a precedent, things will be a lot easier.

For the past several days Ch'iu-lan had been just a burnt-out shell. From morning till night she stood by the window gazing vacantly out to sea. Her face grew visibly emaciated, her eyes were sunk into black sockets.

Grandma Chin and her in-law kept a close eye on Ch'iu-lan. Afraid that she might try to kill herself in a moment of despair, Ch'iu-lan's mother didn't dare go back home, and Grandma Chin didn't dare leave the house.

"Ch'iu-lan, you should listen to what your mother has to say. You've got to think of Chia-hsiung and Yü-chiao. They are still so young. If something should happen to you, what would they do?" Grandma Chin said, with tears welling in her eyes.

"Ch'iu-lan, think this thing through. You're my only daughter . . . " Before she could finish, she broke down and sobbed.

Every time Ch'iu-lan heard Wan-fu's name, her face would twitch with contortion. She would bite her lower lip, struggling to restrain her tears. But in the end she would give up the struggle, and tears would stream down her face.

The two old women were even more apprehensive at night. They strained their ears for the slightest sound. They would wait until all had quieted down in Ch'iu-lan's room. Then they would tip-toe over and peek in to make sure Ch'iu-lan had fallen asleep. Only then could the two old women lay down their groggy heads.

As Ch'iu-lan lay on the bed every night, images of Wan-fu kept surfacing vividly in her mind. It was as if he had come home. She could hear him talking to her, see him puttering around the room. She would then doubt her own senses. Events of the past two weeks did not seem real to her, as if she'd been in a dream. But then she could clearly see her own mother in the house and hear her mother talking. If the whole thing weren't true, surely her mother wouldn't have come all the way from Kaohsiung to say these things to her. At this realization, Ch'iu-lan could no longer suppress the flow of tears. She would wait until the two old women in the next room had fallen asleep, then she would get out of bed and, silent as a ghost, she would drift out to the living room. There she would stand by the window and gaze obliviously at the murky sea, just as she had always done when Wan-fu went out to sea. She had always stood here to see him off, now she was standing here to welcome him home.

The candle on the altar table had almost burnt itself out. Only a tiny flame was left flickering in the wind, turning shadows on the wall into many dancing ghosts.

As she gazed at the hazy beam from the lighthouse that cut through the blackness, scenes of days with Wan-fu floated into her mind. She thought of the days yet to come, of the family with four mouths to feed, their food and clothing, the children's education, and numerous other foreseeable and unforeseeable difficulties. All these responsibilities would fall on her shoulders from here on. These burdens would be hers alone. Pain and apprehension bored into her heart as if an army of ants were gnawing steadily away inside her chest. She understood now why Ch'iu Yung-fu was determined to fight the comapny to the end; it wasn't just the matter of one human life, it involved the fate of an entire family! Two streams of tears flowed steadily down her cheeks.

VII

"Chyang! Tongkwang!" "Chyang! Tongkwang!" These tragic jarring notes of gong and drum, intermixed with a crowd's clamor, broke the midday silence. Grandma Chin had been hanging out laundry under the hot sun. Startled, she looked up and saw people approaching from around the bend, carrying a coffin. Behind the pallbearers was a gong-band. A woman dressed in hemp funeral clothing, leading several children, followed behind the band. A crowd of people brought up the rear. "Chyang! Tongkwang!" The gongs and drums sounded all along the road, as the procession approached the Fishermen's Union building.

"Someone must have died and they're having a funeral," thought Grandma Chin. "But I haven't heard of anybody dying in the past few days."

She couldn't take her eyes away from the procession. In a short while the procession reached the front entrance of the Ch'ing Ch'ang Fishing Company. The pallbearers suddenly came to a stand-still. The people bringing up the rear circled around. The gong band intensified its earth-shattering "Chyang! Tongkwang! Chyang! Tongkwang!"

"Good Lord, what are they up to?" Grandma Chin was baffled.

Just then, her in-law came out of the house and stood by Grandma Chin, watching.

"What's going on?" she asked.

"I don't know. They're carrying a coffin, but it doesn't look like a funeral procession."

After a few moments, they saw, to their puzzlement, the pallbearers walk through the doorway into the office of the Ch'ing Ch'ang Fishing Company. A crowd pushing in from all directions soon blocked the road. Gradually a long line of cars formed, extending back in both directions.

"What are they up to?"

As Grandma Chin stood there puzzled, she suddenly saw Chia-hsiung come charging up the steps carrying his bookbag, shouting, "Granny! Granny!"

"Good Lord! Chia-hsiung. Slow down. What are you trying to prove running so fast?" Grandma Chin scolded in a voice that betrayed her affection.

Chia-hsiung stopped in front of Grandma Chin. Huffing and puffing, he tried to catch his breath and talk at the same time.

"Granny . . . Uncle, Uncle Yung-fu . . . he's leading a bunch of people . . . carrying a coffin . . . to the fishing company."

"Really? That's incredible! Good Lord! Yung-fu." Grandma Chin looked at Chia-hsiung wide-eyed and mumbled to herself as if in disbelief.

"It's true! It's true! I'm not lying," Chia-hsiung continued excitedly. "They say K'un-cheng's dad's body is in the coffin. Someone found it on the beach!" As he spoke, Chia-hsiung slung off his bookbag and handed it to Grandma Chin.

"I'm going back to watch. Uncle Yung-fu is getting really tough. He's shouting for Lin to come out if he's got any guts. I'm going down to watch. Man! Uncle Yung-fu's really tough."

Chia-hsiung flew down the steps. As he ran down the street, Grandma Chin could hear him yelling the curses he had picked up from the men, "Lin, you shit-eating scum. You ingrate cur! Damn you! Come out and look if you have any conscience. Damn you! Tell your boss to get his ass out here and look!"

Grandma Chin suddenly felt a fire flaring up in her chest. She trembled violently as if an electric current had just coursed through her entire body. Hot tears sprang to her eyes.

"That's right! We've got to fight like this, or else we fishermen will always be treated like dirt. Only 30,000 *yuan* for a human life and the fate of a whole family. It's inhuman, it's downright inhuman!"

In a voice trembling uncontrollably she turned to the house and called out, "Ch'iu-lan, Ch'iu-lan . . . "

She found Ch'iu-lan standing by the window, watching the commotion in the street. Tears were already coursing down her face.

CHEN JO-HSI

(1938–)

Chen Jo-hsi (born Chen Hsiu-mei) comes from a proletarian background. Born into a family of carpenters, she was raised in Taipei. In the socially mobile post-1949 Taiwan society, she graduated in Western Literature from National Taiwan University in 1961. Like most of her contemporaries, Chen Jo-hsi came to study in the United States after graduation. She attended Mount Holyoke College and Johns Hopkins University, and received an M.A. in English Literature in 1965. In 1966, she and her engineer husband Tuan Shih-yao "returned" to mainland China to dedicate their lives to the revolution. They were caught in the political maelstrom of the Cultural Revolution. Their earlier dreams and visions shattered, they left China in 1973. After a year in Hong Kong, they lived in Vancouver, Canada, until 1979, when Chen Jo-hsi joined the Center for Chinese Studies at Berkeley, California.

Chen Jo-shi's writings can be divided into two stages, reflecting two distinct periods in her life. During the years from 1958 to 1962, her writings demonstrated a good knowledge of native and Western literary traditions and skillful though self-conscious craftsmanship, but they were not yet informed by a rich first-hand life experience. There followed a hiatus of over ten years, seven of which Chen Jo-hsi spent in Cultural Revolutionary China. When she reemerged in 1974, with her first story about the Cultural Revolution, "Mayor Yin" (Yin hsien-chang), her writing was no longer a conscious effort. The characters and stories in her mind sought a way to flow from her pen. Chen Jo-hsi was no longer the author; rather the stories, now informed by her momentous first-hand experiences, told themselves through her art. Some critics argue that Chen Jo-hsi's post-China stories are not as skillful as her earlier ones, but this shortcoming is more than compensated for by the immediacy and conviction of the later stories. Chen Jo-hsi has sometimes been called a dissident writer because of her negative views of China. However, her Cultural Revolution stories are not in any sense motivated by a political mission, and they are all the more convincing because they are not. Another feature that distinguishes Chen Jo-hsi's stories from dissident writings is that they were not written in China, but after she had left the country, at an objective distance from the events and circumstances depiecte.

Chen Jo-hsi's better-known stories from her first period are collected in **Stories by Chen Jo-hsi Selected by the Author** (Chen Jo-hsi tzu-hsüan chi, 1976). Her Cultural Revolution stories appeared first in *newspaper supplements and magazines, and were later published in the two collections* Mayor Yin *(Yin hsien-chang, 1976) and* Old Man *(Lao-jen, 1978). Her writing about the Cultural Revolution reached its culmination in the novel* The Repatriate *(Kuei, 1978). It is likely that her writing will take a new direction in the near future.*

"My Friend Ai Fen" (Nü-yu Ai Fen) first appeared in United News *(Lien-ho pao) in 1978 and was later incorporated into the collection* Old Man.

My Friend Ai Fen

Translated by Richard Kent and Vivian Hsu

IN THE AUTUMN of 1967, when I gave birth to my first child, I met Doctor Ai Fen in the delivery room.

The first time a woman gives birth she often cries out in pain and feels the hardship is unendurable. After screaming and crying out for several hours in the labor room, by the time I reached the delivery table I suddenly lost all strength. Only then did they find another doctor to come and insert an acupuncture needle into my ear, and then finally delivered the baby. When I heard the infant wail, I let out a sigh, "So painful! After this, I never want to give again!"

Immediately, the woman obstetrician lectured me. "Even a bowel movement takes some exertion, how can you expect childbirth to be painless?" Thereupon she turned her back to me.

The doctor who had inserted the acupuncture needle, however, bent down and whispered in my ear, "Don't mind her. Giving birth *is* painful. Even I haven't been willing to have one so far!"

Feeling as if I had just met an old friend, I grasped her hand, which rested on the edge of the delivery table, expressing without words my thanks. This was Dr. Ai Fen: forthright and sympathetic. I was weak from giving birth, and I spent more than a week recuperating in the hospital. As luck would have it, it was Ai Fen's turn to check on the patients. Seeing each other every day, we had the chance to become well acquainted. Her aunt had been in the United States to study in the 1940s; during the Great Leap Forward she had become terribly disillusioned and committed suicide. Ai

Fen had loved her aunt very much; perhaps it was for this reason that, when she heard I had just returned from America, she was especially good to me, often stopping by my room to chat, if only for a moment. By the time I was to leave the hospital, we had long since passed the usual bounds of a doctor-patient relationship and had become close friends.

Ai Fen was the youngest gynecologist I met in Peking; she was only twenty-six at the time. Though her thick hair was cut very short, it wouldn't entirely stay in place under her white cap; always a few locks stuck out. What's more, a smile always hung about the corners of her mouth, giving one a feeling of unrestrained warmth. The professional solemnity that customarily belongs to doctors seemed completely absent in her. In fact, out of her uniform, she became one of the prettiest young women in all of Peking. She was of medium height, and her figure was ideal—not an ounce too fat or too thin. Her tailored, lined jacket of brightly printed cotton fit so well that the curves of her bodice were just subtly noticeable. In an era when Chiang Ch'ing wore drab military dress to "present herself as a model," Ai Fen's manner of dressing was tantamount to rebellion. At that time, most women, afraid of incurring such critical labels as "infatuated with vanity" or "pursuing the life-style of the bourgeois class," intentionally stored away their more attractive clothes and wore only large and baggy shirts and trousers. But Ai Fen was not very keen on political matters. According to her, she did not aspire to "make herself a martyr or see her name engraved in gold"; she only wanted to "get along from day to day." For this reason, she always wore her best clothes: under the long white physician's coat were trousers of very fine material, the cuffs perfectly pressed; her leather shoes, though somewhat worn, were still polished to a bright sheen.

Ai Fen did not have a northerner's round face. Her cheekbones protruded a little but her jaw was small and square, giving her face a well-proportioned, trim look. But what was most striking was her complexion: white with just a trace of red. In winter when the north wind would blow, her cheeks looked as if she had put on rouge; that radiance could rival the red peonies in Chungshan Park. Besides this, she had a pair of almond-shaped eyes with bright, shining pupils. Her only flaw was her flat nose, but her smiling lips diverted people's attention from it, imperceptibly compensating for this defect. Because Ai Fen's appearance and style of dress radiated an aesthetic sensibility, when she revealed that her husband was an artist, I wasn't surprised at all.

"Hsiao* Fan likes to paint portraits," she told me. "Unfortunately

---

*An adjunct to a person's name to express intimacy. Originally, it meant "little."

he doesn't have any models, so all he can paint is me. Not only is he tired of painting me, but I can hardly stand to look at myself anymore!"

Not long after I left the hospital, Ai Fen brought her husband to our hotel to see us and the baby. Hsiao Fan had a slender build; his skin was very dark, like ink splashed too thickly on a sketch; the bridge of his nose rose up straight below a pair of deep, bright eyes, revealing the melancholy, emotionally charged temperament of a poet. Ai Fen said it was this pair of eyes that had swept her off her feet. Hsiao Fan dressed heedlessly, surprisingly the opposite of Ai Fen: the top button of his jacket undone, gray slacks covered with ink stains, cloth shoes, the original color already unrecognizable. But the sloppiness of his appearance did not at all diminish his charm. Moreover, one year of living in the topsy-turvy world created by the Cultural Revolution had added an element of resentful cynicism to his bearing. Hsiao Fan's father had been with the famed antique emporium Jungpaochai for years; he was skilled at carving seals, good at calligraphy, and possessed a profound knowledge of Chinese painting. Influenced by his father, Hsiao Fan majored in traditional Chinese painting at the Central Arts Institute, but had also worked at Western painting; his artistic interests were wide-ranging. Unfortunately, not long after his graduation, the Cultural Revolution started up; and thereafter he was continuously occupied with revolt and self-criticism. He churned out political and propagandistic paintings, but had not painted one picture which he could like himself.

Though I knew little about traditional Chinese painting, I sympathized with his pain at the neglect of our artistic heritage. At that time, traditional Chinese painting was considered in the same light as Chinese opera: both were criticized as worthless. Of course it was said that if traditional painting could undergo the same "face-change" as opera, it might also have room to survive. For example, take an overhanging cliff with a cascade, add two red flags, and entitle it "Chingkang Mountain"; or put several Red Guards beside a dangerous cliff or a clear stream, and claim such a grouping expressed the theme: "Follow the route of the workers, peasants, and soldiers," etc. When I mentioned such an idea, Hsiao Fan shook his head, saying that this would be blaspheming art.

"I won't paint then!" he announced, seemingly giving up all his ambition. "To be involved with art is dangerous enough: choosing to do traditional painting is just like being thrown into a wrong reincarnation, to be given the death sentence!"

Remembering that he liked to paint portraits, I tried to persuade him to change his subject matter. "Then paint Chairman Mao. That's guaranteed not to backfire. If you paint just one good one you could become celebrated!"

Turning to me, hands clasped respectfully in front of him, he said, "Don't bother to flatter me!" His lips formed a crooked line, displaying a sour smile. "I paint the human body, not portraits. If I were to paint Chairman Mao, even if I put the old man in swim trunks, that could still get me dragged off to the torture chamber!"

On the spot he gave examples of disasters that resulted from painting Mao Tse-tung. A painting not true to life—the color a bit gray and dark—brought upon the artist the accusation of "uglifying the Red Sun." A woodblock on the theme of "to cross the great sea, rely on the helmsman" had given rise to the cynical suspicion that Chairman Mao was represented as "renounced by the masses and deserted by his closest comrades," and the artist was beaten and taken to a "cattle stockade," all because the background was not crowded with the masses, even though Chairman Mao was rendered with marvelous vividness. Apparently, flattery also wasn't easy; usually it brought on more trouble than it was worth. No wonder, then, that Hsiao Fan only dared to follow the others and paint propaganda posters that were all alike, with the result that his aspirations and spirits sank; Hsiao Fan's only consolation was in drinking.

At that time we lived in a hotel that accommodated returning overseas Chinese and was stocked with cigarettes and wines, the likes of which far surpassed those which the city markets offered. One reason Hsiao Fan came anxiously to meet us was to ask us to buy him a bottle of Erhkuot'ou, an inexpensive but fairly good wine. Ai Fen herself never touched a drop, and she also didn't like her husband drinking so much; the two of them often quarreled over this. But except for drowning his sorrows in liquor, Hsiao Fan did not know how to allay his sense of bitter disappointment. The Cultural Revolution had not only broken his life's routine, but had also shattered his aspirations. Previously, he only had to follow along mouthing the slogans, and he was able to maintain the carefree life of a resident in Peking: in the summer going to the North Sea Park to row boats; in autumn, to the Fragrant Mountain to see the red leaves; and there were even special places to sample tea and enjoy the flowers. But when the Cultural Revolution broke out, its affirmation that "to rebel is correct" threw Hsiao Fan into an unprecedented state of mind. Young people were suddenly permitted to challenge authority, and so sharply that they could not be checked. However, from a certain time on, the prohibitions began to be issued one after another. First the "bad elements" were forced to "stand aside," or were considered fit only for carrying buckets of glue on the streets to paste up slogans. In the end, Hsiao Fan realized that the Revolution had done nothing for him aside from denying his own worth. At first he didn't dare paint what he wanted. Now, even if he felt like painting, he could find no inspiration. His future so uncertain, little wonder that he sought consolation from the bottle.

On New Year's Day of 1968, the two of them came again to see us. My husband bought a bottle of sorghum wine as a treat. Hsiao Fan kept praising the wine and in a flash downed half the bottle. His dark face and neck flushed the deep purple of an eggplant, and his eyes got so bright they looked as if they could spit fire. Suddenly seized by a desire to draw, he grabbed a pencil and stationery from the desk. Facing Ai Fen, he quickly sketched her. Ai Fen, who was no drinker, had, at my prompting, taken two swallows of wine. Her eyes were so red she could hardly keep them open, and she leaned diagonally across the sofa. After coaxing my child to sleep, I immediately came over to look at Hsiao Fan's sketch. Rendered in a few supple, deft strokes, the sketch showed a nude, voluptuous woman in a drunken pose in the style of Yang Kuei-fei, and it caught the spirit perfectly. My husband remarked that it resembled one of Matisses's preliminary sketches for the painting "Nude"; at this, Hsiao Fan was very pleased with himself. I showed it to Ai Fen. After giggling for a while, she tore it into pieces.

On May First, the Labor Day holiday, Ai Fen had the day off and invited me to eat dumplings in a famous restaurant at T'iench'iao. As I poured the soy sauce, Ai Fen abruptly informed me that Hsiao Fan had been sent to work at a neighborhood-organized soy sauce factory.

"To make soy sauce?" I hardly knew what to think. "Soy sauce and painting are a million miles apart!"

"No kidding!" Ai Fen responded, with an expression that showed her exasperation and depression. "He tangles all day long with soy beans and brine. His whole body smells of the stuff! And the salty, thick smell in his clothes—I just can't wash away! At night, in bed, unless he takes everything off, I won't let him come near me."

"This is just temporary discipline through manual labor," I said quickly in order to console her. "China's artists still have a future; we have never been a people to ostracize art."

Ai Fen only shook her head and sighed, "We can't look into the future, so there's no point in talking about it. All those who have any connection with art or literature will probably be sent to the country soon. Hsiao Fan himself is talking that way every day. I'm afraid sooner or later we'll end up divorced."

The word "divorce" gave me a start. But from her knitted brows and the worried look in her eyes, I could tell that she wasn't joking.

I counted to myself: they had been married only a little more than two years. Though I had heard often about their little tiffs, when things were going well between them, they were inseparable, more lovey-dovey than any other couple. How could Ai Fen have such a change of heart as soon as Hsiao Fan was demoted to work in a factory?

"Ai Fen, it was out of love that you two married. Why, then, have your feelings cooled so quickly?"

"Our conception of love these days is different from yours," Ai Fen responded, in a tone of voice that made me feel separated from her by a whole generation, while in fact she was only three years younger. "If a husband and wife can't live together, what's the use of this love? The romatic 'Romeo and Juliet' notion has long ago been condemned here! If Hsiao Fan is sent to the country then I must go with him unless we divorce. But what about my father, who is about to retire, and my mother, who is in poor health? They have only one daughter. Naturally, they want me close by."

Confronted by this pragmatic problem, I felt lost for words. In order to make clear to me, though, that at one time she had put a lot of stock in love, there in that noisy restaurant Ai Fen confided all the details of her first love. Apparently, her first boyfriend was her classmate in college. Right from their freshman year they captivated each other. By their junior year they were known throughout the campus as an inseparable couple. However, in the second semester of their fourth year, when they went into practical training, the students were all caught up in the question of where they would be assigned after graduation. At this time, another girl in their class—whose father was a high-ranking cadre and thus had no worries about being sent away from Peking—suddenly butted in and made it clear that she had set her eye on Ai Fen's boyfriend. Because his class background was bad, he feared being assigned to some distant province. Half-reluctantly, he finally gave in to this cadre's daughter. When it came time for graduation in the fifth year, naturally the pair of them was installed in a clinic for ranking cadres in a suburb of Peking.

"Originally I was destined to be assigned to some distant place. Who could have guessed that at the last moment our hospital needed a gynecologist and, by sheer luck, I was able to stay in Peking. But four years of a love-relationship went down the drain, and there was no way to salvage it. Aside from a good political background and connections, the other girl wasn't better than I in any respect. She just happened to cast a covetous eye at my lover and stole him away. This is the kind of love we have!"

Even though several years had passed, bringing up this episode of her first love filled Ai Fen's voice with bitterness and jealousy. I could easily imagine how broken-hearted she must have been at the time. She had even thought of suicide, but her professional training and her sense of responsibility for her family, in the end, overcame this terrible idea. It was during her internship that Hsiao Fan dropped into her life. His fiery courtship softened the blow of having been jilted. Perhaps stemming from a desire for revenge, or perhaps only in order to forget the pain and bitterness of losing a lover, she disregarded her mother's advice and married Hsiao Fan right after graduation.

"My mother is old-fashioned in her thinking and believes that if an artist doesn't become famous, he'll be poor for the rest of his life. And Hsiao Fan's lackadaisical ways didn't please her either—the only thing that made her feel the least bit content was that I could come home often. Because my parents' home is close to the hospital, when I'm on nightshift, it's fairly convenient to go back and forth. My father-in-law used to live in a big house with a courtyard, but when the Red Guards confiscated the property, they moved the whole family into two and a half rooms. Including me, there were six people, so we were really cramped! Hsiao Fan made only forty-eight dollars a month, and he gave it all to his parents. Even the pocket money for his cigarettes and wine came out of my earnings. He's destined to be able to support only himself, and he knows it. If I really want a divorce, he won't hold me back."

I thought that this was just a transient feeling of insecurity in Ai Fen. I didn't for a moment take this matter of divorce seriously.

That year, the situation in Peking changed rapidly. Chiang Ch'ing's directive to "attack culture, defend the military" burned like an unending brushfire, while Lin Piao's declaration that "political power is the power to suppress" was even more widespread. In order to gain power, the rebel faction engaged in militant struggle throughout the year. This eventually gave Mao Tse-tung the excuse to turn against old friends and to station both worker and proletariat propaganda teams at every educational level, to snatch away the rebels' power base, and to impose a "proletarian dictatorship" on them through purges, liquidation, and forced confessions, to step up the Rustication Movement, whereby the main forces of the Red Guards were dispersed to the rural villages. The Rustication Movement gradually touched all walks of life, even neighborhood committees received mobilization orders. Suddenly in Peking everyone was apprehensive. That entire summer I didn't see a trace of Ai Fen.

A few days before the Autumn Festival, I went out to buy a few things and ran into Hsiao Fan at the Hsitan Market. He was wearing bibbed overalls; a pair of slip-on sleeve covers peeped out from the frayed cuffs of his jacket; and an absolutely filthy blue cap sat crooked on his head. At first I was afraid it wasn't he, and I didn't dare to call out, because he had his arm around a young woman worker. The two of them seemed completely carefree, as if they were out for a stroll. But that dark face and that high-bridged nose I'd recognize anywhere. As I stood there in a stupor, Hsiao Fan caught sight of me. Quickly casting aside the girl's hand, he hurried across the street to chat with me. I asked him about Ai Fen. He said that recently she had been filling in on the night shift for a colleague and, because it was more convenient from the hospital, had moved back with her parents. I then asked him about his work at the soy sauce factory. He drew down the corners of his mouth contemptuously and let out a bitter laugh. Then, pretending not to care, he shrugged his shoulders and replied, "Work is work. What's there to say about it? I just live from day to day. Who knows when they'll send us down to the country. And when they do we'll just pick up our bed-roll and start walking."

Because Hsiao Fan didn't bother to introduce his friend, I felt embarrassed that she should just stand there waiting. On the pretext that I needed to get home to feed the baby, I left without further ado. All the way home I thought about the intimacy between Hsiao Fan and his young woman friend; I felt indignant for Ai Fen's sake. And yet I felt Ai Fen's casually moving back in with her parents wasn't right either. After all, even the best couples have their rifts after a while.

Since both Ai Fen and Hsiao Fan were only newcomers at their work units, had no children, and had families in Peking itself, they had had little chance of being allotted their own living quarters. Hsiao Fan's parents believed that the daughter-in-law was duty bound to live with her husband's family and help with the housework. Unfortunately, in such a cramped apartment it was difficult for a couple to have any privacy. How could Ai Fen, who had been pampered since childhood, put up with that? She had continually pestered Hsiao Fan, wanting them both to go live with her parents. But Hsiao Fan was filial by nature and wasn't about to hurt his parents' feelings. Their living arrangement must have had something to do with the discord in their marriage.

On the day of the Autumn Festival, Ai Fen unexpectedly called and asked if, as a favor, I would buy a bottle of brandy for her father. I promised to, and then added that I'd run into Hsiao Fan—but didn't mention anything about that woman.

"I've moved out on the Fans!" Her anger came through over the phone. "And I'll never move back!"

"You two had a fight?"

"Not this time. I'm at work in the delivery ward right now. I'll tell you all about it when I drop by to pick up the brandy." She hurriedly hung up the phone.

Close to evening she came to pick up the brandy, but had to hurry home to pass the holiday with her parents; there really wasn't any time to sit and chat. I accompanied her to the bus stop, hoping to snatch a few brief moments to try to persuade her to return to her in-laws' home. She shook her head and refused, saying she had already sent in a formal application for a divorce to the authorities.

"You say you didn't have a fight. So if you two were getting along, how can you be so heartless?" I asked, in a somewhat accusatory tone.

"Of course you wouldn't know. One night he came home dead drunk. He kept shouting some woman's name, it was really obscene. His whole family heard him!"

I thought of the woman I saw him with at the Hsitan Market. And though I almost brought it up, I managed to hold my tongue. Instead I asked her if she had gotten any actual proof.

Ai Fen laughed coolly, and suddenly became magnanimous, her jealousy completely vanishing. "I guess he's fooling around with some woman from the soy sauce factory. He's always had a soft spot for girls, and he fancies himself to be like Chia Pao-yü,* a lover of beauty. He doesn't turn down any comers either. Even in a real hag, he can find some modicum of beauty! I hope this time around he's able to find some woman from a good class background. I myself am like a clay Buddha crossing a river—can't even guarantee my own safety!"

The Red Guards may have destroyed the "Four Olds,"† but that seems to have had no effect on me. Whenever I hear the word "divorce," it is as if something I've swallowed has gone down the wrong way; it just sticks in my throat. I couldn't restrain myself from trying to say something that might save their marriage.

"Even if I closed my eyes to Hsiao Fan's fooling around with another woman, I'd still want a divorce," Ai Fen said stubbornly, as if she'd already made up her mind.

According to her, the Rustication Movement was far fiercer than the papers reported. Not only did departments and schools take it as a chance to dismiss a batch of deadwood, even law-abiding citizens were banished to the country. The slogan of the day was: "We have a pair of hands like everybody else; why stay in the city and

---

*The main protagonist in *The Dream of the Red Chamber*.
†Old thoughts, culture, customs, and habits.

eat for nothing!" Unemployed dependents were mobilized to the country, but those who were considered "bad elements" were singled out and given "permission" to leave first. And on the pretext of promoting "concern for one's spouse," when one person was sent down, his whole family inevitably followed.

"Our hospital already has encouraged everyone to enlist voluntarily in the Rustication Movement. Who would be so idiotic? But if your spouse is sent to the hinterlands, you too must take a stand: Do you support or oppose the movement? Of course you support it! And how? You all move out to the country to "settle your family happily!" At the hospital two of my colleagues have already handed in their 'pledges,' requesting to be sent with their spouses to the country. When the Revolutionary Committee broadcasted this through the hospital, saying that it was a triumphant victory for Mao Tse-tung thought, everyone's flesh crawled. A colleague in our own delivery ward has also submitted a 'pledge.' Ever since then she's looked as if her soul has left her body. Though the hospital hasn't handed down the official approval yet, she's already like a sentenced convict, completely collapsed. Today we delivered a baby after the mother had an extremely hard labor. When the infant let out the first wail, she said, 'Cry, go ahead and cry. Why not?' If this kind of remark were reported, that colleague could be charged with harboring 'negative tendencies' in the future! Just think, if I don't raise the matter of divorce now, if and when Hsiao Fan is ordered to leave, I'd be forced to take a stand, and the choice would not be up to me then!"

I recalled her first love affair and worried that history might repeat itself.

"Ai Fen, be more cautious. What if Hsiao Fan doesn't get sent down to the country. If you raise the matter of divorce prematurely it might bring it on for real."

She smiled futilely and said, "You may escape this time, but you won't the next."

In the evening haze two yellow headlights appeared in the distance. The bus was approaching. In the pressure of the moment I asked the most important question. "You still love him, don't you?"

"I used to believe in love and gave myself without reservations. I don't feel the same way anymore." In her indirect answer, her tone of voice had a faint sadness to it, like that of the dusk falling all about us. "I only hope to find someone with whom I can talk, someone to live out my days with in peace. But even this is difficult: we just don't have any control over our fates!"

The bus came to a stop. Ai Fen pressed my hand and, without saying goodbye, mounted the steps. I slowly walked back to the hotel and, for the first time, realized that in Peking autumn at twilight could be terribly desolate and gloomy. I couldn't blame my friend's rather heartless and pragmatic attitude toward marriage. In reality, she was a very sentimental person. It was just that something was inexorably working against her, so that all her passion could find no safe object. I heaved a deep sigh for my friend.

With the start of winter, the task of "cleansing the ranks of bad elements" became more earnest and the atmosphere more turbulent. This political storm was even more threatening than the cold winds from Siberia. Aside from going to work and attending meetings, people kept close to home and didn't dare to have much contact with friends. One day, having caught a cold, I went to the hospital to see a doctor. Since I was there, I detoured over to the obstetrics wing, hoping to catch Ai Fen. She wasn't in the examining room, though. As I was leaving, I glanced over the "big character posters" along the corridor. I noticed that the Obstetrics Section had singled out one of the senior doctors for having "a serious historical problem" and was currently focusing its bombardment on him. There were also a couple of other posters criticizing a certain "backward Doctor X," asserting that she coveted ease and comfort, and contrived to avoid joining the Rustication Movement. The poster went on to claim that she neglected her political studies and was tainted with capitalist thinking up the extent of "violating the law." She was called on to carry out with the greatest despatch a soul-searching self-criticism, to be followed by a full public confession. Because I'd stayed at the hospital and was close to Ai Fen, I knew a little about the doctors in the Obstetrics Section. As soon as I read the posters, I knew the doctor with a "historical problem" was the head of the section, because during the Japanese occupation he had treated the invaders. The accusations about the "backward element," however, confounded me. Though Ai Fen herself had admitted that she was "backward," she wasn't the type to break laws or regulations.

Since the time Ai Fen had come for the brandy, I had had no news of her. I missed and worried about her. So one evening, toward the end of the year, I quietly went to visit her in the suburb outside of Ti-an Gate. In spite of the fact that it was a dark, winter night and I had never been to her house, the moment I entered the courtyard, I could identify which door was her family's. I had heard, early on, that Ai Fen's father loved flowers. There by the doorway was a wooden frame with over ten or twenty pots of flowers and plants. I had chosen to go in the evening in order to avoid people's noticing. By coincidence, that evening Ai Fen wasn't on duty. Outside, she and her mother were washing the dishes and putting out the cooking fire. She seemed delighted to see me and pulled me right into the house and introduced me to her father. Mr. Ai had been an editor at the People's Publishing House. But with the start of the Cultural Revolution, he was shunted aside and now did only odd jobs at a printing company. Although he still liked to drink, he didn't dare to compose or recite poetry anymore. Instead, he practiced calligraphy, copying Wang Hsi-chih's *Lan T'ing Hsu.** Brushes, ink, an ink stone, and a thick ream of writing paper lay piled on the desk. Although he was not yet of retirement age, Mr. Ai's hair was already completely white, and the wrinkles between his eyebrows formed deep furrows. His shoulders hunched forward slightly, as if he were under an unbearable burden. His expression, however, was refined and gentle, and his manner remarkably tranquil and serene.

Ai Fen's mother had followed us into the house. Ai Fen had long ago told me that her mother was timid and leery by nature. For quite some time she had suffered from nervous disorders and migraines; she also chattered incessantly. Sure enough, after just a few minutes of small talk, she immediately began to pour out her complaints to me. Originally they used to live in spacious quarters, she said. But each time there was a new "movement" they were forced to give up a room. Now they were reduced to only three small rooms, piled with the chests and furniture she couldn't bear to part with, so that every movement in the house was restricted. I tried to comfort her with old aphorisms like "it's not as good as the best, but still better than the worst." But she still shook her head and kept on sighing. Suddenly she changed the subject and started in about her daughter wanting to get a divorce, complaining that Ai Fen was too willful. At first Ai Fen's mother had not particularly liked her son-in-law, but now she deplored the divorce even more, feeling it wasn't honorable. Thus her son-in-law had become suddenly priceless in her eyes.

"Hsiao Fan always yields to Hsiao Ai. Such a sweet temperament. Where would she find another like him?" Mrs. Ai grumbled to me.

Beneath the thirty-watt light bulb, Ai Fen could only look at the floor, silently putting up with this. Ai Fen's father didn't stop his wife from complaining, but while sipping his tea he cleared his throat several times, as if to remind his wife not to be so tedious. But the old woman paid no attention. Instead, she moved her chair closer, lifted her tea cup, and prepared to pour her heart out to me. I used to blame Hsiao Fan for being too proud to live with his wife's family. I now knew otherwise.

---

*A literary work by Wang Hsi-chih, a fourth-century writer and master of calligraphy.

"Come and see my room." Taking advantage of an instant when her mother was sipping her tea, Ai Fen pulled me away.

Her room was on the side of the house. Aside from the single bed, desk, and chair, there was not much space left. Although the room was small, like it's occupant's appearance, it was meticulously neat and tastefully decorated. The matching print of the bedspread and curtains pleased the eye; their pink color added a touch of warmth and brightness to the otherwise drab, neglected four walls. Above the head of the bed hung a free-brush painting of a peony, the brilliant red of the petals radiant against the dark green of the stems and leaves. Just as I was about to ask her if this was Hsiao Fan's work, I heard her sit down and let out a sigh. Noticing that her cheekbones had grown more prominent and her face thinner, I hastened to ask her whether her work was too hectic.

"Add the meetings to the time on duty, and you get a typical twelve-hour day!" She immediately began to let out her grievances. "I've never seen so many women having babies! All we know about is furthering revolution; we don't know how to get a handle on birth control. Now the result is upon us! From last summer the birth rate has continuously broken all records. In one particular night I alone delivered twenty babies! The maternity ward was filled to bursting, and a few of the mothers had to sleep in the corridor. We couldn't even keep up with feeding the infants, let alone changing diapers. According to the inside story, the population is already approaching nine hundred million. Nine hundred million! Just think of it. Birth control simply must be made a national policy. The more I deliver babies, the more I can't bear to have one myself. These days, not having a child is the greatest contribution to our country. Often as I deliver the babies, I also try to impart to the mothers the rationale behind birth control. But what's the use? I speak 'bitter words with a kind heart,' and people still label me as a 'backward element'!"

So those two posters were aimed at her! The moment I discovered this I couldn't help but feel terrible for her.

"Life is really difficult!" she continued to grumble. "Take me, for example. Because I don't have a good class background, I don't dare be an activist even if I wanted to. I only hope to make no mistakes. I can't hope for any great honor. Every time a movement comes along, I just hope to get by unscraped. To have a mundane, uneventful life, that's good enough. But even that was not to be! Out of caution, I finally joined the radical organization, and now they say I'm just shifting with the tide. What doctor doesn't 'open the back door' sometimes? I did it, and I am accused of breaking the law. It's utterly unfair!"

The story was that Mr. Ai's boss, an old party cadre, had a daughter who traveled as a Red Guard for half a year all over the country to "spread the revolution." She came back and discovered she was pregnant. This old party member asked Ai Fen's father for help. One day while Ai Fen was on shift, she cleared the way for his daughter to have an abortion privately. Before the Cultural Revolution there was a rule that before a woman could get an abortion, a letter of approval from her department was required. In order to obtain that letter, an unmarried woman had to undergo self-criticism and submit a confession to her department. It inevitably led to a scandal.

"She was only seventeen and didn't know a thing. She didn't even know the father of the child. How could she write a confession? What's more, to have such a record on file to follow her wherever she goes would become a terrible burden. How pathetic! What doctor wouldn't 'open the back door' in a case like this? The woman colleague who pasted the poster criticizing me has a husband in the northeast. She was pregnant even before she went to visit her husband. Didn't she herself get a colleague to give her an abortion on the sly?"

"Why didn't you put up a poster criticizing her?" I suggested indignantly.

"How could I dare to do that?" she asked. Then as if swallowing her anger, "Everyone thinks she's got it with the second top man of the hospital's Revolutionary Committee. That guy was originally just a technician in the lab. He didn't join the party until 1965, but, relying on his ability to talk big, he took to leading the revolt. Now that he's become an official, he's all high and mighty. He has a wife in some rural section of Honan, but he even gave up his annual home leave on the pretext that he's busy with 'advancing the revolution, promoting production.' Just think, for a man of thirty, something fishy must be going on. In fact, after he became an official, he immediately moved out of the single men's dormitory and moved into an office at the hospital, saying that it was more convenient for his work. Many times people have seen a light still on in the office at midnight and have even heard a woman's laughter. Of course no one dares to breathe a word about it; even if someone were to accuse him publicly, he can't be touched. Vice Chairman Lin Piao has decreed that relationships between men and women be considered a 'small matter' and that 'a small matter can do no harm.' This has practically become the favorite homily of the radicals. Hmph, the way I see it, the morals of this new group in power is even more 'capitalist' than the old 'capitalists.' "

"He really should be dragged onto the stage and 'struggled' against." I too became angry. "This is one of those officials who set fires while the common people can't even strike a match!"

Ai Fen's face was full of indignation. We were sitting very close together on the bed. She suddenly bent forward to look outside the doorway, and then leaned her head closer to mine, whispering, "This fellow seems to have his eye on me. As soon as my request for a divorce reached his desk, he immediately sent for me. He glibly asked me all sorts of questions. He urged me not to make this decision too hastily, but to think it over for a while, all in the manner of a leader truly concerned about his people. Since then, whenever we're alone, he flatters me. I even suspect it was he who leaked the fact that I had illegally given an abortion, contriving to put pressure on me."

I was so startled that I clutched her hands. Only after a long while could I open my mouth to suggest with a stammer, "Withdraw the request for a divorce right away!"

"If I don't get a divorce, what do I do when Hsiao Fan's sent to the country? Or perhaps the hospital will send me down to the country. If so, it wouldn't be any good to drag him along. Hsiao Fan's even more reluctant to leave Peking than I am!"

Good lord! I suddenly thought of Homer's *Odyssey*. It seemed as if Ai Fen was caught between Scylla and Charybdis, in a dilemma with no way to turn. "What are you going to do?"

"Just wait it out," she smiled sadly and forced herself to be stoic. "I'll only make an oral report. I'll never submit a written statement. A written report is iron-clad evidence. Once it enters your file, it will become a baggage you carry around for the rest of your life; you'll never be able to shake it off. I'm only twenty-seven. I still have more than half a lifetime to live. No matter what, I can't pick up that baggage."

"Your family doesn't know anything about this, do they?" I thought of the tranquil expression I had just seen on her father's face.

"They only know that I've been criticized on posters for having opened a 'back door.' My father had been criticized by a whole wall of posters last year, so they're already used to it. But don't let any of this leak out to them. I'm afraid my mother might get sick if she begins worrying about me."

I nodded my head earnestly.

"After this whole thing blows over, I'll come visit you all. For the time being, we'd better keep a distance for a while. You know what I mean, don't you?" she asked, holding my hands.

Of course I understood her situation. I immediately got up, said good-bye, and slipped out of the courtyard.

For several months after this Ai Fen didn't come to see me. Although I was anxious about her, I kept my promise not to visit her. At the beginning of April, my husband and I were abruptly assigned to a post in Nanking. Just before we left, unable to restrain myself, I went to the hospital to take a look. I first registered as a patient. Then I headed down the corridor to read closely all the big character posters on the walls. The "cleansing of the ranks" seemed to be at its tail end. A couple of posters were aimed at the director of the gynecology section. The rest were all in fervent support of movements like "discard the old, adopt the new," "tighten the ranks, cut out the slack, send technical workers to the country." I didn't see Ai Fen, so I asked a nurse whether she was around.

"Doctor Ai is on sick leave. She won't be in to work for a whole week." When the nurse mentioned "sick leave," her nose and eyes wrinkled up and her lips were curled in a mocking smile.

Startled, I asked her what was wrong with Dr. Ai. But she paid no attention to me and just chattered with the other patients. Having had the door slammed in my face, I hurriedly rushed to Ai Fen's home outside of the Ti-an Gate. On the way I continuously blamed myself for having neglected my friends.

Her mother was watering the flowers and plants at the doorway. Recognizing me, she put down the watering pot and immediately led me into the house.

"I hear Ai Fen's sick. What is it?" I asked impulsively.

"Nothing serious," she started her spiel. "This headstrong child! She went ahead and had an abortion without even telling me! You know, I've been waiting to have a grandson every day. Her father says that it's all because I have spoiled the child ever since she was small."

Hearing me come in, Ai Fen called to me from her room and stopped her mother's grumbling. She was lying on the bed, huddled up in a pink quilt. Her hair hung down loosely on her forehead. Her face was a greenish white. She looked sickly and haggard.

"You're a doctor yourself. How could you be so careless?" As soon as her mother turned her back, I scolded her.

"Doctors are human too," she said, shifting herself and the quilt to let me sit on the bed.

I was relieved to find that she still had some spirit. I couldn't help mocking her, "This is like having your boat capsized in a drainage ditch—how did you ever get yourself into such an incredible mess!"

We looked at each other and laughed.

I'd never met a doctor more enthusiastic about promoting the use of contraceptives than Ai Fen. She even used herself as a guinea pig. Whenever Shanghai or Peking came out with a new contraceptive, she was often among the first to try it out. I remember when

I'd just given birth to my child, she recommended a kind of contraceptive cream which only had to be applied daily in small
amounts near blood vessels, like on the wrists or behind the ears. I
was timid and didn't dare to try it recklessly. When I finally plucked
up my courage to use it, she told me the cream wasn't effective after
all. The doctors had shifted to trying out a contraceptive injection.
An injection once a month was both simple and trouble-saving.
However, these shots evidently had some bad side effects: they
caused menstrual irregularity. The injection method was soon
abandoned, and something else new was tried out. There were so
many techniques, I simply can't keep them all straight now.

"Did you try out some new contraceptive that wasn't effective?" I
was curious.

"No, I was just careless." Then she sat up, reached for a comb on
the table, and began to comb her black, shining hair. On the wall
beside the bed hung a framed picture of her family—herself, her
mother and father. I discovered there was one new picture this
time—a portrait of Hsiao Fan from the waist up. It occurred to me
that if she'd gotten pregnant, her relationship with Hsiao Fan must
have changed for the better.

"Ai Fen, how could Hsiao Fan bear to let you have an abortion?"

But she avoided my questioning eyes and concentrated on combing her hair. After quite a while she answered, "I didn't tell him."

I sighed, feeling sorry for her, but secretly blamed her for being a
bit heartless. I often thought that if they had a child, they probably
wouldn't be seeking a divorce. "Is he still at the soy sauce factory?"

She nodded and said, "It's fortunate that he's there and not in his
original work unit. So at least this recent round of 'cleansing of the
ranks' hasn't touched him."

Setting down the comb and putting on her quilted jacket, she
talked about him. They had become good friends now and no
longer quarreled. He often came to see her. Even her mother was
getting used to the smell of soy sauce and no longer complained
about her headaches; in fact, she couldn't praise him enough. Hsiao
Fan didn't try to keep his dalliances from her. Ai Fen was obviously
a little jealous, only she didn't admit it.

"It looks like you both still love each other," I insisted without
any hesitation. "When the high tide of this Rustication Movement
is over, you should promptly withdraw the divorce petition."

"That won't work. Our reconciliation is built on the security that
separation has brought us. If we tried to live together again, the
problems would only recur."

The topic of her divorce made me suddenly think of that second
in command at her hospital, that glorified lab technician who tried

to take advantage of her plight. I asked her in a low voice, "You didn't write a self-criticism, did you?"

She too whispered in reply, "No."

I felt so relieved for her sake. Clasping my hands, I exclaimed, "Thank heaven! Thank heaven!!"

My concern moved her, and her appreciative eyes wandered over me for a moment. Then suddenly she motioned me closer and leaned forward herself—our heads were almost touching.

"I gave him certain favors, and now things are cleared up. There just wasn't any alternative. I had to do as the circumstances dictated."

She didn't explain what favors, and I didn't want to ask her. Actually I was afraid to ask. Seeing this expert on birth control laid low by an abortion, how could I ask her anything?

Usually lively and talkative, Ai Fen also grew silent at this moment. Her almond-shaped eyes gazed vacantly at the printed curtains in front of her. The delicate April sunlight was blocked out by the curtains; and the little room seemed as if it had gathered a whole winter's cold darkness, a chill that could not be driven away. Having tidied her appearance, Ai Fen looked less haggard. Nevertheless the paleness of her face and the lifelessness of her eyes revealed melancholy and distress. This was the first time since we had gotten to know each other that I had ever seen her with this kind of expression. She was truly like a free, soaring bird that had suddenly broken its wing, its spirit drastically curtailed.

I told her that my family would soon move to Nanking. She was happy for me and yet couldn't bear to part with me. She said that after I left she wouldn't be able to find anyone else to talk heart-to-heart with. When I was about to go, she disregarded all my pleas and insisted on dressing herself and seeing me off at the bus station. On the way, both of us were too dispirited to talk much. But before I departed, Ai Fen gave me a warm, captivating smile and warned me, "I'm not the kind of person who writes, you must know that. If we want to talk, we'll have to wait until the next time we see each other. I wrote too much before—those years when I first fell in love. The love letters I wrote then would be enough to fill a book. I had really written myself dry. Now all I can write are prescriptions for my patients. As far as letters go, I can't write a single word."

Sure enough, Ai Fen didn't answer any of my letters. In 1971, though, we got news of her from a friend of hers traveling south to visit his family. Passing through Nanking, this friend visited and brought along two boxes of Peking candied fruits which Ai Fen had sent for our child. According to her friend, Ai Fen was now formally divorced, and would soon be joining a circulating medical team that would travel around the country for a half year. As for Hsiao Fan, this person knew nothing about what had become of him.

In the beginning of 1973, I was in Peking on a business trip. One afternoon I went to the hospital especially to see Ai Fen. She was on duty in the delivery ward. She was elated to see me and insisted on taking me home for dinner. So after she got off work, we first took a bus to Taohsiangts'un in Wangfuching. Ai Fen bought a stewed chicken and had it cut up. And I bought a bottle of Hsifeng wine for her father. Then, carrying wine and meat, we returned to her house outside of Ti-an Gate.

It had been several years since we'd last met. Her father and mother were still the same. Only Ai Fen had changed a little. She had gained some weight which gave her an attractively full figure. Her breasts thrust forward like those of a young nursing mother. Her face had rounded out, her cheeks like pomegranates in full bloom in May. Ever since Nixon's visit to Peking the year before, when Chiang Ch'ing wore a Western-style dress to receive the foreign guests, such fashions for women in Peking had gradually returned.

Ai Fen dressed even more stylishly than before. A red quilted jacket with small printed flowers was set off by turquoise woolen slacks. On her feet were brand new leather shoes. The gloves and scarf she took off were bright colored and eye catching. As I sat beside her at dinner, I kept smelling the scent of rouge. She was still all smiles, but now they had a quiet grace to them which, like her movements and bearing, reflected experience and maturity.

Her mother still complained about her migraines and the crowded apartment. She made a point of mentioning her daughter's divorce, saying that their neighbors were gossiping about Ai Fen. But because her father's coughs kept interrupting, I really couldn't understand what Mrs. Ai was saying. As soon as we finished dinner, Ai Fen left the dishes and pulled me into her bedroom.

The room, like its occupant, had also changed, with many things added. The most distinctive addition was a charcoal drawing which had replaced a traditional painting above the head of the bed. The drawing showed a nude in profile. The face was subtly but intentionally obscured, but the figure reminded me at once of Ai Fen as she was in the 1960s. The artist was undoubtedly Hsiao Fan.

Ai Fen saw me gazing fixedly at the drawing and she hastened to tell me, "Because of this drawing, I don't dare open the curtains. The door has to be tightly shut, too. If someone should see it, I'd be in big trouble!"

"You're really gutsy, Ai Fen!" I exclaimed. I deeply admired her courage to enjoy and appreciate art; yet, at the same time, I suspected it was this drawing that had brought on her neighbors' gossip.

She giggled and pressed me to sit on the bed. She removed a pair of paint-spotted work trousers from a chair and sat down.

I noticed the curtains were indeed closed, but they had been changed to a gold print. The bedspread too had been replaced with a light yellow one. And besides the old pink quilt, there was now a light purple one. The wall in front of the bed was plastered with colorful posters from the "model operas." Ai Fen's room was so colorful that it rivaled the Fragrant Mountain in autumn. I turned around to look closely at the picture frame on the wall beside the bed, and I saw that Hsiao Fan's photo had been replaced with their wedding portrait. Ai Fen hadn't forgotten their former love after all, even though they were now divorced. From the moment we met again after the long separation, we had talked about everything under the sun, everything except Hsiao Fan. Now that I saw the drawing and that photograph in the room, I no longer could hold my tongue. "Where's Hsiao Fan now? Do you see each other often?"

"Not only that, he practically regards this place as his second home. My mother is completely carried away with him; she even takes him for her own godson."

As Ai Fen talked, she gestured with her head toward the work trousers that she had moved to the table beside her. She spoke casually, as if she were talking about the most ordinary occurrence. It was only then that I noticed the toothbrush intermixed with the paint brushes on the table, and underneath the table lay a pair of sneakers with the toes turned out. It appeared that Hsiao Fan often shared Ai Fen's bedroom.

Recalling the way her mother grumbled about the divorce at the dinner table, I surmised that she hoped they would remarry. Many people who had been forced into divorce because of the political situation during the high tide of the Cultural Revolution were now starting the procedures for remarriage. After all, divorced women were still rather discriminated against. Ai Fen was already over thirty, so her chances of marrying someone else would inevitably dwindle year by year. Since she got along so well with her former husband, I too thought "putting back together the broken mirror" was a good idea.

Moreover, Hsiao Fan had escaped the misfortune of being sent to the country. In 1972 he was transferred to the Propaganda Department of the Peking Municipal Committee. The political movements went on year after year, but he had lost all interest in them. In fact, he began to take time out again to paint privately the things he loved. Just before Nixon came, Chou En-lai invited many old artists to the foreigners' guest house to paint landscapes, flowers, and birds. That made those who had studied traditional painting feel somewhat vindicated for a while. After that, Chiang Ch'ing had her lackeys instigate meetings to criticize "black painting" on some pretext, and to throw cold water on these artists. But the seeds of revival in art had already sprouted. On the faith that "a brushfire can't entirely burn away the grass, with the spring breeze it will regrow," artists had regained enough hope to wait it out. Now that Hsiao Fan had a future, Ai Fen's marriage could be saved. I decided to try to give my friend a boost from the sidelines.

Just as I was plotting my approach, Ai Fen changed the subject to the currently popular "model operas." Her eyes frequently wandered to the wall in front of her. It was plastered with colorful posters from several of the operas, "Taking Tiger Mountain by Strategy," "Shachiapang," "On the Docks," and others. When Ai Fen spoke of "Taking Tiger Mountain by Strategy," her almond-shaped eyes shone brightly and, like a true opera fan, she fixed an enamored gaze on the wall poster. This surprised me greatly. How could she possibly be fascinated by Chiang Ch'ing's "model operas"? In the past she seldom even went to hear traditional Peking opera. As I was wondering this, I saw that Ai Fen had finally shifted her gaze away from the poster. With an expression of irrepressible happiness, she blurted out, "I might remarry."

"Good!" I was so happy that I grabbed her hand and squeezed it. "I was just thinking, you and Hsiao Fan . . . "

"It's not him," she winked her eyes mysteriously.

"Ah, then who is he?" I didn't think Ai Fen could change so dramatically.

Seeing me gaping like a simpleton, Ai Fen giggled and deliberately flaunted her secret like a mischievous little girl. Having laughed for a while, she regained her composure and informed me. "Hao Kuang, 'Hao' as in Hao Liang, and 'Kuang' meaning 'bright.' That's just his stage name, but I'm used to it. He performs with the Experimental Peking Opera, following Hao Liang's style, and he was once received by Chiang Ch'ing! Come, I'll show you his photo."

From the pocket of her padded jacket, she fished out a small plastic jacket with a monthly bus ticket in it. On the other side was Hao Kuang's photo. Of course he looked exactly like an opera star, and from the photo I could sense his stage presence: the elegantly featured face was looking upward, smiling with his teeth just showing; his expression was rather self-assured. I still liked Hsiao Fan, and for a moment was reluctant to see Ai Fen throw herself into a stranger's arms. But everyone has a right to pursue his or her own happiness. For Ai Fen's sake, I was prepared to accept her lover with open arms.

"Not bad!" I congratulated her. "'Model opera' performers have got it made these days! I didn't expect that you'd find another artist to fall in love with. I thought this time you'd choose a doctor."

Ai Fen smiled blandly. "You and my mother sing the same tunes. She always hoped that I'd marry a doctor. It's as if that was the most stable and secure profession. But I'm not a seventeen- or eighteen-year-old girl anymore. I can't afford to be so choosy! Actually one profession is the same as another. Even someone high and mighty like Lin Piao—the second in command in the whole country—can be toppled overnight."

"Does your mother like Hao Kuang?" I asked Ai Fen.

She shook her head. Apparently, her mother was traditional-minded and felt opera singing was not a proper occupation, even worse than painting. She'd sooner have her daughter remarry an artist than marry an opera singer. Thus whenever Hsiao Fan dropped in, she always welcomed him. However, when Hao Kuang occasionally visited, if her daughter didn't urge her, she would not even ask him to stay for a meal. Her mother thought that at her daughter's age a semi-arranged marriage would be the best route: it was more reliable to get a general sense of the potential bride-groom's background even before meeting. But Hao Kuang fell into Hsiao Fan's old groove, a match of the "love at first sight" variety. This made Ai Fen's mother guarded from the start.

Ai Fen said that she and Hao Kuang met each other purely by fate. In 1972 she had traveled around the country with a circulating medical team. Hao Kuang and his troupe were performing up north. By chance, at Changchiak'ou they met each other. People from Peking who bump into each other while away from the city feel a special warmth, even if they're total strangers. At the time Hao Kuang was interested in her, but she felt nothing special for him. Then last summer Hao Kuang returned to Peking. Immediately he searched her out at the hospital and, from then on, had courted her like a whirlwind. At first, because Hao Kuang was two years younger, Ai Fen still had reservations. But finally she couldn't resist his passionate pursuit and gave in.

These past two years her mother had asked people all around to introduce prospective husbands to her daughter. Ai Fen had reluc-tantly gone to two such arranged meetings, but nothing came of them. She would never consider old bachelors working in the prov-inces, widowers with children also intimidated her—she never wanted to be a mother herself, how could she possibly take good care of other people's children? The young and handsome Hao Kuang contrasted favorably with these other prospects; naturally he won Ai Fen's heart easily. Her father was open-minded; he thought marriage should be his daughter's own decision. That left only her mother grumbling.

"Your mother will come around, Ai Fen," I predicted with confidence. "Isn't it always true that the more a mother looks at her son-in-law the more she likes him?"

"I'm not worried about my mother's passing objection; I worry about myself."

For those trapped in a net of emotions, it is hard not to worry about gains and losses. A bewildered and troubled expression suddenly floated across her face.

"Having weathered two stormy emotional entanglements," she admitted candidly, "I've become somewhat timid. I have this fear that if I offer my whole self, I might end up shattered again. I think this is my last time to stake everything on a single roll of the dice. The dice already have been thrown, but my heart is still on tenterhooks. Love came too smoothly. I'm lucky, but I almost don't dare believe it's all true. You've got to meet Hao Kuang! We can all go out to have Mongolian fire pot. I'll treat."

I gladly accepted the invitation. That evening, Ai Fen, holding my arm, saw me to the bus stop. On the way she kept talking about Hao Kuang this and Hao Kuang that. The whole evening I had held myself back from asking more about Hsiao Fan. Finally I couldn't bear it anymore, so I interrupted, "You and Hao Kuang are in love, but isn't Hsiao Fan terribly hurt?"

"Not at all." She spoke in a light tone of voice. "Hsiao Fan has vowed to remain single. He is determined to paint the rest of his life. You wouldn't know it, but whenever his inspiration to paint rises, he even forgets to go to work. A family is actually a burden to him."

"Has he met Hao Kuang?"

"Once. His impression wasn't bad either. Hsiao Fan agrees that I should remarry soon. He said that I'm the kind of woman who can't live without men."

"Hsiao Fan has become your bosom buddy!" I said. "You might as well go ahead and get married."

"That's what I've been thinking too." she said and grasped my hand tightly as if to express the sincerity of her intention. "But I don't know why, when Hao Kuang asked me the last time, I was stumped. You know? The way he speaks is just like my boyfriend in college. Even the words he used when he proposed to me were exactly the same! Ah, just wait 'til you meet him!"

I really wanted to meet Hao Kuang. Especially since I'd heard how much he resembled Ai Fen's unforgettable first boyfriend, I became very curious. However, at that time Hao Kuang was busy performing in "On the Docks," and it wasn't until the day I was to leave Peking that Ai Fen was able to arrange the dinner.

At dusk the three of us met in a small restaurant on the corner of East Fourth Street. The place was so small it could accommodate only two tables. Set in the middle of each was a brass fire pot as big around as the circle formed by two people linking hands. On the side of each was inscribed the title of the last Ch'ing emperor's reign, and each pot's belly was so red it shone. Judging from the elegant ancient style, they were surely antiques. The mouth of each pot was divided into six sections by thin mesh dividers. Each customer would cook his own mutton in his section of the pot. The rich juices from the meat flowed into the other sections and could be enjoyed equally. This was a truly socialist way to eat. It was just into March and the weather was gradually warming up, so not many people were inclined to patronize the fire pot. We three had a table all to ourselves, and thus the accommodations turned out to be very spacious, even more comfortable than in the famous restaurants at the Tungfeng Market. This little place, praiseworthy for its excellent quality at low prices, had been chosen by Hao Kuang; he was obviously a connoisseur of Peking's eating spots.

Though not particularly tall, Hao Kuang had bright, clear eyes, finely-drawn lips, and his manner of speech had a way of magnetizing his listeners. He possessed a certain magical charm which people found irresistible. He came from a middle-peasant family in the suburbs. A person from such a background belonged neither to the "Five Red Elements" nor the "Five Black Elements"; the way Hao Kuang put it, he was politically neutral. This kind of safe, neutral position not only allowed him to have an unencumbered spirit, but also gave him a superior and independent sense of self-confidence. He had been a fan of Peking opera since childhood. Early on he learned to play the Chinese fiddle and grew up playing it and singing. In time he passed the entrance exam to the opera company. This profession matched his disposition, and he was well satisfied with his lot. When Chiang Ch'ing advocated "model operas," Hao Kuang saw it as an irreversible trend and was glad to change over and support it wholeheartedly. He was so fired up about his work that he not only put great effort into performing, but also enjoyed talking about it at length.

Hao Kuang ordered two tall glasses of beer and chatted about the ins and outs of his performance career as he drank. Because the "model operas" were much in vogue all over the country, Hao Kuang had left his footprints over half of China. When he spoke of the things he had done and seen, he was absolutely enthralling. I was so captivated by his stories that several times I overcooked my pieces of mutton.

I asked Hao Kuang which role he was best in. Ai Fen hurriedly butted in, "Yang Tzu-jung, right?"

Hao Kuang gave a slight smile. His self-assured expression was the best answer to my question. I surmised that, with his medium build, to play the tall and straight Yang Tzu-jung, he probably had to wear platform shoes.

At this time he looked around the restaurant and, seeing that there was no one nearby watching, he suddenly lowered his voice and said to me, "Ai Fen saw my poster at Changchiak'ou where I was performing. Not to brag, but that color poster of me pasted on the walls was even bigger than Chairman Mao's—and caught many more eyes!"

Hao Kuang's youthful, self-assured spirit was something totally new for a somber, heavy-hearted intellectual like me. His self-confidence alone left me far behind in the dust. On stage, with his make-up and costume on, I could imagine that he was even more overpowering. It was no wonder that Ai Fen, who worshipped heroes, would be fascinated by him. As she sat beside the fire pot, her eyes lingered on his face the whole time. With red lips slightly parted, she took in every word he uttered. I had heard that he was two years younger than Ai Fen; and knowing her educational background and professional training—not to mention her hard knocks in love and marriage—I had originally expected to see a "older sister-younger brother" kind of love between them. Who would have expected that, once in front of him, Ai Fen's calm maturity, like the slices of mutton thrown into the boiling soup, would shrivel into a ball instantly and allow itself to be gobbled up without the least resistance. Whenever Hao Kuang reached the most self-congratulatory parts in his stories, he would fix his gaze upon her, as if he were opening himself up especially to her. She too embraced him with her eyes, without holding back in the least, allowing herself to follow him without the least resistance. That meal she ate very little and didn't touch the beer. But when we walked out of the restaurant, a bright red flush spread across her cheeks to her ears. Her almond-shaped eyes glistened like a melting pond in early spring. Her body was even more docile and limp, and she kept leaning against him. Hao Kuang was naturally chivalrous, as if to protect her, and even held her handbag for her; he was most attentive.

I was to take the late train south. Ai Fen, afraid that I couldn't manage to get on the train with my luggage, insisted on seeing me off. They both accompanied me to the hotel to pick up my suitcases, and then we took a bus to the Peking Railway Station. While Hao Kuang was buying platform tickets, Ai Fen suddenly asked me, "What do you think of him?"

"He's really eloquent," I replied honestly. "And very charming."

Ai Fen agreed completely. "Ah, the way he talks resembles so completely my first boy friend. It's as if every word is chosen and said only for you to hear; and because it's what you want to hear, it makes you unable to resist. I can't help but give in totally!"

"Get married quickly!" I urged. "You're already inseparable. What are you waiting for?"

As I expected, she didn't wait much longer. The summer of that year, I wrote to her to say that we had decided to leave the mainland. She made an exception and answered my letter, informing me that she had just gotten married. As for my leaving the country, she didn't mention a word.

Since then, I haven't had any more news of Ai Fen. But every time I think of her, the scene in the restaurant, where she became intoxicated without having touched any alcohol, floats vividly before my eyes. I silently wish her happiness in her marriage. In 1976 I heard the news that Chiang Ch'ing was toppled, and the "model opera" also collapsed in the wake of her downfall. I sighed over Hao Kuang's misfortune. Later I heard that Hao Liang was being "rectified"; I could not help but fear for Hao Kuang, and worry even more about Ai Fen. When I wake from my dreams in the middle of the night, the same question often enters my mind: Is Ai Fen's marriage still untroubled?

GLOSSARY

Authors and titles of stories are arranged alphabetically. Where the author goes under a pen name, his legal name, if known, is given in parentheses. For the sake of consistency, all Chinese characters are given in the unsimplified form.

I. AUTHORS

艾　蕪　Ai Wu (T'ang Tao-keng 湯道耕)
陳若曦　Chen Jo-hsi (Chen Hsiu-mei 陳秀美)
陳映真　Ch'en Ying-chen (Ch'en Yung-shan 陳永善)
西　戎　Hsi Jung
蕭　紅　Hsiao Hung (Chang Nai-ying 張迺瑩)
老　舍　Lao She (Shu Ch'ing-ch'un 舒慶春)
凌叔華　Ling Shu-hua
落花生　Lo Hua-sheng (Hsu Ti-shan 許地山)
白先勇　Pai Hsien-yung
冰　心　Ping Hsin (Hsieh Wan-ying 謝婉瑩)
宋順康　Sung Shun-k'ang
鄧友梅　Teng Yu-mei
田　濤　T'ien T'ao
草　明　Ts'ao Ming (Lo Ts'ao-ming 羅草明)
王　拓　Wang T'o (Wang Hung-chiu 王紘久)
吳組緗　Wu Tsu-hsiang
楊青矗　Yang Ch'ing-ch'u (Yang Ho-hsiung 楊和雄)
於梨華　Yü Li-hua

II. TITLES

安樂鄉的一日 A Day in Pleasantville
六月裏的玫瑰花 A Rose in June
在懸崖上 At the Precipice
同根生 Born of the Same Roots
毛毛蟲 Caterpillar
張嫂 Chang Sao
燈心絨 Corduroy
春桃 Garbage Gleaner
小劉 Little Liu
望君早歸 May He Return Soon
女友艾芬 My Friend Ai Fen
暮 Nightfall
老隊上迎親 Old Team Captain Welcomes a Bride
牛車上 On the Oxcart
離 Parting
雨 Rain
迎春曲 Spring Is Just around the Corner
女人 Two Women
西風 West Wind

SELECTED BIBLIOGRAPHY

I. References

Gibbs, Donald A. *Subject and Author Index to Chinese Literature Monthly* (1951–1976). New Haven: Far Eastern Publications, 1978.

Gibbs, Donald A., and Yun-chen Li. *A Bibliography of Studies and Translations of Modern Chinese Literature 1919–1942*. Cambridge: Harvard University Press, 1975.

Hsia, C. T. *A History of Modern Chinese Fiction*. New Haven: Yale University Press, 1961. Second revised edition, 1971.

Tsai, Meishi. *Contemporary Chinese Novels and Short Stories, 1949–1974: An Annotated Bibliography*. Cambridge: Harvard University Press, 1979.

Yang, Winston L.Y., and Nathan K. Mao, eds. *Modern Chinese Fiction: A Guide to Its Study and Appreciation*. Boston: G. K. Hall & Co., 1980.

II. Major Sources of Translations

Chi, Pang-yuan, et al., eds. *An Anthology of Contemporary Chinese Literature, Taiwan: 1949–1974*. Taipei: National Institute for Compilation and Translation, 1975.

Chinese Literature. Peking: Foreign Languages Press, 1951–.

The Chinese Pen. Taipei: Chinese Center, International P.E.N., 1972–.

Hsia, C. T., ed. *Twentieth-Century Chinese Stories*. New York: Columbia University Press, 1971.

Isaacs, Harold, ed. *Straw Sandals*. Cambridge: MIT Press, 1974.

Jenner, W. J. F., ed. *Modern Chinese Stories*. London: Oxford University Press, 1970.

Lau, Joseph S. M., C. T. Hsia, and Leo Ou-fan Lee, eds. *Modern Chinese Stories and Novellas: 1919–1949*. New York: Columbia University Press, 1981.

Lau, Joseph S. M., ed., with the assistance of T. A. Ross. *Chinese Stories from Taiwan: 1960–1970*. New York: Columbia University Press, 1976.

Renditions. A Chinese-English Translation Magazine. Hong Kong: Centre for Translation Projects, The Chinese University of Hong Kong, 1973–.

Snow, Edgar, comp. and ed. *Living China*. New York: John Day, 1937.

Wang, C. C., trans. *Contemporary Chinese Stories*. New York: Columbia University Press, 1944.

III. Translations of Works by Individual Authors

For a more complete list of translations of the works by Lao She, Wu Tsu-hsiang, Hsiao Hung, Lo Hua-sheng, Ping Hsin, and Lin Shu-hua, consult Gibbs and Li, *A Bibliography of Studies and Translations of Modern Chinese Literature, 1919–1942*.

Ai Wu
Homeward Journey and Other Stories. Peking: Foreign Languages Press, 1957.

A New Home & Other Stories by Contemporary Chinese Writers. Peking: Foreign Languages Press, 1955.

Wild Bull Village: Chinese Short Stories. Peking: Foreign Languages Press, 1965.

"Return by Night." *Renditions*, no.7 (Spring 1977).

Chen Jo-Hsi

Chen, Jo-hsi. *The Execution of Mayor Yin and Other Stories from the Great Proletarian Cultural Revolution.* Translated by Nancy Ing and Howard Goldblatt. Bloomington: Indiana University Press, 1978.

Ch'en, Lucy H. *Spirit Calling: Tales about Taiwan.* Taipei: Heritage Press, 1962.

Kao, George, ed. *Two Writers and the Cultural Revolution.* Hong Kong: The University of Hong Kong, 1980.

"The Last Performance." In Lau, *Chinese Stories from Taiwan: 1960–1970.*

"Ting Yun." Translated by Chi-chen Wang. *Renditions*, no.10 (Autumn 1978).

"The Tunnel." Translated by Chi-chen Wang. *Renditions*, no.10 (Autumn 1978).

Ch'en Ying-chen

"My First Case." In Lau, *Chinese Stories from Taiwan: 1960–1970.*

Hsiao Hung

Hsiao Hung. *The Field of Life and Death.* Translated by Howard Glodblatt and Ellen Yeung. *Tales of Hulan River.* Translated by Howard Glodblatt. Bloomington: Indiana University Press, 1979.

"The Family Outside." In Lau et al., *Modern Chinese Stories and Novellas: 1919–1949.*

"Hands." In Lau et al., *Modern Chinese Stories and Novellas: 1919–1949.*

Lao She

Kao, George, ed. *Two Writers and the Cultural Revolution.* Hong Kong: The University of Hong Kong, 1980.

Lao She. *Cat Country.* Translated by William A. Lyell. Columbus, Ohio: Ohio State University Press, 1970.

Lao She. *Rickshaw.* Translated by Jeanne James. Honolulu: University Press of Hawaii, 1979.

Renditions, no.10 (Autumn 1978). This issue has a special section on Lao She.

"Black and White Li." In Wang, *Contemporary Chinese Stories.*

"The Glasses." In Wang, *Contemporary Chinese Stories.*

"Liu's Court." In Wang, *Contemporary Chinese Stories.*

"The Philanthropist." In Wang, *Contemporary Chinese Stories.*

Ling Shu-hua

"Embroidered Pillows." In Lau et al., *Modern Chinese Stories and Novellas: 1919–1949.*

"The Eve of the Mid-Autumn Festival." In Lau et al., *Modern Chinese Stories and Novellas: 1919–1949.*

"The Helpmate." In Wang, *Contemporary Chinese Stories*.
"A Poet Goes Mad." *T'ien Hsia Monthly*, 4.4 (April 1937).
"What's the Point of It?" *T'ien Hsia Monthly* 3.1 (August 1936).
"Writing a Letter." *T'ien Hsia Monthly* 5.5 (December 1937).

Lo Hua-sheng
"The Merchant's Wife." In Lau et al., *Modern Chinese Stories and Novellas: 1919–1949*.
"Yü-kuan." In Lau et al., *Modern Chinese Stories and Novellas: 1919–1949*.

Pai Hsien-yung
Pai, Hsien-yung. *Wandering in the Garden, Waking from a Dream*. Bloomington: Indiana University Press, forthcoming.
"Li T'ung: A Chinese Girl in New York." In Hsia, *Twentieth-Century Chinese Stories*.
"Winter Nights." In Lau, *Chinese Stories from Taiwan: 1960–1970*.

Ping Hsin
"Boredom." In Yn Yu Kyn, *The Tragedy of Ah Qui and Other Modern Chinese Stories*. London: George Routledge and Sons, Ltd., 1930.
"The First Home Party." Translated by Richard L. Jen. *T'ien Hsia Monthly* 4.3 (March 1937).

Wu Tsu-hsiang
"Eighteen Hundred Piculs." *Chinese Literature*, 1959, no.11.
"Fan Village." In Hsia, *Twentieth-Century Chinese Stories*.
"Green Bamboo Hermitage." *Chinese Literature*, 1964, no.1.
"Let There Be Peace." In Lau et al., *Modern Chinese Stories and Novellas: 1919–1949*.
"Young Master Gets His Tonic." In Lau et al., *Modern Chinese Stories and Novellas: 1919–1949*.

Yang Ch'ing-ch'u
Yang, Ch'ing-ch'u. *Selected Stories of Yang Ch'ing-ch'u*. Translated by Thomas B. Gold. Kaohsiung, Taiwan: Tun-li Publishing Co., 1978.
"Enemies." In Lau, *Chinese Stories from Taiwan: 1960–1970*.

Yü Li-hua
"In Liu Village." In Lau, *Chinese Stories from Taiwan: 1960–1970*.

IV. Studies of Women in Modern China

Croll, Elisabeth. *Feminism and Socialism in China*. London: Routledge and Kegan Paul, Ltd., 1978.
Freedman, Maurice, ed. *Family and Kinship in Chinese Society*. Stanford: Stanford University Press, 1970.
Pruitt, Ida. *A Daughter of Han*. New Haven: Yale University Press, 1945. Reissue by Stanford University Press, 1967.
———. *Old Madam Yin*. Stanford: Stanford University Press, 1979.
Signs: Journal of Women in Culture and Society, vol.II, no.1 (Autumn 1976). Chicago: The University of Chicago Press, 1976.

Smedley, Agnes. *Portraits of Chinese Women in Revolution*. Old Westbury, N.Y.: The Feminist Press, 1976.

Wolf, Margery. *House of Lim*. New York: Prentice Hall, 1968.

———. *Women and the Family in Rural Taiwan*. Stanford: Stanford University Press, 1972.

Wolf, Margery, and Roxane Witke, eds. *Women in Chinese Society*. Stanford: Stanford University Press, 1975.

Yang, Martin C. *A Chinese Village*. New York: Columbia University Press, 1945.

Young, Marilyn B., ed. *Women in China*. Ann Arbor: Center for Chinese Studies, The University of Michigan, 1973.